THE ROBERT COLLIER LETTER BOOK

THE

Robert Collier

LETTER BOOK

by
Robert Collier

ROBERT COLLIER PUBLICATIONS, INC.
1248 N. Lamont Dr.
Oak Harbor, WA 98277
360-679-8981 Phone or Fax
www.robertcollierpublications.com

0-912576-21-9 HARDCOVER
0-912576-20-0 PAPERBACK

To

MASON BRITTON
whose idea this was and to

FRED STONE
Who made it possible, this book
is dedicated

PREFACE

This is not a textbook, calculated to show the beginner how to take his pen or typewriter in hand and indite a masterly epistle to some fancied customer.

It is for the business man who already knows the theory of letter writing but is looking for more effective ways of putting it into practice.

It covers all the necessary rules, of course, but it does this informally. Primarily, it is the log book of a long and varied experience. It shows successful ways of selling all manner of products, from coal and coke right on down to socks and dresses. But through all the differences in products and appeals, runs this one connecting thread — that while products and reasons for buying may vary, human nature remains much the same; that familiarity with the thing you are selling is an advantage, but the one essential without which success is impossible in selling, by mail or selling in person, is a thorough understanding of human reactions.

Study your reader first—your product second. If you understand his reactions, and present those phases of your product that relate to his needs, then you cannot help but write a good letter.

It may be said of this book that it does not give enough examples of unsuccessful letters. But most of us can find plenty of these in our own files. And isn't it true that we are far less concerned with why a letter failed than in finding out what it is that makes a letter successful?

The first book on business letter writing I ever read was the "Business Correspondence Library" published by System a good many years ago. To it, and to "Applied Business Correspondence" and other books by Herbert Watson, I owe most of my theoretical knowledge of letter writing. Those familiar with Watson's writings will recognize many of his theories in the early chapters of this book. I gladly give acknowledgment to him as the one on whose writings the groundwork of my own education in direct mail was laid.

To John Blair, President of the New Process Company of Warren, Pennsylvania, I am indebted for numberless opportunities to test my pet ideas in the only crucible that gives dependable results—actual letters sent to prospective buyers—and for the perfect records that enabled me to see which theories were workable, which better forgotten.

For many of the short paragraphs used as examples of good starters, graphic descriptions, or proper closers, I am indebted to writers like Ad-Man Davison and Ben Sweetland and to such magazines as Printers' Ink and System.

To all of these I give acknowledgment and express sincere appreciation.

THE AUTHOR

New York, N. Y.

CONTENTS

FOREWORD

When I agreed to write a foreword to this practical book about selling, which does much to de-bunk the subject, I did not know that the author had used me so frequently as Exhibit A. Naturally I feel somewhat embarrassed at endorsing his studies, since we traveled the road of mail order experience so much of the way as "buddies." I can't help but think it would have been a better book if he had called me Mr. Sears Roebuck, or Mr. Montgomery Ward, or some other well-known name that stands for big profits and big success. However, if he wishes to take the chance of marring an otherwise useful book, that is his affair.

To anyone immersed in the great game of business, there never ceases to be a thrill in landing an order. Multiply that thrill 100 or 1,000 times, and you have a picture of what a big day means to one who depends upon the incoming mail for success in business. I suppose there must be plenty of excitement in turning over to the "big boss" an order for $50,000 worth of something from one customer, but I doubt whether it can be compared with the feeling that you have influenced through your own eloquence a thousand minds to do something you wanted them to do, so that they all responded with signatures, in one day, backed by healthy pocketbooks.

Of all the forms of selling, direct mail is the most intriguing. Certainly it appeals strongly to the student mind. I have known men to be devoted to it, and very successful at it, who probably would have starved if they had been forced to take a sample case and show their wares to their customers face to face. Of all forms of selling, it gets the quickest results because the mails travel faster than salesmen, the mails don't get sick or temperamental, nor do they have to wait for an interview. The direct mail appeal gets there and back while another salesman is packing his grip. It offers great opportunity for showmanship with striking illustrations and color printing. It makes certain that all the best selling points are covered, whereas a sales representative may often miss a few and is quite likely to focus on a weak one he likes best, even sometimes inventing some doubtful ones of his own. In direct mail the management can check all extravagant claims. Direct mail shows a low selling cost too—if it works at all—and has the advantage of showing you quickly whether your merchandise is marketable, so that you can plan and get your campaign under way while the season is on. I say, "If it works!" Of course, it will work if one has the patience to find the right approach. Sometimes you hit it by accident, but usually you hit it by hard study, backed by experience. Mr. Collier has generously poured his experience into this book to save the reader the pitfalls yawning for old-fashioned business men, who are so apt to spend their postage money on good literature with sophisticated dictionary words and involved appeals, instead of headlines with punch, backed by simple homely argument.

A well-known copywriter and direct mail expert used to say, if you can sell books and service through advertising, you can sell anything. This probably explains why Mr. Collier shows you so many examples of successful book selling, making his point with the more difficult demonstration material. It must not be inferred, however, that the methods which he describes apply only to publishers' problems, because it is undoubtedly true that the same technique can be applied to sell anything from peanuts to real estate, and is being applied every day. If you have an article with merit, and there are enough human beings who want it or who can be made to want it, direct mail will find them quickly and at a low cost, in good times and in periods of depression. Moreover, it can be used in connection with other forms of selling without conflict. Your high-salaried road-men to the contrary notwithstanding, you can use direct mail methods not only to help them sell your product, but to sell them as well—and make them like it.

The publishers are pleased to call this a "book," but I should call it a "course of study," because it covers the subject so completely and unfolds food for thought in easy steps with logical sequence just as a good teacher would do the job. I believe many will join me if I nominate Robert Collier to the chair of Direct Mail Engineering at some progressive institution of learning. If this suggestion is adopted, we shall see in a few years a new attitude on the part of the weary public on receipt of circular letters. The bright, refreshing, circular literature of those days will be opened and read because it will be newsy and interesting, instead of dull and drab, as so much of it is today—but how about our pocketbooks after these compelling letters make us sign up for everything which Mr. Collier's disciples want to sell us under this new order of things?

Fred Stone

I

What Is It Makes Some Letters Pay?

What is there about some letters that makes them so much more effective than others?

A letter may have perfect diction, a finished style; it may bristle with attention-getters and interest-arousers; it may follow every known rule; yet when it reaches the Hall of Judgment where the reader sits and decides its fate, it may find itself cast into the hell of wastebasket-dom, while some screed lacking any pretense of polish or the finer arts of correspondence, blandly picks up the bacon and walks home with it. Why?

Because getting the results you set out to accomplish with a letter is no more a matter of rule of thumb than is landing a fish with a rod and hook. You know how often you have seen some ragged urchin pull in fish after fish with the crudest of lines, when a "sportsman" near by, though armed with every piscatorial lure known to man, could not raise even a bite!

It's a matter of bait, that's all. The youngster knew what the fish would bite on, and he gave it to them. Result? A mess of fine fish for dinner. The "sportsman" offered them what he had been led to believe fish ought to have—and they turned up their fishy noses at it.

Hundreds of books have doubtless been written about the fine art of fishing, but the whole idea is contained in that one sentence: "What bait will they bite on?" Thou-sands of articles have been written about the way to use letters to bring you what you want, but the meat of them all can be compressed into two sentences: "What is the bait that will tempt your reader? How can you tie up the thing you have to offer with that bait?"

For the ultimate purpose of every business letter simmers down to this:

The reader of this letter wants certain things. The desire for them is, consciously or unconsciously, the dominant idea in his mind all the time.

You want him to do a certain definite thing for you. How can you tie this up to the thing he wants, in such a way that the doing of it will bring him a step nearer to his goal?

It matters not whether you are trying to sell him a rain-coat,

1

making him a proposal of marriage, or asking him to pay a bill. In each case, you want him to do something for you. Why should he? Only because of the hope that the doing of it will bring him nearer his heart's desire, or the fear that his failure to do it will remove that heart's desire farther from him.

Put yourself in his place. If you were deep in discussion with a friend over some matter that meant a great deal to both of you, and a stranger came up, slapped you on the back and said: "See here, Mister, I have a fine coat I want to sell you!" What would you do? Examine the coat with interest, and thank him for the privilege or kick him and the coat down the nearest stairs, and blister both with a few choice adjectives in the process?

Well, much the same thing happens when you approach a man by mail. He is deep in a discussion with himself over ways and means of getting certain things that mean a great deal to him. You butt in (that is the only term that describes it) and blandly tell him to forget those things that so deeply concern him and consider your proposition instead. Is it any wonder he promptly tells you where to head in, and lacking the ability to reach you, takes it out on your letter instead?

Then what is the right way to approach him? How would you do it if you were approaching him in person? If he were talking to some one, you'd listen for a while, wouldn't you, and get the trend of the conversation? Then when you chimed in, it would be with a remark on some related subject, and from that you would bring the talk around logically to the point you wanted to discuss. It should not be much more difficult in a letter. There are certain prime human emotions with which the thoughts of all of us are occupied a goodly part of the time. Tune in on them, and you have your reader's attention. Tie it up to the thing you have to offer, and you are sure of his interest.

You see, your reader glancing over his mail is much like a man in a speeding train. Something catches his eye and he turns for a better look. You have his attention. But attention alone gets you nowhere. The something must stand closer inspection, it must win his interest, otherwise his attention is lost—and once lost, it is twice as hard to win the second time. Again it's a matter of bait—you may attract a fish's attention with a gaudily painted bauble, but if he once nibbles it and finds it made of tin, you will have a hard time reaching him again with anything else of the same kind.

Every mail brings your reader letters urging him to buy this or

2

that, to pay a bill, to get behind some movement or to try a new device. Time was when the mere fact that an envelope looked like a personal letter addressed to him would have intrigued his interest. But that time has long since passed. Letters as letters are no longer objects of intense interest. They are bait—neither more nor less—and to tempt him, they must look a bit different from bait he has nibbled at and been fooled by before. They must have something about them that stands out from the mass —that catches his eye and arouses his interest—or away they go into the wastebasket.

Your problem, then, is to find a point of contact with his interests, his desires, some feature that will flag his attention and make your letter stand out from all others the moment he reads the first line.

But it won't do to yell "Fire!" That will get you attention, yes of a kind but as far as your prospects of doing business are concerned, it will be of the kind a drunken miner got in the days when the West wore guns and used them on the slightest provocation. He stuck his head in the window of a crowded saloon and yelled " Fire!"—*and everybody did!*

Study your reader. Find out what interests him. Then study your proposition to see how it can be made to tie in with that interest. Take as an instance, the mother of a month-old baby. What is most in her thoughts? Imagine, then, how a letter starting like this would appeal to her:

> After baby's food and baby's clothes, the most important thing you have to decide upon is the little cart baby is going to ride in—is going to be seen in is going to be admired in.
>
> Never a child came into the world but was worthy as good a cart, etc.

Or if you were the father of a six- or eight-year-old boy, wouldn't this get under your skin?

> Your boy is a little shaver now. He thinks you are the most wonderful man in the world. You can fix his boat, mend his velocipede, tell him wonderful stories.
>
> But it will be only ten or twelve years until he goes to College. The fathers of the other boys his chums will go to see them. There will be a Railroad President, perhaps; a great Banker; a Governor.
>
> And you will go; and your boy will say, *"This is my*

father, boys."
How will he feel when he says it? Will he be proud of you?

Or take any one of the following starts. Can't you just see your reader nodding in interested agreement, can't you picture the way they would carry him along into a description of the thing offered, how they would make him want it, how they would lead him on to the final action?

To a Druggist

After you have run up front half a dozen times to sell a couple of stogies, a package of court plaster and a postage stamp; to change a five dollar bill for the barber, to answer the phone and inform Mrs. Smith that Castoria is 25¢ a bottle, and assure Mrs. Jones that you will have the doctor call her up as soon as he comes in, then take a minute for yourself and look over this proposition. It's worth while.

To a Householder

Doesn't it beat the Dutch the way thieves, pick-pockets, hold-up men and burglars are getting away with it these days?

There were over 1500 house burglaries last month in our dear old city; 92 business burglaries; 122 street hold-ups; 11 offices held up; 309 automobiles stolen, and the Lord only knows how many watches and purses taken on the streets. A good insurance policy against burglary and theft is a pretty cheap investment these days. Call me on the phone now, and I can have your valuables covered by noon.

To a Farmer

Any man who owns a cow loses a calf once in a while.

If you own a herd of a dozen or more, you are probably losing one or two calves a year. We know of breeders who were losing every calf—some sixteen—some over thirty a year.

And these breeders stopped their losses short — just like that — through the information given in our . . .

4

To a Merchant

"She didn't buy anything."

How often is this little tragedy repeated in your store? Your time is valuable your overhead expense runs on — and it costs you real money when a prospective customer walks out of your store without making a purchase.

To a Mother

About that boy of yours—

He is arriving at the age when his spirit of manliness asserts itself. You find him imitating his father's manners — he is using your embroidery scissors to shave with—he is no longer ambitious to be a policeman, but has his eye on the Presidency. Among the serious problems with him today is this: He is beginning to want manly, square-cut, "growing-up" clothes. He is no longer satisfied with ordinary boys' clothes, He wants something "like father's."

To a Motorist

If you have ever driven your car in a rainstorm, you know how annoying it is—dangerous, too—to have your wind shield clouded with water. How many times have you narrowly avoided accidents under these conditions? With the — Cleaner attached to your car, all you need to do is turn a button in front of you, and instantly every drop of water in your field of vision is swept from your wind shield. The glass is left clear and clean.

To a Doctor

What a clutter of books a doctor can get around him, and what a fearful outlay of money they will come to represent if he doesn't use great discrimination in their purchase. I don't suppose there is any class of people—and I have customers among every class you can think of—who appreciate more than my medical friends the marvelous savings I am able to make them on all standard sets, reference books, etc.

To a Housewife

After you have your breakfast dishes washed, your floors swept, and your beds made up, I should like to have a moment of your time.

You are an excellent judge of what is good to eat, and know when you are getting what you should from your grocer to be saving and yet to set your table with healthful and dainty dishes for your family...

To Any Man

Are you like Mr. Fuller in that you dislike to shave with cold or luke-warm water?

Mr. Fuller always grumbled when the water was cold. Usually it *was* cold. You know how the ordinary hot water system works early in the morning.

But the Fullers found a way out of their troubles. Now-nowadays, no matter how early they may arise, there's always steaming hot water the instant a faucet is turned.

To Insurance Agents

Did you ever, as a kid, sneak up alongside an old mill pond and heave what Penrod might call a "good old rock" far out into the middle of its placid surface—just for the fun of seeing all the mud turtles on all their sunny legs drop off into the water with one loud, individual PLUNK?

If the humble mud turtle formed no part of the back-yard fauna of your youth, I reckon there was something mighty similar to engage your budding talents. Just as you find now, in your grown-up days, that the pursuit of your business aims often involve the same emotions that lent interest to your activities in the eyes of your early neighbors. For example: We want to point out to you a few of the prospects that are basking along the banks of the...

Bait—all of them. Find the thing your prospect is interested in and make it your point of contact, rather than rush in and try to tell him something about *your* proposition, *your* goods, *your* interests.

6

II

How to Arouse That Acquisitive Feeling

To go back to the very beginning, what is the first thing to do in writing any business letter?

Before you put pen to paper, before you ring for your stenographer, decide in your own mind what effect you want to produce on your reader—what feeling you must arouse in him.

If you want your readers to say, as the crowds did of Demosthenes' famous rival: "What a clever speaker!" — then it is quite all right to start with catch-phrases and the like. But if you want to emulate Demosthenes, whose hearers forgot all about him in their interest in his message, then your whole effort must be centered on arousing the feeling in them: *"Let's go!"*

For back of every successful letter, as back of every sale, is a created feeling that impels the reader to act as you want him. It is the whole purpose of every business letter, whether it be sales, collection, adjustment or complaint, to make your reader *want* to do the thing you are urging upon him.

How are you to arouse that feeling in him? How would you have to feel yourself before you would place such an order as you have in mind, before you would grant such an extension, before you would send a payment to this man in preference to all others, at a time when it was an effort to send a dollar to any one?

What would you want first to know? What about the propostion would interest you most? What would you feel you had to gain by accepting? What would you lose by refusing?

They say the Parisians have a formula for love letters: "Begin without knowing what you are going to say, and end without knowing what you have said." That may be good medicine for love letters, but it was never meant for business. Though, to do the Frenchmen justice, such of their letters as appear in print indicate that while they may not know what they are going to say, they have a pretty clear idea of the emotion they want to arouse in their reader, and they leave no stone unturned in the doing of it.

And after all, isn't that the whole purpose of a letter? Books have been written about the importance of attention, and interest, and argument, and clinchers, but aren't these mere details? When you

7

come down to it, isn't the prime requisite arousing the *feeling* in your reader that *he must have* the thing you are offering, or that he can not rest until he has done the thing you are urging him to?

Consider the two following letters, for instance. The first follows all the rules. It wins attention, it creates interest, it describes what it has to offer, it has argument, conviction, clincher, yet it was only moderately successful, whereas the second letter literally pulled its head off. Why the difference?

Because the first letter was aimed only at the intellect, whereas the second, while it tried to convince the intellect, aimed its real appeal at the emotions! And when it is action you want, go after the emotions every time!

The Finally Revised, Illustrated
Edition of WELLS' HISTORY in 4 vols.
At 1/4 less than the Original Price of Two!

DEAR READER:

At last H. G. Wells' famous "Outline of History" has been put into its finally revised form, illustrated with 100 famous historical paintings, and brought out in four regular, library-size books.

A million copies of the Outline were sold in the bulky one and two volume editions. A million more people wanted it, but they waited for a lighter, more easily handled volume. Here it is—a brand new edition, freshly revised, of four standard library-size books, for *25% less than the price of the original two-volume set.*

And that isn't all.

For a long time Mr. Wells felt that parts of his history needed re-writing—that other parts should be clarified, and the whole thoroughly revised. This was his chance. Starting from the very beginning, he changed every single page of the text, re-wrote whole chapters, added page after page of additional matter. This is his final revision. In discussing this edition with a friend while in America, Mr. Wells said that the revisions would make the original English edition look like a Stone Age effort.

There are a hundred new illustrations, reproductions from historical paintings from the great art galleries of the world. Not only New York, but the Art Stores and Galleries of London and Paris were searched through for these. It is the finest edition of the "Outline of History" that has ever been brought out. Yet you may have it—if you mail the enclosed card at once—at an amazingly low price.

One-Fourth Off!

Think of it! Finally revised, printed from brand new, clear, readable plates, with a hundred new pictures besides those that were in the discarded editions, and bound up into 4 beautiful, library-size volumes—all for 25% less than *the original two-volume set would cost you even now in any book store!*

Here is our offer:

H.G. Wells' remarkable History, the most engrossing story ever told, being the complete romance of Mother Earth, bound up into 4 regular library-size books, illustrated with a hundred famous paintings, and A year's subscription to the Review of Reviews,

Both Together for $12
payable in easy, never missed payments of $1 a month, or $10.50 cash.

Wells begins with the dawn of time. Before there were men. Before there were even reptiles. In broad, magnificent strokes he paints the picture, bringing you straight down to today. In a few vivid pages, he brings the whole past back to life, and makes you live through it. More—he makes it all one connected story, shows you the thread of human purpose binding men together the world over from one age to another.

And the Review of Reviews makes the history of today as alive and interesting as Wells makes the years behind

9

us. Without waste of time, it gives you the boiled-down sap of world events, equips you to discuss national and international affairs intelligently, enables you to read your daily paper with real interest and understandingly.

Only One Condition We Make.

There is only one condition—that you send in your card within ten days after you receive this letter. Such an unusual offer as this cannot be held open long. We can give you but the one chance.

Mail the enclosed card, without money, and we will send you, subject to a week's free examination, the new 4-volume Wells' "Outline of History" at 25% less than the original 2-volume price. At the same time, we will enter your subscription for one full year of the Review of Reviews.

Remember, you don't risk one penny. If for any reason you are dissatisfied with the History, if you don't feel that it gives you the utmost of book value and satisfaction, return it at the end of the week at our expense, send 25 cents for the copy of the magazine delivered to you, and cancel the order.

The enclosed card obligates us only—*Not You!* Signing and mailing it puts the burden of Proof up to us.

May we hope you will *mail it today?*

Earnestly yours,

Your LAST CHANCE
to Get These 4 Volumes For 25% LESS
Than the Price of the First Two!

DEAR READER:

Do you know what is the really significant thing about all these pre-historic fossils and ancient civilizations that

10

have been dug up in the past few years?

—Not the fact that the Dinosaur eggs found in Mongolia may be 10,000,000 or 100,000,000 years old.

—Nor whether the Temple of the Moon-God in Ur of the Chaldees was built before the Tower of Babel, or the Temple of the Sun-God in Mexico was more ancient still.

—Not even whether mankind dates back to the primitive Ape-man of 500,000 years ago, or sprang full-grown from the mind of the Creator.

Not these things. They are, after all, of little consequence to us now. The really significant thing is that from them men are, for the first time, beginning to get an understanding of that infinite "life-principle" that moves the universe— and of the untold possibilities it opens up to them.

You read in Wells' "Outline of History" how for millions of years this "life-principle" was threatened by every kind of danger—sudden climactic changes, lack of food, floods, earthquakes, droughts, volcanic eruptions.

But to it each new danger was merely an incentive to finding a new resource. Pursued through water, it sought land. Pursued over land, it sought the air. To breath in the sea, it put forth gills. Stranded on land, it made lungs. To protect itself from glacial cold, it grew fur. In temperate climes, hair. Subject to alternate heat and cold, it produced feathers. To meet one danger it developed a shell. For another, fleetness of foot or wing. But ever, from the beginning, it showed its power to meet every creature need.

All through the history of life and mankind you see this same directing Intelligence—call it Nature, call it Providence, call it what you will—rising to meet every need of life.

No man can read Wells' without realizing that the whole purpose of existence is *growth*—that life is dynamic, not static. That it is ever moving forward—not standing still. That electricity, magnetism, gravitation, light, are all but different manifestations of the same infinite and eternal energy in which we ourselves live and move and have our being.

Wells' gives you an understanding of your own potentialities. You learn from it how to work with and take advantage of the infinite energy all about you. The terror of the man at the crossways, not knowing which road to take, is no terror to the reader of Wells. His future is of his own making. For the only law of infinite energy is the law of supply. The "life-principle" that formed the dinosaur to meet one set of needs and the butterfly to meet another is not going to fail in your case. You have but to understand it—to work in harmony with it—to get from it what you need.

Your Last Chance To Get Wells' At The Low Price

The low price we have been making on Wells' "Outline of History" was made possible only because we contracted for 100,000 sets at once.

Because we were willing to take the risk of paying the royalty on that vast quantity in advance, because we had previously sold over 150,000 copies of his one-volume edition, Wells reduced his royalties on these sets to a mere fraction of his usual amount.

But we can't hope to sell any such quantity again. We can't risk manufacturing on any such huge scale as to bring our costs down to anywhere near the present low figures.

Of the 100,000 sets we contracted for, 95,000 have been sold. Less than 5,000 are left. And if you had seen the orders streaming in at a 500-a-day clip last season, you would realize how quickly these 5,000 sets will melt away.

While we still have books left, we want them to go to our own old customers and friends. We cannot, of course, discriminate against outsiders; we must fill the orders as they come in. But we can urge you to speak for your set now.

Here Is Our Offer:

Send the enclosed card—without money—and we will forward to you, post-paid, a set of Wells' "Outline of History" for a week's *Free Examination*. Open it up anywhere. Read a few pages. Then try to lay it down! If you don't find, as the New York Tribune put it, that "It's the most exciting book ever written," *send it back*. Scarcely one man in twenty has been willing to part with his set, once he's opened it!

The payments?—You will laugh at them! $1 a month for 12 months for this magnificent set of Wells', and a year's subscription to the Review of Reviews magazine.

You know the Review of Reviews. You know that it gives you the best that can be gotten in science, literature, drama, politics, philosophy and thought, in books, in international questions. In brief, it gives you all that is necessary to keep your mind alert and well-informed on the affairs of the day. It furnishes you the basis for sound conversation and clear thinking. It places you and keeps you among America's "Intellectual Aristocracy."

Not tomorrow, nor after lunch—for things to be done after lunch are frequently not done at all—but now, while this letter is before you, pencil your name and address on the enclosed card and drop it in the mail.

Then the orders may come and the books may go—by the hundreds—but you will be sure of your set by immediate prepaid shipment.

"It's been worth more to me than a College course," wrote one reader.

"If you can read but one book during the year," said President Hopkins of Dartmouth, "that book should be Wells' "Outline of History."

The enclosed card brings it to you for a week—*free.*

Why is it a tabloid newspaper will outsell a clean, well-edited sheet by ten to one? Why? Because its appeal is to the sob sister, to the emotions. Why is it a Billy Sunday or an Aimee MacPherson can crowd great tabernacles, while your ordinary clergyman preaches to empty pews?

Emotion! The religion that brings masses of converts, that sweeps whole cities, is not an appeal to the intellect—but to the emotions! When Mohammed first preached his doctrines, they were sane and moderate—and they attracted few converts. He added the emotional features—*and swept over half the world!*

You may not be trying to start a new religion, but you do want action of some kind. And to get action, you need to arouse emotion on the part of your reader. You may convince his intellect that the thing you want him to do is right and is for his best advantage, but until you arouse in him an urgent desire to do it, until you make him feel that whatever effort it requires is of no account compared with the satisfaction it will bring him, your letter is lacking in its most important essential. It may have everything else, but if it lacks that faculty of arousing the right feeling, you might as well throw it away. It will never make you money.

Fifteen years ago there was a young fellow in a small Connecticut town with a book—and an idea. The book had been written for serious-minded men, to help show them the way to success. But letters and advertising telling of this marvelous secret of power had left their readers cold—so cold that the original publisher had failed. The young fellow had been his bookkeeper, and had bought the plates and stock at the sale of the publisher's effects.

You see, this young fellow had an idea he could sell that book. He believed that a mere description of its contents, such as had been used in the letters and ads, was not enough, that the important thing was to arouse the reader's desire through an appeal to his ambition. He had only $200 left, but he decided to gamble those $200 on sell-

14

ing the book.

To make a long story short, he did it. He spent his $200, and from them he got $2,000 worth of direct orders by mail! That $2,000 was the start of a small fortune. He promptly spent every cent of it in selling more books, pyramiding his receipts like a stock gambler does his winnings. In the fifteen years that have elapsed since then, that young man has sold more than $2,000,000 worth of books. His name is A. L. Pelton. The book was "Power of Will." And he sold his two millions, as he did his two thousands, by making his appeal—*not* merely to the intellect, but to the emotions.

And his case is typical of every great mail success. What sold the "Book of Etiquette?" It had been gathering dust on the shelves of Doubleday, Page & Co.'s stock room for ten to fifteen years when Nelson Doubleday suddenly brought it to life and sold a million copies. What caused the sudden demand? Not, you may be sure, any wave of culture or politeness sweeping over the nation, but simply the *fear* aroused in the readers of Doubleday's letters and advertisements that some unconscious gaucherie might cause them embarrassment.

Why do people buy reducing belts, face creams, hair tonics? Why do they diet and go through arduous exercises? Not because their reason tells them they need these things, still less because they like them—*but because their emotion of vanity impels them!*

Appeal to the reason, by all means. Give people a logical excuse for buying that they can tell to their friends and use to salve their own consciences. But if you want to sell goods, if you want action of any kind, *base your real urge upon some primary emotion!*

III

Getting News Interest into Your Letters

What the world wants, and has wanted since the beginning, is *news*—something to flag its jaded interest, something to stir its emotions.

Tell a man something new and you have his attention. Give it a personal twist or show its relation to his business and you have his interest.

Do you know how Wells' "Outline of History" was first put across? On its news value! "The Oldest Man in the World," "Was This the Flood of the Biblical Story," "The Finding of Moses," and so on. Newspaper headlines, all of them. News interest in every one of them. Rich man, poor man, beggar man, thief—all stop to read if you can put news interest into your letters.

"When the Rattlesnake Struck!" Can't you see yourself reading on to see what happened? Well, that is what thousands of others did every time that headline was used. It sold hundreds of thousands of O. Henry books.

"Will a Yellow King Rule the World ?" Which one of us would not be startled enough by such a headline to read on and see if there was any reason to fear that such a thing might ever really happen?

"What is the Unpardonable Sin in all Nature?" Can you imagine any reader so blasé as not to go on at least a few lines further to find the answer to that question? And if you can lead him on those few lines, it is your own fault if you can not make your story so interesting that it will carry him right down to the last line and the order blank or card that follows it.

A business man is no different from any other kind. Watch him on his way to the office. Compare the time he gives the financial and business news with the way he eagerly devours the details of the latest murder or scandal, or the attention he gives the "sports" page. He wants news interest. He will get it in his business as far as he can, but if it is not there, he will look outside his business for it.

So if you want his attention, go after it as the newspaper paragrapher does. He knows he has to compete with a thousand other distractions, so he studies his reader and then presents first that side of his story most likely to attract the reader's interest.

16

You have to compete in the same way for your reader's attention. He is not looking for your letter. He has a thousand and one other things more important to him to occupy his mind. Why should he divert his attention from them to plow through pages of type about you or your projects?

You have, we shall assume, decided upon the emotion your letter must arouse in your reader to get him to do as you want. You know that every man is constantly holding a mental conversation with himself, the burden of which is his own interests—his business, his loved ones, his advancement. And you have tried to chime in on that conversation with something that fits in with his thoughts. But some propositions do not lend themselves readily to this. What are you to do then? Look for news value! Look for something in or about your proposition of such news interest that it will divert the reader's mind temporarily from his own affairs, then bring it back by showing how your proposition fits in with those affairs or is necessary to their successful accomplishment. How are you to do it?

Perhaps the best way to explain that is to show a few examples of the way it has been successfully done. Here are some typical openings which get the reader's attention and lead logically on to a description of your proposition:

Do you know what was Socrates' chief characteristic? It was his pertinacious curiosity, his desire to know the why and the wherefore of everything, his questing for fundamental reasons.

It was this curiosity that helped make him represent the highest achievement of Greek civilization. It is that same questing for fundamentals that makes the Bland Advertising Agency so invaluable when a new product is to be introduced, a new field opened, and a new method tried.

In the city of Baghdad lived Hakeem, the Wise One, and many there were who came to him for counsel, which he gave freely to all, asking nothing in return. One day there came to him a young man, who had spent much but got little, and asked: "Tell me, Wise One, what shall I do to receive the most for that which I spend?"

Hakeem answered: "A thing that is bought or sold has no value unless it contains that which cannot be bought

17

or sold. Look for the Priceless Ingredient."

"But what is this Priceless Ingredient?" persisted the young man. Spoke then the Wise One. "My son, the Priceless Ingredient of every product in the market place is the honor and integrity of him who made it. Consider his name before you buy."

For 25 years, Squibbs has been making, etc.

What is the eternal question which stands up and looks you and every sincere man squarely in the eye every morning?

"How can I better my condition?"

That is the real life question which confronts you, and will haunt you every day till you solve it. Read carefully the enclosed booklet, and see if you don't find in it the answer to this important life question which you and every man must solve if he expects ever to have more each Monday morning after pay day than he had the week before.

Your grandfather in his buggy traveled no faster than Caesar; in individual transportation he was almost as limited as a citizen of Rome.

Suddenly—the automobile—and our generation is unshackled! With a car, miles shrivel up into minutes, and the humblest family leaves its doorstep to own the continent.

All day long, from the minute your mind takes the trail early in the morning, until you quit the game late at night— you are figuring on ways to sell more goods, to win more trade, to possess more executive ability, to be a bigger business builder.

This is the one great heart and soul aim of which you are ever conscious—the mastery of your business, the rising to supremacy in your line, the steady year in and year out increase of financial income. You'd willingly spend a few minutes to learn new ways of directing and developing your mental energies so as to cut out waste motion

18

and make every move count for 100% progress.

Did you ever stop to think that the average man's brain wastes more energy than the worst old rattle-box that ever squandered good steam? It's the knowing how to apply your brain-power—how to think, how to reason, how to conserve mental energy, how to concentrate, that alone can make you a leader in your profession.

And it was to teach you how to think, how to concentrate, how to apply the basic fundamentals of all science to your own daily problems that the Blank Course was written. It shows you, etc.

It was payday in Connellsville, Pa., and I was sitting in a local store, talking with the owner—
When a laborer came in.
He said he wanted so-and-so, that he, etc.
So I thought this: You want more business—want your store recognized as the, etc.

If you are tired of a salaried job, if you want to get into a big-paying, independent business of your own, I have a proposition that will interest you.

Here's a little "inside information" that we're passing on to you, because you are a home-maker, and as such it concerns you.

We got a little low on summer stock the other day, so our buyer, Mr. Smith (he's full of ideas and enthusiasm) went to the source of supplies, and we just got a letter from him, thus: (Then give the news of some special buy that enables you to offer a wonderful bargain.)

What is it worth to keep baby's milk sweet? By making your refrigerator measure up to that all-important job, you make it measure up to all other jobs.

Some time today or tomorrow or next month, in practically every commercial office in the U. S., an important executive will sit back in his chair and study a list of names on a sheet of white paper before him.

Your name may be on it. A position of responsibility is open, and he is face to face with the old, old problem—"Where can I find the man?"

The faces, the words, the deeds, the possibilities of various employees pass through his mind in quick review, and he realizes once again how little an employer really knows about their hopes, their ambitions, their particular ability to handle more important work. That is where the Blank School can help him—and you.

What has given the high values to Iowa farm land? Corn. What has given the rapid advance in farm values to all the central western states? Corn. What is the biggest factor in making the farm lands of lower Louisiana advance? Corn. Why? Because they are in the "corn belt."

If your expenses were doubled tomorrow, could you meet them—without running heavily into debt? If you had to have more money on which to live—to support those dependent upon you—could you make it?

You could if you had the training afforded by our Course. It has doubled other men s salaries. It can do the same for you.

For 20 years I was an exile, shunned by people on every hand, unwanted in the business world, impossible socially, a mental and physical wreck, a failure at everything. I was despondent, almost devoid of hope. Life to me was a burden.

And then I learned to talk! (And so on with description of a course to cure stammering.)

Right around New Year's, most of us are somehow thinking about what we'll accomplish within the next twelve mouths. Often we get to figuring and planning and laying it all out beforehand.

So maybe it will mean a lot of inspiration to you, as it did to me, to read.

I have come to look upon it as a pity that circumstances should ever combine to place men of much ability in a position where they are not obliged to begin with a struggle for existence. For most individuals are so constituted that they are obliged to do so. The saving event in many a man s life is the blow that takes away the props that have supported him, and leaves him to look out for himself. Many persons have told me that this is true of their own lives, and we know it is true of ours. So instead of railing against the fate that makes it necessary for you to dig in and make something of yourself, thank God for it, and start now getting ready. The Blank Course will fit you, etc.

The old gentleman who resigned from the Patent Office in 1886 because, as he said, everything had been invented, had nothing on the most of us. There are times when we all begin to feel that mechanical equipment is about as perfect as man can make it.

Take lubrication for instance. In spite of the thousands of dollars wasted in furnishing six ounces of oil to a bearing that needs only one, production men are satisfied—until, of course, some one comes along and shows them where 500% can be saved.

Making production men dissatisfied with their lubrication equipment is our business. Here is a new kind of Bolshevism that pays all around.

You've got to have more money. Your salary, without income, is not enough. The man who depends upon salary alone to make him rich, well-to-do or even comfortable, is making the mistake of his life. For the minute you stop working, the money stops coming in. Lose a day and you lose a day's pay—while expenses go right on.

Don't you think it's time you got Nature to work for you? A dollar put into a peach orchard will work for you days, nights and Sundays. It never stops to sleep or eat, but keeps on growing, growing—from the very minute you put your money in.

A small moss lamp is sufficient to heat an Eskimo's igloo—because its walls are insulated. Minute particles of "dead air," held captive in the snow blocks, provide natural insulation—the most efficient known to science.

But present-day homes of ordinary construction waste two-thirds of the heat that comes from the furnaces. One-third of this heat naturally escapes through windows and doors. The other third is unnecessarily wasted. It escapes easily through uninsulated walls and roofs. Ordinary building materials cannot hold heat in. Celotex stops heat waste.

There's a bank here in Chicago—not much larger than yours—that secured over 280 new savings depositors last month! And secured them, mind you, on the sole strength of business-getting circular letters, without the aid of a single solicitor! That's why this letter is as vital to you as though it were a certified check. For it tells how, etc.

Suppose a good job were open where you work. Could you fill it? Could you jump right in and make good, or would the boss have to pass you up because you lacked training?

The man who is offered the big job is the man who has trained himself to hold it before it is offered to him.

Don't take chances on being promoted. Don't gamble on making good when your opportunity comes. If you want a big job that carries responsibility and pays good money, get ready for it! Pick out the job you want in the work you like best. Then start right now to get, through the Blank Correspondence School, the training that will prepare you to hold it.

If you do as Arnold Bader did—he lives five miles north-east of Monticello—you will have very little trouble with your clover, and you can start a patch of alfalfa that will grow.

When a man, 42 years of age, who has been working for others all his life, decides to go into business for himself— and when, in a few short months, he so solidly establishes his business as to outdistance competitors who had the advantage of years of experience—there must be something about his method of doing business that other men would like to know about at once.

In the January magazine, you will find the story of how John Jones succeeded, what he did, etc.

Pay-day—what does it mean to you? Does your money go 'round? Or does it fail to stop all the gaps made by last week's or month's bills?

Last week according to actual, certified reports on file in our office—300 men got their salary raised as a direct result of becoming more proficient from studying ABC courses.

Don't you think it's time that salary raise was coming your way?

The old saying: "There is strength in numbers," certainly does not apply to the wearing apparel of the woman of today.

Could anything be more disappointing to a well-dressed woman than to pass an exact counterpart of the coat which she is wearing, on some other woman?

Exclusiveness is the keynote of our women s coats; therefore we cannot permit any duplicates. That's the reason our Women's Coat Salon, etc.

"How's the garden? "—is the morning greeting at the suburban station. Many estate owners are planting potatoes on all their available ground. Others, not so ambitious, are growing only enough for a table garden.

Under these conditions, House and Garden magazine assumes a new importance. It has already established a reputation for clear, usable garden information. Now, it is a guide book for the subject uppermost in everyone's mind.

You get more pay for each working hour now than you did the first day you worked. Why? Because you put more value into each hour of your time. You have developed your efficiency.

Your business efficiency grows out of your business ideas, and these come from your business knowledge. If you enrich your knowledge with the tested and proven experience of other men, you save yourself valuable time and the needless labor of studying out that which is already known. You add other men's business knowledge to your own efficiency. You get the material out of which to make new and original ideas.

It is these new ideas that make and break records. They mark the difference between the man who gets paid much and the one who receives little. And it is the material for these new ideas that you find in System, the Journal of Modern Business Management.

25 or 30 years ago, back in the days when we traveled by the Dobbin and Dashboard route, men used to say — "Well, I reckon life insurance is a good thing, but you have to die to win.

Times have changed. And so have life insurance policies. Today there are at least 17 ways you can put life insurance to work for you, right now, in your own lifetime, and reap rich rewards without sacrificing the protection value of the policy.

No matter what business or personal undertaking you have in mind, there is probably a policy that will help you carry out the program easily, quickly, economically—and at the same time protect those dependent upon you.

Frankly, I'd like to discuss the matter with you, etc.

There is one type of letter that is always interesting news, provided the product you are offering has an established market. That type is the price-reduction, money-saving offer. Here are a few such letters that have proved particularly effective:

Monday, March 6th—mark the date on your calendar now! It is the date of a sale you will not want to miss. A sale of women's white Spring frocks at $12.50.

It is such an interesting event that we want to tell you a few things about it. Most of the dresses are, etc.

At the close of a busy season, we find ourselves with 137 sets of the beautiful Gold Star edition of Oliver Cromwell's works slightly damaged from stock-room handling—so slightly you would have to make a close inspection to discern the damage, but still—you know how it is—they cannot be sold as perfect books.

So rather than send them back to the bindery and give the binders the profit of re-binding, we have decided to let the advantage go to a few booklovers—people like you who love good books for the books' sake and not for trifling details about them—and to offer these 137 sets at just what they would be worth with the covers ripped off!

At certain periods of the year, we have special events in this store which we do not advertise. In order that we may personally advise you of such sales, we would like to have your name and address. Won't you please therefore give us this information at the bottom of this card, and either send or bring it to the store at the first convenient opportunity?

On the 1st of October, the rate of the Business Week will go up $1 a line. If you place your order before the 30th of this month, you can buy space to be used any time before January 1st at $— a line. After the 30th, positively no orders will be accepted at less than the new figure. As a matter of fact, our circulation entitles us to the higher rate now.

That one extra dress you so badly wanted, but thoughtfully and economically decided not to buy—that smart afternoon frock, or the pretty street dress, that you longed for, but resisted because to buy it then would have been extravagant—is now, you will be happy to learn, turned into a matter of plain, common sense economy!

For to make space for spring stock that is coming earlier than we were prepared for, we must cut the prices on our complete and beautiful line of winter styles to the point that will make it almost an extravagance not to take advantage of the wonderful values.

We are enclosing in this envelope our check for $6.20 payable to Smith Bros. Readers. This means that if you endorse the check and return it to us before Dec. 10th, we will send you $6.20 worth of these readers, whichever ones you may choose!

On the back of the check, you will find complete list of all our Readers, Grades 1A to 6B. If you wish to order additional quantities at this time, you can apply the enclosed check against our bill as part payment.

You will probably be able to buy an Ever-ready Bag next year—10 years from now—

But, you can never buy it again at its present price of $14.85. That price is about to go up to $20. The special low-payment, free-on-approval club is about to close for good.

This is your chance.

The card herewith brings the newest bag, etc.

Of course, there are ways of flagging the reader's interest even before he gets to the first line of your letter. Putting a catch-phrase on the outside of the envelope is one. The Literary Digest employs this method on most of its mailings, so you can be sure they have found it effective, for no experienced user of the mails keeps up any practice that does not justify itself in increased orders on the record sheet.

As a rule, such catch-phrases on the outside of envelopes are effective only on third-class mail, to catch the reader's eye and arouse enough interest to get him to open your letter. The Review of Reviews has used them numbers of times to great advantage. In the O. Henry sale, they used such catch-lines as: "When the Rattlesnake Struck," "The Fateful Kiss," "If This Happened on Your Wedding Night." In selling Simonds' "History of the World War," they had several that worked well, such as "And they said we wouldn't fight!" and "Retreat, H--l! We just got here!" Another, for a health course, was "'If the darned fools only knew!' said Roosevelt."

All these helped to get the reader inside the envelope. Their purpose was the same as the newspaper headline— to arouse the reader's curiosity and make him go further into the story. So they have to be judged like any other headline, by the one standard—how successful are they in doing their job? And the only way to find that out is to test them against other headlines, or against plain corner cards.

Even on third-class mail, we often find the plain corner cards better, and on first-class, it is almost invariably so. You see, the only object of a 2 ct. stamp is to make the letter seem like a personal message, and to put a catch-phrase on the outside of the envelope defeats that object at once.

So a pretty safe rule to follow is—if you want to use an attention-getter on the outside of the envelope, save half your postage by sending your message third class.

One of the most effective stunts we have seen used to get a man to look inside the envelope was the idea of a young friend of ours. He watched trade papers, house organs and the like for pictures of men connected with different organizations. Then, instead of addressing the man by name, he pasted the man's picture on the front of the envelope and under it wrote: "Care of Such and Such a Company," and the address. It was subtly flattering and it won attention—favorable attention, too.

Folders often lend themselves to such attention-getting stunts even better than envelopes, for their size gives more room for illustration. In effect, they are advertisements sent through the mails, and they have to compete for their readers' interest in the same way as advertisements in a magazine. And their success or failure depends upon the same factors of attention-winning illustration and headline, interest-arousing start, clear description, logical argument and clincher, with coupon or card that makes ordering easy.

These are the more obvious ways of getting attention. Often they are so exaggerated that they defeat their own purpose. Quieter and usually more effective ways may be found in the letter itself, in the circular enclosure, or in the post card or order form.

Some offers lend themselves to a pictorial, colored letter-head. When Nelson Doubleday first offered his Little Nature Library, he used a plain letterhead. By litho-graphing a nature scene of birds and woods and flowers across the top and down one side of his letterhead, he actually *doubled* the number of orders received from his letter! And the Little Leather Library increased their proportion of orders by almost as much.

On the other hand, we have seen numbers of offers which have pulled better results on a plain letterhead than on a colored, pictorial one. To be effective, pictures must not merely be attractively done—they must add essential back-ground that would not be possible without them.

As an instance, at one time we offered a set of large gravure prints of famous pictures. By tipping in the upper left-hand corner of the letterhead a small reproduction of one of these prints, we added nearly 50 per cent to the pulling power of the letter, and sold the prints (which had been gathering dust for years) at a goodly profit.

The same thing held true in selling calendars—a small reproduction in full colors of the picture we were using on the calendar, greatly increased the returns.

Where a business is built around some one personality, as in the case of Elbert Hubbard, his picture on the letterhead often adds 10, 15 or 20 per cent to the pulling power of his letters. We found that to be so in testing different offers for John Blair, head of the New Process Company of Warren, Pa. And the same thing has been true of a number of people we have worked with.

Another effective attention-getter was to tip on the letter-head a sample of the product we were offering. When it was traveling bags, we gave a sample of the leather, to show how tough and long-wearing it was. When it was a topcoat or overcoat, we attached a sample of the cloth, so you could prove for yourself its wool content, see its attractive color and design, get the *feel* of it.

Then there is the fill-in, and the way the letter is folded, and the circulars and order card inserted. We frequently found that even so unimportant a thing as the fold made a difference in the orders. Folding the letterhead out, using the military fold so that only the salutation and first line of the letter showed when the reader picked it up, has increased orders for us at times by as much as 10 per cent.

Indenting the main paragraph helps, too. We have found it a more effective way of calling attention to a special point of interest than either underlining or capitals.

Even the postage stamp has an effect upon the attention accorded a letter. Two red 2-ct. stamps pull more replies than one 4-ct. stamp. One red 2-ct. stamp pulls better than two green 1-ct. stamps. A brown 1 1/2-ct. stamp looks much like a 4-ct. stamp, so it pulls better than a green 1-ct. stamp, but no better than two 1/2-ct. stamps!

As for the metered mail and postage indicia, experience varies, but in our own case, we have found postage stamps more effective than either. To show what a difference color makes even here, we know at least one post office that permits the use of black ribbons in running 1-ct. metered mail, and this 1-ct. metered postage has frequently outpulled 2-ct. stamp or meter!

These are minor details, of course, and not to be considered in the same breath with the start of the letter, the description, the argument or the close. But when you have written a successful letter, when you have your appeal right and are looking only for ways to get more orders, then you will be surprised at how these little minor details can make that order record mount!

IV

Word Pictures That Make People Want Your Product

Now that you have your reader's interest, what are you going to do with it? Start a series of firstlys, and secondlys and thirdlys, like the old-time Preacher, and put your reader to sleep, losing all the advantage you have worked so hard to gain? Go into a long-winded description that tires him out before he is halfway through? Or lead him gently from one point of interest to another, with word pictures so clear, so simple, that he can almost see the things you are offering him?

Getting your reader's attention is your first job. That done, your next problem is to put your idea across, to make him see it as you see it—in short, to visualize it so clearly that he can build it piece by piece in his own mind as a child builds a house of blocks, or puts together the pieces of a picture puzzle.

The mind thinks in pictures, you know. One good illustration is worth a thousand words. But one clear picture built up in the reader's mind by your words is worth a thousand drawings, for the reader colors that picture with his own imagination, which is more potent than all the brushes of all the world's artists.

And the secret of painting such a picture in the reader's mind is to take some familiar figure his mind can readily grasp, add one point of interest here, another there, and so on until you have built a complete word picture of what you have to offer. It is like building a house. You put up your framework. You add a roof, floors, sides, windows, doors, stairs, until you have your structure complete. You would not start with one side, or the roof. You get a solid foundation first; then you add to it logically, piece by piece, until you have your finished building.

Just so it is in building word pictures. Washington Irving gave a classic example of this in his description of the schoolmaster in "The Legend of Sleepy Hollow."

> He was tall, but exceedingly lank, with narrow, sloping shoulders, long arms and legs, hands that dangled a mile out of his sleeves, and his whole framework most loosely hung together. His head was small...

Can't you just picture that gawky, homely figure, with its ill-fitting clothes and shambling gait, the whole giving a scarecrow-like effect such as you see occasionally even today, where some youthful bumpkin seems to have sprouted so fast that arms and legs and Adam's apple have out distanced the rest of his anatomy in the race for development, until now they seem but a weak web holding together a bunch of limbs, with ham-like hands and arms at the ends.

Thousands of sales have been lost, millions of dollars worth of business have failed to materialize, solely because so few letter-writers have that knack of visualizing a proposition—of painting it in words so the reader can see it as they see it.

Yet the ability to do that is perhaps the most important factor in a successful letter, for it means describing your proposition in terms of things the reader knows. Westcott gave a good example of this when he had David Harum tell some "horsey" friends about *The Lost Chord.*

> It's about a feller sittin' one day by the organ, an' not feelin' exac'ly right—kind o' tired and out o' sorts and not knowing' jes' where he was drivin' at—jes' joggin' along with a loose rein for quite a piece, an' so on; an' then, by an by, strikin' right into his gait and goin' on stronger and stronger, and fin'ly finishin' up with an A-a-a-men that carries him quarter way 'round the track 'fore he can pull up.

You see, your sale must be made in your reader's mind. Before you can get his order, it is necessary for you to register a sequence of impressions in his mind, the combined result of which will be to make him want the thing you are offering more than the money or trouble it costs him. And the method of registering those impressions lies in first picking something with which he is familiar, and building on that.

To describe apples, for instance, as "like those with which Eve tempted Adam," is to use a simile that will strike a familiar chord with every one. "Honey such as Cleopatra served to Antony," brings in another familiar allusion that almost any one would recognize.

"As rich in appointment as Croesus in coin of the realm." "Satisfying as sinking a ten-foot putt on a rough green." "As much chance as a gold-fish on a cat farm." "Like a home run in the ninth inning with the bases full." "Like painting a battleship with a tooth brush." "Thick, creamy chocolate coatings that give you that 'moreish' feeling." "The company with a good product that does not advertise is like a man who whispers to himself on a desert." Every one of these stirs a familiar memory and thus gives you a definite impression to tie your story to. It is the difference between having a foundation to build upon and resting your edifice upon shifting sands.

Further along in this book we shall give you numbers of instances of the way the writer has used this idea in describing various products he has helped to sell. Meantime, we give below a few good examples of how others have done it:

About a Ginger Ale

The lore which enters its making is akin to the lore of the wine-makers of France—a formula and process handed down from father to son. Only three men know the secret of its charm and vivacity, its mellow glow and friendliness. You will find in it stimulation like that of mountain air.

Silverware

The cheerful hum of voices, the steaming kettle, the cup that cheers, and Silver plate with its satiny surface catching every light.

A Room

It seemed, partly because the ceiling was low, to be very spacious; the walls and ceiling were of a kind of dusky amber hue; a golden brown was everywhere the prevailing tint. The tiny curtains, the long settees into which one sank, the chairs, the shades of the mellow lights—all were of some variety of this delicate, golden brown. In the middle of the room stood a square table.

A Rug

Under her feet a rug so thick that she felt her shoes must be hidden in its pile.

A Laundry

A goodly part of the delight of a dinner is in linen white as almond blossoms. Napery, to be at its best, should be laundered carefully and skillfully. Many discerning housewives entrust their fine table linen to the White Laundry. In it, the constant thought is not "how quick" but "how well." But with all our care, we do save time for you, too.

A Book

If you are one of the live, wide-awake men who welcome the rush and tumult of great daring and big adventure, who believe that there is nothing better for tired brains or tired bodies than the healthy, blood-tingling, mind-quickening stimulation of a good story, then .

Hawaii

Four days beyond the Golden Gate, the Hawaiian Islands lift their crests of misty jade above a sparkling sea. Four nights away, the orange moon floods Moana Valley with its spell, and the ghosts of gorgeous flowers spread a witchery of perfume in the shadows. Four days away, the long combers, creaming on Waikiki's bar, race shoreward, and golden-skinned surf-riders, young gods and goddesses of the blue deep, speed across the amethystine waters.

Someone waits to drape a lei of jasmine on your shoulders. Someone waits to sing the husky croon, "Aloha oe," to echo in your heart for years. Why don't you go and capture your dreams?

A Ham

This mark certifies that the hog came from good stock, that it was corn-fed in order that it might be firm and sweet — that it was a barrow hog, so that the meat would be full-flavored and juicy—that it was a young hog, making the ham thin-skinned and tender—well-conditioned and fat, insuring the lean of the ham to be tasty and nutritious. This mark certifies that the ham was cured in sugar, pure saltpeter and only a very little salt, thus bringing out all the fine, rich, natural flavor of the carefully selected meat, and preserving it without "salty pickling."

A Real Estate Development

From every standpoint of the amusement industry and the real estate promoter, Boca Grande is a dead town. It always has been dead and probably always will be. That is why it appeals to many live people.

It doesn't quarrel with any of the bigger and better movements. It simply lets them alone. It has no Chamber of Commerce, no dredges or sand-suckers, and nothing proposed for 1931. Boca Grande is simply a haven for those who prefer to roll their own in the way of amusement. Providence did a perfectly satisfactory job in the way of making this a lovely place to swim and fish and golf, and we who have been wintering here since long before the boom came and went, let it go at that.

You might like Boca Grande a lot. Many clever people do. It is an adventure in naturalness. Let us send you a book about it. It is a very nice book, and not too much exaggerated.

An Electric Refrigerator

Just a few degrees below the temperature of an ordinary ice-box is a colder zone that affects the keeping of foods in a remarkable way. It is the zone where moisture crystallizes out of the air as frost, leaving the air dry, crisp and snappy. At this lower temperature, the air takes on a frosty sting. This is the zone of So-and-so, produced by So-and-so electric refrigeration.

A Gas Burner

The Blank Heat-Spreading Burner is a nest of small jets, and is so designed that the heat is spread evenly over the entire bottom of the utensil. Combustion is so perfect that all the fuel is burned. You get the full benefit of every atom of gas. The bottom of the cooking utensil rests only seven-eighths of an inch from the burner top. There are no deposits of carbon to be scoured off.

An Oven

This is the Blank Oven, built on the principle of the Dutch oven, with the "baker's arch" to prevent air pockets. The patented heat spreader at the bottom assures even distribution of heat, and guards against your roasts and baked things being underdone on top and burnt on the bottom. On the door of the oven there is a heat indicator which shows how much heat there is inside.

And here are a few from England which tend to show that our cousins across the water are not as deficient in humor as the "funny papers" would lead us to believe. Certainly their descriptions would be hard to improve upon.

A Plum Cake

It was in one of those sweet old country houses where they put little bunches of lavender with the linen that we first tasted the plum cake of our dreams—glorious stuff, rich, fragrant and incredibly plummy. We admit now that our mouth was too full when we asked for the recipe, but we were overwrought and excited; anyhow, let bygones be bygones, they gave us the recipe for our customers.

The dear old housekeeper, with her ringlets and black taffeta, took us to the still room to show us how to make it, and told us fascinating things; how brown-shelled eggs are best, and how it is most auspicious to make such a cake when the moon is in its second quarter. That is why you so often see our chef on our roof in Piccadilly anxiously scanning the heavens on fine nights.

Turtle Soup

When we speak of turtle soup, our voice becomes very tender—do not think us unmanly. We have in mind the spiced turtle soup we make for those who feast regally. As you gaze into its depths, you see luscious calipee and morsels of calipash gleaming darkly through the soup that is so rich and yet so wondrous clear. Then there is our special turtle soup, cleared of all heaviness and fat, that brings roses back to the cheeks of delicate people.

Once a rival, maddened by jealousy, came and spoke lightly of our turtle soup. We killed him. It was wrong of us, for we held no game license that season, but it shows we are not unmanly.

Cakes

We have these cakes made at a little rose-covered country house, by people steeped in the sweet lore of home-made cake-craft. We will not even let them come to London for a holiday, for fear they should be contaminated by modern methods. So there they bide, unhurried and at peace, with bowls of rosewater at their elbows, and little sprigs of rosemary and great crocks of buttermilk, making glorious cakes full of the goodness that is England.

Could such cakes as these be made within earshot of a London motor-bus? We trow not.

A Cheese

There is in England one incomparable herd of glossy little Guernsey cows that give milk that is about one-third cream. It is from this wonderful herd that we obtain our butter. That is why there is no mistaking its golden charm.

With all humility, we say there are few, if any, cheeses as good as ours to be obtained in England. For many years we have obtained them from the same prize dairy.

We have kept a few of last year's Cheddars for those who love the ripe splendour of well matured cheese.

Do not be misguided by the mirthless Stiltons made in hissing factories by pale youths who cycle madly to the cinema when freedom hoots from the powerhouse.

Our real farm-house Stiltons will show you why the name is venerated by mankind. Each cheese is made in the homestead of a Leicestershire yeoman, from great pans of cream, and aprons full of cowslips for the coloring. When such cheeses as these enter the dining rooms of clubs, the faces of brigadiers soften, and admirals give little plaintive cries of love.

Chinese Ginger

Fat-root ginger with its generous warmth curbed by sweetness. And then there is the syrup—lazy in its richness.

Ham

Deep-sheathed in ivory-white fat, and close set with rosy meat...

The eating of them makes a man realize how fond he is of all his relatives—well, practically all.

Bacon

When the fragrance of its frying rises through the area, passers-by give savage cries and raven at the railings. This is one of the disadvantages of living in town.

The fascination of our bacon lies in the secret manner of its curing. It is mellowed in the suave smoke of certain rare woods and old-world herbs. Bacon with meaning and beauty in every mouthful. Often we stand for hours before a side of our wonderful bacon, musing in deep reverie, and finding therein our greatest happiness.

Put life into your descriptions—life, and when possible, a smile. Give your reader something that will stir him out of his indifference, arouse his emotions. You never see "Standing Room Only!" signs in front of an art museum or a public library or a theater where educational films or travelogues are being shown. But just try to get into almost any good movie around eight o'clock of an evening! Why the difference?

Because most people cultivate their intellects only under the lash. They revel in emotion at any and all times.

So give them a thrill! If you want to describe your mustard, weave it into a story. Tell how the girl planned this picnic lunch; of the loving care that went into every bit of it; the touch of this; the flavor of that; the delicious ham; the savory mustard; and then how the boy forgot them all just in the delight of being with her.

Tell about the man so poor he did not have a penny even to buy his boy the velocipede he had been begging Santa to bring him; so after the little tot had gone to bed, Dad sat down with his pocket knife and some old lumber and carved out a sort of wooden velocipede that not only delighted the boy's heart, but when shown to a toy manufacturer, put Daddy beyond the reach of want for the rest of his days.

Tell how the rubber tire owed its inception to the efforts of a young veterinary to make a more comfortable wheel-chair for his invalid mother; how the first mowing machine consisted of a number of scissors with one side nailed to a board, the other connected to a string which opened and shut them. Get the story back of your product. Give your reader a laugh or a tear or a lump in his throat. Stir up his emotions! You will have no trouble interesting him then!

Compare the following advertisements, for instance. The first three are good ads and pulled a reasonable number of orders. They were successful, as advertisements go. But their appeal was solely to the intellect. Once we had tried the style outlined in the last four ads, we discarded the other kind entirely, for the emotional type tripled and quadrupled our returns.

No. 1.

Roosevelt said, "Mr. Frank H. Simonds' "History of the Great War" is a very remarkable work, and I look forward eagerly to the appearance of the remaining volumes. It is not too much to say that no other man in this or any other country can quite parallel the work that Mr. Simonds has done. It is hard to say what most to admire; the really extraordinary grasp of the essential facts of the war which is shown; or the transparent clearness with

38

which the facts are brought out; or the entire fairness and impartiality of the conclusions."

No. 2.

Colleges Study This History

Yale University has ordered 400 copies of selected chapters from Simonds' "History of the World War" for use as a textbook in its history classes. Ex-President Hadley says of it: "I have had so much pleasure from what Simonds has already written about the war that I shall be particularly glad to have the results of his observations and conclusions in a more permanent form."

Once in a generation, perhaps, there appears a man with the gift for making history vital, alive, interesting— a man like Ridpath or Macaulay—a genius that combines a natural gift for language, a natural gift for history and a natural gift for facts with great vision and the ability to make you see and be thrilled by his vision.

Frank H. Simonds is this generation's Ridpath—this war's Macaulay. His tale is simple and direct enough to captivate children, yet so profoundly true as to hold the greatest scholar.

No. 3.

Ever since the day in July, 1914, when one flaming editorial of his startled the world with its prophecy of the great war, Simonds has been the one pre-eminent writer on the war. He is quoted by newspapers the world over. The British Government has had his articles reprinted and distributed broadcast. The French Government has conferred upon him alone of all the Historians of the war the Cross of the Chevalier of the Legion of Honor. The Greek Government has made him an Officer of the Royal Order of the Redeemer. The King of Rumania has named him an Officer of the Royal Order of the Star of Rumania.

To no other writer did statesmen and generals so freely and frankly give information. No other military critic was so often quoted or so highly regarded as an authority. Multitudes based their opinions upon his judgment. His words governed the hopes and fears of millions.

So it is wonderful indeed that you can now have the whole story of the war in its final form written by him, with interesting special articles and illuminating sidelights by the greatest military, naval, and political leaders of America and Europe.

No. 4.

*"My right has been driven in, my left has been driven in —consequently with all that is left of my center, I will now attack.' -*Foch.

That is the terse report that General Foch sent to Joffre at the crucial moment of the battle of the Marne. Told that his troops were worn out by the three days of continuous fighting—" Tired?" he cried. "So are the Germans. Attack!" And attack they did in gallant style. He drew together all his exhausted divisions, all his reserves, and at the very moment when the enemy thought him routed, he smashed against the Prussian Guard in a violent, desperate assault, broke through its lines, crushed them—and saved Paris!

How Much Do You Know of This Brilliant Leader?

Do you know that he is everywhere considered one of the greatest tacticians the world has known? Do you know that it was he who saved the channel ports of Calais and Dunkirk, and thus made possible the uninterrupted passage of men and supplies from England? Do you know that he was the man who took in hand the Italian defense just at the moment the Austro-German drive was at its height, and not only saved Venice, but changed almost certain defeat into glorious victory?

The History of the Great War

Gives a detailed account of these exploits as well as the whole story of the war. You read in it of the heroic stand, etc.

No. 5.

A Rude Awakening
(The illustration for this ad showed the
Kaiser seated, with a huge firecracker

40

labeled "A.E.F." just ready to go off behind him.)

The Kaiser has again and again assured his people they have nothing to fear from America—that all we shall ever be able to get past his U-boats is a few divisions of troops and some shiploads of supplies—that the tales of huge armies being formed, of mountains of munitions being manufactured, of flocks of aeroplanes and great fleets of ships, are just "American bluff."

What a Rude Awakening Is in Store for Him

Already our men are in the battle line by the hundred thousand; already our Navy has definitely checked the U-boat menace. Soon we shall have more than a million men in France and two million more are in training, and our shipbuilding alone will more than replace any future losses from submarines and mines.

But to definitely defeat the German Military Power, to win the war and make the world safe for the next hundred years, will take every bit of energy, every ounce of force that we can muster; and one of the first things necessary to get the most out of our enormous resources is to know all about the war—what led up to it, how it began, through it all. Where can you find all this? In, etc.

No. 6.
The Terrible Year
This, according to the German plan, was to be "The Terrible Year." The German High Command realized the necessity of getting a decision before the full American strength could make itself felt, so their strategy was to keep hammering the Allies until they had pounded their way through to Paris or the English Channel, and forced the Allies to accept a German peace.

But the Americans Turned the Tide
Against all the German expectations, America solved her transport problem so speedily, so successfully, that she was able to pour men into the fighting by the hundred thousand right at the crucial moment, turning German

41

victory into overwhelming disaster.

Not only did Our Boys stop the German and hurl the Prussian hordes back over the Marne, but it was their energy and dash that enabled Foch to counterdrive so successfully, capturing thousands of prisoners and literally mountains of munitions.

The History of the World War gives you in vivid, pulsing narrative, etc.

No. 7.

The Coming of the Yanks

The battle of Chateau-Thierry was at its height. The Germans were pouring in such a hurricane of shot and shell, liquid fire and poison gas that the French Poilus, staunch veterans though they were, had begun to give way before that storm of destruction, and the never-ending hordes of on-rushing Huns.

Already the French Commander was preparing for a hurried retreat. Already he had ordered his hospital, with its hundreds of wounded, moved to the rear. The outlook was dark indeed—the road to Paris and the heart of France seemed open to the invader, when suddenly from over the hill behind the French lines came the sound of martial music—of thousands of fresh young voices singing—singing cheerily, confidently, exultantly—

> *The Yanks are coming,*
> *The Yanks are coming,*
> *The Yanks are coming over there!*

And through the mist and battle smoke broke the long lines of Americans, their guns at the charge, their bayonets fixed, every man singing—exultant at the chance to get at the foe.

They went at the Germans like so many wild-cats. They killed them with bayonet, with rifle butt or with knife. They charged right into the face of machine guns —tore them apart—choked the gunners with bare hands!

In two short, glorious hours, the whole war was won. In two hours that will rank in history with Waterloo or Gettysburg, the Germans woke to the fact that they had not a chance—that they were fighting against something

42

too big for them to meet—a spirit so high that no force of theirs could stop it.

The full story of Chateau Thierry has never been written. Not in any newspaper or magazine can you find the things our boys did that day. It is only around some confidential table where men high in the counsels of our Allies meet that the truth is freely told.

But now at last you can know the full story of that wonderful battle—of how our boys brought it home to the Germans that the end had come. It is a stupendous story. It will make every American heart beat faster. You can read it, just as it really happened, in

Simonds' "History of the World War."

V

Motives That Make People Buy

Most people are like automobiles. They can be pushed or pulled along, or they can be moved to action by starting their own motive power from within. In either case, *you* must provide the fuel. And the only fuel that will start the sort of action you want from within is *desire.* Arousing that desire in your reader is known as the gentle art of exercising persuasion.

What is persuasion? Nothing but finding the motive that will impel your reader to do as you wish, then stirring it to the point where it is stronger than his inertia, or his economical tendencies.

To do that, you must show how he is going to benefit, and you can not do it unless you have the faculty of putting yourself in his place. Would *you* be richer, healthier, happier for having done the thing you ask? Would it help your standing with others? Would it enable you to do anything, write anything, say anything better than you could before? Is it something every one should have? Would it gratify any passion? Would it enable you to help those you love? Would it prevent loss of money or the respect of others?

Only the new letter-writer selects the arguments that are nearest to hand—the viewpoints that appeal to his own selfish interests. The experienced writer asks himself such questions as those above, then picks the motive that is strongest and presents it from the viewpoint of the reader alone. He shows what it will do for the reader, what it will add to his prestige, to his power, to his comfort, to the well-being of those he loves.

Description of your product is necessary. But description, no matter how interestingly done, will never sell your product by the thousands. It is what it will do for the one who buys it that counts!

There are six prime motives of human action: love, gain, duty, pride, self-indulgence and self-preservation. And frequently they are so mixed together that it is hard to tell which to work on more strongly. A man may want a new car, for instance, solely from a feeling of pride in its fine appearance, but unless money is a matter of no moment to him, pride alone will seldom make him buy.

To make that pride motive so strong as to sweep caution to the

44

winds, you must reinforce it with a touch of self-indulgence, a measure of love and duty for wife and family, and a large dash of gain. Show how the old car hurts his standing, how repair bills and higher gas and oil consumption eat into the difference in price, how he can effect some saving now that will not be possible a month or a year later.

The more motives you can appeal to, of course, the more successful you will be, but it is important that you differentiate between the motive that makes him desire a thing and the one that impels him to take the action you desire, for the whole purpose of your letter is to make your reader act as you wish him to. He may not want to pay a bill, for instance. He may need the money badly for himself, and all his inclinations may be towards keeping it in his pocket. But if you can "sell" him the idea that his credit means more to him than the possession of that money or anything it can buy him, you have touched the right motive.

What has he to gain by doing as you wish? What to lose by refusing?

"If some one were to make your boy a thief," read a National Cash Register Company letter. "Feeling as you do about your own boy, is it right to put temptation in the way of other men's boys ?"

Love and pride and duty are all intermingled there, with the added inducement of gain implied—of saving the losses from petty thefts and the like. But love is the dominant motive.

Love is always the strongest motive. You have but to read the papers to see how men are every day giving everything they have for it—riches and honor, life itself. Yet love is one of the most difficult motives to effectively work into a letter. Because it is so universal, it has been harped upon to such an extent that the letter-writer has to be more adroit in its use than with any other motive.

Gain, now; that is easy. True, it has been worked to death, too, but we are a gullible race, and we are much readier to believe that some one is unselfishly interested in helping us to make or save money, than that he will go out of his way to further the well-being of those near and dear to us.

Tell a man, for instance, that you have only two cars left in stock, or ten suits in his size, or a hundred sets of books, and when the new stock comes in the price will be advanced 25 per cent, but since he is an old customer you are holding one of these for him at the old price, and he will believe you. But try to tell the same man that your only reason for trying to sell the "Book of Knowledge" or the "Junior Classics" is your ardent love for and interest in the well-being of children, and he will laugh at you. He may buy these books if the good they will do his children is adroitly presented to him, but he resents having his love for them used as a leverage to dig money out of him for you.

Here is a skillful appeal to pride that was used with great success in the days before the automobile had crowded the horse and buggy off the road, and that can still be adapted to many another product just as successfully:

Mr. John Jones,
Jonesboro, N. C.

DEAR SIR:

Mr. Smith, our factory manager, just came in with your inquiry of Jan. 1st. He read it to me and said:

"You remember Mr. Jones, don't you? He stands pretty high over there in Jonesboro where he lives—lots of folks know him. If Mr. Jones could drive one of our buggies around and tell his friends and neighbors who made it and how well satisfied he is with it, we could sell a lot more buggies in that neighborhood this coming year."

Then he suggested an idea which I know will please you immensely, Mr. Jones. Here it is:

I am having made to order for my own personal use just about the finest buggy that money can buy. Here's a blueprint of it. See the extra strength I've built into the wheels. Note the triple ply springs that make riding easier. Mr. Smith just said: "Mr. Jones would surely be delighted with a buggy like yours. Why don't you offer him this one? You can make another for yourself."

He thinks that if I send you my built-to-order buggy, you as a man who knows buggies, who knows what materials and finish ought to go into good buggies, will surely be pleased with it and certainly be envied by friends and acquaintances of yours who will see and admire my buggy when you drive it. I know Smith is right. So I've decided to act on his suggestion and let you have the buggy I've taken such great personal pride in designing.

Now, Mr. Jones, if an extra-fine buggy one built specially to order for the President of the Columbus Buggy Co. would interest you—if such a buggy, with its longer wear and smarter appearance, would be worth a few dollars more to you—if you'd like to drive a buggy you'll be proud of all your life, just fill out the attached form, send it back by return mail, and I'll ship you a buggy like mine at once, or if you say so, I'll send you the buggy now being made for me, and make another like it for myself.

Of course, clothes don't make the man. But you know yourself how helpful they are in getting him a hearing.

It is likely that Tom Edison or Charlie Schwab could wear any kind of clothes and not suffer particular loss of prestige if the suit happened to be shabby or a misfit.

But most of us have to be a bit more careful. Aside from what our friends might think of us, we don't feel right ourselves unless we have the consciousness of being well-groomed.

Through a fortunate purchase of fine wool, we are able to offer this MacCarden Motor Robe at a special low price of $9.85—about $5 or $6 less than you would expect to pay for a good robe in a retail store. We have been notified, however, that future wool will cost us much more; and we cannot hope to continue the $9.85 price when our present supply is gone.

Just glance over the enclosed folder and think for one moment of the absorbing, fascinating story that goes with it —education in the highest sense, entertainment in the most educational sense. People who have read this new, finally revised edition of the Outline are saying that it has done more for them than a College education. A College education costs you probably $5,000 and four years of your life. Wells' wonderful work is sent to you on approval, and you will read the four books as absorbedly, as quickly as so many novels.

One of the oldest firms in the rubber business—a factory which makes tires that are as good as any in the world— wants to see if car owners will buy their tires "direct" if he will sell to them at just about the price dealers now pay.

This tire manufacturer knows that such a saving can be made if a lot of unnecessary selling expense and middlemen's profits are wiped out. So he's going to test out the motoring public by offering the very best tires he makes direct to car owners through our selling organization which operates by mail all over the country.

And to quickly find out if men really want to save 25% on the best tires that can be made, he is having us rush out this August letter to a few selected car owners,

We have just 790 of these double-texture, all wool Great coats to sell at this low price. When they are gone, your chance to save on your Winter Ulster will go with them. But while these 790 last, you can get as perfect-fitting, as good-looking, as fine-quality a Winter Overcoat as ever you would want to wear, at an almost unheard-of bargain.

As Resident Buyers for a number of out-of-town stores, we are making the rounds of the manufacturers every day, and whenever they bring out some "special," whenever they close out some small lot, whenever they finish copying some designer's model-gown, *we get it!*

You know yourself what bargains you can pick up even in the stores just by shopping around. Imagine, then, what we can do when we are daily shopping among the manufacturer's themselves. A fourth off, a third off, even a half off the regular wholesale price is nothing unusual, for manufacturer's have no time to bother with these small lots, and they give them to us at practically our own price.

The result is that we can offer you some of the season's loveliest and most distinctive models, in all sizes, in the most fashionable colors and materials, *at actually less than their regular wholesale prices!*

Nearly every man can look back—and not so far back with most of us—and recall cases where some little slip lost him opportunity or prestige, cost him the favor of some one whose good opinion he valued, turned what might have been a valuable friendship into enmity or indifference.

But there is no need to lose more such opportunities. For just as a physician may read medicine, just as a lawyer may read law, just so may you now read the science of culture—that science of good breeding which includes etiquette but yet is above and beyond all etiquette.

One of the best opportunities for the use of persuasion is in collection letters. As a matter of fact, it is our opinion that there are only two ways to collect old accounts. The first is persuasion. The second is the threat of court action or loss of credit standing.

Our own idea is that the most effective collection series is one that alternates these two. When you send out a strong threat you frighten a certain number of delinquents into paying, but you make the others so mad they swear they will never pay. Send another threat on top of that and you just make them madder. But use persuasion and you smooth down their fur, get a number of payments, and have things all set for another effective threat.

Here are a few samples of persuasive collection letters:

You remember how Abraham Lincoln walked many weary miles from the grocery store where he earned a mere pittance, in order to bring to a poor old woman the few cents change she had forgotten and left on the counter.

And how Mark Twain, because his name happened to be associated with that of an unsuccessful company, took all its heavy debts upon himself, and, though an old man, paid every one.

It is this "I-will-owe-no-man-a-penny" spirit that builds up and strengthens self-respect and personal integrity—and makes a credit reputation that bulwarks a man in time of need. It is because we find just such good old-fashioned honesty as this in 99% of the folks with whom we do business, that we feel sure of the payment

49

of your account, even though it has been neglected recently.

Unless you have conducted a similar business, you can hardly conceive of the mass of detail involved in handling many thousands of these $1 and $2 accounts. The difference between profit and loss on such a business depends upon the promptness of collections more than on any other one thing.

I know you will not consciously be instrumental in working a hardship on any concern with which you do business, and I am quite sure that when you see your failure to remit promptly is doing just that, you will sending a check by return mail.

Back in the Stone Age, records were carved on a stone slab. When the debt was due, Mr. Creditor presented the account in a very polite fashion—holding the slab in one hand while in the other he carried his stone mallet. The debtor had no alternative.

Then civilization moved on until the debtor's prison was the deciding factor as to whether a debtor would pay or not. But now it is a different proposition—*credit*. Every kind of business, large or small, must build its foundation on its credit standing. Concerns liquidating their obligations at maturity build their credit standing to the highest point attainable, while those who allow their obligations to run along month after month without payment, decrease their credit standing until it is nearly obliterated.

Again, as perhaps in your case, there is the business man who is too busy with matters of more importance, and the work of looking after his financial and accounting details is delegated to some other person who lets these important factors ride without considering the detrimental effect they have on your credit standing.

Your name in red ink on our records is something we want to avoid. You do, too, I am sure. Here is the way the account now stands:

John Johnson—Bills Receivable—$25.00

But unless we receive a check by the 17th, here is the way our bookkeeping department will have to enter it.

(Red Ink) John Johnson—Account Overdue $25.00

The bad feature about this entry is the effect it has on our credit man, and the credit men of all the other stores that belong to our Association. But then your check before the 17th prevents all this.

The records in the case show that your account has been PAST DUE for 90 days, and that you have failed to return the goods or make payment, or to advise the Blank Company of cause for delay. The records also show that though written repeatedly, you have shown no inclination to liquidate your indebtedness. You have COMPELLED them to turn the account over to the Legal Department to take such action as may protect the interests of the company.

That you may be fully cognizant of the law, I wish to advise you that obtaining goods with an intent to defraud constitutes a criminal act and if such fraud is proved, the person committing it is liable to imprisonment.

Your case is now on the records of the Legal Department, and will come up for attention in one week unless you make remittance to the Blank Company.

It is to be hoped you will, for your own protection, make payment if you desire to avoid the annoyance, publicity and cost of a lawsuit. You remember a famous English Jurist is reported to have said that if a man claimed the coat on his back, and threatened to sue him for it, he'd give him the coat rather than risk losing his waistcoat, too, in defending the lawsuit.

If that is true when you are in the right, how much more true it must be when the facts are so strongly against you as in the present case!

Summed up, arousing the right motive comes down to making the reader want what you have to offer, whether that be merchandise or money or credit or merely a clean bill of health—*not* merely for what it *is*, but for *what it will do for him!*

When you can get him thinking along those lines, when you can bring home to him the advantages that will accrue to him from doing as you wish, in so effective a way that he wants these more than anything or any trouble they may cost him, then you can feel that you have demonstrated the gentle art of exercising persuasion.

VI

The Proof of the Pudding

Out in a little town in northwestern Pennsylvania is a mail order house which built a business from scratch, to over a million dollars a year on one basis only—*proof.*

They described their products to the best of their ability, they followed the usual rules of attention and interest, but for their main argument they used *proof.*

One of their most effective letters read:

> When 10,000 men from all over the country send all the way out here just to get a raincoat, there must be something unusual about these coats. And when a man like John Jones of such and such a street in your town [and here they gave the name of an actual buyer in the town, frequently a man whose name was well known] not only sends for a Blank Coat, but is so well pleased with it that he writes: "Your Blank Coat is not only the finest quality and the best fit I have had in a coat for a long time, but an unusual value. I haven't been able to find its equal in our local stores at twice the price."
>
> When thousands of well-dressed business and professional men from all over the country write us letters like that, and when more than a dozen of your own fellow townsmen have sent for this same coat, and liked it so well that they gladly sent up $14.65 for it and felt that they were saving $10 to $15 each when they did it—don't you think it would be worth your while to at least look at so unusual a value, especially when the enclosed card will bring one to you in your exact size without one penny of cost or one bit of obligation?

Testimonial

In the beginning, of course, it was more difficult. They had no ten thousand customers to refer to. So at the start they depended for their proof upon the "free-examination, no-money-until-you-have-tried-it-for-a-week-plan. That helped to establish confidence. And

53

as fast as they got an order they did their utmost to turn it into a satisfied customer from whom they could get a testimonial. The testimonials were bait, and with them they tempted every man in the town or state where the writer lived.

That the idea was sound was proved by the results. Tucked away off in a corner of Pennsylvania, in a town no one had ever heard of, without capital, without special advantages of any kind, they built their business to a volume of over a million dollars. Why? Because statements which, coming from themselves, would have been laughed at, were accepted at face value when they came from the mouths of their customers.

Perhaps even this alone might not have been convincing had they not backed up these statements with the "free-examination, no-money-until-you-have-tried-it-for-a-week" idea, which showed that they not only believed the statements to be true, but had every confidence in the ability of the goods to back them up.

Every sales letter must have argument or proof of some kind, but all the argument in the world is not equal to proof such as this: "You know Jim Jones, who lives over on Vesey Street, a few blocks from you. Here is what he says . . . But we don't ask you to take his word for it. We don't ask you to believe even such men as this Senator, and that Congressman, and a nationally known banker or lawyer or whatnot. Try it for yourself and see! The enclosed card brings it to you without cost and without obligation, for a week's *free try out.*"

What is it that sells patent medicines by the millions every year? What is it that makes men swallow gallons of nasty, unpalatable nostrums, pounds of seaweed, and yeast cakes put up in all manner of forms? *Proof!* A man describes your symptoms with such exactitude that you think he must have taken a look down your epiglotus, then assures you that one dose or a dozen pills or cakes of yeast relieved him of every trace of his ailment.

What is there for you to do but to try some of the same? If the remedy was so efficacious with him, you naturally reason it will not do any harm to try a little of it yourself. And so the sales go on.

We are a credulous people, but we have become so accustomed to hearing every one claim that his product is the best in the world, or the cheapest, that we take all such statements with a grain of salt. Let some third person make the statement, however, apparently from excess of enthusiasm over the wonderful value or service he has received, and we prick up our ears. Let that be backed by positive proof and we are ready to risk our money.

For that reason, it usually pays to put a testimonial into every letter you write. I know one unusually successful mail order man who will not let even a collection letter go out of his house without a testimonial in it. And I believe he is right. For why doesn't your customer pay his bill? Frequently because he is not satisfied with your product, not quite sold on the idea that it is as good value for the money as he had expected. More than any one else, he needs to be convinced of this, and what surer way to convince him than through the mouth of some one who has used it?

True, testimonials are in rather bad odor of late, due to the way advertisers have run after celebrities and bought their endorsement of everything from chewing gum to pajamas. But there never will be a time when a testimonial, which has the ring of truth about it, will not be a potent factor in dispelling doubt in the mind of a hesitant customer.

VII

Supplying That Impulse

Watch the crowd in front of a sideshow. At just the critical moment in the barker's talk, his assistants on the outside of the crowd start a general push forward towards the ticket window.

In every sale, whether in person or by mail, there comes that same critical moment. Your prospective customer is almost convinced. You have his attention, you have aroused his interest, you have just about persuaded him that he must have the thing you are offering, you have proved to him beyond question that it is the best or the cheapest; but he is not quite ready to sign on the dotted line. Caution, inertia, call it what you will, urges him to hold back. Desire, the appeal of a bargain, is goading him on. He is hesitating, teetering, first this way and then that. Too much urging will make him draw back. Too little will leave him where he is. What are you to do?

Give him a push without seeming to do so. Like the circus barker's assistants, supply the impulse that will make it easier for him to go forward with the crowd than to stand still or draw back. How are you to do it?

You already know the motive it is necessary to arouse to make your sale, so look for some easy preliminary task on which you can set that motive busy. Then see if you can make it easier for your customer, already started, to keep going forward rather than stop and turn around and go back.

In personal selling you find examples of this every day. What does an automobile advertisement try to make you do! Buy a car? Not at all. "Come and look at our beautiful new models "—that's all. "No obligation whatever. It will be a pleasure to show them to you.

You go, and what happens? Does the salesman urge you to buy? No, indeed! He shows you around most readily, notes the car you like, gets you to sit in it, to feel the clutch, to sense all the comfort and luxury of it. Then he asks if you would like to drive it out to the country next Sunday "Just to see how beautifully it runs." He has it in front of your house at the appointed time or a little before. He gives up the driver's seat to you at once. He says nothing about a sale just calls your attention to the gentle purr of the motor, to the way it breasts the hills, to this little comfort and that knickknack. And when he gets you back to your door, he gently insinuates: "Now, what time shall I send it around tomorrow," or "Well, let's take a look at the old car now, and see how much we could allow on it." And almost before you know it, you have a new car.

That is salesmanship. And that is the sort of salesmanship you must put into every letter. Just remember that nearly every man balks at making a decision that is going to cost him money. He wants time to think it over. He hates to commit himself definitely. So humor him. Tell him frankly: "Don't decide now. Plenty of time for that later. Just fill in your height, your weight and your collar size on the enclosed card, and we'll send you a Keep dry Coat in your exact size. Try it out. *Wear* it for a week. Take it down town and compare it with anything you can find in your local stores. *Then* decide."

Don't you see how much easier that is? Nothing to worry about, no decision to make—just take a look at the coat when it comes. If it fits nicely and you like it, wear it down town and compare it for value with coats in the stores there. After all, there is nothing final about it. If you change your mind, you can easily send it back.

But when the coat comes, what happens! You may be away, or the weather is warm, so you do not wear it. And it lies around the house for a week or two. Then along comes a bill. My, you will have to get at that coat and try it! You get it out. You are reasonably well pleased. You wear it a few times and get some spots on it. Seems a shame to send it back then, and anyhow, many of those who bought it said they could not equal it at twice the price. Of course, you have not had the time or energy to go in and compare prices yourself. Oh, well, it's a pretty good bargain, and too darned much trouble to send back now whether it is or not. Box it came in is probably thrown away. And so another sale is made. Not just the best kind of sale, of course, but probably the average sale.

Certain it is that the same principle holds true of almost any kind of selling. A friend of ours, for instance, sells yachts, some of them priced at over a million dollars. Do you suppose he goes or writes to J. P. Morgan and says: "See here, J. P., that old yacht of yours is getting a little down at heel. The mud guards are scratched and the upholstery is getting moth-eaten, and as for the engine— it's so wheezy that when you start from the float, every old tub around ups anchor and poles away, for fear you will bust and spread yourself over the landscape before you reach Hoboken. Honest, J. P., the

57

original Model T Ford couldn't rattle worse than that contraption you call a yacht. Better let me enter your order for a real boat, old scout. Now how about it?"

This man has been instrumental in selling more than $25,000,000 worth of yachts, but I do not think any of them were sold in just that way. No, indeed. When a man gets on his prospect list, nothing crude like that ever happens to him. He gets some interesting little circulars showing pictures of the latest in yachts, with just an adroit suggestion of how fine it would be to forget the office for a few weeks or months, forget the work-a-day world, and go cruising through the Caribbean, or around the South Sea Islands, or wherever life and adventure beckon.

Then after a few of these, the first time a new and especially attractive boat is ready for its trial cruise, Mr. Prospect receives a special delivery letter or telegram some-what along these lines: "New Asterbilt yacht ready for trial spin next Thursday, the 10th. Mr. Asterbilt is making up special party for a few pleasant hours on Sound and begs that you and Mrs. Prospect will honor him. Boat leaves Yacht Club dock at ten sharp. R. S. V. P."

Does Mr. Prospect answer? And especially Mrs. Prospect! I give you three guesses. And when they are safely aboard, along with a number of other "big business men and their wives—mostly prospects like themselves—are things made comfortable for them? I'll say they are! It is perfect luxury afloat.

Nothing so gross as a salesman ever approaches them on a trip like that. True, they are shown over the boat by *officials* of the company. And every point of interest is called to their attention, even as with the automobile salesman. They go through the salon, the cabins, even down to the engine room so spick and span it would not seem out of place as an adjunct to a drawing room. They take the wheel a while, get the feel of the boat, begin thinking of all the things they could do if they had one like it.

And just about then, along comes one of these officials with a picture of the new boat they are building for Mr. Van Spiffiingen - a very wonderful boat, but some people prefer a bit more speed, or more beam, or whatnot, and Mr. Prospect has a chance to air his preference. And isn't that peculiar, but they have a boat in the building with those very features. Here are the plans. And before he knows it, Mr. Prospect has signed on the dotted line and is now Mr. Customer, soon to take a party out on a trial spin on his boat.

Wherein is the difference? The yacht sale runs into bigger figures

58

and employs a bit more finesse—that's all. In its essence, it is the circus barker and his helpers all over again. And though the method may vary, the psychology back of it is necessary in every sale that is made.

Particularly is this true of selling by mail. Why should you buy a coat from John Blair, whom you have never seen, when there is a perfectly good store a couple of blocks away, where you can look over the stock of coats, try on as many as you like, and if you fail to find one that fits you exactly, you can have one altered until it does. Why should you take the trouble and risk of sending for a coat by mail when it is so much easier to get one at home?

For two reasons only: first, because you are convinced that you save money by so doing. Second, and just as important, because John Blair makes it even easier for you to get his coat than to go to the neighborhood store. And the same principles apply to every sale made by mail. Just listen to these few typical examples of successful ways of "supplying that impulse."

Don't decide about buying now. You can do that later. Simply return the special FREE TRIAL Card, and by return mail will come the Blank machine, all charges prepaid. Then, after 6 days' examination—after you have had plenty of chance to try it and prove it—if it is not all we say and more, send it back at our expense. We'll pay the charges both ways. Could we give you any stronger evidence of our faith in the Blank machine?

Let me just prove what it will mean to you. This will not entail the slightest obligation on your part. Fill out the card and mail it—that's all. We'll do the rest.

Figure it out for yourself—harness, feed, labor, veterinary bills—all the items your horse and wagon delivery cost you.

Quite a sum, eh!

Now if you'll pick up that pencil you were figuring with a moment ago, and fill out the attached card, we'll tell you all about Ford motor trucks—how they are increasing efficiency and decreasing costs for people in your line of business, folks you know personally.

59

Just send the enclosed card today. It doesn't obligate you in the least. We are only too glad to thoroughly demonstrate. No harm done if you don't keep it.

Just fill out the enclosed slip and mail it, and the samples will be on the way in time to start this department with next Saturday's sale. Remember, you risk nothing all you have to think about is your profit.

This puts you under not the slightest obligation. It simply gives us the chance to submit figures that you can check against the prices you have been paying—we're always glad to do that anyway, whether we get the particular job we figure on or not.

After a thorough examination and 10 days' trial, if you are convinced that you want an Excelle, you need send us only $5 then, and the balance in conveniently arranged payments over the next nine months. But if you don't want to keep the Excelle, remember you can return it without question, for you are under no obligation in accepting this free-trial offer in this way.

This won't put you under the least obligation. If we can't show you that it is to your interest to take up this matter, it is our fault not yours. Just mail the card and let us put the facts before you. You must wear the smile of satisfaction, or it's no sale. That's our guarantee on every machine. Can you ask more! On that understanding, will you mail the enclosed blank?

Take us at our word—put us to the test—give us an opportunity to prove our claims to you. Use the post card enclosed fill it out and send it to us.

A modern and actual Aladdin's lamp lies in the return card attached. Rub it with your pencil and your wish for full and complete particulars without obligation will come true.

Remember, an order is simply an opportunity for the Blank to sell itself to you. There is no sale—no obligation to keep it—until you have used it in your own home for 30 days and are satisfied. Just let it show you what it can do.

John J. Jones, Chairman of the Board of the great Associated National Banks, was once asked how he managed to handle such an enormous volume of daily work demanding important executive decisions. "I never need to give more than one hour to the consideration of any question, however important," he answered, "because first, I get all the facts before me, and the time to decide is while the facts are fresh in mind."

Because you are likely to agree with Mr. Jones' sound con-elusion, we are sending for your convenience a form on which to register your decision upon the important facts which this letter has placed before you. And there is a stamped, addressed envelope enclosed to bring it back to us, so that you may receive your first benefits from your decision with-out a minute's unnecessary delay.

Signing and sending the enclosed card puts the burden of proof upon us, and incurs no obligation.

I'm willing to do my part. Are you willing to put me to the test? Just fill in on the enclosed card the size tire your car takes—and watch results!

So don't file this away to think over. There's nothing to puzzle about, because you don't have to send one penny or promise anything, other than that if you don't like the Blank you will return it at the end of the week. That's easy, isn't it!

To prove it, all you have to do is fill in, sign and mail the card. After 30 days, you can return the Blank if you want to.

Try it out. Never mind what we say about the uses your clerks will get out of it—*find out*! It is easy. Just send the card.

Use this machine at our expense for ten days. If you like it, keep it. If not, send it back to us, freight collect.

This trial won't obligate you in any way, nor will it cost you a penny.

Will you check, on the enclosed card, the particular types of merchandise which would interest you most? In doing this, you will both acknowledge receipt of our catalog, and also enable us to keep you on the list for certain data of interest.

And remember, the book is free. To each of the first thousand manufacturers subscribing to the Blank Magazine, we will send a cloth-bound copy of this splendid 300-page book without charge. And even the magazine is no expense, for the $2 you pay for it will come back to you many times over before you have read half of the 12 issues.

We enclose letter the Railway Company wrote us. Please return it in the enclosed stamped, addressed envelope, and tell us what you think of our plan.

Tucked away in the inside pages of this letter, you will find a convenient postcard. Your name and address on that card will bring samples of Morco Flavors. These powerful, concentrated flavors possess three times the strength of ordinary extracts. You require only one-third the usual quantity. That's where the big saving comes in.

Take it home. Use the Quick-Lite 10 days. If you don't think it the most wonderful light you ever saw—if it isn't everything we claim it to be, just take it back to the dealer and he will refund your money. We give you this "10-day Visit" offer as an absolute guarantee of complete satisfaction. There are no strings to it. Buy a lamp. Use it

10 nights. If you don't want to keep it—if you would rather continue to use other means of lighting—take the Quick-Lite back to your dealer and get your money.

That's all you have to do—put your name on the enclosed card now, while this free 10-volume book offer is still open. We guarantee your satisfaction and delight. For if after receipt of books you are not more than pleased, send them back at our expense, and any money you may have paid will be returned at once.

Your reader, in short, is interested, but hasn't quite made up his mind. He balks at putting his name on the dotted line. "Some other time" "Tomorrow!" That little word "Tomorrow—" Mañana "—is said to have been the cause of the Spanish people's decline. Certainly it has cost many a salesman and sales letter-writer his job, for more than all other causes put together, it has lost sales.

So do not give your prospect the chance to spring any "Mañana" upon you. Beat him to it. Tell him not to decide now—*on your main proposition*. Instead, put his mind to working on some minor point—and you will find that a favorable decision on it will, in three cases out of four, carry the major proposition along with it!

VIII

How to Put a Hook into Your Letters

As the tail is to the kite, as the rudder is to the ship, so is the close to any important letter. It may be a perfectly good letter aside from that. It may fit right in with the reader's thoughts, it may win his interest, it may spur him to action, but if it does not tell him *what* to do, if it does not provide a penalty for his not doing it, your prospect will slip away from you like a fish off the hook.

There is just one reason why any one ever reads a letter you send him. He expects a reward. That is the key to holding his interest. All through your letter you keep leading him on, constantly feeding his interest, but always holding back something for the climax.

You come to it. You make your special offer. Your reader is impressed. He promises himself he will give it favorable consideration. But you do not want favorable consideration. You want an order or a payment. How are you going to get it? Start your impulse, as outlined in the last chapter. Good! But if that does not work, what then? *Provide a penalty!*

There are only two reasons why your reader will do as you tell him to in your letter. The first is that you have made him want something so badly that of his own ertia he reaches out for your order card to get it. The other is that you have aroused in him the fear that he will lose something worth while if he does not do as you say.

It may be a delinquent debtor in fear of loss of credit standing or of court action. It may be a buyer fearing to lose his chance at a bargain. It may be the merchant fearing to lose your trade. It may be the ambitious youngster fearing to lose an opportunity for advancement. But unless your close can arouse in your reader the fear that he will lose something worth while if he does not do as you tell him, you will get no results.

So when you want to inspire fear, *be definite*! Be specific! If you are threatening suit, tell your reader that unless you have his remittance or a satisfactory explanation by a certain date, the account goes to your lawyer. If you are going to advance your price, and want to corral all the orders possible at the old figure, set a definite date for your advance. Or if you have only a few articles left, give the exact quantity. It carries conviction, as you can see from these two examples:

> On the 1st of October, the rate of the Messenger will go up to $1 a line. If you place your order before the 30th, you can buy space to be used any time before January 1st at 75¢ a line. After the 30th, positively no orders will be accepted at less than $1 a line. As a matter of fact, our circulation entitles us to $1 a line right now.
>
> Don't let this letter be covered up on your desk. Send the enclosed reservation right now, or instruct your advertising agent to reserve the space for you, and make sure of this big bargain.

> Only 46 sets left! The success of our special offer surpassed all expectations. It will be necessary to issue another edition at once. The style of binding will be changed, but otherwise the two editions will be the same. As we don't want to carry two styles on hand, we are willing to let you have one of the remaining 46 sets at the old price, although the increased cost of paper, printing and binding has forced us to raise the price of the new sets more than 50%!

Make your reader feel that this is his last chance—keep your penalty dangling before his mind's eye, the money-saving lost, the opportunity missed. Put into your close the fear of consequences.

Finally, tell him *what* to do. Don't leave it to him to decide. We are all mentally lazy, you know, so dictate his action for him—get your suggester to working on him. If he is to do certain things, describe them. Tell him to put his name on the enclosed card, stamp and mail, or pin his check or dollar bill to this letter and return in the enclosed envelope. Here is the way others have done it successfully:

> "Now, what am I to do?" you ask. Simply send your order to me personally. Just say—" Make my suit as you agreed in your letter."
>
> If you wish other samples or further information, we shall be more than glad to furnish them. But send your

order first. Remember, we have material on hand sufficient for only 95 suits. While they last, you can get a made-to-measure, tailored-to-fit suit of our regular $75 quality, for only $37.50. But to do so, you have to be prompt.

Don't send me any money after the 1st. If you do, it will surely be returned, unless you are willing to pay me the new price of $50 a share instead of $40.

I have some regard for the men who made inquiries when our project was young before it fairly got under way. That is why I am including you in this offer— because you were one of our original inquirers.

Remember, no acceptance of your old price after the 1st. The stock is even now worth $50.

Such wonderful opportunities will of course be snapped up quickly. Our doors will open at 9 o'clock Monday morning, and to have the widest range of selection, you should not put off your visit a moment later than absolutely necessary.

It was necessary to place this large order to secure the sets at the lowest possible figure. Knowing that the number would exceed our weekly sales, we decided to offer these extra sets to some of the ambitious young men who have been writing us.

If you will fill out the enclosed scholarship blank and mail it right away, we will send you one of these handsome sets FREE, express prepaid. But this offer must be accepted before the 30th of this month. At the rate Scholarship Blanks are now coming in, it is more than likely that the available sets will all be gone by the 30th. It is necessary therefore that you. send your application at once.

The demand has been large and there are only a few copies left but one of them will be yours when you have O.K'd and mailed the enclosed card.

But you must act now. There are only 2700 copies of

this book still on hand and no more can be printed at less than double the price. So pin your money to this letter and mail it today.

Remember, he who hesitates nowadays never gets a flash at fortune. The men who made millions in Texas oil lands are the men who dared, who went ahead unafraid, who plunged in on their own judgment—and didn't wait.

The saying that everything comes to him who waits may have been true a hundred years ago, when people had plenty of time to wait for the good things of life. But today the only one that things come to is the man who goes after them. The enclosed blank is your reservation for some of the good things of life. Will you mail it *now*—TODAY?

It has been proved that seven times out of ten your average business man will read the opening paragraph of an ordinary letter that is palpably not from a customer, take a cursory glance at the middle, and then jump to the last paragraph to see what it is all about, and how much it costs. So it is essential that you put a hook into that last paragraph.

Remember, too, that a successful close has two parts. The first is the persuasion and inducement. It shows your reader the gain that is his by ordering, the chances of loss he takes by delay. It emphasizes the guarantee and minimizes the cost.

When your reader gets that far, he is almost ready to act, but your close lacks a hook. What must he do to get all these things? *Tell him!* Make it so plain and easy he will not have a reason for not ordering. If you do not, you have not finished your letter, and lacking the barb of that hook, your reader is likely to lapse from his "almost ready" attitude back into indifference.

IX

The Six Essentials

To sum it up, every good letter contains these six essential elements:

1.   The opening, which gets the reader's attention by fitting in with his train of thought and establishes a point of contact with his interests, thus exciting his curiosity and prompting him to read further.

2.   The description or explanation, which pictures your proposition to the reader by first outlining its important features, then filling in the necessary details.

3. The motive or reason why, which creates a longing in the reader's mind for what you are selling, or impels him to do as you want him to, by describing—not your proposition but what it will do for him—the comfort, the pleasure, the profit he will derive from it.

4. The proof or guarantee, which offers to the reader proof of the truth of your statements, or establishes confidence by a money-back-if-not-satisfied guarantee.

5.   The snapper or penalty, which gets immediate action by holding over your reader's head the loss in money or prestige or opportunity that will be his if he does not act at once.

6. The close, which tells the reader just what to do and how to do it, and makes it easy for him to act at once.

These rules, of course, are for the man or woman who is studying the art of writing resultful letters. After a time, they come to be a sort of second nature, so that you weigh each of these features without being conscious that you are doing so. You may even mix them all up into one grand goulash, so that to the beginner they will seem to be not there at all, but they or their close relatives are in every successful letter.

Rules, however, are merely the start. They are the mechanics of a letter. Real letter-writing only starts there. It is getting the feel of your message that counts. I remember the first sales letter I ever wrote. I knew as little about the writing of letters as any one who ever took his typewriter in hand to tackle the job. But I was full of an idea, and it came out all over that letter. And that is what counts.

I was doing mining engineering at the time, in a little town called Powellton, in West Virginia. We had an unusually good vein of gas coal, which was called the Powellton Seam; and the 200 old style, beehive ovens, with which we turned out Powellton Coke.

Like all the other mines in the district, we depended for business upon brokers in the big towns. They would contract with the large users for so many carloads of coal or coke, of a certain general grade, and then place their orders with whichever mines made them the lowest price, allowing them the greatest margin. The result was that all the mines were in much the same boat, whether their coal happened to be better or worse. When times were good they bid against each other for laborers, and between the lack of them and the lack of cars they were able to run the mines only three or four days a week. When times were bad they underbid each other for the little business available, and managed to work only one or two days a week.

That condition had been general for a good many years, with our mines as with practically all the others in the district. And there was no reason to think it would not continue indefinitely, as, in fact, it has with many of the mines in that district.

But from much cogitation, there one day dawned upon us an idea so obvious you will wonder why we did not think of it first thing. It was this: We had an unusually good grade of gas coal and a splendid coke. There must be certain purposes for which that coal and that coke would produce far better results than any other made. If we could find these purposes, the businesses that needed coal and coke for them would cheerfully pay any reasonable premium for our particular product, and not only would we make more money, but we would cease to be dependent upon the whims of the brokers and would be sure of a regular volume of orders through good times and bad.

So we started experimenting, and found that for gas-making purposes we had easily the best coal in the district. Figured on the basis of cubic feet of gas produced, to say nothing of the by-products, any gas company could well afford to pay from 25 to 33 per cent more for our coal.

That was all we needed. From that moment, every gas company within a radius of several hundred miles was our target. We disregarded the usual "per ton" prices to a great extent, centering our whole argument upon how many cubic feet of gas they got from each pound of coal, and what that gas cost them, including the delivered price of their coal.

How much are you paying per cubic foot for your gas? [was the basis of our letters]. If we can show you how to cut the cost by a fourth, are you interested enough to *prove* it? The Blank Gas Company of Cincinnati *has* cut its costs by more than that, and here are the figures as given in a letter from their Superintendent. [Here we quoted exact figures and costs]. The Bank Company of Indianapolis and [here we mentioned four or five other companies well and favorably known to the trade] have had similar experiences. We'll be glad to send you the exact figures from each if you will take the time to read them.

But better than any figures from other plants is this chance to write new figures of your own in your plant. Send the enclosed card, without money. On receipt of it, we will ship you a carload of Powellton screened gas coal, our regular standard quality.

Test it. Try it any way you wish. At the end of your tests, figure how much gas you get per pound of coal, *and what that gas cost you!* If you don't find that the Powellton Coal has saved you at least 25% on your cost, then that carload we send you won't cost you one cent. But if you do see where you can save from 25 to 33% of the cost of your gas, then you are to give us your contract for all the gas coal you use for the next year, at a price of $1.25 per ton f.o.b. Powellton, W. Va.

Remember, no saving—no cost. But if we save you 25%, we get your contract. Is it a go?

I knew none of the rules of letter-writing. I could not have told you the difference between a clincher and a monkey wrench. But I was bubbling over with enthusiasm for our idea, and that enthusiasm must have permeated our letters, for we got so many orders from gas companies, it kept us humping to fill them all. And what was more to the point, they stuck. When I left Powellton, we still had on our books nearly every gas company we had ever put there.

One would stray away now and then, of course, lured by the siren song of a bargain. When that happened, we said nothing—just got a few average samples of the other man's coal and sent them, with samples of ours, to a laboratory for comparative test. When the reports came back, we carried them out in figures of the cost of the coal and the final cost of the gas per cubic foot and sent the result without comment to the superintendent or other responsible executive of the gas company. In most cases the business was soon on our books again.

The coal problem solved, we set about finding a similar solution of the coke question, for the gas companies preferred screened coal, which meant that all the dust coal or slack was left us for cooking purposes.

We had made frequent analysis of our coke, of course, and knew that it was unusually low in sulphur, phosphorus and ash. So we set out to see which type of foundryman considered these qualities most valuable.

We soon learned that to the maker of steel rails, phosphorus was anathema, so we had little difficulty in persuading the Ashland Steel Company that a coke as low in Phosphorus as ours was easily worth 25 cts. more a ton than any other they could buy. 25 cts. a ton doesn't sound like much, but when you multiply it by sixty to ninety tons a day, which was what the Ashland Steel required, it soon runs into money.

That was a good start so, much encouraged, we looked around for others. And in the makers of stoves and ranges we found possible customers who were quite as particular about sulphur as the Steel Company had been about phoshorus. In thin castings like those needed in stoves and ranges, sulphur means bubbles and cracks, and costs more money than any saving in price can possibly make up for.

But stove founders were, for the most part, located pretty far away from us, and other good cokes just about as low as ours in sulphur content were as readily available to them. To get their business on other than a price basis, we had to find some better argument than low sulphur content.

We worked on that for quite some time, talked to different founders to get a line on their problems, studied numerous books on the subject and finally stumbled on the answer almost by accident.

It happened that we had been figuring on a big contract with the Bucks Stove and Range Company of St. Louis. They were one of the most efficiently run concerns in the business, and they wanted the best, regardless of what it cost. So before placing their contract, they bought a carload of coke from each of half a dozen concerns whose analysis and claims seemed to indicate that they were in the running.

71

We had shipped them a carload and intended to run out to St. Louis in order to be on the spot when the contract was awarded, so that if it seemed that a last-minute reduction of 10 or 15 cts. a ton would turn the scales in our favor, we could throw it in. When lo and behold, without notice of any kind, in came the contract by mail at the price we had originally quoted!

To say that we were pleasantly surprised was putting it mildly. But we didn't let either our pleasure or our surprise get in the way of the fact that here was probably the answer to our problem. If our coke stood out so well in a comparative test that we had landed the Bucks order without effort, in the face of the best cokes and the best salesmen that the Connellsville could show, then there must be something unusual about our coke that every other stove founder ought to know. And we lost no time in setting out for St. Louis to learn what it was.

And here is what we found: Its high carbon content and low ash gave Powellton Coke a heating power that would melt an unusual amount of iron and a structure that supported a phenomenal weight, with the result that where a good coke did well to melt eight or nine tons of iron to one of coke, ours melted as high as fifteen tons of iron to one of coke! Figuring the price of the coke at $7 a ton delivered, it cost the Bucks Stove and Range Company 80 to 90 cts. to melt a ton of iron with ordinary coke, whereas with Powellton Coke it cost them only 47 cts.! Can you wonder that they gave us the order without urging or bargaining?

Our problem was solved, and, as is often the case, through no skill of ours. The Lord had been good to us in the kind of coal he gave us, and instead of patting ourselves on the back, we should have been kicked for not cashing in sooner on our products' peculiar advantages. But we were too happy over having found the answer to do any worrying about what was past and done with. It took us just about three days to get a letter into the mails to every stove founder within five hundred miles of us. This, you must remember, was back in 1907 or 1908, when Bryan was still a name to attract attention anywhere.

When Bill Bryan first sprung his 16 to 1 ratio upon a waiting world, founders and business men generally called it visionary and impractical—said it wouldn't work.

So when Bill Smith, Cupola Foreman for the Bucks

72

Stove & Range Company of St. Louis, proudly strode into the President's office with his report of a 15 to 1 melt, he wasn't surprised to meet with only skepticism on the part of that official.

"You're getting your politics mixed with your melting figures!" accused the Boss. Bill may lack some of the eloquence of his namesake, but no one ever accused him of running away from a scrap. So the upshot of it was that the President agreed to be on hand at the next melt.

Sure enough, Bill's figures proved to be right! They didn't equal Bryan's 16 to 1, but they averaged a good 15 tons of iron to every one of coke!

Of course, Bill modestly disclaims the credit. "Any one could do it with that coke," he says. "It's got a structure that'd carry the Eiffel tower. And as for sulphur bubbles— it just never heard of such words."

And that's the reason Powellton Coke gets the Bucks Stove & Range contract this year, in direct competition with and after thorough tests of every good coke on the market. That's the reason the Gallipolis Stove Company, the Huntington Range Company and a dozen others have been using Powellton Coke for years.

Of course, some of them stray away occasionally. We're none of us proof against the siren song of low price, but when they begin to figure the cost of their coke in tons of iron melted, as the Bucks Stove & Range Company did; when they find that on this basis Powellton Coke is costing them only 47¢ a ton of melted iron against 80¢ to 90¢ for any other brand, and when they add to that the cost of scrap castings due to sulphur and phosphorus, they always come back, and it's a long time before they stray again.

If you figure your coke cost, *not* on the delivered price of the coke, but on tons of iron melted—if you are buying high carbon heat-content, and not sulphur, ash and phosphorus— we have some figures that will interest you.

May we send them?

That letter brought home the bacon. For a while we had almost a monopoly of the stove and range business in our territory. We did not keep it altogether, because good coke structure depends largely upon skill in making the coke, and other ovens with the right kind of coal succeeded in making almost as good a coke as ours. With intensive study, they found ways of loading the furnace so that their coke would melt just about as high a percentage of iron as ours.

But do not imagine we were resting on our laurels, or out playing golf all this time. We realized it would not be long until some one caught up to where we were then, so we tried to keep at least one good jump ahead.

We tested not only our coal and coke, but different ways of screening the one and making the other. We tried cooking longer and shorter periods, charging the ovens with bigger or smaller charges—everything, in fact, that we could think of that might make our product better.

And we did not stop with our own product. We had numbers of experiments made in the more effective use of our coal and coke. We had never heard of the rule that a letter should talk—not about your own product but about the pleasure or profit your customer will get out of it, but we had learned from long experience that coal and coke were drugs on the market and could only be sold on a price basis, whereas cubic feet of gas, or thermal units of steam, or melted tons of iron were things that sold themselves.

In line with our idea of making every possible improvement in our product, we got a few books on letter-writing and applied the principles outlined in them to our letters. I remember the first set of books we got. It was System's "Business Correspondence Library "—three volumes—and it became our Bible for direct-mail work. Looking back on it now, I do not believe we could have found a better ground-work for our studies. Certain it is that it helped us to sell many thousands of tons of coal and coke, when without it we might have lost the sales. I think it is out of print now, but next to Herbert Watson's "Applied Business Correspondence," I believe it has helped more men to a knowledge of how to use letters for profit than any set of books ever written.

John Blair, founder of the New Process Company of Warren, Pa., once told me the same thing. His introduction to good letter-writing came from the same little set of three books—after he had made his bow with a few successful efforts of his own, about which more anon.

To go back to our interrupted labors: Starting in 1907 or 1908, and continuing for five years, we sold practically all the products of our mines and ovens by mail. We used dozens of different letters and circulars, with all kinds of variants upon the one appeal, but unfortunately my book of letters was lost a few years ago, and the company had then changed hands, so the only sample I have to show is the letter quoted above.

It was about this time I had the good fortune to meet Thomas H. Beck, then sales manager—now president of Collier's. He had been sales manager of Proctor & Gamble, the Ivory Soap people, where he was responsible for as revolutionary an idea in its way as was ours of selling cubic feet of gas and tons of melt.

Soap flakes, it seems, were sold to laundries by the barrel of so many pounds weight. One barrel of soap was considered much like another, so sales were made almost entirely on price. Then it occurred to Tom Beck to have Ivory Soap flakes analyzed and the results compared with analysis made in their laboratory of all the competing brands. What was his surprise and delight to find that the competing brands contained something like (let us say) 15 per cent water, to only about 5 per cent water for Ivory!

If a barrel of soap cost $2, a laundryman could pay Ivory $2.20 and be getting his actual soap content for the same price per pound that he was paying the $2 competitor. If in addition he was paying $1 a barrel for freight or delivery service, that made an extra premium of 10 cts. he was handing to Ivory's competitor.

It did not take Tom Beck more than half a minute to figure out the possibilities that this opened up. As soon as they could be got into the mail, he had letters on the way to every laundry in his territory asking them whether they were buying soap or water, suggesting that it might be cheaper to get their own water from the faucet rather than have it freighted all the way from the factory to them, and then be charged for it at soap prices in addition.

To say that he started a furor among soap makers is putting it mildly. The net result to him was that it enabled him to land the far bigger job with Collier's, and to me that it gave me a sympathetic ear into which to pour an idea I had long been nursing for selling Collier books by mail.

Which takes us into another chapter.

X

How It All Began

P. F. COLLIER & SON had been publishing books since 1885, selling them through salesmen, directed by some thirty-seven branch offices.

In the two or three years prior to 1913, they had made six different attempts to start a department for selling books by mail—all without success. One man spent $25,000 and sold eighteen sets of books. So when I, with no knowledge of bookselling and no background but our coal and coke sales, suggested that I had an idea which I believed would sell books successfully, it is no wonder the "powers-that-be" laughed at it.

It happened that P. F. Collier was my uncle and was responsible for my education, but he had always told me he did not want me in the business until I could bring something to it they could get nowhere else. For that reason, I had never before tried for a place with Collier's, but now I felt I had an idea they could use, so by letter and in person I kept trying to sell it to them.

In Tom Beck I found a sympathetic listener, for Proctor & Gamble are large users of coal, and he had seen many of the letters in our campaign and thoroughly approved the idea of them. So with his help, and that of the Vice-President, G. J. Kennedy, I finally sold them the idea of a six months' tryout.

It was not on any munificent basis, you can be sure of that. I was to have a drawing account of $25 a week, and to receive a commission of 5 per cent on any sales I made by mail. To leave a good, secure, salaried job for an uncertain chance like that takes optimism of a high order, but I was young and single, and just fool enough not to know any of the things that could not be done, so I jumped at the chance.

Luckily for me, I found a good mentor at Collier's in the person of Bruce Barton, who was then the assistant sales manager in charge of advertising. It was not any part of his duties to lend me a helping hand, but he went out of his way to do it. And to his suggestions and kindly criticisms I owe it that the very first letters and circulars we tried were complete successes. How complete, you can judge by the fact that the profits on our first six months' sales were 34 1/2 per cent, and I was making so much money on the 5 per cent commission that the arrangement was promptly cancelled and I was put on a good, living salary.

Collier's had been selling the "Harvard Classics," Dr. Eliot's famous Five-Foot Shelf of Books, for about six years then, and it was their best seller, so of course I started my efforts with it. Their salesmen covered all the big towns, however, so my efforts had to be confined to the little towns and the rural communities, for even after we proved what could be done by mail, Collier's never forgot that their house had been built by salesmen, and they never allowed our mail efforts to interfere with the agent sales.

It was for this reason I left them after five years—to get a bigger field of activity, but meantime they were better than any post-graduate college course.

There was Tom Beck, one of these master salesmen you meet once in a lifetime. He could sell any man or group of men practically anything. I have seen him go into meetings where every man was opposed to his idea and come out with every one's approval of his plan. You might not agree with him—but you could not resist him. You had the feeling: "Well, the thing is not practicable, but if Tom Beck gets behind it he'll put it over!"

Then came Bruce Barton, peer of any advertising writer I have ever seen. He used to sketch out the skeleton frame-work of his ads and then give them to me to fill in. It was a liberal education in advertising writing.

And then came George Kennedy, who had started his collection experience ringing doorbells and collecting 50 cts. a month installments on Dickens or Thackeray or some of the old, original volumes Collier's put out. He had been in the business almost as long as old P. F. himself, and P. F. Collier was the man who started the installment sale of books in this country! What George Kennedy did not know about parting the reluctant debtor from his money certainly is not known to many.

I went with Collier's on the first of July in 1913. On the ninth of August we dropped our first circulars into the mail. They consisted of an illustrated four-page letter, the first and fourth pages carrying the letter, the inside pages the illustrations and circular copy.

The letter was sent under first-class postage without fill-in, and a stamped post card went with it. Including postage, the whole thing cost us about 4 cts. in the mail.

You can believe we watched for the returns from those circulars with fear and trembling. We had mailed 10,000 of them, mostly to advertising leads that were from one to two years old, and which had been in the hands of two or more salesmen and been returned as unsalable.

When the orders began to mount up from these old leads, the salesmen who had turned them down—and the whole sales department—sat up and began to take notice. For our first letter to those old discarded inquiries brought back 4 1/2 per cent of orders for a $39 set of books!

Four and one-half per cent meant that, with letters at 4 cents. each, our orders were costing us less than $1 apiece. Can you imagine that, on a $39 set of books? No wonder we showed a profit for those six months of 34 1/2 per cent!

The trouble was that we soon came to the end of those old discarded leads, and after that, the salesmen didn't let go of them so readily. But while they lasted, the "pick-mailings" were easy. Here is the first letter we used on them:

If Dr. Eliot of Harvard Were to Say to You—

"Come around to my home to-night. I want to show you some books that I believe you'll enjoy; they are interesting, entertaining, yet they will give you all the essentials of a liberal education, even if you can spend only fifteen minutes a day with them."

You'd go, wouldn't you, and the next morning you'd hasten to get copies of these books.

Now that is, in effect, just what Dr. Eliot has done. From his lifetime of reading, study and experience—forty years of it as President of Harvard University—he has chosen a Five Foot Shelf of just the few books, and only the few, that are really essential to the Twentieth Century American.

Just 15 Minutes a Day, and Then—

And this is what he says to you: "I believe that the faithful and considerate reading of these books will give any man the essentials of a liberal education, even if he

78

can devote to them but fifteen minutes a day."

Think of it—*The Essentials of a Liberal Education,* under the personal guidance of Dr. Eliot, who has trained more men for success and is a greater authority on books and reading than any other man in the world today. What other books, or who else, could offer you so much?

Dr. Eliot's work is complete. You owe it to yourself at least to examine the result—the fruits of his 40 years' experience as President of Harvard University. They are not the mere product of his genius—they are the finished utterance of the human race.

Examine the Books for a Week—at Our Expense

Don't send a cent of money. Simply drop the enclosed card in the mail and the complete set of Harvard Classics will be shipped to you from our nearest Branch Office AT OUR EXPENSE. Keep them for a week; browse through them; read them; enjoy them. We won't urge you to buy them either then or now, because we realize that it is up to you to make up your mind in your own way as to just what the books will be worth to you. If you decide to keep them, you can pay for them as you like, even as little as $2.00 a month; if not, you can return them at the end of the week without question at our expense.

Here is your chance to avail yourself of Dr. Eliot's wonderful knowledge and experience to prepare yourself for life. You owe it to yourself to at least SEE and EXAMINE this Library that he selected to speed you on the road to a bigger, broader success. The card brings it to your door, charges prepaid. Merely put your name on it and drop it in the mail.

But remember, in the great book of Time there is but one word—" NOW "—so drop your card in the mail *now.*

Very truly yours,

The inside pages showed, on the left hand, a great pile of books, piled all over each other until they practically hid the background of the Harvard University buildings. On the right hand was the orderly row of the Five-Foot Shelf, with the Harvard Library behind it. The keynote of the copy was a quotation from Emerson: "In the Bibliotheque Nationale in Paris are a million books. A man might read from dawn to dark for fifty years, yet die in the first alcove."

And what would he get as a result of his fifty years' reading? A heterogeneous collection of facts, unrelated, of no particular value to any one or anything. In the "Harvard Classics," on the other hand, just a few minutes a day would give him the orderly outline of all that man has learned—in effect, a liberal education.

Our first letter having pulled so well, we tried a number of others to determine how many follow-ups we could profitably send on these old leads. On the series we finally worked out, our second letter pulled about 2 1/2 per cent, our third 1 1/2 per cent, our fourth 1 per cent and our final one 2 per cent.

Here is letter No. 2. With it we enclosed a circular, which is reproduced after the letter. Following it is the post card that accompanied them.

> *Will you Examine "The Harvard Classics "—Dr. Eliot's Five Foot Shelf of Books—*
>
> If we send you a set at our *own expense* FOR A WEEKS EXAMINATION?
>
> We don't ask you to decide now whether you will want to keep the set. All we want you to do is EXAMINE the books for a week in your own home—see for yourself what a wonderful field they open up to you—judge whether they will be worth seven cents a day to you in pleasure, in profit, in actual mental growth.
>
> ### The World's Civilization on a Book-shelf
>
> For years Dr. Eliot has felt that all the books really essential to the Twentieth Century American could be contained on a Five Foot Shelf, and when—after 40 years as President of Harvard University—he gave up active work, he set himself the task of picking out from all the myriads of things which have been written and said during the past five thousand years, just those few works of

the greatest thinkers in every field which most vividly picture the thought and achievement of the human race since the world began.

The result is literally the putting of the World's civilization on a single book shelf. From the many writings of the greatest thinkers Dr. Eliot has picked those few characteristic works which cover their main ideas, which best express their basic thoughts. He has made it possible for you to have the *best works* of each of them without having to burden your shelves with the *complete writings* of all.

Just Fifteen Minutes a Day—

And this is what Dr. Eliot says to you: "I believe that the faithful and considerate reading of these books will give any man the essentials of a liberal education, even if he can devote to them but fifteen minutes a day."

Think of it! THE ESSENTIALS OF A LIBERAL EDUCATION, in only fifteen minutes a day, under the personal guidance of Dr. Eliot, the best teacher and the greatest authority on books and reading in the world today. What other books, or who else, could offer you so much?

A Saving to You of $433.05

There are fifty volumes in the Harvard Classics, and they contain 418 complete works by 300 of the greatest writers the world has ever known. Bought separately in even the cheapest editions and bindings, these 418 works would cost you $472.05, yet we offer them to you, uniformly bound in silk cloth stamped in gold, with footnotes, reading guide and an encyclopedic index of 76,000 subjects, at only 9¢ for each of the 418 works—$39.00 for the set complete in fifty volumes, and you can pay for them just as you like—even as little as $2.00 a month.

An Encyclopedia of References

Lawyers tell us that in their pleas, editors in their editorials, teachers in their teaching, clergymen in their sermons, and business men in their occasional talks, they are getting to depend in a wonderful degree on this key to the world's thought.

You see, it not only gives you the best thought of the world's Masters on most important subjects, but every thought, every period, every subject even remotely touched upon, is made instantly accessible through the wonderful Index that is appended to volume 50—an Index that contains 76,000 references.

Examine the Books for a Week—at Our Expense

Don't send a cent of money. Simply drop the enclosed card in the mail and the complete set of Harvard Classics will be shipped to you from our nearest Branch Office AT OUR EXPENSE. Keep them for a week; browse through them; read them; enjoy them. We won't urge you to buy them either then or now, because we realize that it is up to you to make up your mind in your own way as to just what the books will be worth to you. If you decide not to keep them, you can return them at the end of the week without question at our expense.

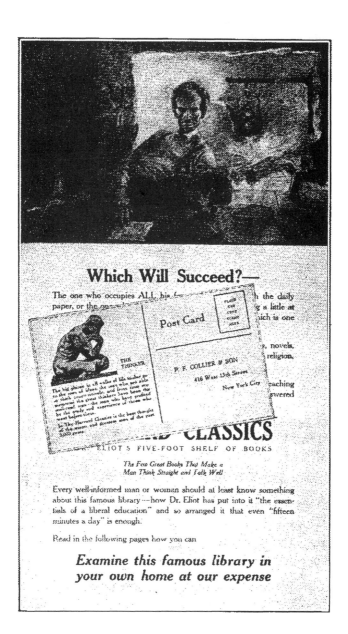

Letter No. 3 is one that came into the series later, after the start of the World War. Like the two before it, it is built around the one idea enunciated by Carlyle: "All that mankind has done, thought, gained or been—it is lying in magic preservation in the pages of books." But it takes guidance to find the right books, and in Dr. Eliot, for forty years President of Harvard University, we had found the guide par excellence.

Its enclosure, which follows, added measurably to its pulling power—in fact, it has been our experience that a good circular will add from 25 to 33 per cent to the pulling power of almost any letter. After the circular follows the order card—the same, except for the copy on the front, as on follow-up No. 2.

The Harvard Classics Contain a Liberal Education

They are the crowning educational achievement of Dr. Chas. W. Eliot, representing the results of his lifetime of reading, study and teaching—40 years of it as President of Harvard University.

They contain that literature of the world which broadens the horizon, liberalizes the mind and enables the busy Twentieth Century American to become really well-read and well-posted in just a few minutes a day.

The World's Civilization on a Book-shelf

There are fifty volumes in the Harvard Classics, and they contain 418 *complete works* by three hundred of the greatest writers that have ever lived. From all the myriads of things which have been written and said during the past 5,000 years, Dr. Eliot has chosen those few works of the greatest thinkers in every field which most vividly picture the thought and achievement of the human race since the world began.

Examine the Books for a Week—at Our Expense

Don't send a cent of money. Simply drop the enclosed card in the mail and the complete set of Harvard Classics will be shipped to you from our nearest Branch Office AT OUR EXPENSE. Keep them for a week; browse through them; read them; enjoy them. We won't urge you to buy them either then or now, because we realize that it is up to you to make up your mind in your own way as to just what the books will be worth to you. If you decide not to keep them, you can return them at the end of the week without question at our expense.

But the War—?

Just bear in mind what President Wilson, the greatest leader of thought the world has ever known, wrote a short time ago to the President of a Western College who asked him if our colleges should close and general education be neglected at this time.

"By no means should our schools and colleges be closed during the period of the war, and general education be neglected. Never in History have educated, cultured men and women been so needed as they will be in the next few years to carry on the work of reconstruction and peace."

Here is your chance to avail yourself of Dr. Eliot's wonderful knowledge and experience to prepare yourself for the after-the-war problems. You owe it to yourself to at least SEE and EXAMINE this Library that he selected to speed you on the road to a bigger, broader success. The card brings it to your door, charges prepaid. Merely put your name on it and drop it in the mail.

But remember, in the great book of Time there is but one word "Now" so drop your card in the mail now.

Very truly yours,

For No. 4 we used a large mailing folder, recapitulating all the arguments of the three letters and containing only a post card.

No. 5 is going to be a surprise to many people. It is long—oh, how long! Four whole pages of closely type-written stuff! Who would ever read it? Yet people did, evidently, for from a low point of 1 per cent on the previous circular, and 11 1/2 per cent on No. 3 letter, the orders jumped up to 2 per cent! And all efforts we tried, to make a sixth or seventh or eighth follow-up pay, were practically fruitless. So we called this our "mopping-up letter" and filed away the leads.

Here is the letter. Only a post card went with it.

A Saving to You of $413.05

Brentano's, the largest retail Booksellers in the World, quote these 418 works in even the cheapest editions and bindings at $4792.05.

THE LOWEST PRICE AT WHICH THE HARVARD CLASSICS will ever be sold has now been reached in the new Silk Cloth Edition, costing only one-eighth the price of the original sets.

I have put aside one hundred sets of this edition for the specific purpose of FREE EXAMINATION. This letter is your opportunity to examine one of these hundred "Free Examination Sets" in your own home.

It is the final bedrock price to you, and IT HOLDS GOOD FOR ONLY A SHORT TIME LONGER. I write you because, with all that you have heard and read ABOUT the Five-Foot Shelf of Books, you have never yet seen them. You have never yet had the privilege I now offer you of actually handling the volumes, reading in your own home one or two of the 418 masterpieces, proving to your own satisfaction the wonderful completeness of the 76,000-word index, surprising yourself that fifty books so well made and so serviceably bound can be sold AT SUCH A PRICE.

Just read the extract quoted below from letter from the Manager of Brentano's, the great retail booksellers, whose main office, you know, is at the corner of Fifth Avenue and Twenty-seventh Street, New York City:

"We are returning herewith your list of items made up from the Five-Foot Shelf of Books. This list of books embraces about 300 authors and their works.

"The same can be supplied in regular editions in cloth binding for $472.05, with the exception of about fourteen to twenty authors which were published during the 14th to the 18th centuries and exist only in very rare editions and very costly. Same can only be had for reference in European Libraries, as copies are seldom found in the open market."

Their itemized quotations are exceedingly interesting. Volume 1, for instance, which contains Franklin, Wolman, Penn, can be duplicated in three little volumes of Everyman's Library at 50 cents each or only $1.50 (Harvard Classics price $1.10). But volume 8, containing the nine greatest Greek Dramas by Aesehylus, Sophocles, Euripides and Aristophanes, would cost $10.60 to duplicate, while volume 39, which contains some of the most prized possesions of the British Museum and the Bibliotheque Nationale, Paris, has rarely been reprinted and is almost unobtainable now except in the Five-Foot Shelf of Books AT ANY PRICE.

First, therefore, I should like you to satisfy your own curiosity as to how it is possible for us to manufacture and sell $472.05 worth of literature in uniform binding, with footnotes, glossaries, introductions, etc —at just one-eighth that price. I should like you to see one of these free-examination sets for this reason first.

But it isn't merely of figures that I want to speak to you. I should like you rather to think of the Five-Foot Shelf in terms of TIME, which to the busy modern man is not only money, but is more valuable than money. Look at the Five-Foot Shelf from the standpoint of the time it will save you and your wife and your children.

You have a letter or a paper to write, or a speech to make; some member of your household has a paper for a woman s club; one of the children has a topic assigned at school; some subject is discussed in the newspapers and you want to read up on it; where can the material be found at a moment's notice? Nowhere that I know except in the Index of the Harvard Classics.

Take the subject "Health," for instance, and see what has been prepared for you. This is an actual extract from the Index:

"HEALTH, Antoninus's care of, ii, 197; Burke on pleasure and idea of, xxiv, 36, 38; Carlyle on, xxv, 423—4, 435—6; Carlyle on care of, 402—3; Channing on, xxviii, 366—7; Descartes on, xxxiv, 50; Epictetus on care of, ii, 160 (118); Hunt on, xxvii, 307; More on, xxxvi, 213—14, 215; Locke on importance of, xxxvii, 9, 10; Pascal on use and misuse of, xlviii, 374; Pope on, xl, 443; rules of, xxxvii, 10—28; unconsciousness of, xxv, 338—48; Woolman on care of, i, 244—45.
   "HEALTH, by Pinkney, xxviii, 394—45.
   "HEALTH, to Ane I Loe Dear, vi, 590.
   "HEALTH, Here's His in Water, vi, 191.
   "HEALTH, Here's to Thy, vi, 28—9.
   "HEALTH, Regimen of, Bacon's, iii, 85—6.
   "HEALTH, to them that's Awa, vi, 477."

Remarkably suggestive, isn't it? So on every one of the other 75,999 subjects you have at your finger tips the information that it would take you hours or even days to gather from scattered volumes.

But neither time nor money is the proper word with which to picture The Harvard Classics. The real word is pleasure, self-satisfaction, the delight of mental growth. Look at one of these hundred free-examination sets from this standpoint. Shut your eyes for a moment and let these 418 friends take you by the hand, carry your imagination away with them. You will travel down the Nile with Herodotus; or roam the Spanish Main with Drake; see the great Grecian dramas in the Ampitheatre of Athens; hear Cicero denounce Catiline in the Roman Senate; follow Cellini through the thrilling intricacies of his dealings with Princes and Pontiffs; stand with Columbus on the Santa Maria as he sees the blue haze which is the new world; see Harvey as he discovers the circulation of the blood.

A few minutes a day of pleasurable reading—a book for each evening corresponding to your mood—and at the end of the year you will have a wider appreciation of literature, and art, and poetry, and science, and philosophy, and discovery, than you could possibly obtain in a lifetime of ordinary haphazard reading.

It is in this spirit that I want you to be when you turn over the pages of one of these free-examination sets. Thinking of your own pleasure and that of your household, and weighing the trivial cost of these MASTER-PIECES against the cost of other things of life as compared with the satisfaction that they bring, I want you to say to yourself: "Is this a good investment—in money, in time, in pleasure, in mental growth?"

"But," you may say, "what of the War?" Just bear in mind what President Wilson, the greatest leader of thought the world has ever known, wrote a short time ago to the President of a Western College who asked him if our colleges should close and general education be neglected at this time.

"By no means should our schools and colleges be closed during the period of the War, and general education be neglected. Never in History have educated, cultured men and women been so needed as they will be in the next few years to carry on the work of reconstruction and peace.

Here is your chance to avail yourself of Dr. Eliot's wonderful knowledge and experience to prepare yourself for the after-the-war problems. You owe it to yourself to at least SEE and EXAMINE this Library that he selected to speed you on the road to a bigger, broader success. The card brings it to your door, charges prepaid. Merely put your name on it and drop it in the mail.

But remember, in the great book of Time there is but one word—" NOW' '—so drop your card in the mail NOW.

Very truly yours,

IMPORTANT! The Price of The Harvard Classics will soon be advanced.

Paper, Ink, and Binding have more than doubled in cost since the material used in the manufacture of these books was bought. Our present stock will last only a short time longer, and then our prices must be increased to keep pace with the costs.

Take advantage of the present low costs by mailing your card NOW.

Nothing remarkable about any of these letters, is there? You have seen as good or better ones many a time. But they had this virtue. They brought back what they went after—the orders. In the five years I was with Collier's they sold many hundreds of thousands of dollars worth of books.

Why? Because they set out with a definite goal in mind and they made every word carry them one step nearer that goal. Take letter No. 1 as an example. What is its purpose?

1. *To winnow out from the mass of readers those few who can be sold the idea of "culture," the value of higher education.*

If Dr. Eliot of Harvard were to say to you—" Come around to my home tonight. I want to show you some books I believe you'll enjoy; they are interesting, entertaining, yet they will give you all the essentials of a liberal education, even if you can spend only fifteen minutes a day with them."

Can you imagine any start more likely to attract the attention and arouse the interest of a man culturally inclined, who had not enjoyed the benefits of a college education? You know many such men, and you know how many of them feel that they are handicapped through lack of the cultural advantages a college gives. In the back of their minds always is the fear that they are a bit inferior to their college-trained friends. So how they would welcome the idea of a talk with so famous an educator as Dr. Eliot! How they would jump at the idea of a college reading course under his guidance! Therefore how well that idea fitted in with the mental conversation going on in the back of their minds!

2. *The ease of it!* They have had opportunities to take night courses in schools and colleges that would, in time, give them every educational advantage that would have been theirs had they spent four years in college. But this entailed so much work. And an expenditure of time out of all proportion to its value to them in dollars. So they passed it by.

But along comes the chance to get all the essentials, under the guidance of one of the greatest educators the country has known, *in only fifteen minutes a day!* Dr. Eliot has used his forty years of experience to pick the few worth-while books from all the millions that have been written, and edit them so that in a few minutes' pleasurable reading each evening, they can make up for the four years in college they missed.

3. *The free trial, no money or risk.* It is made so easy for the reader to examine the books, without obligation or risk of any kind. Naturally his curiosity is aroused to learn what books Dr. Eliot considers essential. He would like to see them, to glance through them, perhaps read a page here and there.

Well, here is his chance to do it without a penny of cost. Perhaps he has already read some of the books. Perhaps he is nearer the standard of his college friends than he had thought. It would be nice to see, anyway, and as long as it does not cost anything to have a look--

No. 2 letter starts right where No. 1 left off: "Will you examine the "Harvard Classics" if we send you a set at our own expense for a week's free examination?"

Don't decide now whether you want to buy them or not. Plenty of time for that later. Just browse through them for a week and see for yourself how interesting they are, what absorbing entertainment, what marvelous education.

Think of it! The world's civilization on a bookshelf! All that mankind has done, thought, gained or been--within the compass of a five-foot shelf of books! Can you afford *not* to look at it?

Education in the highest sense, entertainment in the best sense, all made possible in fifteen minutes a day. And then the price! A saving of $433.05 from the regular bookstore price of the same works in separate editions. That alone makes it a bargain well worth any man's money.

Then as an added inducement, it is a book of reference as well, an encyclopedia in itself. Surely it is worth your while at least to send for these books and look them over!

Then followed the Lincoln folder, with its appeal to ambition, its description and argument in its center pages, its proof of value in the reproduced letter from Brentano's on the last page.

Nos. 3 and 4 are reiterations of the same line of argument in different words and different pictures.

No. 5 is the old standby—the last-chance offer. It plays up the saving, it repeats all the advantages that are yours if you act now, all you may lose by delay. It emphasizes the no money—no risk, then makes it so easy for you to order that it seems a shame not to take advantage of the opportunity.

In short, it tried to such good purpose to follow the rules laid down in the previous chapters, that even as the fifth letter in the series, it brought back $39 orders at a cost of less than $2 an order! Than which there are few quicker methods of making money.

XI

The First Olive

IN EVERY business, it is an axiom that the first sale is the hardest. It is like the first olive out of the bottle, or a maid's first kiss—after it, the rest come easily.

And nowhere is this truer than in selling by mail. When you try by mail to interest a man in your product, your most difficult task is to win his confidence, his belief in your statements. That is the reason for the free-trial offer. That is what makes necessary the money-back guarantee.

So when you have made one sale to a man, your hardest job is done. From then on, your real profits should begin. Where it may have cost you 10, 20 or even 50 per cent of your selling price to make the first sale, your second one should seldom cost you more than 5 or 10 per cent. Why? Because your customer believes in you! You have sold him something; it has proved to be all you claimed for it; therefore he feels safe in trusting anything you may say to him in the future.

That is why the big mail order houses will cheerfully spend several dollars to get a customer's first order. That is why experienced users of the mail oftentimes offer to the general public only small units of sale like $1 or $2, knowing that a man will much more readily take a chance on a low-priced item with some one he does not know, and that a satisfactory transaction at this low figure tends to establish confidence just as surely as a big sale.

The New Process Company of Warren, Pa., as an instance, used a $1 lot of initialed handkerchiefs to build a customer list quickly. Wm. H. Wise & Co. of New York sold the "Elbert Hubbard Scrap Book" at $2 or $3; and then to the resultant customers, they sold a good many thousand sets of the $100 "Little Journeys!"

At Collier's, we started with our highest priced sale, solely because we happened to have on hand a couple of hundred thousand old inquiries which had expressed an interest in that set. Then, after we had won their confidence, we sold them other sets.

The first was the "Harvard Classics Shelf of Fiction "—a logical follow-up to the "Classics" themselves. There were twenty volumes, in bindings to match the Five-foot Shelf. A first circularizing of the "Classics" buyers brought something like 10 per cent of orders. Since the circular in the mail cost us less than 3 1/2 cts. each, 10 per cent meant that our orders were costing us only about 35 cts. apiece, or less than 2 per cent of our selling price!

That is nothing unusual for a first follow-up to customers who have been sold by mail. Once you have won your customer's confidence with an article that has done all you promised for it and more, you should be able to sell 10 per cent of your customer list any related product. Of course, if you keep going back at them every month, as the New Process Company frequently does, you are not going to sell 10 per cent each time. But if your offering is something a large percentage of your customers can use to advantage, you will get a profitable volume of orders every time.

To realize this, you have only to look at the letter and circular which pulled such good returns on the "Harvard Classics Shelf of Fiction." There is nothing outstanding about either of them. The circular especially is not at all what I would send if I were making the offer now. There is little about it to intrigue the interest. Just compare it with some of the circulars we used on Wells' "Outline of History," or O. Henry, or Simonds' "History of the War." Yet it pulled. Why? Because in selling them the "Harvard Classics" we had already won the readers' interest in any later related offer we might make. For that reason, an ordinarily good letter, with a rather uninteresting circular, pulled extraordinarily profitable returns. Here is the letter:

YOU ARE AN OWNER OF THE HARVARD CLASSICS-
So you will be mightily interested to know that Dr. Eliot has just added a Two-Foot Shelf of Fiction—20 volumes—to his famous Five-Foot Shelf of Books. It is called—

The Harvard Classics Shelf of Fiction

In it are forty-five of the most famous novels of the greatest writers of all time. Seven different countries are represented —Russia, France, England, Germany, Spain, Scandinavia, and America—each by its most noted authors, each author by his best stories.

95

So good are these wonderful romances of fiction and history, so great has been their influence, that they can truly be called an essential part of the reading of every Twentieth Century American. They supplement and round out the Harvard Classics, covering as they do a field almost untouched in the original Five-Foot Shelf of Books.

Special Offer
To
Harvard Classics Owners

A special edition of the Harvard Classics Shelf of Fiction has been made up for Harvard Classics owners. Because of its wealth of criticisms, sketches, and essays by noted authorities it has been called the "Commentators Edition." While it lasts we can offer you the complete set of the Harvard Classics Shelf of Fiction in 20 volumes, bound in silk cloth, gold stamped, at a saving of 44% compared with Brentano's actual quotation reproduced on the back of this letter; and payable in just a few months by very small monthly payments; or with a discount for cash.

Examine the Books for a Week—at Our Expense

Don't take our word for the value and interest of these great stories; don't take as final the judgment of Dr. Chas. W. Eliot, President Emeritus of Harvard University and probably the greatest authority on books and reading in the world today. Examine the books for yourself—read in your own home one or two of the forty-five wonderful stories— then decide. It costs you nothing to SEE the books—the enclosed card will bring them to you for a *week's examination.*

SEND NO MONEY. Merely ask to *see* these stories that Dr. Eliot has selected for you—the Twentieth Century Busy Man, from out of all the fiction of the World. The enclosed card brings them. Put your name and address on it now and drop in the mail.

But remember, this special offer to Harvard Classics owners holds good only, until the "Commentators Edition" is exhausted, so drop your card in the mail *now*.

Yours very truly,

Later follow-ups on the fiction books considerably increased the percentage of sale, but all depended for their effectiveness upon their tie-up with the interest already created by the "Harvard Classics," so they seem hardly worthy of inclusion here.

Much better, from the point of view of a good piece of mail selling, was our folder offering the "Junior Classics", the Two-foot Shelf of Books for Children. Imagine how such an approach as this would appeal to the parents of any growing youngster:

> You know how the little folks just love a good story, how they'd rather listen to one than eat or play or sleep, how they beg you, sometimes, to tell them a story, to read to them.

What parent has not had that experience? What parent will not nod his head in agreement with every word? You have your reader's interest. Now you point out—what he will also agree with—that the children *will read* something, and it is what they read now that has the greatest influence on their after-life; it is their heroes, the men and women who are made to seem to them wonderful and worthy to pattern after, who form your children's characters.

How important, then, that they should have the right reading, and here is the chance to get for them the 846 best stories for children from the literature of the whole world, picked by two famous educators, Dr. Eliot and Dr. Neilson.

From there on, proof, persuasion, bargain and free trial follow in swift succession. Everything is made easy. Which is probably the reason this folder pulled as high as 8 per cent on some lists. Here is the folder itself:

> *You Know How the Little Folks Just Love a Good Story—*
> How they'd rather listen to one than eat or play or sleep—
> how they beg you, sometimes, to tell them a story, to read
> to them.

They will read something, and it's what they read now that determines what they are to be—it's their heroes, their ideals, the men and women who are made to seem to them wonderful and worthy to pattern after, that form your children's characters—that have the greatest influence on their after-life—that spell the difference, frequently, between success and failure.

If you could pick out from all the literature of the world just the stories of folk-lore and fable, just the tales of fiction and history, just the poems, that would give your children the right ideals, that would stimulate them to their best efforts, that would give the best groundwork for their later studies, and if you could have the advice of the best-read man and the greatest educator of his day as to that reading, you'd feel that no price was too high to pay for it.

You *can* get just those stories, tales and poems—846 of them—gone over by the best-read man and the greatest educator of his day, Dr. Charles W. Eliot, for forty years President of Harvard University, approved and indorsed by him. They are bound up into ten volumes, and you'll find Dr. Eliot's suggestions as to the training of your children in his introduction to the set.

The 846 Best Stories for Children From the Literature of the World

All that is best in mythology and folk-lore, fairy tales and legends, historical romances of chivalry, stories of courage and daring, animal and nature stories—in short, all that is best in the literature of childhood from every race and every land is included in these Junior Classics— stories that the first mothers told at nightfall to their little ones, the Folk Tales and Myths of the Far North Country, the Br'er Rabbit Stories of our own Southland.

The tales of Greece and Rome have a volume to themselves, and in them the child comes to know as familiar friends the great characters who, in high-school days, he will meet again between the covers of text-books. Then follow the stories of the heroes and heroines of chivalry. Shakespeare's heroes and heroines, too, are here in selected plays, retold and rearranged to make easy reading for children.

"Alice in Wonderland" is in the company, and "Robinson Crusoe and "Joan of Arc" and "Evangeline." The stories that never grow old are here—" Aladdin" and "Sinbad the Sailor" and the heroes and heroines of Scott's best stories. Scores, literally hundreds, of the wonderful people of childhood—they are all here, ready to become the delightful associates of your own boy and girl.

Save $30 and Have the Best

There are 846 stories, poems, tales, and essays in The Junior Classics—" The Children's Two-Foot Shelf of Books "—a story each night at bedtime for nearly three years.

Purchased separately in the various bindings of the original publishers, these 846 masterpieces would cost $30.00 more than the price we ask for them in uniform bindings—the best product of the bookmaker's art.

Bound up into 10 volumes, in durable cloth binding, the price of these 846 stories, tales, and poems is only $16.00, payable at the rate of $1.00 a month; bound in three-quarter Autumn Leaf Leather, the price is $24.00, payable $1.50 a month, a discount of 10 per cent being allowed for full cash payment.

Each of the 10 volumes has its colored frontispiece—a reproduction of a celebrated painting, and there are scores of illustrations (an art education in themselves).

The 846 masterpieces have been arranged by Professor Neilson, head of the English Department at Harvard University, in reading courses which make them a real training in the appreciation of great literature, and a stepping-stone to the classics of the adult world.

A home training planned by the greatest educators to develop character and insure success—that is The Junior Classics in a single sentence.

And sold at less than a third of what the individual parts would cost.

"My Mother Never Read to Me"

Pity the man or woman, who, looking back over life's journey, must say, "My mother never read to me." To him one of the richest joys of existence has been denied; school work would have been easier, life's tasks more meaningful had there been the background of idealism and mental uplift gained in his first plastic years in his own home.

It is for the boy or girl who covets this rich experience, for the parent who WANTS to draw close to his or her child through the pages of great literature, but who is perplexed as to just WHAT OR HOW TO READ, that The Junior Classics is offered.

"Give me a child until he is seven years old," said Cardinal Newman, "and I care not who has him after."

Give your boy or girl for the first years of his life to the great ideals and noble thoughts of literature. Make his or her heroes not the rude figures of the Sunday supplements—but the great characters, men and women, who have made history. Fill his or her mind with such images and ideals, and you need not worry for the future.

It was to do THIS for the mothers and fathers and children of America that the leading educators of America gave of their best to The Junior Classics, and that Dr. Eliot agreed to lend his splendid reputation and influence to their success.

101

"There is no University," says a celebrated authority, "like a mother's reading to her child."

That is the inspiration of The Junior Classics. For the mother or father who CARES what his child may become, who CARES, that is, as much as three cents of money and five minutes of time a day, this splendid library lifts an enormous burden.

For here, authoritatively selected and scientifically arranged, are the works that for generations have proved their power to mold character, make school work easier, insure success.

Henry Clay said: "A wise mother and good books enabled me to succeed in life. She was very poor, but never too poor to buy books for her children. It is a mean sort of poverty that starves the mind to feed the body."

Did You Ever Hear the Story

Of the youngest governor Minnesota ever had—the late Governor John A. Johnson? He was talking one day of his start in life:

"The man who influenced my career more than any other," he said, "lived in our little home town. He lent me the right books; he taught me what to read and how. Much of what I am I owe to that man—and to those books."

THE RIGHT BOOKS—because their influence came into the life of that simple small-town boy at the critical period of his boyhood, ambitions were awakened and purposes stirred which brought him finally to the governor's chair. Without them he might have been content to remain forever behind the counter of the store where he started work; it was the books coming to him in the molding years of youth that showed him the world and taught him how to conquer it.

Dip into the biography of almost any man or woman who
has reached success and you will find this story of good
books repeated. Franklin, Jackson, Clay, Lincoln—none
of these men ever had the advantage of a good schooling;
all of them owed their great success in life to the influence of good books.

Examine the Books for a Week—at Our Expense

Don't take our word for the value and interest of this set.
Don't take as final the judgment of Dr. Eliot, the foremost
educator of his day. Let us LEND you the books for a
week without cost and without obligation. Examine them
for yourself. Read in your own home a few of the 846 stories and poems in The Junior Classics; *then* decide
whether these stories will be worth two or three cents
each to your children —in pleasure, in profit, in mental
growth.

Remember, you are under no obligation to keep them. We
send the books to you, prepaid, for one week—to read, to
examine, to talk over with your family. If you like them,
send us only $1.00 at the end of the week, and $1.00 a
month until the set is paid for; if not, return it without
question at our expense.

SEND NO MONEY. Merely ask to see these stories that
have been approved for your children by Dr. Charles W.
Eliot, President Emeritus of Harvard University, who has
directed the training of more successful men than probably any other man in the world.

The enclosed card brings them to you. Merely drop it in
the mail.

After the "Junior Classics," we worked our lists on half a dozen
other sets of books, principal among them, "The Story of the Great
War," Lodge's "History of Nations," and Shakespeare.

103

Here is a typical letter on the war story, written early in 1917, when it looked as though the end might come any minute:

After the War—What?

Do you know what will probably happen after this World War? Are you familiar with the fundamental conditions which underlie the development and progress of nations?

Do you know what actually happened after other wars—in England, for instance, after the Napoleonic campaigns? In our own United States after the Civil War? To belligerents and neutrals after the Franco-Prussian War? In international trade after the Russo-Japanese War?

Do you know whether peace sends the price of commodities up or down? Makes money "easy" or scarce?

Do you know if any Nation actually faced bankruptcy, or repudiated a war debt? Or how war debts affect taxation? How often have you wished that you could speak with authority, backed by absolute knowledge, of the real inside facts of this World War—of its probable outcome and its effects upon our trade, our institutions and our standing.

THE STORY OF THE GREAT WAR

What Led Up to It—How It Began—Through It All

Contains the facts that you, as a business man, must know. It tells the full story of this greatest crisis in the World's history—a crisis that affects you and me almost as closely as the nations of Europe.

Do you for one moment imagine that any nation or group of nations can contract debts amounting to sixty billions of dollars without affecting the entire credit system of the whole world? Do you suppose that fourteen million men can be killed, wounded or lost without affecting labor and capital everywhere? Do you think that the whole map of Europe can be changed without disturbing the even tenor of our ways?

This Is America's Opportunity

War is blazing the way for America to commercial supremacy. However long the war may continue, Europe must eventually reconstruct. Thousands of square miles of territory, now in ruins, must be rebuilt. Millions upon millions of people must be clothed and fed.

You are a business man. Put the question squarely up to yourself. How much do you really know about the resources of the different countries of Europe, their wealth in men and material and food stuffs—what likelihood there is of any country being forced to give in.

Is Germany Really Starving?
Is Revolution Likely in Austria or Russia?
Can Great Britain be Blockaded by Submarines?

The answers to these questions are all to be found in the five volume story of the Great War. Without these answers how can you form an intelligent opinion as to what will happen? How can you plan ahead for your own business future?

Heretofore we Americans have had a deep sense of self-sufficiency. We haven't had time or inclination to know how the rest of the world lived. *But now we must know.*

England, Germany and other nations, reaching out after commerce and new markets, studied countries and peoples and conditions. So the American business man, the manufacturer's and the merchant and the salesman, must inform himself if he would develop—if he hopes to make the most of present opportunities.

105

"The World's Great Events"—
—*10 volumes*—

With the 5 volume "Story of the Great War," cover the whole history of the World from the dawn of civilization to the present day. The two sets together bring the entire world home to you. They tell you about all the peoples of the earth. They show you many a parallel to the present great struggle in the history of other nations during the past five thousand years.

They bring out the absolutely important facts and figures about every nation that you must know—not dry facts dryly stated, but thrilling facts told in an intensely interesting narrative that make these histories read like the most enticing of fiction.

The leading historians of the world wrote these histories. Into a few attractive, easy reading volumes are condensed all the mass of material which in old time histories occupied many volumes and cost hundreds of dollars.

There are five copiously illustrated volumes in the Story of the Great War, beautifully bound in 3/4 leather, and ten in the World's Great Events, bound in a rich dark brown cloth. While the present edition lasts, we can make you a special combination price on these fifteen volumes of $2.20 apiece—$33.00 for the two sets payable at the rate of only $1.50 a month, a discount of 10% being allowed for full cash payment.

This offer holds good, however, only while the present edition lasts, for paper, ink and binding are going up by leaps and bounds and the price of our next edition will have to be raised accordingly.

Examine the Books for a Week—Free

Don't take our word for the value and interest of these great books; don't take the word of the thousands of scholars and statesmen and business men who have

106

bought and commended them; let us LEND the books themselves to you for a week—FREE—so you can see for yourself how intensely interesting they are, what a wonderful field they open up to you.

Remember, you are under no obligation to keep them. We send them to you by prepaid express FOR A WEEK'S FREE EXAMINATION. If you like them, send us $1.50 at the end of the week and only $1.50 a month until paid for. If not, re-turn them without question at our expense.

But remember, too, that our present prices will hold only until the stock now on hand is exhausted.

Now Is the Time

After the War is over, anyone can say what the outcome has been, what effect Peace has had upon our industries but hindsight of this kind is seldom very valuable. It is the man who can judge of these things now—the man with foresight who can plan ahead and be ready for the opportunities when they come that will forge into the front rank of American business and professional men.

NOW, while every edition of the newspapers is centering your interest on Europe—Now when the knowledge will be of infinite value to you is the time to acquire that knowledge not only of the full story of this War, but of the effects of previous wars on trade and credit and labor and capital.

SEND NO MONEY. Merely ask to SEE these books that tell all the essential facts in the History of the World in the most interesting and authoritative way imaginable. The card brings them. Drop it in the mail—Now.

Yours very truly.

That letter pulled about 3 per cent on our customer lists, and about 1 per cent on such lists as doctors, lawyers, accountants, engineers and other occupational names. It was mailed under 1 ct. postage, so the letter-circular and card cost only about 2 3/4 to 3 cts. in the mail, which gave us a cost of about $1 an order on a 3 per cent pull, and $3 an order at 1 per cent. Considering that the "History" sold for $33, there was a goodly margin of profit at both figures.

Lodge's "History" was older and had little of timely appeal, so we did not do so well on it. From the following letter we got about 1 per cent of orders on our customer lists, and from the folder which follows the letter, we got about 3 1/2 per cent from occupational lists.

There was a profit in both these figures, for both letter and folder were very inexpensively done, the letter costing less than 2 cts. in the mail and the folder less than 2 1/2 cts. But the results did not run into big figures.

A HUNDRED YEARS AGO ALL EUROPE WAS IN ARMS AGAINST NAPOLEON— Today almost the whole World is arrayed against the Kaiser.

Napoleon ended his days on the rocky isle of SL Helena. Will the Kaiser do the same?

It is much the same old story. One nation tries to impose its rule by force upon all the others—one man tries to dominate the World. Xerxes, Alexander, Caesar, Napoleon, the Kaiser —all dreamed of World domination, all attained some measure of success—but what was feasible in the times of Alexander and Julius Caesar is utterly impossible in these days of universal enlightenment. "The World Must and Will Be Made Safe For Democracy."

After the battle of Waterloo Belgium and Holland and Luxembourg were set up as neutral states. Do you know why?

Have you ever heard the long story of diplomacy and intrigue that lay behind the Triple Alliance and the Triple Entente?

Do you remember the Agadir incident?

Have you ever read an impartial account of the Reconstruction period that our Southern States went through after the Civil War? Do you know that many of the States of Europe will have to experience this same Reconstruction after the present war?

Do you know that trade and credits and money standards are being affected in much the same way as by previous wars, though of course on a vastly greater scale?

It is just another case of History repeating itself. All of the various phases of reconstruction and readjustments in commerce and trade and credits can be judged of from the experience of past wars; you can use real foresight, you can safely plan ahead, if you will but profit by the lessons of History.

NOW, while every edition of the newspapers is riveting your attention on the problems of the war—NOW, when the knowledge may be of infinite value to you, is the time to acquire that practical working knowledge of history that the forward-looking American of today must have.

In a new kind of history, written for the modern busy man under the supervision of Senator Henry Cabot Lodge of Massachusetts, you will find in interesting narrative form just the essential facts about each Nation that you need to know. It is the only collected history of the World that devotes a whole single volume to each of the larger Nations, giving fully and in detail the story of each, and it brings that story down to the very opening of the present stupendous struggle.

The Lodge History of Nations brings out the absolutely important facts about all the warring nations that you must know to understand the causes and sequence of this greatest struggle in history.

It brings out facts and figures about each nation with statistics and data that cannot be readily or conveniently located elsewhere—not dry facts dryly stated, but thrilling facts told in an intensely interesting narrative that makes these histories read like the most enticing fiction.

The Lodge History of Nations was originally published by the Snow Company of Chicago at prices ranging from $120.00 a set to $625.00, and it has never before been sold at less than these figures.

However, publishing as we do some five million books a year, we have manufacturing facilities that the Snow Company did not have, and because of these we have been able to print the complete 25 volumes of the Lodge History of Nations on special water-marked paper from the same plates as the finest De Luxe sets, at a price of only $44.00—two-thirds less than the lowest price named by the Snow Company—and you can pay for the books as you like, even as little as $2.00 a month.

Examine the Books for a Week—at Our Expense

Don't take our word for the wonderful value and interest of this great set of Histories. Don't take the word of the thousands of satisfied owners. Examine the books yourself for a week in your own home without cost and without obligation—THEN DECIDE.

SEND NO MONEY. Merely drop the enclosed card in the mail and the complete set will be sent you immediately AT OUR OWN EXPENSE for a week's examination. If, during that week, you can see where the books will be worth 7¢ a day to you in pleasure and profit, accept them. If not, return them without question at our expense.

But at least ask to SEE this set that Ex-President Andrew D. White of Cornell University calls—" The Best World History by Modern Historians.

Yours very truly,

110

There followed after these Shakespeare, Dumas, different Memoirs and the like. The Memoirs letter started with the story of the drummer boy's wife who saved the Czar and his army from the Turks, hinted at a dozen other interesting incidents of the kind, touched upon de Pompadour, whose true story makes the legend of King Cophetua and the begger maid seem tame by comparison, and showed how her sinister motto—" After us, the deluge "—led logically to the Revolution and the Reign of Terror, just as the rottenness of the Czars brought similar scenes to Russia more than a hundred years later.

Needless to say, such stories won reader-interest and brought back orders in profitable volume, but none of them compared in sales with the "Harvard Classics" and "Junior Classics."

These were our standbys. With the reputation of Dr. Eliot back of them, we were able to go to every country town and hamlet and leave at least a few sets of these sterling works. But excepting on inquiries that the salesmen were unable to sell, we were not allowed to touch the larger towns and cities, where most of the population lives and where most of the reading is done.

For, contrary to general belief, our experience was that it is far easier to sell the dwellers in the cities by mail than it is the farmer. This is true even of such merchandise as coats, shirts, ties and other wearing apparel. It is far more true of books.

So our sales were limited. It was hard to get highly profitable percentages of orders from telephone books and automobile registrations. The occupational lists paid well, but there were comparatively few of them in the rural communities. While as for the most profitable lists of all—the buyers of other sets published by concerns like the Review of Reviews, Putnam's, Doubleday, etc—we were barred from using them by our geographical restrictions, because they could not take the time to sort over their lists and address our circulars only to rural communities.

For these reasons, our sales amounted to only about $250,000 a year, when if we had had the whole country to draw upon, they should have run into the millions. So when the Review of Reviews offered me the sales managership of their mail selling, I jumped at the chance to show what could be done by mail when all the hobbles were off.

111

XII

Selling $2,000,000 Worth of O. Henry Stories

For more than thirty years, the Review of Reviews has been selling magazines and books by mail. For almost as long they have been noted for the effectiveness of their sales literature, and few indeed are the ideas that either Charles D. Lanier or Fred Stone have not tried. But in the Fall of 1918, the management of the business was taking so much of their time that they had to delegate the copy writing to some one else, and the choice fell upon me.

The joke of it was that the thing they had in mind particularly for me to work upon turned out to be merely a minor seller, whereas the one that was supposed to be sold out was our main leader for two whole years.

When I went with the Review, O. Henry's short stories had been selling in set form for about six years, and of late the results had fallen off badly; so I was told not to bother with it, but to see what I could do with Frank H. Simonds' "History of the World War," and to put every-thing I had into pushing Harrington Emerson's "Institute of Efficiency."

Well, I spent several weeks writing circulars on both of these; then, while they were being printed and got ready for mailing, I picked up some of the O. Henry stuff and idly jotted down a letter and circular, merely to fill in time. When they were finished they seemed rather good to me (to Messrs. Stone and Lanier, too), so we decided to try them on a small test.

During the next twelve months we sold more than 50,000 sets of O. Henry, amounting to more than $1,000,000! Of the Efficiency Course, we sold less than $150,000

We used several different letters on O. Henry and a number of ads, but the basic appeal was the same in all. First, we took it for granted that our reader had heard of O. Henry and knew something of the intriguing humanness of his stories. So we wasted no time with introductions, but started our letter with a "bargain" appeal— a bargain and a "hurry-up." For the hurry-up, we had several different premiums. Jack London was the most popular of them. If you would send your order right away, you would get free with your set of O. Henry, five volumes of Jack London's famous stories.

An old dodge, of course, but why worry whether a scheme is old or new when it brings a million dollars worth of orders? Here are some of the letters and circulars that proved most effective:

A SAVING TO YOU OF $108.00

The original edition of O. Henry was snapped up at $125.00 per set, yet here we offer you a special edition, printed from the very same plates as the original sets, and containing every word, every illustration, for less than one-seventh the price.

THE LOWEST PRICE AT WHICH THE WORKS OF O. Henry will ever again be sold has now been reached in the new silk cloth edition, costing less than one-seventh the price of the original sets.

This is the final bed-rock price to you and it holds good only until this special edition is exhausted. I write you because with all that you have heard and read ABOUT the works of O. Henry, you have never yet SEEN them. You have never yet had the privilege of ACTUALLY HANDLING the volumes— reading in your own home some of his wonderful stories proving to your own satisfaction the marvelous genius of the man, the depth of his understanding and sympathy.

The whole English-speaking world is going wild over O. Henry. In the past three years, his stories have broken all short story records since books have been published.

College presidents, great lawyers, kings of finance, leaders of the nation, soldiers and sailors, clerks and working girls— people from every class, young and old, rich and poor, men and women, are all hastening to get the stories that mean delight to everyone.

Fifty or more of O. Henry's stories have been made into photoplays, and now crowd the best movie theatres. In the colleges, they are the favorite textbooks of short story writers. Secretary Daniels took a test vote at Annapolis on the most popular author, and O. Henry led the list— Jack London coming second. In Camp Libraries every-where, the great demand of our soldiers and sailors has been for O. Henry.

Jack London—Five Volumes—Free

Second only to O. Henry in popularity is Jack London, so if your order comes in promptly, we will send you FREE, with your set of O. Henry, a five volume set of the works of Jack London, description of which you will find in the folder enclosed. The number of these sets that we have, however, is exceedingly limited, so we can promise to send the five FREE volumes of Jack London to you only if your order for O. Henry comes in immediately.

Examine Both Sets in Your Own Home for a Week—at Our Expense

Send no money. Merely put your name on the enclosed card and drop in the mail and both of these sets will be sent to you.

Remember, there is no obligation of any kind attached. The postal order is simply an opportunity for the books to sell themselves to you. There is no sale—no obligation to pay for them—until you have tried them out for a week in your own home and are satisfied. Just let us send the books for examination. The card brings them. Merely put your name on it and drop in the mail.

But remember too, we've only a few of these free sets of Jack London on hand, and we will have to make it "First come, first served," so if you want one for your Library, send in your card NOW.

Very truly yours,

IMPORTANT! Paper, ink, binding and labor have more

than doubled in cost since this edition of O. Henry was printed. As long as it lasts, you can get your set of O. Henry at this low price, with the Jack London FREE, but this is the last edition we shall ever be able to make at such a low price.

So take advantage of the low pre-war costs by sending in your card NOW!

To Love, Honor and Obey!

SHE was the daughter of one of the State's great pioneers—soldier, ranger, cattleman—a man who had had a big part in making that country.

And she was marrying a coward, a spendthrift, a gambler—and a cheat?

Why she did it no one knew—least of all Luke Standifer. But one day she told him. And then Luke—but—

What he did may make you laugh or make you weep—but he cut the Gordian knot.

It is a story that for subtlety, for thrilling action and intense interest, has seldom been excelled. Yet it is only one of 274 such tales by that Master of the Short Story—

O. HENRY

$500.00 IN PRIZES TO O. Henry READERS!

First Prize—$250. Second Prize—$100. Third Prize — $50. And ten prizes of $10 each. Simply write us a letter saying which is your favorite O. Henry story, and why you like it best. For the thirteen best letters, we will give the prizes listed above. See last page for rules of the competition.

DEAR SIR:

The other day someone asked Judge Ben Lindsey, of Juvenile Court fame, if he wouldn't name his favorite O. Henry story.

"My favorite O. Henry story," said the judge "*is all of them.* No writer ever had greater knowledge of human nature, and the charm of his stories makes it possible to read them over and over again."

Have you got your set yet? Most everybody else in this country seems to have. More than four million volumes of these inimitable stories have been sold to American readers in the past few years.

Universities are planning tablets to O. Henry. Text-books of English literature are including his stories. Theatrical firms are vying with one another for the right to dramatize them. He is the biggest, finest, most fascinating writer of the short story the world has ever known.

Did we ever tell you what W. P. Colburn, Superintendent of Schools at Rhinelander, Wisconsin, said of O. Henry?

"I hope nobody will ever again send me a whole set of books like these you sent, at least at one time. For four days it has been impossible to get anything done about the house. Nobody will come to meals, or go to bed, or do anything else on time, but read O. Henry."

We have no desire to upset your household, but it happens that we have left over from last year's big sale a few hundred sets of the 7-volume edition of Oppenheim's best stories. We are going to open this season's subscription to O. Henry by giving away—FREE—as long as they last—one of these 7-volume sets of Oppenheim with each set of O. Henry.

More than 350,000 families now own these fascinating O. Henry tales. The first edition was a limited one at $125. Every set was snapped up before it was printed.

The new library edition contains everything that was in that limited edition. It gives you a chance to get the stories for which these people paid $125 *for less than a fourth that price*—AND IN ADDITION, *to get FREE the 7-volumes of Oppenheim's best stories.*

116

Send No Money

Simply sign and mail the enclosed card. It will bring you both sets—the 192 volumes of O. Henry, containing his 274 complete stories—and the 7 best novels of E. Phillips Oppenheim FREE.

We pay all the charges. When you get your set, look over its fascinating pages. Read it for a week. Dip into it. Enjoy it.

If at the end of the week you don't think the stories are worth even their original price—*which you are lucky enough not to have to pay*—send the books back. Otherwise 50 cents a week makes them your own—an endless source of inspiration and delight and pride.

Send the card now—today without money—while you can still get the 7 Oppenheim volumes FREE. *This is your last chance.*

Sincerely yours,

P. S. The sumptuous Keratol binding, more durable than leather, costs only a few cents more a volume and has proved a favorite. For this luxurious binding, just change the payments as indicated at the bottom of the order card.

RULES OF THE COMPETITION[1]

1. This competition is open to everybody, whether an owner of an O. Henry set or not.

2. The prizes will be:

$250.00 *for the First Prize*
100.00 *for the Second Prize*
50.00 *for the Third Prize*
And 10 *prizes of 10.00 each*

117

3. Entries must be submitted in the form of a letter of from 150 to 200 words. State simply which is your favorite O. Henry story and your reasons for liking it best. The literary style of the letter won't matter one way or another.

4. All letters must be postmarked on or before midnight of March 15, 1922. Prizes will be awarded on March 25, 1922.

5. Letters may be typewritten or hand-written, but if the latter, they must be written legibly. Judges will take into consideration neatness and legibility in awarding prizes.

6. Competitors may submit as many entries as they like, but no one competitor will be given more than one prize.

₁ These rules appeared on the last page of letter.

7. *What is wanted primarily* in these letters is to ascertain, if we can, what it is about O. Henry that appeals to so many people. No writer of the short story since the world began ever had so many admirers—so many ardent devotees. We want to know what it is about these stories that appeals most to you.

8. Judges of the competition will be selected from among the personal friends of O. Henry on the Editorial Staffs of the World's Work and the Review of Reviews. No one connected with either magazine will be eligible for a prize. *"When one likes everything that O. Henry wrote, it is difficult to make selections, but I think that 'A Municipal Report' is my favorite."*

You will recognize the first O. Henry letter as being merely an adaptation of one of the follow-ups on the "Harvard Classics." As I saw it, the two letters had much the same job. The "Harvard Classics" letter was the final one of a series of circulars and its job was to sum up the strong points of the others and then, by emphasizing the money-saving, try to get immediate action.

The O. Henry letter had the same job. For six years these same readers had been hearing about O. Henry. Anything they would listen to had to be in the nature of a final appeal —a last chance at the low price or premium or something.

For the real interest, we depended upon our circular— telling enough of each story to whet the reader's appetite and make him want more, but not enough to satisfy his curiosity or enable him to fill in the answer for himself. Glance over the "When the Rattlesnake Struck" opener, or "To Love, Honor and Obey," and see if you don't want to get your hands on the books and find the answers. They contain the essence of all successful circular-writing— they get the reader's attention and interest and make him want to know more. Then the post card makes it easy for him to get more.

Here are two more letters and circulars along similar lines which did their part in bringing home that $1,000,000 worth of orders:

A SAVING TO YOU OF $95

The original edition of O. Henry's works was eagerly snapped up at $125. a set, yet here we offer you the very same stories, printed from the same plates and containing every word of the original set, at less than a fourth the price, AND IN ADDITION, we give you E. Phillips Oppenheim's 7 best novels—FREE!

DEAR SIR:

For years you have heard of O. Henry—you've read the advertisements of his stories and thought that some day you would own a set for yourself. But you've put off the sending from month to month. The time for that is gone. *Now*— TODAY—you must order your set of O. Henry to get the low price and the Oppenheim FREE!

The whole English speaking world reads O. Henry. Universities are planning tablets to him; text-books of English literature are including his stories; colleges are debating his place in literature; theatrical firms are vying with one another for rights to dramatize his stories—he is considered the biggest, strongest, livest force that has broken loose in English literature for many a long year. In short, he is the greatest writer of the short story the world has ever known.

So great is the popularity of O. Henry, so enormous the demand for his books, that we should like nothing better than to continue this offer for all time—but we can't. It costs more than twice as much now to make the sets as it did. Paper prices have quadrupled, labor costs two and a half times as much, binding three times. So we must withdraw this offer, but as long as the stock now on hand lasts, you can get O. Henry at the low price and—

E. Phillips Oppenheim 7 Volumes—Free!

No other writer ever knew so much of the secret history of Europe as Oppenheim. No other writer ever understood so well the hidden forces—the secret intrigues—the startling accidents—the sudden death—that have kept the whole Continent in turmoil for the past generation. He was looked upon as the most dangerous man in England. He was marked down by Germany for private execution, because he knew too much of her plots and intrigues, he suspected too many of her designs.

Fighting—scheming—plotting—mystery—love adventure all these are in his stories and all his marvelous genius is in the telling of them. He makes them so real that you forget everything about you in the joy of them. He lets you into secrets that take your breath away. He shows you the real inner workings of European diplomacy. He holds you enthralled with the romance, the mystery of his tale right up to the very last word.

Your Last Chance to Get a Set of Oppenheim Free!

This is the last edition of E. Phillips Oppenheim we can get at the special price which permits of our giving it free with O. Henry. When this one edition is gone (and there are only a few sets now left) you will be able to get Oppenheim's wonderful stories only at their regular price of $1.20 to $1.75 a volume.

121

Now, while you can, get your O. Henry set with the 7 volumes of Oppenheim FREE! This is your chance. The card brings you both sets—the 12 volumes of O. Henry, contain his 274 complete stories—and the 7 best novels of E. Phillips Oppenheim FREE!

We pay all the charges. When you get your set, look over its lustrous pages, aquiver with romance and action. Then, if you don't think the stories are worth even the price of the original sets—which you are lucky enough *not to have to pay*—send the books back. Otherwise, 50¢ a week makes them your own—an endless source of inspiration and delight and pride.

Send the card now—TODAY—without money while you can still get O. Henry at the low price, and the seven Oppenheim volumes FREE. *This is your last chance!*

Sincerely yours,

34% DISCOUNT FROM LAST YEARS' PRICE!!!

DEAR SIR:

Down—goes the price of O. Henry—back to the pre-war figure! The best paper, the clearest printing, the finest bind that O. Henry has ever had and the pre-war price! The Review of Reviews was the last of the great book publishers to raise its rates. It is the first to bring them down again.

34% Discount from Last Year's Price!

One-third off—that is the difference between the peak price of the post-war years and the pre-war price. Our own costs aren't down yet to pre-war figures, but we feel that the quickest way to get them there is to bring our price to you down where it ought to be.

So we are making this big cut. It is our bed-rock price, and it holds good only on this one edition.

We write you because, with all you have heard and read ABOUT O. Henry's stories, you have never yet SEEN them. You have never yet had the privilege we now offer you of ACTUALLY HANDLING volumes—reading in your own home some of these wonderful tales—proving to your own satisfaction the marvelous insight of the man, the depth of his understanding and sympathy.

Marvelous indeed are his tales—bits of life they are really, about you and me. He finds romance everywhere— around the corner—in the department store—in the shop—in the street car. He had a sympathy for everything that was real, a kindly belief in the good that is in all of us. His appeal is universal. He writes for you whether you live in New York or Kokomo. He makes you his friend with his first story, and then tells you a thousand others.

"Through the Shadows with O. Henry"

It has long been known that there was a mystery in the life of O. Henry. It remained for Al Jennings—sheriff, outlaw, bronco buster, adventurer and staunch friend of O. Henry —to uncover it for us. For the first time he tells fully the story of those dark early days in O. Henry's life which cast their shadow over his later success.

For O. Henry lived a life crowded with vivid incidents. Hotheaded adventure—stirring romance—these were his in that part of his life which he so carefully guarded from the public. He was afraid the public would misunderstand. But here the story is told so understandingly, so tenderly that when you have read it, you will love O. Henry not less, but more!

This is no polished masterpiece of style. It was written by an ex-outlaw, ex-train-robber—the friend of Theodore Roosevelt and General Miles—and the most devoted friend O. Henry ever had. It has in it the rarest of all qualities—the ability to tell a story so thrillingly, so movingly, that you forget the author in the man of whom he tells.

We were able to get only a small number of copies of this famous book. While they last, we are going to give one of them with each set of O. Henry—FREE!

Now, while you can, get your O. Henry set at the pre-war price of only 50 cents a week, and one of these few copies of "Through the Shadows with O. Henry "—FREE. Never again can we make you such an offer. Don't miss it. Put your name on the enclosed card and mail it *now*—TODAY!

Yours truly

P. S. There are many old admirers of O. Henry who feel that his works are worthy of the very best setting, and therefore they want their sets bound in more sumptuous style. We have made for them a real edition deluxe bound in full levant grained leather. Our manufacturing department set out to make this set suitable for a place alongside of the other classics in the costly libraries of elegant homes. By making 1,000 of these sets we have succeeded in making the price astonishingly low for books of this character—only $3 a month for 10 months or $27.00 in one cash payment. Remember this is for the full leather binding. If you want O. Henry to use and enjoy, the regular cloth edition contains all the stories, is handsomely made and costs less. See order form enclosed.

125

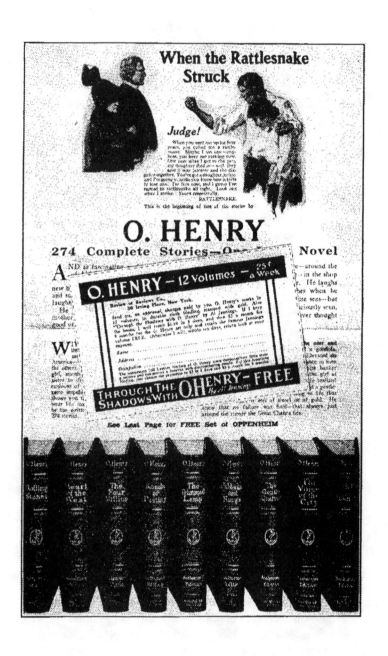

126

One million dollars worth of sales in a single year on a set that was supposed to be just about dead was pretty good, but the real test came with the second year. Could we keep it up?

It looked for a while as though we could not. We tried several variations of the original appeals, but they would not work. Circulars which, the previous year, pulled 2, 3 and even 4 per cent, were down below 1 per cent. Advertisements which had brought us orders for $1 and $2 apiece, suddenly climbed to $5 and $6. Something was wrong.

We tried all the different ways we knew, analyzed the results from every standpoint, and 'finally hit upon this: One of our most effective headlines in the previous year's ads had been—"Before the Price Goes Up!" After it, we went on to explain that paper, binding and labor were jumping skyward by leaps and bounds, that we had on hand some thousands of sets manufactured at the old low rates, and that when these were gone, the price would have to go up.

The argument was true, and prices of other commodities were rising so rapidly that people recognized its truth. But when the price did actually go up at the beginning of the second year, sales dropped to the point where they were no longer profitable.

So we decided to try another kind of hurry-up, and the one we hit upon was: "Last Chance to Get Jack London *free!*" Mind you, we had been giving Jack London (or Oppenheim or the mystery and detective stores, or some other premium) for some six years, and people had come to expect it. They had grown tired of hearing of raises in price, probably no longer believed further raises possible, but the threat of losing the premium was something different.

Strange as it may seem, putting in that one line changed the results over night. Back went the sales to the previous year's figures. Ads pulled again. And circulars—*how they pulled!* For the second time we sold $1,000,000 worth of O. Henry books in a single year!

The letters we used were not essentially different from the previous ones. They merely specialized on price and last chance!

Aside from that, they went over much the same ground as before. They had to, for in sales extending over seven years, pretty nearly everything had been said about O. Henry that could be said.

So we put our main dependence upon our hurry-up for the orders. And the hurry-up did the work.

In other words, as Mr. Lanier used to say often, it is not the copy that counts so much as the scheme back of it. In him and Fred Stone I had two as astute teachers as ever an ambitious user of the mails could ask for. They had been using the mails to sell books and magazines for twenty-five years, and what they did not know about it was not worth knowing.

I had youth and enthusiasm and a flair for copy that seemed to bring home the orders. They had the experience and judgment to guide these into the proper channels. And, too, Fred Stone had the genius for handling people and organizing work without which those thousands of orders would have been a liability instead of an asset. So we got through our second year.

That ended the big sale on O. Henry. Two million dollars worth in two years seemed to just about saturate the market. At any rate, it saturated the available lists of bookbuyers, for though we kept trying for the next several years, the O. Henry sales never again went over the $100,000 mark for any one year. Then the Literary Digest brought out the complete set in one volume to use as a premium with their magazine, and that put an end to the set sale for good.

What was responsible for this big sale? The same thing that is responsible for any sale—making your reader want it! We did not ask him to take our word for the interest of the O. Henry stories, or their value to him as cross sections of human nature—we gave him enough of the stories themselves to arouse his own interest. We gave him enough, but not too much. Then we told him that everybody was reading them, that they were the equal of a university course in practical psychology, that even without their story interest they were worth all they cost just as a study in human nature. And finally, we gave him a reason why he must order at once, or lose a really worthwhile premium that would otherwise be his free. In short, we aimed first at making the reader want the stories for themselves alone. When we felt we had succeeded in that, we gave him as many excuses for buying them as we could think of, and a real reason why he must do it right away. And lastly, we made it easy. We sent him a post card that brought the books to him without cost or obligation for a week's free reading. We told him he could browse through them as much as he liked, see for himself how interesting, how invaluable, the books would be to him. *Then* decide!

You might think that would result in a heavy percentage of returned sets. But it did not. Our average returns of O. Henry sets ran around 10 per cent, and the highest they ever went was 14 per cent. That's not bad, especially as most of them came back in perfect condition and needed only re-wrapping and re-boxing to be used again.

The payments, too, were good. Ordinarily we took the time to look up each order in our files and in the records of the Mail Order Credit Association, where the credit experience of some fifteen or twenty companies is pooled. But when you are getting as many as 3,000 orders in a single day, you cannot always take the time to do this. So during the rush we shipped everything that looked good to us without investigation, and looked up only the doubtful ones.

Ordinarily we wrote off 30 per cent of our gross business to cover returns, cancellations, collection expense and losses. That our judgment was not so bad in picking the good orders is proved by the fact that we had to increase that 30 per cent by only 3 per cent during those two years of rush times, and the saving in time and clerical expense more than made up for that.

It is not safe to assume, as so many do, that 90 per cent of the people are honest: In the early days of selling by mail that was true, but people have learned how easy it is to get goods on credit by mail, and the unscrupulous ones have taken advantage of it, with the result that there has grown up a class of professional curiosity-seekers and "dead-beats "—people who send for everything that can be secured without a down payment, and hold on to it until forced by threats of post-office action or court judgment to return it. The Mail Order Credit Association has records of more than 300,000 of these—men and women who have fleeced two or more of its members, in some cases *all* of its members! *If you guard against these*, then you can safely assume that 90 per cent or more of these who order your goods are honest—*but not until then.*

XIII

A War History That Sold

What became of the test on Simonds' "History of the World War,"
and the Emerson "Institute of Efficiency," while all this O. Henry
selling was going on? You have probably asked that question several times while reading the last two chapters.

They were not neglected, you may be sure, even though they were
outshone. Messrs. Lanier and Stone were too good business men to
ever keep all their eggs in one basket. The time when one product
was going best was always the time they were testing most assidu-
ously to find something else to take its place when it was sold out.

The Efficiency Course tests did only moderately well. We sold
perhaps $150,000 worth of them a year for the next two or three
years, but never enough to get wildly excited about. Compared to
the sales we were making on books, the results from the letters on
this course pale into insignificance. But just as samples of "Success
Course" letters, we give a few of them here:

YOU'VE GOT TO HAVE MORE MONEY—
Living expenses—food, clothing, rent, amusements—
have doubled or more than doubled in cost.

How can you increase your earnings enough to keep up
with these increased costs? How, without speculating or
gambling or changing your line of work, can you double
or triple your income in a reasonably short time?

There is only one way you can do it—and that is by using
ALL of your powers—100% of your abilities—instead
of the 10%, 25% or 50% used by ninety-nine men out of
a hundred.

Professor William James, one of the world's greatest psychologists, says: "As a rule, men habitually use only a
small part of the power which they actually possess.
Compared with what they ought to be, they are only half

awake. Their fires are damped, their drafts are checked. They are making use of only a small part of their possible mental and physical resources."

SUCCESS, in short, is simply a matter of INTELLI-GENT DIRECTION OF YOUR OWN POWERS. All the essentials of success are within you, they are simply awaiting proper development.

Our industrial captains, our merchant princes, our financial kings, our intellectual leaders—all started their careers with a mental and physical equipment no greater than that of the average man's. They made their success by using ALL of their powers instead of the small percentage utilized by the average man.

Now, be honest with yourself—what is the barrier that blocks YOUR progress to the things you most desire in life? What is it that keeps YOU from making more money? Isn't it INEFFICIENCY—failure to use to capacity the powers with which you have been endowed?

Efficiency—100% use of your talents—would bring you immediate advancement—would enable you to double or treble your income, especially now when there is so great a demand for big men to fill the many big jobs that have been created or left open by the War. With Efficiency behind him, ANY man, regardless of previous training or education, can hold down the biggest jobs in the business world today. "Ordinary ability, properly developed," says Theodore N. Vail, President of the American Telephone and Telegraph Company, "is all that is necessary to reach the highest rung in the ladder of success.

That ability you have; the development must come through Efficiency. Properly directed, the latent ability in you will enable you to reach any height to which you may aspire to realize ambitions that now seem impossible of attainment.

For anything that you have to do, whether it be the building of a skyscraper, the managing of an office, the winning of a bigger job, there is but one efficient way—one best way— of doing it. Efficiency will point out to you that one best way.

Efficiency is COMMON SENSE applied. It shows employers how to increase profits. It shows employees how to increase their earnings. It shows the professional man how to get more out of the day's work and out of life. Efficiency, however, is a science with definite laws, and the average man is no more familiar with its vital principles than he is with the principles of any other science of which he has made no study.

In the Emerson Course you learn from a master of Efficiency the fundamental principles that are responsible for all successes in life and business. Not only do you learn these principles but you receive actual training in their application.

Harrington Emerson is rightly regarded as the central figure of the world-wide Efficiency movement. He was the first to draw the attention of the nation to the elimination of industrial waste, first to formulate and apply the principles of Efficiency to industries, and first to conceive of the application of these principles to the individual.

For twenty years Emerson made notes and collected data for a Course in Efficiency for the individual. During this time he and his associates were in close touch with every scientific and technical advance, collecting and recording over 25,000 examples of modern progress in Efficiency.

Then for two years competent assistants traveled with him and aided him in building up the Course. When it was finally finished, after being re-written a dozen times, Dr. Walter L. Hervey of the New York Department of Education was engaged to go over the Course word by word with Mr. Emerson s assistants, to be sure that everything which modern scientific educational methods could add to it should be added.

Experts in home study courses and the science of Efficiency were engaged to organize the Emerson Institute, which watches over the work of the students, helps them over the hard places, incites them to give their best to the study and get the best it has to give; which answers any and all questions and insists on seeing that the Course really accomplishes Mr. Emerson's purpose.

Thousands of dollars in money and the time of some of the highest paid men in the country were freely spent in preparing the Course. It represents the knowledge and experience gained in forty years of work in over two hundred plants, many of them the largest of their kind in the whole world. For his work in just one of these plants Mr. Emerson was paid $500,000, yet we offer you the results of all his research and experience, made up into twenty-four lessons, for only $1.25 a lesson—$30.00 for the twenty-four lessons; payable $1.00 with order, $2.00 in one month and then $3.00 a month for nine months.

Examine the first three lessons at our risk. The enclosed order form will bring them, each one a week apart— subject to 30 days examination. Read them—try them out--if you are not more than satisfied with the results at the end of 30 days—if you cannot see where they will double or triple your earning power—send them back and your first payment of $1.00 will be refunded immediately and in full.

Remember, Mr. Emerson is no mere theorist or dreamer. He is a wide-awake world-famous professional man, one of the busiest business engineers in the country. In his very first big job, the savings affected reached the enormous sum of $1,500,000 per year, while the amount paid him for his services was $150,000. The Western Union Telegraph Company, The Gorham Mfg. Company, The Mutual Life Insurance Company, The Corbin Lock Company, The Yale & Towne Mfg. Company, and scores of other nationally known concerns have themselves sub-scribed to the Emerson Course in Personal Efficiency for large classes of their employees. The Scovill Mfg. Company of Waterbury, Conn., alone gave us a class of 324 men, for which they paid us $11,080.80.

Merely attach your check or a dollar bill (which will be returned to you after you have seen the lessons if you decide not to go through with the Course) to the attached order form and mail in the enclosed envelope. The first lesson will go forward immediately and the next two will follow a week apart.

Remember, this order is simply an opportunity for the Course to sell itself to you. There is no sale—no obligation to keep it—until you have tried it out in your own home for 30 days and are satisfied. Just let us send the first three lessons for your examination.

But remember, too, in the great book of time there is but one word-"Now"-so send the order now while you think of it.

Sincerely yours,

If you are to find the best, easiest and quickest way to the desirable things of life, you must begin by developing efficiency in the handling of time. So Lesson Two of the Emerson Course in Personal Efficiency is devoted to keeping a record of your time.

This record will measure your progress and show its direction; it will warn you of wrong methods and ineffi-cient operations; it will show the way to short cuts and furnish a basis for all future work in efficiency develop-ment.

We are mailing Lesson Two to you today, although your first payment of $2.50 has not yet reached us. However, $2.50 a month —8¢ a day—is so trifling a sum compared with the dividends in actual money that this Course will pay you —and pay you immediately—that we are sure your failure to forward your first payment has been due merely to over-sight on your part. Day after day letters pour into us telling of revolutionized lives, increased earnings, greater health, savings in time, in money, in effort—greater efficiency— greater happiness.

There is the merchant who increased the business of his store thirty-six thousand dollars a year as a result of Efficiency.

There is the man who had to borrow the money to subscribe for the Course and who is now, as a result of Efficiency, the president of a large pneumatic tool company out in the Northwest. This man thinks so much of the Course that every year, at Christmas time, he gives a number of them to his friends.

There is the young fellow just out of school working for a salary of $35.00 per month. Through the Course he got the training that enabled him to fill a position paying $250.00 per month.

One man writes: "I'm fifty-eight and I've just begun to live." Another says "I've been born anew as a result of Efficiency." One man tells us of increasing his monthly earnings over 1,000 per cent; another of tripling his business before finishing the Course.

For everything that a man wishes to do, whether it is the building of a skyscraper, the writing of a novel, the managing of an office, the winning of a bigger position, there is but one efficient way—one best way— of doing it.

The purpose of the Emerson Course is to enable you to find that one best way so that you can accomplish easily and quickly the things you have to do as well as the things you want to do.

Efficiency is a Science with definite laws, and the average man is no more familiar with its vital principles than he is with the principles of any other science of which he has made no study.

You are probably doing the best you can, but the question is, are you doing all that you are capable of doing—ARE YOU MAKING FULL USE OF YOUR POWERS?

Think of the times when you've yearned for a bigger future —when you've grown impatient with the barriers that seem to hold you down—when you've heard of the career of some acquaintance whom you knew to be inwardly no more capable than yourself! Here's your chance to equip yourself for success, as few men are equipped, under the guidance of probably the greatest Efficiency engineer the world has ever known—at a cost to you of only 8¢ a day—$2.50 a month.

Surely, you will not hesitate to spend that amount for the best services of a man to whom the great corporations of the country have paid as high as five hundred thousand dollars, for similar work in their organizations. You realize the necessity of Personal Efficiency if you are to get ahead. You can see the danger and risk of leaving the question to chance or convenience. You know that indecision—putting things off—is dangerous. Here is your chance to start today. Don't put it off—don't wait until tomorrow. You know they say that word "Tomorrow" has been the cause of the Spanish people's decay. When you want a Spaniard to do anything he always says "Tomorrow." And tomorrow is never here.

TODAY—that's the word for you. Pin your check or money order for $2.50 to this letter and return in the enclosed envelope. DO IT NOW.

Sincerely yours,

If the world's greatest Efficiency Expert—

After forty years' experience in re-organizing and getting maximum results from Factories, Stores, Offices, Railroads and Mines, were to offer you the results of all his years of experience—

if he were to tell you that he would follow you around, check up your every move, show you how you could better your methods here, save time there, accomplish more with less effort and double or treble your earnings—

if he could convince you that by following his instructions, by adopting the fundamental principles he lays down, you could reach any height to which you might aspire realize any reasonable ambition, no matter how impossible it may now seem of attainment, you would certainly consider no ordinary price too high to pay for his services, would you?

Well that is, in effect, just what Harrington Emerson offers you. For forty years he has been the central figure in the world-wide Efficiency movement. During that time he has handled more than two hundred different plants, many of them the largest of their kind in the world, and so great has been his success that some of the fees paid him ran as high as $200,000.

The same principles that he used in directing the work of those great corporations are just as applicable to you, for the principles themselves are fundamental.

And the point where Mr. Emerson always begins, whether he is handling one man or a thousand, is to develop their efficiency in the handling of time. So Lesson Two of the Emerson Course starts with a record of your time.

This record will measure your progress and show its direction; it will warn you of wrong methods and inefficient operations; it will show the way to short cuts and furnish a basis for all future work in efficiency development.

We are mailing Lesson Two to you today, although your first payment of $3.00 has not yet reached us. However, $3.00 a month—10¢ a day—is so trifling a sum compared with the dividends in actual money that this Course will pay you—and pay you immediately—that we are sure your failure to forward your first payment has been due merely to oversight on your part.

Probably you have often wondered how so many men with little education have swept forward to success, while other men with the best of training and seemingly greater ability have floundered around in the ruts of failure. Out of more than four thousand American millionaires, all but twenty started life as poor boys. What power was responsible for the rise of these men from poverty to riches?

These men got there because their ambition was backed by hard work and Efficiency—a combination that no set of circumstances can ever beat. And their careers were marked throughout by their ability to do things, do them better than they had ever been done before—by ability to make every minute and every action count for the most.

Given a high degree of Efficiency, a man can snap his fingers at "luck," laugh in the face of "opportunity" and turn his back in derision on that overworked excuse of the self-acknowledged failure—" pull."

It is this success-making quality of Efficiency that is taught by the Emerson Institute. Here you get the real secret of success. Here you learn what it is that makes men succeed in life. Here you receive careful and scientific training in the qualities you must have to achieve your life aim.

Merely attach your check or money order for $3.00 covering the first payment of this Course to this letter and return in the enclosed envelope. You will look back upon it forever after as the pass-key that opened to you the door of success.

Very truly yours,

Simonds' "History," however, did very well, and while it did not pay out on as large a number of lists as O. Henry, the lists it did work on pulled surprisingly good percentages of orders.

Here again it was the scheme that sold rather than the copy. When I went with the Review, they had sold only 5,000 sets of Simonds' "History" in over two years. In the next two, they sold about 70,000 at from $17 to $25 a set! It wasn't merely more effective copy that made all that difference. It was the plan behind the copy.

We had been trying to sell the books as the most graphically interesting and authoritative history of the war. And they wouldn't go. Why? Because the war was but just over and most people felt rightfully enough, that the facts were not all out yet and they would wait to get their history until the real, inside story was available. So we had to find a reason why they should order at once.

We found it in a premium. Six little volumes of intensely interesting true stories of the war. We offered them free if the reader would send in his order at once. What happened? Instead of 5,000 sets in more than two years, we sold nearly 35,000 in less than one year!

Then the sale dragged. What should we do? What had succeeded on O. Henry? A last chance offer? So the second year we made it "Your last chance to get True Stories *free!*" and sold another 25,000 sets!

Following that, we tried out various premiums, and managed to dispose of some 5,000 to 10,000, but none of them ever showed the vitality of "True Stories." Then, too, the public taste for war stories and war histories showed a sudden and most decisive drop about a year after the Armistice, so we felt that we did well to sell as many histories as we did.

Here are some of the most effective letters and circulars we did it with:

WHILE THEY LAST!
DURUY'S HISTORY OF THE WORLD—FREE!!!

Dear Sir:

For years now you have heard of Frank H. Simmonds—
you have seen his articles in the newspapers and magazines and thought that some day you would own a set of
his "History of the World War" for yourself. But you have
put off the sending from month to month.

The time for that is gone. NOW TODAY—you must
order your set of Simonds' to get with it—

Duruy's History of the World—Free!

It happens that we have left over from a huge edition a
few hundred sets of this wonderful World history, over
3,000,000 copies of which have already been sold. *These
few hundred sets are not enough to sell in our usual way,
so—while 'they last—we will give one of them—FREE
—with each set of Simonds' History.*

In Frank H. Simonds' History of the World War you get
the complete, authoritative, permanent story of the great
War—the only narrative history of the War that has yet
been written.

In Duruy's wonderful volumes, you get the history of the
world before. They show you the glory that was Greece
and the grandeur that was Rome. They guide you through
the Middle Ages, the picturesque days of Feudalism and
the Crusades. They take you through the Renaissance, the
revolution in art, science and letters. They show you the
recent history of Europe and how for a hundred years it
has been shaping itself towards the gigantic conflict just
ended.

Your Last Chance to Get Duruy's History Free!

There are only a few hundred of these sets left—just a

remnant of our last big edition—and they won't last long.

Now, while you can—get your Simonds' history at its regular price—and this greatest of world histories FREE.

This is your chance. The card brings you both sets—the five magnificent volumes of Simonds', illustrated with over a thousand paintings, drawings and photographs—and the four volumes of Drury—FREE.

We pay all the charges. When you get your set of Simond's History, look over its lustrous pages, aquiver with the thrilling story of the greatest conflict in history. Then if you don't think it is well worth the price—even without the four FREE volumes of Duruy—send it back. Otherwise 50¢ a week makes both sets your own—an endless source of inspiration and delight and pride.

Send the card now—without money—while you can get one of these few sets of Duruy's History—FREE. This is your last chance!

Sincerely yours,

141

This letter, as you will notice, offers Duruy's "History of the World" as a premium. It is just an adaptation of a similar letter that offered "True Stories." We wanted to find the most effective premium possible, so we tried half a dozen different ones.

The next letter shows still another premium: Tumulty's "Wilson as I Know Him." Both of these pulled reasonably well, but nothing to compare with "True Stories." Here is the Tumulty letter:

DID YOU EVER GET $10 FOR NOTHING?

Here is your chance!

If your card comes in before January 1st, we will send you—*not only* Tumulty's story of Wilson, for which the New York Times paid $25,000 and which added 50,000 new subscribers to their lists, BUT IN ADDTION, we will send you, *without extra* charge, H.G. Wells' "Outline of History," in the new, thin paper, single volume edition.

In other words, by mailing your order at once, *you get two $5 books without one cent of cost*!

DEAR SIR:

At last—the long silence that President Wilson's friends have maintained in the face of the most astounding accusation ever directed at a man of international prominence has now been broken with challenging answers.

Joseph P. Tumulty, for more than ten years Private Secretary to Woodrow Wilson, has written the inside story of the vital period of his Presidency. He solves questions that have been puzzling the public for years. He discloses Government secrets known only to the innermost circle. He unfolds the record of America's part in the War as viewed by the Chief Executive.

Nothing in American history equal to this story has appeared since Nicolay and Hay's Life of Lincoln.

The New York Times paid $25,000 for the exclusive rights to it in the Middle Atlantic States—the highest price ever paid for such a series. It has brought the Times more than 50,000 new subscriptions.

Because it is so timely, because it throws such interesting side-lights upon the history of the War, we offer it to you FREE with—

Frank H. Simonds'
"History of the World War"

In Simonds' History you get the complete, authoritative, permanent story of the Great War—the only narrative history of the War that has yet been written.

In Tumulty's intimate, fascinating story, you get the secret history of the United States at War—inside facts that the average man has never even dreamed of.

Your Last Chance to Get This Fascinating Volume!

We were able to secure only 1,000 copies of Tumulty's famous book at the special price which enables us to give it FREE with Simonds' History. 1,000 copies won't last long. When they are gone you can get this volume only at its regular price in the book stores—$5.00.

Now, while you can, get your Simonds' History at its regular price, and this most interesting of inside histories—FREE.

This is your chance. The card brings you both sets—the five magnificent volumes of Simonds', illustrated with over a thousand paintings, drawings and photographs—and the big volume of Tumulty's—FREE.

We pay all the charges. When you get your set of Simonds' History, look over its lustrous pages, aquiver with the thrilling story of the greatest conflict in history. Then if you don't think it is well worth the price—even

without the FREE volume of Tumulty's—send it back!
Otherwise 50¢ a week makes both sets your own—an
endless source of interest and delight and pride.

Send the card now—without money—while you can get
one of these few volumes of Tumulty's story of Wilson—
FREE. *This is your last chance!*

Sincerely yours,

After the sale was all over, and neither "True Stories" nor any other premium seemed able to resurrect it, we still sold about 10,000 with the old standby—the damaged-set letter. That is one letter that has never failed us after any big sale. We used it on O. Henry, we used it on the "Photographic History of the Civil War," we used it on Simonds' "History "—and later, as you will see, it worked just as successfully on traveling bags, even on bed blankets for the Warren people!

You see, in selling any big stock of books, you are bound to accumulate a large number of "rubbed" or slightly damaged sets, perfectly good in every respect except that they cannot be sold as new books. Many of them have had the corners "bunged up" in being returned by customers after examination. Many others have a page torn or are thumb marked, but for all practical purposes they are as good as new books. They form the basis for the damaged-set sale.

The trouble with us has usually been that these damaged-set sales so far outpulled any ordinary circulars that the orders kept rolling in long after the damaged sets were gone. On Simonds', for instance, we had some 3,000 actually damaged sets, and we got about 10,000 orders! Those extra orders were not costing us anything, so it was actually profitable to fill them with brand new books rather than turn them down!

This reminds me of a time when we were holding a similar sale at Warren on traveling bags. As usual, we got a lot more orders than we bargained for. One day the shipping clerk happened to come through my office. "How are the damaged bags holding out, John?" I asked him. "Oh, we re getting enough," he said, "but," he confided, "I'm getting darned tired kicking holes in the sides of the packing cartons just to make those bags look damaged!"

Here is the letter that caused all this trouble:

A FEW IMPERFECT SETS AT A BIG DISCOUNT!

DEAR SIR:

In the rush and excitement of selling, in two years, 75,000 sets of Frank H. Simonds' "History of the World War," there was no time to pay attention to technically imperfect or slightly injured sets, except to lay them aside as they appeared.

145

Some of them were wrongly bound, some slightly damaged from stockroom handling—so slightly that you would have to make a close inspection to discern the damage, but still—you know how it is—they cannot be sold as perfect books.

So rather than send them back to the bindery and give the binders the profit of re-binding, we have decided to let the advantage go to a few book-lovers—to people like yourself who love good books for the books' sake and not for trifling details about them—and to offer these magnificent sets at 30% off the regular price!

Only 157 Sets Left!

We have just 157 sets of these books to sell at this low price. When they are gone, it will be impossible to get Simonds' "History of the World War" at less than its regular price, but while these few sets last, you may have one of them at this big discount and you can pay for it in little, easy monthly payments.

Every set we guarantee to be in satisfactory condition. In some cases only one volume is not quite perfect. But as only a definite number of sets were contracted for with paper maker, printer and binder, one "hurt" volume means that a whole set is technically "damaged," even though four volumes are absolutely perfect, and in some cases it takes an expert to find anything wrong with the fifth.

In one case the binder made a mistake, and bound certain volumes of a set with gray linings and the other with blue linings. For all practical purposes these sets are perfect. Some subscribers might even prefer blue and gray linings, as sheets and covers are mainly without a blemish.

We will, of course, ship the books subject to your approval, to be returned at our expense if not satisfactory;—we always do that.

Signing and mailing the enclosed card puts the burden of proof upon us and incurs not the slightest obligation.

But you must act at once—there are only 157 sets left—and the best ones will naturally go to those who reply first. So sit down right now and put your name on the enclosed card and drop it in the mail!

Very truly yours,

147

How is it that a letter which sells histories and O. Henry stories in unusual volume is just as successful in selling bed blankets and traveling bags?

Because the one constant factor in selling is human reactions. We seldom try to sell merchandise. We sell ideas. And my experience has been that a fundamentally sound idea which will sell books in great volume will be just as successful in moving traveling bags or bed blankets or any other merchandise, if properly adapted to them.

The adapting is the job. Many writers make the mistake of thinking that if they copy the wording of a successful letter, their letter is bound to pull too. There is no bigger mistake. The *wording* counts for little. It is the way you adapt the idea back of the successful letter that counts.

The best illustration of this I have seen was at Warren. A couple of men who had been with the Warren company for several years—one in the advertising and the other in the list department—felt that they had all the information they needed as to copy, lists and products, and started a rival mail order company of their own, getting a local merchant to back them.

They used the same lists of names the Warren Company had been using, they copied letters and circulars almost word for word, they offered the same products—yet from the very beginning they were a failure. And in a couple of year's time they passed completely out of the picture. Why? A dearth of ideas. They thought mere words could do the trick. Words are empty sounds. It is the images back of them that counts!

XIV

Books That Many People Know

NOT all the sets published by the Review of Reviews ran into such figures as $1,000,000 sales. The O. Henrys and the Simonds and the Wells are rare birds, and fortunate indeed is the publisher who gets hold of them. There has to be something remarkable about the work itself, as a rule, though it is even more important that there should be something remarkable about the advertising, as Nelson Doubleday proved when he took an ordinary book of etiquette and sold a million copies of it by extraordinary advertising.

Not every book will lend itself to such a sale even with the finest advertising, but the sale of any book can be greatly stimulated by the proper kind of advertising. It is merely a matter of finding the primal human motive your book appeals to—be it love or gain or fear or ambition--and then directing your appeal at that motive.

When I went with the Review they had on hand about 5,000 sets of Rudyard Kipling, the leftovers of a big sale of several years before. The sale over, Kipling had languished for a while. But a new letter brought it promptly back to life, and the 5,000 sets changed hands in a few weeks' time. Not a large matter, of course, but every $150,000 sale helps by that much to swell the grand total.

We could have sold a lot more, but manufacturing costs had gone up so much that Mr. Lanier hesitated to put so much money into a set of books that had, for a while at least, been so hard to move. Here is the letter and circular that moved what we had:

> The long winter evenings are here.
>
> Do you want to make them different this year—want to get more pleasure and profit out of them than ever before?
>
> If you do, then you want something we've got. This is the first letter telling our friends about it. It is the complete works of Rudyard Kipling, the greatest living writer and poet—the first complete collection ever published of all his wonderful stories, tales and poems.

149

And in every single story throughout the 4,500 pages, there is a thrill for you—some mystery of old India, some human tangle that keeps you enthralled until the last word is told--some tale of love or war.

It may be the story of Hans, the blue-eyed Dane and Anne of Austria—it may be about the spy that got aboard an English battleship and the glorious joke they played upon him. It may be a tale of the old Irish who took Lungtungpen, naked as they were born.

It may be one of his stories for children—about Wee Willie Winkle, who marched out alone to fight an Indian tribe--of Mowgli, and man-cub of the Jungle—or Kim, the most precious little imp that ever walked in the pages of a book.

Or, it may be one of his immortal poems that have the lilt and the swing of a martial song--"The Recessional"— "If"—"East is East and West is West"—but there are hundreds of them.

But whatever one it is, if it's by Rudyard Kipling it is a wonderful story or poem—one that will jolt you right out of yourself and into another world and won't let you go until you have finished it.

There are 60 thrilling stories and 35 splendid poems- -the whole beautifully bound in silk cloth, in twenty-five volumes with gilt tops and gold lettering on the backs.

Let us send these twenty-five volumes to you at our own expense for a week's free examination. The enclosed card brings them to you by prepaid express. If you like them you can send us $1.00 at the end of the week and then $1.50 a month for 19 months. If not you can return them without question, at our expense.

Remember, there is no sale, no obligation to keep the books until you have tried them out for a week in your own home and are satisfied. Just let us send them to you for a week's examination.

But remember too, that paper is so scarce that we were able to get only enough to bind up 5,000 sets and it may be months before we are able to get enough more to bring out another edition so if you would be sure of getting a set at the present low prices, put your name on the enclosed card NOW and drop in the mail.

Yours truly,

Wrecked in the Clouds!

RUDYARD KIPLING

Turn to Next Page and See just what Comes to you in these 25 Volumes

Another set which had been gathering dust on the Review shelves for a number of years was the Spanish and Italian Romances. These never had done well. We had about 3,300 bound sets on hand, and unbound sheets enough to make about 5,000 more. With the following letter we cleaned up 3,000 sets at $10.50, and then closed out the balance at $4.98. Considering that the stock had long since been written off, there was a goodly profit in the sales at these prices, especially as the order cost proved to be very low.

WHILE THEY LAS T—53% OFF!
The mind, relaxing into needful sport,
Should turn to writers of an abler sort,
Whose wit well managed, and whose classic style
Give truth a lustre, and make wisdom smile.

COWPER

DEAR READER:

You know how everyone loves a good story, how young and old alike will listen wide-eyed to tales of mystery or romance, to stories of love or adventure.

Here is your chance to get the stories on which the literature of a dozen languages is based—AT A DISCOUNT OF 53%.

In cleaning out our stock-room to make ready for the big new edition of O. Henry soon to be delivered, we found that we had left over some three hundred sets of the famous "Tales from the Spanish and Italian," only one limited edition of which has ever been printed.

The finest flower of four centuries of Spanish imagination, the choicest masterpieces of six hundred years of Italian story-tellers, have here been gathered together into one complete set of eight volumes, beautifully illustrated, bound in silk cloth and stamped in gold. From Cervantes to Ibanez, from Boccaccio to D'Annunzio, the greatest story-tellers of Spain and Italy are here represented by their most delightful works, more than half of them now presented to English readers for the first time.

152

These eight volumes were made up to sell at a price of $15.00. In the post-war deflation, that price was reduced to $10.50, and three thousand sets were sold at that figure.

Now there are only some three hundred left, and three hundred sets are not enough to advertise in our usual way. So, while they last, we make you this offer:

Mail the enclosed card, without money, and we will send you these eight volumes at 53% less than the $10.50 price--$4.98.

There's no margin in that for collection expense, as you can guess, so we ask you to pay the postman or express-man your $4.98 when the volumes reach you. If, after reading them for a week, you are not entirely satisfied— if at the end of that time you are not convinced that this is the biggest book bargain you have ever had—send them back at our expense and your $4.98 will be refunded immediately and in full. There are no strings to this offer. The $4.98 is yours when you want it.

But remember, there are only some three hundred of these sets left, and three hundred won't last long. So send your card Now —this minute! This is your last chance!

Earnestly yours,

On offers such as these, we were content to sell the stock on hand and forget them. But sometimes we deliberately set a small quota for ourselves, when our goal was quality rather than quantity.

When Mr. Stone arranged with Bruce Barton to sell his two books—" The Man Nobody Knows" and "The Book Nobody Knows "—in connection with the Review of Reviews, he set a mark of 25,000 as the number of sales he wanted. Why? Because he felt that he needed just that many more thoughtful, serious-minded readers for the Review to balance the subscription list.

You see, a subscription list has to be planned just as any other list is, with the object of giving to the advertiser a fair cross section of the type of reader he seeks. You don't want all your readers to be men of mature age, you don't want all of them from one business or class or devoted to one interest.

154

The ideal list is a diversified list, a list evenly balanced between all the types that make up the more intelligent classes of American readers.

How are you to get such a balanced list? To an extent you can do it by circularizing certain professions and occupations. But that will never keep your subscription list over 100,000. To get a big volume of subscribers, you must branch out into general lists and then your chance for selection is gone.

So, since you can no longer pick the kind of subscriber you want, you have to so arrange your offer that the type of reader you want will pick you. And that is the main purpose of a premium. Take Bruce Barton's books, as an instance. Who would want these? Only the more seriously inclined reader, thoughtful men and women, seekers for light and truth.

Mr. Stone felt that he needed 925,000 more of that type of reader on the Review lists, so he chose the Barton books to winnow out that wheat from the chaff of general bookbuyers.

To do that, we tried (as we usually did) two letters, each from a quite different angle. In this particular case, both pulled about equally well, so we used first one and then the other. Between them, they sold the 25,000 sets at a profitably low selling cost. Here are the letters and circular:

DEAR READER:

Jesus Christ "the founder of modern business?"

Jesus a master of efficiency in organization, a born executive?

Jesus a sociable man, a cheerful, bright companion with a pat story on His lips—an outdoor man with clear eyes and hard muscles?

Jesus wording the best advertisements ever written?

Yes, this is the Jesus Christ now being introduced to hundreds of thousands of business men and busy women by Bruce Barton.

Barton is himself a brilliant, successful young American

business man as well as a writer. In his book "The Man Nobody Knows" he brings to us, in our daily work, a Jesus we never knew before, one who set examples for us, not in some ideal and impossible way but in our job, managing a bank or clerking, selling automobiles, doing professional work—furnishing something of service.

This is one of the two books Bruce Barton has written which are storming the imaginations and hearts of people everywhere--proving sensations on the movie screen, quoted from in a thousand newspapers, read eagerly by hundreds of thousands of alert, successful men and women, overjoyed to find that so far from being a figure apart from their lives and daily work—sadly incompatible with them—Jesus Christ is one they can like, talk to, work with, get lessons from, even in the very technique of their craft.

This is one of Barton's two books; the other, "The Book Nobody Knows," is, of course, the Bible.

In the same way Barton has brought the Old Testament into our lives and jobs and present day thoughts and standards.

Think of it! A million men and women doing the active work of the world, suddenly finding Jesus Christ and the Bible close to them, useful, part and parcel of their daily lives and of human endeavor to succeed!

Barton's two books interest and aid the rich and powerful; they help any cub salesman to get orders for shoe polish—and to work on principles that lead him toward riches and power.

Now, you who have thought of Christ as an ascetic, a mystic, a physical weakling, a "Man of Sorrows," will want to meet this cheerful, able founder of "modern business." If you can read only two books more in your life, these two must be the ones.

The Review of Reviews takes pride in being the distributor of such books as Wells' "Outline of History" and O. Henry's works, and takes pride in its arrangement with Mr. Barton for an edition of these two books, by which you get them both, with our compliments, simply by becoming a subscriber to "The Necessary Magazine."

Further, the magazine subscription may be paid for in small monthly installments.

Still further, you need send no money at all in ordering; just your signature and address on the enclosed card bring the books to you, and if you have any reason for stopping the order after browsing through the two volumes, you are perfectly free to do it.

Our special subscribers' edition is not sold in the bookstores. The books are regular sized library volumes. The Review of Reviews sells for $4.00 a year. You get the two volumes entirely without cost by simply becoming a subscriber for the Review of Reviews for 18 months at the regular price.

And could you, even aside from these two inspiring books, spend any money more usefully than by subscribing to the Review of Reviews? Such men as Nicholas Murray Butler and Theodore Roosevelt, on the one side, and on the other, miners and alert farmers in the far West, have relied on it year after year to keep them "up to date."

What you read in the newspapers so often gets into a mental jumble. The Review of Reviews straightens it out for you. Dr. Albert Shaw surveys the month's happenings and notable persons for you in his "Progress of the World." Frank Simonds, the clearest and most fascinating writer on Europe's affairs, gives you a clean-cut picture of international happenings and issues. The Review's famous "Current History in Caricature" amuses and instructs you by telling the history of the month with the most successful cartoons from all over the world.

In this day of floods of magazines, with no one able to read one-tenth of them, the department, "Leading Articles of the Month" takes the gist out of the notable features appearing in all periodicals and serves it to you fresh. Besides, there are contributed articles, a magazine in itself, that inform you on just the worthwhile subjects men are talking of, the ones that will help in your life and work.

The less time you have for reading, the more you need the Review of Reviews. Just *it* is enough to keep you up with the times. It is the magazine of magazines.

It is called "The Necessary Magazine" by the largest number of subscribers any monthly of current events has or has ever had—"the intellectual aristocracy of America."

With such a helpful magazine; with two such gifts with it; with nothing to do but sign your name *without cost or obligation,* there is but one thing to remember:

Send the card *promptly* because thousands will lose no time in getting these most desired of current books.

Sincerely yours,

DEAR NEIGHBOR:

Will you set me right on one point about yourself:

I'm wondering if your idea of the Christ is like that of most people—a "Man of Sorrows," sent to this earth to undergo certain sacrificial experiences, glad to get them over with, looking forward always to getting back to His heavenly home.

That is the idea of Jesus that most people have. That is the idea of Him that many teachers have fostered. *But it is not the idea of Him that a careful reading of the Gospels will give you.*

158

A physical weakling? Ascetic? Anaemic? Jesus was a successful carpenter in a day when tools were few and sheer strength took the place of winches and pulleys.

A "Man of Sorrows"? He made people happy wherever He went. The sick, the poor, the sorrowful—all flocked to Him and were sent away happy. Little children loved Him—and were joyous and happy with Him. He was the most popular dinner guest in Jerusalem!

A failure? Why, he was the founder of modern business! For what is the watchword of the successful business of today? What but Service?

And 1900 years ago Jesus preached on the shores of Galilee "Whosoever will be great among you shall be your minister. And whosoever of you will be the chiefest, shall be servant of all." Is there one word of that which does not apply to the well-run modern business? Yet most people think that this idea of giving more than you are paid for is a new idea! It is simply that the world is only now waking up to the *practicability* of Jesus' teachings.

For years people have had the feeling that what a man did on week-days was somehow contaminating. That Church on Sunday was to wipe out this stain so that he might make good in the hereafter. When the fact is that what really counts is not the things you *profess* on Sundays—but the things you *practice* on week-days!

That is what modern business is coming to believe. That is the spirit that animated all of Jesus' words and actions, as portrayed in the most interesting, the most talked about story of Jesus ever written—

"The Man Nobody Knows"
By Bruce Barton

With its companion volume—"The Book Nobody Knows" —it has taken the business world by storm. It shows Jesus--NOT as a "Man of Sorrows," not as a meek and lowly "Lamb of God," but as the greatest of all figures in History, as the Practical Ideal of the modern business man.

"I came that ye might have life and have it more abundantly ."

He differed from the Prophets. He differed from John the Baptist. He brought a new idea into the world—that changed the whole current of History. Would you know what that idea is? Then read these two great books.

They tell you of the greatest thought ever conceived. And it is to further that thought, that we have arranged with Bruce Barton to offer his two inspiring books with the The Review of Reviews at a very special price.

The Man Nobody Knows and The Book Nobody Knows sell for $4. The Review of Reviews is $4 a year. If you will mail the enclosed card at once you can get ALL THREE —NOT for $8, but for only $2 a month for 3 months (or $5.30 in one cash payment).

The Barton books will give you a new and far more inspiring conception of Jesus, of His work and of the Bible. The Review of Reviews will bring to you each month the best of the world's thought and achievements. It gleans from the great mass of newspapers and magazines and really worth while articles and presents the meat of them to you. It is, in short, a Master Key to all that has happened during the previous 30 days.

One Edition Only!

Our arrangement with Bruce Barton is for only one edition of his books at this special price. When that one edition is gone, your opportunity goes with it.

But while that edition lasts, you can see these books, browse through them, read them for a week—WITH-

OUT COST AND WITHOUT OBLIGATION. Just your name and address on the enclosed card are all that is necessary.

There's only one condition—your card must be mailed right away!

Hastily yours,

161

On another occasion, we felt we needed a quite different type of reader—the man of thirty-five, forty or forty-five who feels himself beginning to slip a little, who is no longer as vigorous and full of vitality as he would like, whose muscles are flabby and whose hair is beginning to thin.

How could we pick him from the mass of humanity that reads the papers and books and magazines? He is no longer interested in muscle-building as such. He wants his ease. But he also wants health and vitality and vigor enough to enjoy life as of yore. So we got for him a Course of Lessons fathered by the Life Extension Institute, and with it as our bait we landed some 50,000 readers for the Review of Reviews.

Just see how easily and naturally this letter and circular does it:

A MESSAGE TO YOU FROM THE GREAT MEN OF MEDICINE!

Do You Know?

The five elementary rules of right living?

The ten guiding principles of exercise?

What exercise will keep you in fit condition?

What a normal man should be able to do?

When sunshine is injurious? When it is Nature's most powerful drug?

What causes colds?

How to escape them?

How to cure headache?

What the muscles need most?

What exercise is necessary for women?

How fresh air concerns the skin?

How a watering mouth

GOOD-MORNING, SIR

Remember how you used to plow through great masses of work day after day and month after month, cheerily, enthusiastically, with never a sign of tiring or nervous strain? Remember how you used to enjoy those evenings, starting out as fresh from your office or shop as if you hadn't just put a hard days work behind you?

No doubt you've often wondered why you can t work and enjoy your-self like that now, but solaced yourself with the moth-eaten fallacy that— "As a man grows older he shouldn't expect to get the same fun out of life that he did in his earlier years.

Poor old exploded idea!

Youth is not a matter of time. It is a physical state. You can be just as brisk, just as

162

affects digestion?

What are the vitally important vitamins?

When to take hot or cold
baths?

The body's danger signals- ?

What the heart needs most?

How the eyes may be rest-
ed?

*active, just as light-hearted now as you
were ten or twenty years ago. Genuine
youth is just a perfect state of health.* You
can have that health, and the boundless
energy and capacity for work or enjoyment
that go with it. You can cheat time of ten or
twenty years merely by taking thought, by
learning a few vital facts about your body—
how to eat, how to sleep, how to exercise
right. You need no painful, lengthy exercise;
no weary diet; *just to live a sensible life.*

Modern science tells us that old age is merely our name
for the gradual poisoning of our bodies. Aches and pains
burrow and creeping through the body, a relaxed
abdomen, deepening lines on the face, jangling nerves, a
haunting feeling of dullness and gloom—these outward
signs indicate that actual poisons are being deposited in
blood, tissues and joints; if we eliminate them, we go far
towards eliminating old age; but if in our happy-go-lucky
way we allow the poisons to remain in the body, we look
old and feel old no matter what our age.

For the first time in the history of medicine the leading
physicians and scientists have given their time, study,
instruction and praise to a great popular work that
embodies the very latest medical research and science.
For the first time the world's greatest specialists have
written down in simple, understandable language what
you must do to build up a live, strong body, muscular,
upstanding—to get that virile feeling of red-blooded
energy and enthusiasm that comes only from perfect
health.

*The Review of Reviews Course in Physical Training
Tells You—Free—How to Sweep the System Clean of
Poisons, How to Get Well, Stay Well, and Have a Body
You Can Be Proud of.*
For two years the Life Extension Institute, which has

163

secured through its Hygiene Reference Board of 100 leading Physicians and Scientists the most comprehensive and tested knowledge on these subjects, worked with the editors appointed by the Review of Reviews to get all of the scientific facts in logical order, written in such simple, understand-able language that even the busiest man could instantly grasp its meaning.

Thousands of these Courses, made up into fifteen complete lessons, were sold to business and professional men all over the country at a price of $18.00, and if you could see the letters that come to us every day, telling of renewed health and vigor, of happiness and content brought back into troubled homes, you'd readily believe that they were well worth the price.

But fifteen lessons were too many for really a busy man, so we have condensed all the essentials of the Course into seven interesting, meaty lessons.

These 7 Lessons Given to You—Free!

Because this course in physical training will appeal most strongly only to the more intelligent and wide-awake business and professional men of the country, and because these are the very people that we want as readers of the Review of Reviews, we are going to GIVE this course—ABSOLUTELY FREE with an eighteen months' subscription to the Review of Reviews, at the regular subscription price of the magazine alone, payable, if you like, in little monthly payments of only 50¢.

Some friends have told us that we ought to charge $15 or $20 for this Course—that people would rather pay such a sum than get it free. They repeated the old story of the man who stood on London Bridge trying to give away gold sovereigns, without takers. But we have too much faith in the intelligence and alertness of the kind of people who want to read the Review of Reviews to believe that they will refuse a thing of great value simply because they are not asked to pay a lot of money for it.

When a man or woman receives this Course; uses it, gets health, happiness and efficiency from it; realizes that it has brought, in concise, easily understood, attractive terms, what science has learned to date about developing his body, about proper habits, about what to eat—he "swears by" the Review of Reviews. And that is all there is of value to a magazine property —a body of people who "swear by" it.

Just put this squarely up to your own good judgment. You want to look your best all the time; you want a lithe, strong figure, broad-shouldered, up-standing; you want muscles tough and springy, that will do all you ask of them and then beg for more; you want that feeling of red-blooded energy and enthusiasm that comes only from perfect health. Here in this Course you can get them—not from any quack remedy, but from the sound principles worked out from the vast experience of the greatest Scientists and Physicians of the day.

To prove it, all you have to do is to fill in, sign and mail the enclosed card. At the end of a week, you can return the Course IF YOU WANT TO. Try it out! Never mind what we SAY it will do for you. FIND OUT! It's easy. Just send the card.

Remember, there is no obligation attached.

The card order is merely a chance for the Course to sell itself to you. There is no cost—no obligation to keep it—until you have tried it out for a week in your own home, AND ARE SATISFIED!

Just let the card come forward. It obligates us only—*not you.*

But remember, this offer holds good only while the FREE edition of the Course lasts—and there are just 1,700 sets now left. So put your name on the card and mail it NOW! There's no time to waste.

Yours right cheerily,

There were numbers of such offers—Lincoln, Barnum, Tom Masson's "Best of the World's Good Stories," and a dozen others. All were reasonably good letters as results go (of Masson's stories, for instance, we sold 20,000 sets) but there was nothing especially distinctive about any of them, so we quote below only three typical letters and circulars of the kind.

The first offered a short course in building wireless sets for the home. It was written, you must remember, a year or so after the war, when the idea of wireless in the home was in its earliest stages, and many more sets were being built by amateurs than sold through stores. The following letter and circular sold about 10,000 courses:

Edited and Approved by
MAJOR-GENERAL GEORGE 0. SQUIER,
Chief of the Signal Corps of the U. S. Army

DEAR NEIGHBOR:

If you do as F. J. Caveney did—he lives in a little mining camp up in the North Woods you need never again be shut off, even for a day, from the best in music and entertainment, from the world of sports, from the news of the market, from the events of the day.

No matter where you may be, in city or country, in mountain cabin or camp—news, entertainment, music, education, are literally in the air all about you. You have but to reach out and take what you want.

And you can take of them according to your own tastes--the baseball fan can get the score, inning by inning, play by play; the business man, the record of the markets, the news of the day; his wife, entertainment, opera, lectures, fashions; the young folks, comedy and dance music; the little ones, bed-time songs and stories.

166

The great invention which made the Radio-phone simple and easy as an ordinary telephone was perfected only a short time ago as a result of experiments conducted during the War by the U. S. Signal Corps, working in conjunction with the great electrical companies. It cost the

government literally millions. It is one of the few big dividends to humanity that came out of our vast War

expenditures. When it was perfected, the Radio-phone left the laboratory and moved into the home.

The World on the Wireless

There is no known limit to the distance at which wireless messages can be picked up if the receiving apparatus is delicate enough. The time will come when you can "listen in" on a grand opera at Seville or Vienna as easily as you can on New York; when you can dance to the strains of an orchestra in Paris or St. Petersburg; when you can hear the British Premier address the House of Commons, or the Pope blessing the Pilgrims at Rome.

An Easy Course in Home Radio

Home radio has been brought within the reach of everyone, rich or poor, young or old, flat dweller or mountaineer. Any man or boy can make a set at little expense.

Seven noted engineers and professors have combined to produce a course that shows in easy, untechnical language what to do and how to do it, what to make and how to make it, what to buy if you prefer buying your set, and how to run it.

Edited by Major-General Squier, Chief of the Signal Corps

Because he believes that it can be made one of the greatest forces for good for the youth of the country, because he feels that it will do more than anything else to restore the home circle, Major-General George O. Squier, Chief of the Signal Corps of the U. S. Army, and probably the one man in the whole United States who most thoroughly understands the subject, has helped us to make this Course as reliable, as authoritative, as up-to-the minute as it can be made. He has gone over every word of the copy, corrected, revised, suggested, and the result has his hearty endorsement and approval.

168

The air is full of wireless messages every hour of the day. In the evening, particularly, there are treats which no one ought to miss. Famous people will talk to you, sing for you, amuse you. YOU DON T HAVE TO BUY A SINGLE TICKET—you don't have to reserve seats. All you need to do is to mail the card enclosed, and get these simple lessons. They will open the way for you to the most marvelous entertainment you ever had.

Think of it—one evening's "puttering" on the part of father or the boys will bring you something you can enjoy the rest of your life!

And the lessons are sent you ON APPROVAL, prepaid. If you don't like them, if they are not clear and simple and easy enough for even a child to understand, SEND THEM BACK! Your money will be refunded at once. No quibbling—no questions asked.

But send your card NOW. Every day you are missing something good. Don't delay another minute. Get your ticket now for this perpetual entertainment. Sign and mail the post-card!

Yours for a happy home circle,

It happened that a manufacturer had printed a big edition of Shakespeare in little leather volumes to use as a premium of some kind, and after his sale was over he found himself with some thousands of sets still on hand that he had no use for. So he offered them to us at a ridiculously low figure. We took them and used them to sell with a subscription to the Review of Reviews, feeling that Shakespeare readers were just the type we wanted on the Review list. Here is the letter that did the trick. It not only pulled its 4 per cent, but even better than that figure, with the result that we cleaned up the entire stock in the first circularizing and could have disposed of a good many thousands more. But we could not get them made at a figure that would enable us to duplicate the offer.

SHAKESPEARE
20 volumes in real leather
and gold, pocket size, for
$1.00.

DEAR SIR:

If only 4% of our readers accept this offer, it will take all the sets we have on hand.

If that happens, we cannot make and offer you a new edition at less than five times the price shown above!

These are bed rock facts, that we absolutely guarantee. Read the enclosed circular for the explanation.

We emphasize them because this is such an extraordinary bargain, and unless you act at once you will lose it forever. Sign the enclosed card now and you will get these 20 exquisite little volumes promptly. Put it off and you can't get them at all unless you are prepared to pay five times the price.

Shakespeare, pre-eminent as to all time and all nations, is also pre-eminently the author to have in convenient pocket size. Every sentence, every word is a gem, brilliant and imperishable; every play belongs in just such a bijou jewel-box of a volume as are each these twenty.

Naturally, we are confining this most attractive bargain of years to Review of Reviews subscribers. All you have to do to get in on it is to become a subscriber to the Review of Reviews—a thing that over 250,000 of the best informed people are doing anyhow without any wonderful Shakespeare inducement.

And to clinch it, you have the privilege of returning the books and getting your money back in full, if, on examining them, you wish to do so.

So you can't lose by signing and mailing the card. You can get the best bargain of your life.

But you must act NOW—before these few hundred sets are gone.

Sincerely yours,

If you are already a subscriber to the Review of Reviews, your subscription will be extended a year from its present date of expiration.

Why do people buy magazines? More often than not for relaxation. They get the more serious type like the Review for instruction, in order that they may be posted on what is going on in the world, but they will not read too much instruction at one time. They need relaxation in between. And as the Review does not publish fiction, the best way to supply it seemed to be as a premium. So, as we wanted the fiction to be on the same high plane as the Review itself, we chose for our premium (or, rather, Fred Stone did, for it was his idea) the stories that are awarded the O. Henry prize as being the best of the year. And we sold some 30,000 .to 40,000 copies of them. Here is the way we did it:

To those who want the best for themselves and their young people.

DEAR READER:

IF— you had a committee of wise literary experts picking out for you, from all the ~9≥4,000 short stories published in the last four years, just those that are worthwhile, thrilling, tragic or charmingly witty,—just the stories that are really worth your reading and preserving—

Would you esteem it a service, and would you value having these sixty-four selected master-stories to enjoy yourself and read to others?

172

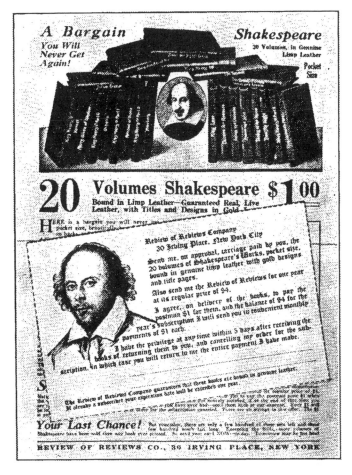
If, further,

*These eight volumes of sixty-four super-stories were
serviceably bound in heavy paper covers, and GIVEN
TO YOU, FREE, as a subscriber to the Review of
Reviews, would you snap up the chance?*

The distinctive achievement in American fiction is the
short story. Gems are appearing every month or so. But
how can you find them, buried in an avalanche of 6,000

173

stories published every year, in a hundred periodicals and books?

The problem cannot be solved by you, but it has been solved *for you* by the Society of Arts and Sciences which has been, through these four years, reading and studying each of this vast number of stories to make the "O. Henry Memorial Award, "—the prizes that go to the really significant, outstanding short stories appearing each year.

In each volume is an introduction showing how and why the prizes were awarded,—of real value and keen interest to everyone who appreciates a "corking" short story and absolutely invaluable to the younger folk whose tastes and standards are forming.

If you are one of those who enjoy a good short story, why have anything less good than the best? It is obvious that no favorite magazine or favorite author can hit the bull's eye every time. In these eight volumes of 1,200 pages are the 64 bull's eyes made out of about 24,000 tries at the target of excellence.

Here are not only the star writers of short stories, but the star stories of each of these artists, selected from all their work. And here and again is a wonderfully gripping tale by some new writer not yet recognized as a star, or the man or woman who tells only one, or only a very few, really great tales. The only test for admission to the galaxy is the question,—will the reader be thrilled, amused, exalted, moved to tears, with true literary art,— and anyone who in any particular story surpasses his fellows is admitted to the prize volume for your delight.

Read this Carefully:

The books will cost you nothing except 10 cents for delivery. Bound serviceably in heavy paper, in a style making them easily worth $3 or $4 for the set of eight volumes, they will be shipped to you on receipt of the enclosed coin card in which place a dime.

At the same time, you will be put on the subscription list of of the Review of Reviews *for eighteen months* (subscription price $4 per year) and you will receive bills for the subscription in little monthly installments of 75 cents.

The Review of Reviews has been for thirty years under Dr. Albert Shaw's editorship, the standard and most widely circulated monthly in the world to keep people up-to-date in literature, politics, public personalities and the large affairs of this earth, with the acknowledged leader of the authorities on European affairs, Frank H. Simonds, contributing to every issue. It is a magazine you *must have* to keep up with the times, and you will find it more than ever necessary in the coming election year with its stirring and puzzling political events and problems and persons. Get with it, at no cost to you, this charming set of books with the most delightful entertainment, and you need have no dull half-hour this coming year.

We have made one sizable edition of this set containing the prize stories of the past four years, but, in our judgment, not one more than will be called for by those receiving this offer.

So if you want the solid and useful value of the magazine and the sparkling entertainment of the prize stories,— utility and pleasure combined,—

Send the coin card at once.

Yours truly,

P.S.

Special Prize for You:

As subsequent volumes appear of stories selected for the "O. Henry Memorial Prizes," one for each year, readers accepting this offer may get them from us, as soon as they are published, *for 60¢* if they are still subscribers to the Review of Reviews, whereas the retail price of the volumes is $1.90 each.

That was our main business keeping the magazine supplied with plenty of live, interested subscribers who ordered from us by mail, and therefore would be most likely to order by mail products advertised in our pages.

But we were not neglecting the book business. Always we managed to keep some set going. There were none to attain the proportions of O. Henry, Simonds and Wells, but by selling 10,000 to 20,000 lots of different authors, we managed to keep the pot boiling.

Two such typical sales were Mary Roberts Rinehart and Irvin Cobb. Of the former, we sold 20,000 sets. Of the latter, 10,000.

Mrs. Rinehart's stories seemed to lend themselves to illustration even better than Cobb's, possibly because among them were some good detective stories. The two Rinehart letters and circulars, and the one describing Cobb, speak for themselves. In both cases, we felt that the authors were so well known and their stories so popular that we needed to waste little time in convincing our readers that they would enjoy them. We had only to tell them what they were getting and then give them a reason for ordering a complete set at once, rather than pick up the books one at a time as they felt the urge to read them.

So in our letters we concentrated on bargain and special offer, using the circular to whet their appetites for the stories themselves.

HALF-PRICE INTRODUCTORY OFFER

DEAR SIR:—

Who are the 192 Greatest Living American Women?

The Officers of the National League of Women Voters were staggered by that question. They called on the Women's Joint Congressional Committee, and the Committee in turn called in such men as Chauncey Depew, Director Johnson of the Hall of Fame, President McCracken of Vassar and President Mezes of N. Y. City College to help them make up the list.

The exact twelve will probably never be decided upon, but by taking those few that practically every one was agreed upon, the fame of one name, at least, was established beyond all question. That name was—

Mary Roberts Rinehart

Ten million magazine readers, hundreds of thousands of movie and theatre goers, scores of thousands of library patrons—all attest her as the most popular, as well as one of the twelve greatest women in America today.

Free and daring—the very spirit of American womanhood— clean and wholesome as Nature itself—she thrills, fascinates, perplexes and amuses you. It's as stimulating as a cold plunge on a hot day just to come under her spell.

The baffling mysteries of "The Circular Staircase" and "The Man in Lower Ten"; the daring humor of "Bab," "Tish" or "When a Man Marries"; the charming love stories and ingenious escapades in any one of a dozen other stories, all capture your interest in the very first page and hold it to the last. No one so jaded but that he will find new and thrilling sensations here.

For the First Time

Although Mrs. Rinehart's admirers are numbered by the millions, curiously enough they have never before had a chance to get her collected works—a full set of her best stories—selected by herself and her publishers.

For the first time you can now get them, and at a cost that seems ridiculously low when compared with the recent war-time figures.

Half-Price Introductory Offer

This is the first collected edition of Mary Roberts Rinehart's best stories, and naturally she wants to make it a success. In order to enable us to offer it to you at a lower price than her books have ever sold at before—in order to make this first edition go like wild-fire—*she has agreed to accept exactly one-tenth of her usual rate of royalty on the first edition of 10,000 sets.*

Paper prices have come down; labor costs are lower, and now with this generous concession of Mrs. Rinehart's, we can make you a price of this one edition actually lower than the pre-war figures—little more than half what these same volumes would cost you in any book store.

And In Addition, if your order comes in at once, we will send you the 3 latest and best volumes of

Conan Doyle—Free!

To start the sale with a rush—to make you order NOW rather than wait for some special occasion like Christmas or a birthday—WE WILL GIVE YOU, if your order comes in at once, these 3 latest and best volumes of Conan Doyle FREE!

15 books—12 volumes of Rinehart and 3 of Doyle—all

178

printed from brand new plates, clear and readable, and beautifully bound in cloth. Bought separately at any book store, they would cost you nearly twice as much as we offer them to you here *on approval,* subject to a week's free examination.

And you can pay for them, if you like, in tiny convenient payments of $1 a month—92.5 cents a week.

Will you be one of the lucky ones? Will you send your card now while you can get the 3 volumes of Doyle FREE? Or will you put off sending the postcard—until this rare opportunity is passed—until you can get these fascinating volumes only at their regular book store prices?

Put your name and address on the enclosed card and mail it now—while you can get not only the low price and convenient terms, but in addition, the 3 famous volumes of Conan Doyle FREE.

This is your last chance!

Earnestly yours,

YOUR LAST CHANCE AT THE LOW PRICE!

FRIEND— That half-price Introductory Edition of the best stories of Mary Roberts Rinehart is just about gone. There are only some 700 sets now left.

No more can we give you the advantage of Mrs. Rinehart's generous reduction of her royalties to one-tenth their usual figure. No more can we get the low prices for paper, for printing, for binding, that we paid for this edition.

Half-Price Introductory Offer

That is what we called it, and that is what it actually is— half the price at which we could now reprint these same books and make them up into another edition.

While these 700 sets last, you can get your set at the special Introductory Price. When they are gone, it will cost you double that.

Free—to Those Who Are Prompt!

In order to clean out this last remnant of the Introductory Edition quickly, we are going to GIVE AWAY, as a premium for promptness, three volumes of Sir Conan Doyle's latest and best stories—some of his greatest Sherlock Holmes tales.

To everyone who will send the enclosed card within ten days, we will give—ABSOLUTELY FREE— these three volumes of Conan Doyle.

This is your chance—the last chance you will ever have to get these best Rinehart stories at half price and the Conan Doyle FREE. There are only about 700 sets all told, and 700 won't last long. Put your name on the enclosed card now and drop in the mail. You will never have another chance!

Yours for ten days only,

"Extra! Extra!
All About the Great Reduction!
Off Irvin Cobb!"

FRIEND:—

What is it that makes people love the spontaneous humor of Mark Twain? What is it about Bret Harte's stories that made him an imperishable figure in American letters? What is it in Poe's grotesque tales that make you read and re-read them, though the chills run down your spine, and your blood runs cold with horror?

Isn't it that one infallible mark of genius—the masterly blending of humor, tragedy, pathos and romance, that comes to but one or two story-tellers in a generation?

Now has come to us Irvin S. Cobb. Take the joyous humor of Mark Twain, the subtle feeling of Bret Harte, the gruesome talent of Poe—mix them together, then add a touch of O. Henry—and you begin to get some idea of his sparkling genius.

Robert H. Davis, Editor of Munsey's, says of him—" Cobb writes in octaves, striking instinctively all the chords of humor, tragedy, pathos and romance. If you desire a perfect blending of all that is essential to a short story, read any of Cobb's stories. In Cobb we find Mark Twain, Bret Harte and Edgar Allen Poe at their best."

181

Cobb is Mark Twain's logical successor. He mixes humor and sage reflection as intimately as the cook mixes the ingredients for the stuffing in the turkey. He has made more people laugh than any man since Twain's day. In his touches of human interest, in the subtle play of his wit and humor, in his vivid portrayal of the life and character of everyday people~ his homely tales are little master-pieces.

The First Uniform Edition!

Hundreds of thousands of Irvin Cobb's books have been sold in all styles and bindings. His humorous contributions have been running for years in the biggest magazines and news-papers all over the country. But there has never yet been brought out a single uniform edition of all his fascinating tales and humorous stories. Now for the first time you can get them—76 different stories, humorous, homely, lovable, serious, grotesque.

We have had his 18 books re-set in new, clear type, bound them up into 10 library volumes in a handsome uniform binding, and now offer them to you in a limited Introductory Edition at—

40% Off the Regular Price

The little folder enclosed shows you the 18 volumes you get —lists for you the 76 stories. Send for them. There is no cost —no obligation to keep them—until you have looked them over for a week in your own home, *and are satisfied!* Then— and then only—you can send us the first small payment of $1, and thereafter $1 a month for only eleven months.

Merely put your name and address on the enclosed card and drop it in the mail. The books will be sent you at our expense. *Do it now,* while this small Introductory Edition lasts, while you can get this complete set of all his entertaining stories, all his wit and humor, at 40% *less than*

182

their regular price!

The card commits us only—NOT YOU! *Use* it!

Yours in waiting,

P. S.   *Two Additional Prizes for Promptness!*

We are bringing out this Introductory Edition now merely to gauge the demand so as to determine quickly how big an edition to make for our regular sale.

You can help us, if you will, by sending in your FREE EXAMINATION CARD at once. To make it worth your while, we offer you these two prizes for promptness.

Mail your card within 10 days after you receive it, and we will send you one of the few sets with Irvin Cobbs own personal autograph on the fly-leaf—

AND IN ADDITION, *we will send you,* FREE, *the two volumes of Tom Masson's "Best of the World's Good Stories," contain the 1,000 best stories, witty sayings and most convulsive anecdotes that he accumulated in his 15 years as Editor of "Life."*

There is a story here for every need, from an after-dinner talk to a political speech, from a salesman's canvass to a director's meeting.

In all of these you will notice a similarity of treatment, the circular being used in every case merely to support and lend greater interest to the letter.

As we see it, a letter, circular and card are just an advertisement, divided into its component parts. An advertisement must compete with all the items of interest around it—with current news, with good stories, with timely photographs. So it puts an arresting illustration at the top, it uses a startling headline to get people to read on, and it saves its reasons why and its hooks and bait until the last.

Put that same advertisement into an envelope just as it stands and it will not pull one fourth as well as when split up into letter, circular and card. I have tried it a dozen times with our most successful ads, and I know. It requires a letter with it to carry the load. The circular may be used to win interest, and for this purpose, the advertisement's headline and illustration are transferred to it, but the reader turns to the letter for his real reason for ordering, and unless you have your hook in it, your chance of getting his order is slim.

We have had an occasional circular which overshadowed the letter, but when it does, it is well to examine your letter and see what is wrong with it. Usually you will find it is weak. For as a general thing, your letter will account for 65 to 75 per cent of the orders you get, your circular for 15 to 25 per cent and your post card or order form for 5 to 10 per cent.

There are variations from these figures, of course, but if you expect big results from your mail efforts, look to your letter for them. If the stuff is not in it, you will never get the results.

Speaking of operations—

XV

How Wells' "Outline" Was Sold

And now we come to the biggest thing ever put across by the Review of Reviews—the sale of II. G. Wells' "Outline of History."

When it was offered to us, the bookstore sale of the two-volume set at $10.50 had already reached 50,000 sets. But it had begun to wane a little, so Macmillan was about to bring out a one-volume edition at $5. At the time they did so, they offered us the chance to sell it in combination with a Review subscription—but to do so, we had to agree to sell 83,000 sets within two years, and pay $25,000 advance royalties to bind the bargain!

Selling 83,000 of anything in two years is quite an undertaking, even for the Review of Reviews, especially when the royalty must be paid whether you succeed with the sale or not. So there was some hesitation about accepting the proposition. Fred Stone and I were strongly for it, and Mr. Lanier was inclined that way himself, so it was finally decided to accept, provided we could first have sixty days in which to test for ourselves the possibility of the sale. This Macmillan agreed to, so we went to work.

At the very beginning there was quite a divergence of opinion as to how Wells' could best be sold. The newspapers had reviewed the history far and wide, and their comments in general were so complimentary that it was felt by some that this was one case where no special effort need be made to sell—all we had to do was to remind people of everything the newspapers and magazines had been saying about Wells, then tell them that here was their chance to get this marvelous history, of which 50,000 had been sold at $10.50, *for a third of that price!*

Those who felt that way were so sure of their position that a letter and circular were written along these lines, and some 10,000 of them were tested. Here they are:

WHAT?
H. G. Wells'
"OUTLINE OF HISTORY"
At One-Third The Original Price!

DEAR SIR:

Suppose a vote were taken of all English-speaking people as to what book of this entire generation is at once the most fascinating reading, the most useful to the reader and the most important to mankind at large. That—

H. G. Wells' "Outline of History"

would not only head the list but have more than twice as many votes as its nearest competitor is almost too easy a prophecy; we wouldn't take up your time to say such an obvious thing except for the following fact that interests you personally:

Mr. Wells' big ambition for this epoch-making work is that it should go to the million readers who would revel in it and get a new conception of their human race and their job in the universe—as well as to the hundred thousand who can afford to pay $10.50 for such a book and who have done so.

Why This Offer Can Be Made

To this end, to enable us to offer the new edition just out, revised by him, *to Review of Reviews subscribers only* for a really low price, and payable in small installments at that, Mr. Wells has agreed to take, on this edition only, *just one-seventh of the royalty paid on the former two-volume edition.*

That this is the most important book distribution this magazine, or any other, has ever made, shows on its face.

We confidently expect to be overwhelmed with orders that will sweep off the entire edition we have contracted for.

We have, therefore (to maintain the balanced proportions of our subscription list), assigned so many copies to each State, and the order form enclosed herewith is for you, is

186

numbered, is not transferable and is not good after ten days from its receipt unless there are copies of Mr. Wells' masterpiece not yet applied for.

The Common Adventure of All Mankind"

Wells' History, starting with the empty dawn of things, tells you in. absorbing story the common adventure of all man-kind—the growth, not only of peoples, but of all nature and life.

Perhaps you do not realize that with all the colossal scope of the Wells' History you are brought closer, face to face with the great characters of history than you or any one else ever came before.

Alexander the Great, Caesar, Cleopatra, Mahomet, Charlemagne, Napoleon becomes real persons, introduced by Wells, and if you do not get some of the heartiest laughs of your life in meeting them face to face, we miss our guess.

Review of Reviews Begins Where Wells Leaves Off

The Review of Reviews, for a quarter century the most widely read monthly of current events in the world, takes up for you where the Wells' History leaves off and pictures your own and world history for you, monthly, for the rest of your life.

It gives you the things you want to know about the world today. It takes from all the great newspapers and magazines everything worth while and repeats the gist of it to you. It ties together the important happenings, puts them in their proper sequence, shows you their relation one to another so clearly, so interestingly, that you wonder how anyone can think himself well informed who sees only the fragmentary reports in the daily news.

No Money—No Risk—but Hurry!

Read the enclosed circular to understand why this is the most talked of and most praised work of our generation.

But most important—sign your name to the enclosed card; that is all. The signed card makes sure you benefit by this Review of Reviews' edition and Mr. Wells' scaling down of his royalty to one-seventh of its former size.

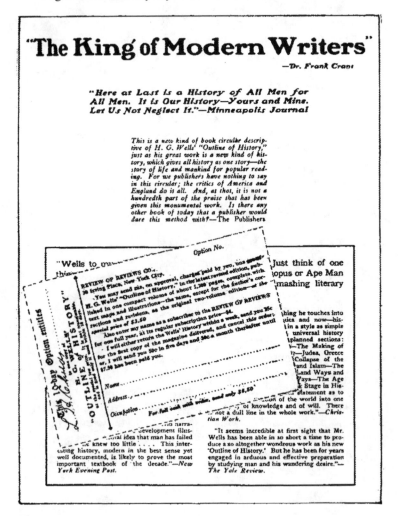

It makes sure the great 1,200 page book, full of maps and illustrations is sent to you, charges paid, and you have the full privilege of returning it within five days after its receipt with not a cent of cost for the opportunity of looking it over.

There are no strings to this offer—your order won't stand unless you want it to.

But send the card now—without money. Tomorrow may be too late!

Sincerely yours,

The results were so disappointing that if our second test had not been all printed and ready for the mail, we should have abandoned the idea of selling Wells' then and there. Luckily, Fred Stone and I had contended from the beginning that Wells' appeal was due primarily to the prehistoric features his history brought out, so the circular ought to be devoted largely to these. And while the first test was being rushed out, I was working on a circular along pre-historic lines. Copy of the first page of it, and the letter and card that went with it, follow:

At Last! H. G. Wells'
"Outline of History"
At One- Third the Original Price!

DEAR SIR:

The enclosed 10-day Option is worth real money, so we have limited it to your own personal use. It is not transfer-able and it is good for only ten days after you receive this letter. If you can't use it, we should appreciate your kindness in destroying it.

For it gives to a selected list of people the opportunity to get the most talked about, the most successful and the greatest book of this generation *at a reduction of two-thirds from the original price!*

189

Think of it a discount of 67% from the price that 50,000 people have already paid! Do you wonder that we regard these Options as valuable?

Here Is the Way of It:

You know, of course, that H.G. Wells' "Outline of History" is the most talked about book in the world today. No matter where you go—no matter what you do—you come across it. Newspapers and magazines the country over are almost a unit in commending it. Literary Critics are exhausting their superlatives in trying to adequately describe it. People everywhere—just regular folks like you and me—are reading it eagerly, avidly, and getting as real enjoyment out of it as though it were the most thrilling of popular novels.

And all because it gives us just those things we all want to know about peoples and countries and rulers, put in such an interesting way, and with such pungent, incisive comment and occasional flashes of relieving humor that, as the N. Y. Tribune puts it—" It is among the most exciting books ever written."

50,000 copies of Wells' "Outline of History" have been sold in the book-stores at $10.50.

50,000 more could probably be sold at the same figure. But H. G. Wells wants to reach ALL the thinking people of this country, and to give us a chance to do that with one big edition, he has agreed to sacrifice 85% of his royalties on that one edition!

An Offer We Can Never Make Again!

The result is such an offer as we can make but once in a life-time—

H. G. Wells' marvelous "History," known and discussed wherever books are read, bound up into a single magnificent volume, fully illustrated, at a price of

190

$3.50!

And—

a years' subscription to the Review of Reviews at its regular price of $4.

Both Together For $7.50

payable in little, never-missed monthly payments of 50 cents, or $6.50 cash.

Wells' "History," starting with the empty dawn of things, tells you in absorbing story the common adventure of all mankind—the growth, not only of peoples, but of all nature and life.

The Review of Reviews gives you the things you want to know about the world today. It takes from all the great newspapers and magazines everything worth while and repeats the gist of it to you. It ties together the important happenings, puts them in their proper sequence, shows you their relation one to another so clearly, so interestingly, that you wonder how anyone can think himself well informed who sees only the fragmentary reports in the daily news.

There Is Just One Condition

Only one condition we make—that you send in your reservation at once.

The plates are all made—the paper is bought the printers are waiting but we can make only one edition at this price, and we want to give every one of our friends a chance at that edition.

So we send you this offer now. Mail the enclosed card, without money, and we will send you Wells' "Outline of History" at the special price, subject to a week's free examination, and enter your subscription for one year of the Review of Reviews.

If for any reason you are dissatisfied with the "History," you can return it at the end of the week, send 25¢ for the copy of the magazine delivered you, and cancel your order.

There are no strings to this offer—your order won't stand unless you want it to.

But send the card *now*—without money. Tomorrow may be too late!

Sincerely yours,

From the first day that the orders began to come in from that circular, there was never a moment's doubt as to whether we were going to sell Wells' "History." Why, on ordinary occupational lists like doctors, lawyers and the like, it pulled 3 1/2 per cent! And as for the good book lists, if we told you some of the percentages that circular chalked up, you would not believe us.

Suffice it is to say that, where we had hesitated about agreeing to sell 83,000 sets in two years, *we sold 90,000 in 4 months!* And the above letter and circular did every bit of it.

True, we tried some magazine and newspaper advertising, but two of the best advertising agencies in the country were unable to develop a single ad that pulled orders at anywhere near the low price we got them by mail. It was only when we took the different pages of the circular, like the one starting: "The Oldest Man in the World," and made page ads from them, that the advertising began to show results. But before that happened we had sold our 90,000 sets by mail.

Each of those sales carried with it a subscription to the Review of Reviews—$3.50 for Wells', $4 for the Review— which means that at 3 1/2 per cent, each circular was costing us 2 1/2 cents in the mail and bringing us 26 cents worth of orders—a selling cost of less than 10 per cent. There was money in that.

But to add 90,000 subscribers to a magazine's subscription list in four months' time is as much as an ordinary magazine can stand, unless it wants to raise its advertising rates, and this the Review did not feel like doing. So it was decided to bind the next edition of Wells' in a fine Art craft and sell it alone. This we did, and sold another 60,000 sets before the year was out!

What next? Many people would have been satisfied with that, but after the way we had been able to sell $1,000,000 worth of O. Henry stories two years in succession, we were not going to give up Wells' without getting a lot more out of it than a single year's sale.

But we had to change our offer. We had been over all our regular lists twice, with different letters and circulars. Now we must get not only a different letter, but a new reason for buying.

It happened that Wells had stirred up so much comment and had received so many criticisms and suggestions, that he had considerably revised the history and added a large number of new pages. So we decided to bring out the new edition in four volumes, and price them at $9 if bought alone, or $12 with a year's subscription to the

Review of Reviews.

Then came the question of how to sell them. The circular was easy, for Tut-ankh-Amen was then very much in the public eye. So, as there was not much in Wells' about him, we based the circular upon his great father-in-law, Ahknaton. But the important thing was the letter. We had already worn out the bargain appeal and the special reservation and all the usual mail order stunts. We had to find something of interest in itself, yet closely tied up with the "History."

After several tries we found it. Here it is. Judge for yourself if it would not have intrigued your interest.

Certainly it intrigued that of our readers, for it sold about $750,000 worth of Wells' and the Review!

DEAR READER

What is the "Unpardonable Sin" in all Nature? What one thing most inevitably brings its own punishment? What most surely spells extinction?

Stagnation—Standing Still!

The Gigantosaurus, that was over a hundred feet long and as big as a house; the Tyrannosaurus, that had the strength of a locomotive and was the last word in frightfulness; the Pterodactyl or Flying Dragon—all the giant monsters of Prehistoric Ages—are gone. They did not know how to meet the changing conditions. They stood still while the life around them passed them by.

Egypt and Persia, Greece and Rome, all the great Empires of antiquity, perished when they ceased to grow. China built a wall about herself and stood still for 1,000 years. Today she is the football of the powers. In all Nature, to cease to grow is to perish.

100,000,000 *Years in One*

It was for men and women who are not ready to stand still, who refused to cease to grow, that Wells set to work on his almost incredible task—to put into one fascinating work all the 100,000,000 years of life and growth that this planet has known.

—To place in your hands the orderly knowledge that men go to College four years to get—and often come away without.

—Not only the History of the world, but the Science of the world. The Philosophy of the world. The outstanding Literature of the world—a vast panorama unrolled before your eyes by the most graphic word-painter of modern times.

And all so interestingly, so absorbingly done that, as the New York Tribune puts it—" It is among the most exciting books ever written." That is what you get in—

H. G. Wells'
"Outline of History"

And that isn't all.
Just glance over the enclosed folder and think for one moment of the absorbing, fascinating story that goes with it—education in the highest sense, entertainment in the most educational sense.

People who have read this new four-volume, finally revised edition of the "Outline" are saying that it has done more for them than a College education. A college education costs you probably $5,000 and four years of your life. Wells' wonderful work is sent to you on approval and you will read the four books as absorbedly, as quickly as so many novels.

Four Volumes for 1/3 Less than the Price of the First
Two!

Although the History has been revised and enlarged; although it was printed from brand new plates, with a hundred new full-page pictures in addition to the two hundred in the discarded edition; and although it is now bound in four usable, library size volumes instead of the original bulky ones, we can, through a fortunate arrangement with the Review of Reviews,

Send to you and a few other New Process Company customers this famous "Outline of History" for 33 1/3% less than the original two-volume edition would cost you even now in any book store!

What is more, you can SEE IT, EXAMINE IT, PORE OVER IT in your own home for a week at our expense. Your name on the enclosed card brings the four volumes to you, postpaid, for a full week's FREE examination.

And the Review of Reviews, too

What the "Outline" is to past history, the Review of Reviews is to current events. It interprets men and movements in terms that every alert American can understand and profit by. It gives you the boiled-down sap of world events, equips you with a background of facts against which to read your daily news.

Akhnaton
Was HUMAN

While This One Edition Lasts!

The low price we are offering on this great History is possible only because the Review of Reviews contracted for 100,000 sets at once.

Perhaps you think that leaves plenty of time for you to get your copy?

With any ordinary book that would be so, but not with Wells. They sold 90,000 copies of his one-volume edition in little over three months, and already nine-tenths of their 100,000 four-volume sets are gone. The remainder won't last long.

At most, we can get only a few thousand sets, to offer among our 258,000 New Process Company customers. Can you imagine how long those few thousand will last?

Will you look over this set now—while you can get the four volumes, revised and beautifully illustrated, at a third less than the original two-volume set would cost you even now in the bookstores—while you can have them sent to you postpaid, without expense, for a week's FREE examination, to be returned "collect" if for any reason you decide not to keep them?

The enclosed card is your answer. Use it while there is yet time!

Yours 'til then,

That ended the second year of the Wells' sale, but it was far from ending the sale itself. For three years we sold it, until our total sales topped the 360,000 mark! Two of the letters we did it with are quoted in an earlier chapter of the book. The last of the really successful ones is given below:

LAST CHANCE AT 25% OFF!

DEAR READER:

One of those discoveries which makes history such startling and interesting reading has just come to light through the deciphering of a stone tablet found on the Sinai Peninsula. Scientists have often cast doubt upon the Scriptural story of the finding of Moses. But this inscription tends to con-firm the account just as we find it in the Bible. Written or dictated by Moses, and translated by Prof. Grimme of the University of Muenster, it reads:

"I, Manasse, mountain chief and head priest of the Temple, thank Pharaoh Hiacheput for having drawn me out of the Nile and helped me to attain high distinction."

Taken alone, this might not be regarded as conclusive proof of the truth of the Biblical record. But it is just one link of a chain that every day is growing stronger. Remember, in "Samuel," how the Philistines killed Saul and hung his armor in the "House of Ashtaroth"? And how, in revenge for his death, King David 20 years later put the fortress of Beth-Shan, where Saul's body had hung, to the torch? The Temple of Ashtaroth and the flame-scorched walls of Beth-Shan, have just been unearthed by excavators working under the direction of the University of Pennsylvania, and the records there inscribed confirm much of the Biblical story.

Another archaeologist, Dr. Ditleff Nielsen, comes forward with finds in the Arabian Desert, which tend to show that the Queen of Sheba was no myth. Whether she herself existed or not, there undoubtedly was such a kingdom—a rich and a vast kingdom—2000 years before Christ.

On a tablet of clay dug up from the ruins of ancient Chaldea has been found an inscription detailing in almost identical language the Scriptural account of the flood. While as for the Tower of Babel, its ruins are still standing!

Discoveries like these, which are daily coming to light, go to show that there is no real conflict between religion and science. Interpretations may differ, but to the broad-minded student of science, as to the broad minded student of the Bible, there is a common meeting ground, and nowhere is it better brought out than in—

H. G. Wells'
"Outline of History"

Wells gives you the one interesting, connected story of the world. It is no mere history in the old, dull sense. Not a mere account of the rise of this nation and the fall of that. It is the history of mankind.

No one but Wells could make so fascinating the story of Man's Progress upon earth. No one else could give so vivid a synopsis of all that is worth knowing in history.

Just glance over the enclosed folder and think for one moment of the absorbing, fascinating story that goes with it—education in the highest sense, entertainment in the most educational sense.

People who have read this new four-volume, finally revised edition of the "Outline" are saying that it has done more for them than a College education. A College education costs you probably $5,000 and four years of your life. Wells' wonderful work is sent to you on approval and you will read the four books as absorbedly, as quickly as so many novels.

Four Volumes for 1/4 Less than the Price of the First Two! Although the History has been revised and enlarged; although it was jointed from brand new plates, with a hundred new full-page pictures in addition to the two hundred in the discarded edition; and although it is now bound in four usable, library size volumes instead of the original bulky ones, we can, while the edition lasts,

Send to you and a few others, this famous "Outline of History" for 25% less than the original two-volume edition would cost you even now in any book store!

199

What is more, you can SEE IT, EXAMINE it, PORE OVER IT in your own home for a week at our expense. Your name on the enclosed card brings the four volumes to you postpaid, for a full week's FREE examination.

And the Review of Reviews, too

What the "Outline" is to past history, the Review of Reviews is to current events. It interprets men and movements in terms that every alert American can understand and profit by. It gives you the boiled-down sap of world events, equips you with a background of facts against which to read your daily news.

While this One Edition Lasts!

The low price we have been making on Wells' "Outline of History" was made possible only because we contracted for 100,000 sets at once.

Of all those 100,000 sets, only a few are now left. We can't hope to ever bring out an edition like that again. We can't expect to ever be able to manufacture and sell on so small a margin. When the few remaining sets are gone, your last chance at those low-cost volumes will go with them.

So don't file this away to think over. There's nothing to puzzle about, because you don't have to send one penny or promise anything, other than that if you don't find these four volumes, as the New York Evening Post puts it, "one of the indispensable books, "—why, just send them back, and that ends the matter.

That's easy isn't it?

I'll be holding one set for you for a few days. But you'll have to mail the enclosed card right away!

Yours 'til then,

200

P.S. If you are already a subscriber for the Review of Reviews or if you prefer a fiction magazine, you may substitute the new Golden Book for 18 months instead of the Review of Reviews one year, for the sale price. Simply change the order card. The Golden Book is the new kind of story magazine that everyone is talking about—The best stories, essays, plays and poems of all time selected by a board of editors as worthy to endure out of all the world's great literature.

That ended the biggest sale of any one set of books that the Review ever had. We have always been especially proud of it, for we worked it up from scratch. There was nothing in any previous campaign to give us an indication of what appeal would go best on it, and as it happened, our most effective appeals were entirely different from anything we had ever tried before.

Of course, it really followed the rules outlined in the early chapters of this book, for with the discovery of the tomb of Tut-ankh-Amen, the people's interest was centered largely on things prehistoric; so when we started our circular or letter with a reference to something of the kind, we were tying right in with that interest.

This was well illustrated by the last two letters, the one referring to the prehistoric fossils and dinosaur eggs, and the other to the unearthing of the stone tablet of Moses. Even after 250,000 sets had been sold, those two letters were still able to stir up interest and add another hundred thousand sales to the record.

The point would seem to be that if you can tie in with what people are thinking about and interested in, you can sell anything. And the particular form that your letter takes is far less important than the chord it happens to strike. We shall touch upon this later with regard to letters selling other products.

The big sale of Wells' naturally brought us a lot of good publicity. To the Review, that meant more advertising contracts. To me, it meant a chance to try a new field-selling, not books, but wearing apparel and men's furnishings of different kinds.

Some fifteen years previously, John Blair of Warren, Pa., had started what is now the New Process Company with $100 of borrowed capital and an idea. The idea came from having worked his way home from college by selling raincoats.

It seems that one of his chums in college had just been willed a raincoat factory and he had proposed to Blair that the latter take the job of sales manager. Blair was ever a modest soul, and he had some doubt of his fitness for the job, so he decided to see how much he knew about selling by taking a trunkful of samples and working his way from Philadelphia to his home in Warren.

The trial was without special incident until he reached Kane, some forty miles from Warren and his last stop. He was showing his samples to a merchant when a customer came into the store. The man seemed in no hurry, so the merchant went on looking over the coats, and finally placed his order. Blair was putting away his samples when the customer strolled over. "Got any black raincoats in that bunch?" the man asked. Blair thought a moment and finally remembered that he had one down at the bottom of the trunk. He hauled it out, found that it fitted, and a sale was made.

Curious to know what any one could want with a black raincoat in that day of tans and grays, Blair asked him why he had picked on black. "I'm an undertaker," the other explained. "When I go to a funeral I must wear a black coat. A dozen times I've been caught in heavy rains and just about spoiled every coat I had. Now she can rain all she wants to!"

That set Blair to thinking. There were 920,000 under-takers in the country, and except in the big cities, every one of them must be faced with the same problem. The big city stores might be able to stock black raincoats in enough different sizes to fit every under-taker, but certainly the small town stores could not. So it meant either wearing an ordinary coat and getting soaked by every heavy rain, or else having a coat specially made at high cost.

If some one central store could cater to all these under-takers by mail it ought to be able to do a tremendous business.

Blair decided to try it. He wrote a letter embodying the idea and offered to supply black raincoats of perfect fit at the same price ordinary raincoats were selling for in stores. His printer trusted him for the letter and envelopes, his chum agreed to make up 400 black raincoats for him in assorted sizes, and he borrowed $100 for the postage. The rest of the work he and his brothers did themselves.

He mailed 10,000 letters, then waited fearfully for the results. They came, all right. His 400 coats melted like snow before the summer's sun. A second 400 went almost as fast, and he had to order a third 400 before the orders stopped coming.

For two years he was content to sell raincoats to undertakers only. Then priests and ministers began to write him and he extended his line to cover them. From that to selling ordinary coats and suits and other items of men's furnishings was but a step. In fifteen years he worked up his gross sales to about $2,000,000 a year.

Then he seemed to reach his limit. During all those fifteen years, his entire sales appeal had been centered around one idea—*personalizing*. In the beginning, he had catered only to undertakers. His customers felt—and rightly—that here was a house devoted to their interests alone. That he understood the undertaker's needs. That they could get better service, lower prices, closer attention from him than anywhere else.

And with each new occupation or profession he added to his lists,

Blair was careful to use that same personalized appeal. He never sent the same letter to undertakers as to doctors or ministers.

He wrote to each as one who specialized in that profession's needs. He quoted testimonials from well-known men in the same line. He won confidence by a thorough understanding of the needs of each profession and occupation, and he brought back the orders with prices and goods that really did represent unusual values.

But there came a time when the old appeals began to lose their pull, when the occupational lists seemed to wear out. So he was forced to turn to general lists, such as telephone users, automobile owners, and the like. How could he make effective use of his personalized appeal on them? You would never guess the way he finally worked out. It showed ingenuity of a high order.

With a gross business of $2,000,000 he had customers in almost every town of any size in the country. And a great many had written appreciative letters, telling what good value they considered his coat, how well it was wearing, and so on. So what did he do but pick every town from which he had one or more good testimonials and write a letter something like this:

"The best value in a Raincoat I have ever had. You've saved me at least $10 on the price I'd have had to pay in our local stores."

The very words of John J. Smith, of 2601 Racine Avenue of your city. Perhaps you know Mr. Smith. If so, you know he is not given to exaggeration. To make such an impression upon him, a coat must be good. And to draw forth a letter like the above, it needs to be a most unusual value.

That it is all of that, the calibre of men who are wearing it is sufficient guarantee. When men like James Brown of 314 Hardin Ave., William Sherman of 14 Sixth St., and Max Jones of 14 Fifth Avenue, will send all the way out here for a Raincoat, there must be something about the coat and the price of it that it would be worth your while to know.

And so on into a description of the coat. That was expensive circularizing, of course, requiring a different letter for each town, but it proved to be so effective that it seemed well worth the extra expense. The year before I went up there, this form of letter pulled so well that John Blair felt safe in contracting for some 20,000 raincoats for Spring delivery, and 40,000 traveling bags for Summer sale.

But along about that time retailers were beginning to awaken to the so-called "menace" of mail order competition. Letters like the one above, intimating that the mail order people could offer far better values than those given in stores, got under their skin, and they centered their efforts upon the men whose names were quoted in them to such good purpose that permission to use them was withdrawn. By the time he started getting his letters ready for the Spring sale. Blair found himself with so few testimonials and names he could use that instead of personalizing by towns and cities he was forced to try it by states, and the results proved most disappointing.

Where he needed nearly 1 1/2 per cent of orders to show a profit, he got less than 1/2 of 1 per cent. Where he had expected to sell well over 20,000 raincoats, he found it difficult to dispose of 5,000. And the traveling bag season started off just as disappointingly.

The result was that the first of June showed them, not the goodly profit of usual years, not the rush of business they had expected, but $80,000 in the red, and an inventory so big that it simply staggered them.

It was then I was given the chance to show what book publishing methods would do in the way of moving merchandise. I had come up long enough before to have had time to send out a couple of tests, and to become familiar with the organization and the products. Now I was to have the opportunity to show whether I was worth my salt.

XVI

How the Bookbuyers Saved a Campaign

THE first thing one learns in selling books is that the easiest man to sell is one who has previously bought books by mail. There are certain occupational lists to which you can sell profitably. You can even, upon occasion, find appeals that sell to telephone and automobile registration lists. But the big percentages come when you circularize lists of people who have bought kindred books by mail.

Naturally, therefore, when faced with the urgent need of quickly disposing of 40,000 traveling bags, the first thing that occurred to us was: why waste money trying to sell these to difficult lists like telephone users, when there are all those millions of bookbuyers offering a virgin field for a product such as this?

So we rushed out a test on a score of good book lists, using the letter we were surest would work on a bookbuyer —an adaptation of the first letter we had used so successfully at the Review of Review on Wells' "Outline of History."

It pulled, of course. The same idea has pulled in selling lots, and houses, and stocks, and every manner of product. Get an idea that is psychologically sound and it will work on anything. This one worked on traveling bags. On a $14.85 offer it pulled 2, 3 and even 4 per cent and better on some lists. It pulled so well that within a week after the results began to show up we were started on a two million mailing—all to good book lists.

You see, including what we had to pay for the use of the lists, our circulars in the mail cost less than 4 1/2 cents each, so even when we got only 2 per cent of orders, our selling cost amounted to but a trifle over $2 on a $14.85 traveling bag, and from that maximum it tapered all the way down to $1 a sale.

There was money in that—so much that when the 40,000 bags were gone we were glad to buy an additional 10,000 and sell them, too. Before the end of the short Summer season, we had disposed of 50,000 traveling bags. And here is the letter that did it:

DEAR SIR:—

The enclosed Special Privilege Card is worth money, so we have numbered it and limited it to your own personal

206

use. If you cannot use it, we should appreciate your kindness in destroying it.

For it gives to a select group of Pittsburgh men the chance to obtain, for only $14.85, a traveling bag which experienced men tell us cannot be equalled in a retail store for less than $20 or $25.

This offer is not transferable. It is being made to a limited number of men in Pittsburgh, for the reason given below:

Three years ago, after many requests from well-known men, a famous designer produced for us a wonderful new Traveling Bag which we christened the "Statler" Bag. Made of GENUINE ENGLISH LEATHER, Beaver grain, and patterned after the finest imported luggage, this new bag won instant favor. Today it has become the biggest-selling bag ever produced—a fact which luggage manufacturers are frank to admit.

In this new "Statler" Bag you will find the MOST IMPORTANT improvement ever put in any luggage. It is equipped with 10 *handy moisture-proof interior pockets*, which give you a special place for each of your toilet accessories—comb and brush; shaving set; toothbrush and toothpaste; even your handkerchiefs, neckties, underwear, shirts and collars!

When you travel with a "Statler" Bag, everything is right at your finger-tips. You can pack your bag in *half* the time it used to take. Bottles can't tip over. Your clothes will not be mussed or wrinkled. There's "a place for everything, and everything in its place."

Now, here is my offer to you:

In order to introduce the *new, improved* "Statler" Bag as quickly as possible, we have allotted 360 bags to be sold to substantial business men in Pittsburgh at a very low Direct-by-Mail price.

You are one of the men selected for this special offer. I would like to send you a "Statler" Bag at my risk, and with no expense to you. I want you to keep it for a full week's *free trial*—actually take it with you on a trip—enjoy its amazing convenience, delight in its *fine appearance.*

After you have used the bag a full week FREE, send it back at my expense—if you are willing to give it up!

But if you like it so well that you don't want to part with it, you can send me—not the high price you would pay in a retail store—but only $14.85, my low Direct-by-Mail price on these 360 bags.

Remember, there is no sale—no obligation to keep the "Statler" Bag until you have tried it out for a week, AND ARE SATISFIED! *Just let us send the bag.*

But remember, too, that bargains like this will be snapped very quickly—and we have allotted only 360 bags to the city of Pittsburgh.

So use your Special Privilege Card NOW—while it saves you time and money.

Yours for mutual service,

P. S. I believe you are likely to know some of the Pittsburgh men who have already purchased "Statler" Bags. When men like these use the "Statler" you can realize it must be a bag of supreme quality.

Hon. Joseph C. Buffington, H.F. Bockstoce, Ass't Treas-
Judge of the U.S. Curcuit   urer
   Court,   The Carnegie Steel Company,
Pittsburgh.   Pittsburgh.
James C. Gray, President,   Norman Wilson Storer,
The Standard Chemical Co., Noted Electrical Engineer
Pittsburgh.   Westinghouse Electric Co.

B.F. Jones Jr., President,
The Jones & Laughlin Steel E.D. McCafferty, Ass't Sec.
Company   H.J. Heinz Company,
                                 Pittsburgh

That little matter disposed of, we got busy on the raincoats. Having more time for these, and having satisfied the powers-that-be that book lists were a gold mine for their products, we were able to test half a dozen different letters and pick the one that pulled best.

Curiously enough, that was one along lines I had never tried before, nor seen tried by any one else. I had read somewhere the account of a manager whose company had been at swords' points with a certain competitor for years. It was very much to the interest of this man's company that the two should get together, but no one had ever been able to heal the breach. Finally, it occurred to him one day that the man we feel most kindly towards is the one we have just done a favor, so he went to see his competitor and asked the rival manager if he would do him a favor. Certain of their customers were taking advantage of their terms. It had to be stopped, but he didn't know how to do it without incurring their ill will. The other manager was more experienced than he. Would he not do him the favor of telling him how he handled similar cases?

The rival manager opened up like a rose to the morning sun and their little talk started a friendship that quickly healed the breach between the two companies.

Well, it occurred to us that there was sound psychology back of the first manager's action, and it ought to work with letters as well as in person, in overcoming indifference as well as enmity. So we tried it on our raincoat letter. It proved one of the most effective appeals we ever had. We have used a dozen variations of it since on a score of different products.

On the raincoats, it pulled so well that during September and October we disposed of not only all the left overs from the previous Spring, but some 20,000 additional coats besides. At a goodly profit, too, for again we got 2 and 3 per cent and better returns, on a product selling for $18.75. Here is the "Favor" letter that did the trick:

DEAR CUSTOMER:

Will you do me a favor?

For twelve years now, you know, we have been selling the famous "Keepdry" Coat direct to the consumer, at a saving of many dollars from the usual retail price.

This year I want to vary our line a bit, so I have changed the fabric to one that looks like a smart topcoat—but will still shed rain. And instead of the usual double-breasted rain-coat model, I'm using a single-breasted topcoat model that appeals to men because it has style, and yet retains that loose, comfortable look of the well-tailored light overcoat.

210

I believe that anyone who ever gets out in stormy or wet weather will like this "Any Weather" Coat better than any raincoat or topcoat he can buy, but you know how it is in merchandising—you can never be sure of such things until after you have sunk a lot of money in them.

Which brings me to the favor:

I want to make sure of the demand—or lack of demand— before we sink too much money in this new coat. So I've come to you as a customer of the house:

Will you try out one of these new "AnyWeather" Topcoats for me for a week—WEAR IT—see how it feels, how it looks, how it compares with topcoats you have bought at $25 or $30? Above all, how it keeps out wind and rain? And then write me?

Needless to say, I'll send you a coat you can be proud to wear anywhere—a coat that will fit you as though made to measure by your own tailor.

I can do it, you know, because we have so much greater a range of sizes than any retail store. Where the retailer carries coats in half a dozen sizes and only one length, we have 57 different sizes and 5 different coat lengths!

More than that—where the ordinary raincoat or topcoat serves but one purpose, this new "AnyWeather" is top-coat, motor coat, sport coat and raincoat—*all in one*! It can be worn on every occasion that a light overcoat is used— *and in a heavy downpour as well*! Every man needs a coat like this for rainy days—for chilly nights— for auto rides.

Stormy days will never again mean chills and colds and ruined clothes if you wear an "AnyWeather" Coat. It will protect your health and your clothes, yet keep you looking and feeling as smartly dressed as ever.

But I did not start out with the idea of selling YOU the

211

coat. I just want to satisfy you that it is one you will be proud to wear anywhere, in any company, in any weather.

If you will fill in the three simple measurements called for on the enclosed card—I'll get one of these new "Any-Weather" Coats off to you at once by prepaid Parcel Post —to be worn for a week *at my risk and expense*—FREE!

At the end of the week, if you should like the coat so well that you want to keep it, you can pay—*not* the $25 or $30 that you are accustomed to paying for coats in stores, not even our low Direct-to-the-User "Keepdry" price of $16.85 —BUT OUR SPECIAL INTRODUCTORY PRICE TO YOU, ONLY $14.85!

Otherwise just send it back at our expense, and in payment for the week's wear, tell me frankly your honest opinion of the coat and its salability.

Naturally, I am not making offers like this to everyone, so whether you accept it or not, I should feel obliged if you would return the card so as to insure against its falling into other hands.

Naturally, too, your opinion will be of value to me only if I get it NOW—before the Fall season has really opened— before we are definitely committed for any great quantity of these new all-weather coats.

Won't you, therefore, fill in the three simple measurements on the card TONIGHT if you can, and mail it? On second thought, better mail it *right away*—while you have it in your hand—so there will be no chance of forgetting it.

I thank you for your courtesy.

Yours for mutual co-operation,

You will notice it could just as easily be used to sell books, or shirts or blankets or some commodity you are interested in. You see, the product is of minor importance. There was scarcely a man in the whole place who did not know more about raincoats than I. But it was not raincoats we were selling. It was an idea—in this case, the idea that by specializing on one grade of coat, one cloth, one style, and making it in every conceivable size, we could not only save you money, but give you a better coat and a more perfect fit than you could get at double the price in stores.

We did not need to know anything about coat manufacturer's to convince you of that. All we needed to understand was human reactions to certain ideas, and these are what we studied.

They worked so well on raincoats that we felt emboldened to try a different tack on the overcoats—selling a real reason for their low price, rather than depending on the price itself to bring in the orders. We have since found that to be one of the most important essentials in selling—to give a convincing reason why you are able to make a lower price than your competitor. Mere reductions are not enough. There are too many ways of skimping on quality and taking it out in a bargain price. You must have a logical reason why your price is low.

The reason given in the letter that follows was true, and it must have sounded convincing, for it sold some 21,000 overcoats in about two months' time, at a cost of $28.75 apiece. A few special ones sold as high as $47, but these were for a new idea we were testing. Here is the letter:

MR. BUSINESS MAN:

You know how most factories are—busy and working overtime eight or ten months of the year, and practically idle the rest.

And those lean months—like the famines of ancient Egypt— eat up most of the profits of the fat ones.

This year we determined to change that.

Instead of letting the Woolen Mills lie idle during January, February and March, we kept them busy weaving the new double-texture, pure wool fabric for "Keep Warm" Ulsters. Instead of letting the tailors twiddle their thumbs during June, July and August, we kept them busy making up this fine quality cloth into the finished coats for Winter, figuring that the low price we could make on these would soon clear out this surplus output.

The result is that, instead of the prices ranging as high as $47.00 at which we used to sell these "Keep Warm" Ulsters in former years—instead of the high prices that customers tell us coats of similar quality would cost them in stores—we can now offer you the new, improved "Keep Warm" distinctive in material and design, correctly tailored in every detail, and as smart as an English Greatcoat—for only $28.75.

You know how important it is to get just the right kind of Overcoat for those bleak, raw days that start in November and continue right through to sleety March.

Neither snow nor sleet, bitter cold or sunny days matter to the man who wears a "Keep Warm" Ulster. It's the kind of Greatcoat for any kind of Fall or Winter weather.

You see, that's where the pure, double-texture wool comes in. The shocks of sudden weather changes cannot penetrate it. Comfortable on mild days because of its lightness—cozy and snug in zero weather because the pure wool repels cold— it keeps your body-warmth in, and it keeps the cold out.

Made in a model that appeals to men because it has style, it yet retains that loose, comfortable look of the well-tailored Ulster coat. And it's lined with genuine Skinner's Satin in the sleeves and shoulders, because the smooth satin makes it easy to put on, and easy to slip out of. You can wear it all day long without having your shoulders sag or ache. Just the kind of coat that a man wants for Fall and Winter wear.

All over the country, men who like to be well-dressed at all times—men like Colonel Ashburn, of the Military Academy at West Point; Governor Holcomb of Connecticut; Chief Justice Teller of the Colorado' Supreme Court, and A. E. Barker, Purchasing Agent of the J. P. Morgan & Company —are taking to this distinctive " KeepWarm" Ulster in place of the ordinary overcoat.

Why, in the past few years, we have sold more than 42,000 of them, and every day brings us letters like this from Charles M. Robinson, Esq., Counselor-at-Law, of New Haven, Connecticut:

> *"An Ulster equal to this one would have cost me at least $50 in a retail store. I have found it to be very warm, and its wearing qualities excellent."*

And this Fall's model is better far, we believe, than any we have ever before offered!

Bargains such as this will, of course, be snapped up quickly. Our output this Fall is absolutely limited to 19,961 "KeepWarm" Ulsters, and among our more than a quarter million customers, they won't last long.

While they last, you can get one of these latest models, smart, new Greatcoats for only $28.75—as fine a quality and a better style than any we sold in the past for as high as $47.00.

Your Overcoat—and Why!

What is more, you can SEE it, EXAMINE it, WEAR IT FOR A WEEK at our risk and expense, without one cent of payment. Merely fill in the simple measurements on the enclosed card and drop it in the mail. We'll do the rest.

Fair enough, you'll admit. And you realize that we couldn't make such an offer if we didn't know that these new "Keep-Warms" will back it up.
But we DO know it, so we're entirely willing to do our part. Are you willing to put us to the test?

Just mail the card. Then sit back and watch results.

We're waiting,

That ended the regular sale. We had eight or nine hundred coats left in odd sizes and colors, so we went back to the book .business again and borrowed from it our old damaged-set letter. Of course, there was nothing damaged about the coats, but the odd sizes and colors furnished just as good an argument, and, as it proved, just as effective bait in landing orders. For instead of the eight or nine hundred orders needed to clean up our stock, we landed close to ten thousand! That was no hardship, you can be sure, for the factory had any number of odds and ends of piece goods on hand, and they were delighted to make them up into coats—at a goodly reduction in costs, too. Here is that old book letter, as adapted to selling odds and ends of overcoats.

790 Left-over Ulsters at a Big Discount!

DEAR SIR:

In the rush and excitement of selling, in the past two months, 21,000 "KeepWarm" Winter Ulsters, there was no time to pay attention to exactly how sizes and colors were running.

The result is that now, with the season near its end, we find ourselves with 790 coats left over—in all sizes—*but without a complete range of sizes in any one color!*

217

There are dark grays and blues and beautiful brown heather-mixtures, in Greatcoats that we sold in the past all the way up to $47.00—really handsome colors, all of them—but we can't be sure which color is here in the exact size that will fit you.

And you know how the Overcoat season is—if these Ulsters are not all disposed of before Christmas, some of them will probably be on our hands until next Fall.

So rather than carry any of them over until then, we have decided to make one sweeping reduction, and offer these 790 smart, distinctive, beautifully tailored Greatcoats— of fine, warm, double-texture pure wool cloth—for only $27.65!

This is the lowest price we have ever made on these all-wool "KeepWarm" Ulster Coats. Just try to find their equal—in style, in workmanship, in fine-quality materi-al—for $40 or $50!

Only 790 Coats Left

We have just 790 of these double-texture all-wool Greatcoats to sell at this low price. When they are gone, your chance to save on our Winter Ulster will go with them. But while these 790 last, you can get as perfect-fit-ting, as good-looking, as fine-quality a Winter Greatcoat as ever you would want to wear, at an almost unheard-of bargain.

If you will just write your name and three simple meas-ures on the enclosed card and mail to us, we will send you a "KeepWarm" Ulster—that will exactly fit you—by pre-paid Parcel Post.

You may keep the overcoat for a full week. Then, if for *any reason at all* you don't care to keep the coat, you can send it back *at our expense.* But if you are so well pleased with it that you don't want to part with it, just send us $27.65, the low price at which we are offering these last remaining 790 coats.

SEND NO MONEY—simply mail the post card. But do it at once, as this opportunity to save money will not occur again.

Yours up to 790,

Notice how readily the idea adapts itself to overcoats, just as though it had never been used for anything else. That is my experience of most basic ideas. If they are good for selling one product, they can be adapted to selling almost any other product.

Notice, too, how simple was the form of circular. This, of course, was intentional, to carry out the idea of there being so few coats left in stock that it was not worth while to print an elaborate circular to describe them.

One of the questions often asked of me is: "What did you do to keep your customer sold after you had received his order?"

An important question, for every one has experienced the reaction that so often comes after you have allowed yourself to be persuaded into signing an order or sending for something by mail. You feel that maybe you were too precipitate and begin to look around for ways in which you can back out.

We met that problem by using every opportunity to re-sell the customer on his purchase. In acknowledgment letters, in bills, in the enclosure that went with each product, we had in mind the truism that the sale is not made until the goods are paid for, so we tried to put salesmanship into each of these. Here is a sample of one of them—the enclosure that went with the overcoat and was seen even before the overcoat was uncovered:

DEAR CUSTOMER:—

A man has to be well-dressed these days—correctly dressed. And "correctly dressed" means conservatively dressed— dressed in accordance with the standards set by men of high repute.,

One underlying thought has always been back of every KeepWarm" Ulster we have sold—one of correctness, as well-groomed men express and endorse it.

"KeepWarm" Ulsters are made for the man who seeks well-styled, conservative clothes, with good wearing qualities and finest workmanship, rather than the "ultra fashionable" styles that appeal to some men. Our merchandising policy—buying, selling and advertising—is controlled by this "correctness" idea.

You can wear the "KeepWarm" Ulster we are sending you, with the comfortable assurance of being well-dressed—of knowing that your coat is a part of you and that it ex-presses you at your best.

Sincerely yours,

P. S.—A customer often writes us that some friend wants a coat exactly like the one he bought of us. So we have printed a "Friend's Order Blank" on the back of this folder. There is only one condition attached to it—it should come in right away to get the advantage of the low $27.85 price.

Of course, these were not the only offers we mailed during those seven months. They were the high lights. In addition, we sold tires, shirts, underwear, ties, and a dozen other items, but the sale of none of these reached the proportions of the traveling bags and coats.

Shirts came nearest to it—in fact, later on shirts came to be one of our biggest sellers. We shall touch upon them in the next chapter, for our mailing on shirts during that first Fall was more in the nature of a test than a separate mailing. It showed such promise, however, that we decided to make a big mailing on it in the Spring.

Tires sold reasonably well, but their margin of profit was so narrow that we never went after that business in a big way. Here is one of the successful letters we did use:

MR. CAR OWNER:

"Enclosed find check for 25% of your Tire Bill."

If we said at the beginning of this letter that we were enclosing- our check for $3.00 to $12.00, you would be interested and doubtless highly pleased. You would certainly read on to see why we were so liberal.

Instead of an actual check, we'll tell you in a few words how you can save that amount of money *on every tire you use.*

One of the oldest firms in the rubber business—a factory

which makes tires that are as good as any in the world—wants to see if car owners will buy their tires "direct" if he will sell to them at just about the price dealers now pay.

This tire manufacturer knows that such a saving can be made if a lot of unnecessary selling expense and middle-men's profits are wiped out. So he's going to test out the American motoring public by offering the very best tires he makes— DIRECT to car owners, through our selling organization which operates by mail all over the country.

And to quickly find out if men really want to save 25% on the best tires that can be made, he is having us rush out this August letter to a few selected car owners.

If the response to this advertising is not tremendously large, the manufacturer's plan will be discontinued immediately. That would be too bad from a money-saving point of view; but it will show that people would rather continue buying tires in the old way even at high-er prices.

On the other hand, if the response is large, this plan of sending tires *direct-to-the-user* (by parcel post) will be continued and you can always get your tires through us at a great big saving.

This Is a Free Trial Offer

If you mail the enclosed card at once, we'll send you at our own risk and expense one or more tires for a week's FREE EXAMINATION. You can measure them, heft them, and compare them for bigness and strength and resiliency with any tire you know. See if you recognize' their make. There's no better Cord Tire in America today.

At the end of the week—if you're satisfied that they're as fine tires as ever you've seen—you can send us the low Direct-to-the-User price given on the inside of this letter. Otherwise, just send them back at our expense.

There's only one condition to this offer—you must take advantage of it at once. For, naturally, the results of this experiment in direct-selling will be of use to our manufacturer only if he can follow them up promptly, while the heavy driving season is still on in August and September. Naturally, too, since everything is ON CREDIT (no cod., no "express collect," no cash in advance) we had to carefully select the people to whom this free-trial offer is being made, so if you cannot use the enclosed card, we should feel obliged if you would either return or destroy it.

Returning the postcard without delay (regardless of whether your answer is YES or NO) will be an act of courtesy that will be personally appreciated by the president of one of America's oldest (1857) rubber companies.

Very truly yours,

P.S. To keep him from getting "in wrong" with jobbers and dealers and garages while this test is being made, the manufacturer's is making just a slight change in the tread design on his tire and is having the sidewalls show up the name of the tires as "New Process Super Cord" instead of using his own well-known name—but the tires are absolutely identical in construction with the very best and largest cord tires that this noted manufacturer makes. You will recognize their high quality (and maybe their manufacturer) as soon as you see them.

The last offer of the season was our Christmas mailing. It was the only mailing of the year in which we offered a choice of a variety of different products, and for that reason, it was about the least successful of all.

For here is a strange fact, which has held consistently throughout all my experience in selling by mail: If you offer one article you will get twice as many orders as if you offered a choice of two or more articles!

You see, making a choice involves hesitation. And in selling by mail, the customer who hesitates is lost to you. I have seldom known that rule to fail. Even in giving free premiums, we found that offering the customer a choice of two or more premiums cut the orders in half.

So I have always been an advocate of selling one thing at a time— a traveling bag or a coat or a set of shirts at a unit price for the lot. But at Christmas time I was over-ruled. All the others felt that we would get more orders by offering a big variety of gifts. In later years we learned differently. But this time we made up a little catalog and offered a choice of any or all the articles in it. It did not pull nearly as well as our single product offers, but it paid. Here is the letter and booklet:

DEAR CUSTOMER:

Christmas comes in just a few weeks, and if I know anything about daddies, husbands, uncles and big brothers, that means something to you.

May I help you pick out suitable gifts for your family and friends?

*Right here in your hand is a little booklet just crammed full of good things that men of all ages appreciate—*fine shirts of madras, flannel or English broadcloth; neckties, bath-robes, hosiery of fine silk or warm wool, golf balls, books, etc.

Then for your wife and the other women folks there are silk stockings, silk umbrellas, lingerie, furs, appliances for the home, jewelry, and many other thoughtfully selected gifts which women cherish.

For that youngster there are good things that all he-boys gloat over—footballs, baseballs and gloves, outfits for tennis and things for the vigorous, sturdy chap that loves the out-of-doors. For his quieter sister, we have just the type of dolls and books that she will love and cherish.

Silverware
    Luggage
        Pearls
            Clothing
                Electrical Appliances
                    Toys
—all are here—at prices surprisingly low! And if you make your selections now, while our stock is at its best, they'll be shipped the very day your order is received.

Take this letter and booklet home with you this evening— better still, go over it right now! You will be amazed how quickly you will find exactly the Christmas presents that will mean most to your relatives and friends.

And you will be even more amazed at how much money you can save.

Everything Comes on Free- Trial

Keep each article a full week—examine it for quality and value—satisfy yourself that it is just the gift for the friend you have in mind—THEN DECIDE. Send back any article you don't care for! You'll not be out one penny.

Now don't file this away to "think over." There's nothing to puzzle about, because you don't have to send one penny or promise anything, except that you will send the gifts back in a week if you don't like them.

That's easy—isn't it?

By using the enclosed order-form you kill two birds with one fountain pen. *You save a good many dollars on your Christmas gifts, and you're relieved of all that bothersome burden of Christmas shopping in stores.*

Where's that pen?

That ended the sale for the year. It changed the figures on the balance sheet from $80,000 in the red on June 1 to $121,000 net profit December 31. And it proved a number of things, among them that the best mail order buyer is one who has already bought other products by mail, and that it is ideas that sell goods—not mere descriptions of the goods themselves. Ideas are the only things that count, and the idea that will sell vast numbers of books can be used just as effectively in selling raincoats or traveling bags or overcoats or shirts!

Those were the important things we got out of that seven months' sale. And they were the factors responsible for the big strides we made in the next two years.

XVII

A Giant of the Mails

IN THE book business, January and February are the best months of the year. This is especially true of inspirational books, for people make their good resolutions the first of the year, hence they are far more likely to embark upon courses of study than after those resolutions have been forgotten.

In selling merchandise by mail, however, we found January and February the poorest months of the year. Stores hold their bargain sales then, so it is hard to show a great enough saving between their offerings and those you can make by mail, to induce people to go to the trouble of sending away for the things they want.

Another little-known factor in mail selling is that people will buy by mail far more readily before the season for that product has begun, or at its very start; but once well under way, they turn to their local stores. The reason for this must be that when the time has come when they actually need a thing, they don't feel like risking any possible delays in delivery. They want what they want when they want it. But beforehand they are willing to send for things and try them, figuring that if they are not what they like, there is plenty of time to return them and get something locally.

So, excepting small mailings on left-over Winter products, we devoted our time in January and February mostly to tests. Of course, we could not expect anywhere near as good results as when a product was in season, but we usually managed to get a fair indication of the pulling power of a circular by always using a yardstick, *i.e.*, by testing against each new circular we were trying, a thousand of the last successful circular we had used on that product. If the new one outpulled the old in this off-season, we felt reasonably sure it would do the same when the season came around again. If it did not, we discarded it and tried again.

There were always plenty of products to test, for we had to be continually on our guard against old products losing their appeal, and to keep feeding in new ones to take their places. The previous Christmas, for instance, we had tested pearls and perfume, with the idea of using one or both of them for our Christmas offer the following year. Both showed promise, the perfume especially coming

227

through with so many orders that we mailed some hundreds of thousands the following Christmas. Here were the two offers:

DEAR MADAM:

Will you try this experiment?

Ask your jeweler to show you a perfect deep-sea pearl. Put the enclosed Deltah manufactured pearl alongside it. Then try to tell them apart!

The jeweler can do it—with the aid of his magnifying glass. But neither you nor any other person not an expert in precious stones can distinguish the natural from the manufactured pearl.

In lustre, in weight, in iridescence, in color, the little pearl we are sending you will measure up to all the requirements of the genuine deep-sea jewel. Step on it! It will stand the weight of an ordinary size man. Boil it in hot water! It will come out lustrous, with the soft opalescence that only a pearl can give. Weigh it! You will find it heavy, firm, indistinguishable in any way from the natural pearl, except to the expert with his magnifying glass.

Most society women, most of the stars of stage and screen, have duplicates of their costly deep-sea gems made up in these manufactured pearls to wear at all public functions. For no one can distinguish them from the genuine.

The only difference apparent to the naked eye is in the price—and you save that big difference.

In New York, in Paris and London, Pearls are the vogue this year. They are being worn for every occasion, with almost every conceivable costume—with evening gowns, for parties and afternoon teas, for street, for shopping.

The "Carmen" necklace of Deltah pearls, from which the enclosed pearl was taken, was made to sell in retail stores at $21.00 and is so advertised in national magazines at the present time.

But if you will mail the enclosed card right away—before the heavy Christmas rush begins—we will send you this famous necklace, in the favorite 24-inch "Opera" length, fastened with a diamond clasp of white gold and genuine diamond, for only $15.75.

Not only that, but we will send it to you *for a full week's free trial,* without one cent of payment, to be tried out, to be examined, to be WORN for a week at our risk.

If for any reason—or no reason you are not more than delighted with it, send it back and you'll not be out one penny.

Naturally, we can't make offers like this to every one, so even if you don't take advantage of it we should feel obliged if you would return or destroy the card. Naturally, too, you will have to take advantage of it right away, before the heavy Christmas rush begins.

May we hope you will mail back your card *now*—
TODAY?

DEAR MADAM:

Who would ever dream that exquisite Narcisse
Perfume—perfume so lovely that its heady fragrance will
amaze you, yet so marvelously delicate and all-pervasive
that it seems like a breath from the flower gardens of
sunny France—who would ever believe that such perfume could be had for a dollar or less an ounce!

$1 an ounce! Why, you would pay more than that for just
ordinary, unknown perfumes at the corner druggists perfume that would seem flat and dull and lifeless alongside
this exquisite Narcisse.

The most delightful, the most captivating sweetness ever
extracted from flower petals and imprisoned in crystal —
that is Narcisse. Faint yet compelling, this liquid fragrance is like golden sunshine mellowed by stained glass.
The lore which enters its making is akin to the lore of the
wine makers of France—a secret handed down from
father to son for generations.

A fragrance that intrigues you—a delightsome, refreshing fragrance unlike that of any perfume you have ever
known. The essence of music and laughter, the sweetness
of flowers on a dewy morn—all magically imprisoned in
crystal.

Graded the way perfumes are usually graded, Narcisse
would retail for $4 to $5 an ounce. In fact, in the fashionable shops of Palm Beach, Newport and Fifth Avenue,
Narcisse *is* sold at $5 an ounce.

To offer even the small quantity we have at less than $1
an ounce is such a remarkable event that we have decided to confine it to just the wives of our customers. To

230

them we are making this offer:

If you will mail the enclosed Free- Trial Card at once, I will send you an 8-ounce bottle of Narcisse, postpaid, for examination. Break the seal, open it up and TRY *it! At the end of the week,* SEND IT BACK *if you are willing then to part with it.*

But if you don't want to part with it, send me—NOT the $5 an ounce, at which Narcisse Perfume is priced in many fashionable shops—BUT ONLY $7.85 FOR THE FULL EIGHT OUNCES!

This holds good, though, only on the small quantity we now have on hand. The enclosed FREE-TRIAL CARD must be used at once.

Yours if you are prompt,

In the Bald Eagle Mountains

HIDDEN away in the Nittany Valley is a peculiar spring of pure cold water. Perennially it disappears for eleven months at a time. Usually during the Spring freshets, the clear, cold water that is hidden away deep in the earth, is forced to bubble to the surface, and those who know that the spring is "flowing" again, come from miles around for its water.

For it is said that on moonlit nights the nymph Narcissus comes to drink of this spring, and that after her coming the water has strange healing properties.

Certain it is that at no other time are the flowers of the Narcissus quite so beautiful, their fragrance so captivatingly sweet. To capture that delightful fragrance, to imprison it in a sun-kissed amber liquid in vials of crystal—that is what has been done for you in—

231

At the same time we tested a new variant of the old damaged-set letter, with a view to using it the following December on whatever overcoat stock was left after the regular sale. Copy of it follows. It pulled almost as well as the damaged-set letter quoted in the last chapter, so we put it aside for later use. Here it is:

A Few Overcoats at a Great Saving

DEAR CUSTOMER:

I can save you a good many dollars right now—if you haven't bought your winter overcoat yet.

Already this winter we have sold 21,631 "KeepWarm" Ulsters—at prices ranging up to $48.75. Now there are only 582 of these good Ulsters left—not enough to do any heavy national advertising about—yet we don't want to carry them on our inventory until next Fall.

Rather than offer them to some jobber at a "bargain" price, I'm going to offer them to my old customers—yourself and other men who have bought raincoats, traveling bags, etc., from me in the past—at a real old-fashioned bargain price, only $24.95.

In other words, I'm giving *you*, rather than some city jobber, the benefit of the bargain. Remember that my seven-day free examination privilege holds good. You send no money in advance. You are free to return the "KeepWarm" Ulster if you don't like it for any reason, particularly if you don't think it's worth $40.00 instead of only $24.95.

Certainly you can use another overcoat this Winter—most of the cold weather is still ahead. Or you'll need a new overcoat this Fall. Just between you and me—isn't a saving of $15.00 worth enough to you to get your coat right now?

This is my one and only offer at this low price. I've only 582 coats left. If you are not keeping warm in one of them a week from today, you'll be the one to blame—not I. I am giving you a wonderful chance to get a genuine "KeepWarm" Ulster now at a fraction of the regular price. Just think, for only $24.95 you can get an all-wool, handsomely-tailored, satin-lined Ulster that will keep you warm and well-dressed this Winter and all next Winter, too!

Simply fill in the postcard, mail it today without any money, and I'll send your proper size in a 'KeepWarm" Ulster right away by Parcel Post.

But remember this—I have only 582 Ulsters left at $24.95. To protect myself I reserve the right to telegraph you if your order reaches me after your own size is all gone. To be sure of getting one of these "Keep Warm" Ulsters, send for your size at once!

Sincerely yours,

P. S. These 582 coats are the very latest ones made this Winter—the last word in style and tailoring—pure-wool cloth, plaid back, Skinner's Satin lining, etc.

Then we took up shoes and socks and ties and underwear and all manner of products. From the sales point of view, there were few products in men's wearing apparel that we were not able to bring back orders for in profitable volume. But when it came to the actual sale, it sometimes developed that it was so difficult to fit customers satisfactorily that the products had to be ruled out.

Shoes were one of these. Several times we tried shoes and brought back orders in profitable number, but when it came to fitting people, our orders dwindled by half. Possibly we did not have the right shoes or the proper method of sizing. Whichever it was, more than half the shoes we sent out came back. So we quickly abandoned that line. Here is one of the letters that brought in the orders:

DEAR SIR:

What size shoe do you wear?

233

If you will pick out the most comfortable pair of shoes you have, and pencil on the enclosed card all the markings from just inside them near the top, we'll promise to send you as easy-fitting, as stylish-looking, as comfortable a pair of shoes as ever you've had on your feet, at a price lower far than you've paid for good shoes since the war.

Their style will speak for itself. Their fine leather, too. But only months of wear under everyday conditions will tell you the full story of comfort and service that is built into every pair of "Double Wear" Shoes.

For "DoubleWear" shoes are designed for comfort according to Nature's own plan for the feet. There's a graceful swing to the toe. The sole rests firmly against the ground and yet flexes with every motion of the foot. The arch fits snugly. In short, they fit everywhere—bind nowhere look like far higher priced shoes—and WEAR that way.

Will you try this test?

Fill in the markings from your most comfortable shoes, on the enclosed card. Then see if we can't give you as easy-fitting, as stylish, as good-looking a pair of "DoubleWear" Shoes—*regardless of what you paid for yours!*

Costs nothing to try, and if you can get as easy-fitting, as good looking, as serviceable shoes at a third less than you are now paying, it's worth saving, isn't it?

We're ready to send them, without one cent of payment, for a week's FREE inspection. Are you willing to put us to the test?

We'll be here—waiting,

Another "dud" was athletic winter underwear. It sounded good, and our customers evidently' thought so too, for they ordered it in goodly quantities; but oh—how they returned it! And when I had tried a suit on one of those cold, blizzardy days that are so frequent in north-western Pennsylvania, when the wind blowing down from the lakes has an edge like a knife, I knew just how our customers must have felt. And I did the same as they— I went back to my long ones.

But as an example of a letter that brings in the orders, the athletic union suit letter has a right to a place. So here it is:

"Oh! It's Great to Get Out in the Morning!"

DEAR NEIGHBOR:—

Those bracing, snappy Winter days will soon be here.

Do you want to make them different this year—want to get more vigorous, happy, red-blooded enjoyment out of them than ever before?

Then put away those shivery BVD's or other light underwear and get "Keep Warm" Athletics.

Remember when you were a youngster, how you used to coast and skate all day long and far into the night with never a thought about the cold?

Wool—that's what did it! Only "KeepWarm" Athletics are not the scratchy, uncomfortable woolens you wore then. They are the finest Australian Lambs' Wool, with all the warmth and absorptive qualities of wool, but mixed with just enough high-grade Southern cotton to give them softness, fleeciness and strength.

How Athletes Protect Themselves

What Have I to Say?

Why, just this, Mr. Blair.

If those "KeepWarm" Athletics are all you claim, I'd like to see them. So send along a box — *at your own risk and expense* — for a week's FREE EXAMINATION

At the end of the week I will either send you the special price of $11.95 for 4 suits; or else I'll return them — *at your expense.*

Name..

Address...

City... State....................

Name of Firm
Connected With...................................... Position
or Title.....................

Your Height ....ft. ....in. Weight........lbs. Chest
Measure...............

For the vital organs of the body must be kept warm. Cold "gets to a man" unless he's amply protected from neck to knees. But nowadays, when men work so much indoors, they like to have their arms and legs free. And they ought to. Nature never intended our legs and arms to be heavily covered. Look at the animals—their fur grows no heavier on their legs in Winter than in Summer—*only on their bodies.*

"KeepWarm" Athletic underwear offers the double advantage of warmth for the vital organs and freedom for legs and arms. And wear! "Keep Warm" Athletics might be called the suits that put the "Wear" in "Underwear."

Just take a look at them! Costs nothing to do that. The enclosed card brings them to you in a factory unit of four to a box at the special Direct-to-the-User price of $11.95. Try to buy their equal in stores at less than $4 to $7 a suit!

But never mind what we SAY about them—look them over for yourself. You'll find a new kind of winter comfort, and a new way to save money by buying DIRECT!

Yours for the straightest route
—the Direct-by-Mail Line.

Why did I not find that out before I wrote the circulars? Principally because it would have done no good if I had. The manufacturer had "sold" the buying department on the idea, so it had to be tried to be proved feasible or other-wise. Individual opinions counted for little with us, no matter whose they were. It was not one of us we were trying to sell. It was the consuming public. So the only voice we heeded was the voice of a customer.

But most of our tests were not so sterile. There were bath robes, for instance; and woolen socks; and winter underwear of the regular kind; and motor robes; and a number of other products that we shall come to presently.

March marked the beginning of the regular mailings. March, in other words, ushers in Spring, and Springtime means first raincoats, then shirts and Summer underwear, then traveling bags and the like.

So we started the Spring mailings with a letter on topcoats. But we had found that the feature of a topcoat which had the greatest pulling power was its rainproofness; so we called our topcoat first "The Keepdry," and later "The AnyWeather." Of course, as always, we tried several different letters, but here is the one that got the palm:

DEAR SIR:—

If you are thinking of buying a Spring topcoat, a raincoat, a motorcoat, a light-weight overcoat—

Don't!

For you can buy them all in a "Keepdry" *at one low Direct-by-Mail price.* The "Keep dry" is all these coats in one. It is the ideal coat for Spring, but good for any season—and for many seasons. For everywear—everywhere.

Light and smart as a sportcoat—the "Keepdry" sheds the hardest rain. Distinctive in cut, material and design, correctly tailored in every detail—the "Keepdry" protects you from the heaviest downpour.

For between the smart gray cloth of the outer fabric and the handsome plaid lining is a thin film of pure rubber—soft and pliable as silk, but rain-proof and water-proof.

Out at the Country Clubs, or in town on business—wherever smartly dressed men go in cloudy weather, you see the "Keepdry." For it keeps a secret. Most raincoats are just plain raincoats—only that and nothing more. The "Keepdry" conceals the fact that it is a raincoat until the rain begins.

Every man needs a coat like it for rainy days—for chilly nights—for auto rides. With a "Keepdry" in your wardrobe you are equipped for any weather. Why, every day sees letters coming to our office like this one from Mr. A. J. Duteil, Vice-President and Treasurer of the

Southern Ohio Portland Cement Company—

"I never got as much comfort and satisfaction out of any coat as I have from the 'Keep dry.' I had been looking for such a garment for years—a coat I could wear on all occasions and be proud of."

The lowest price at which we were able to figure these good coats last Spring—or for several years before—even on huge quantity production basis, even after leaving out all needless salesmen and figuring our costs Direct-to-the-User, was $17.85 to $23.50.

But you know how most factories are—idle or working only part time for 2 or 3 months of the year; while the overhead, rents, interest charges, salaries, etc., go merrily on. This year we decided to change all that, so we kept the "Keepdry" factory steadily busy at full time, making up "Keepdry" Coats for the Spring.

The resultant saving we can now pass on to you.

Instead of the $17.85 to $23.50 price we had to charge last Spring and in previous years, or the high price that customers tell us they would have to pay in stores, we can now give you a new, improved "Keep dry," better than any we have ever before been able to offer, for only $14.65.

There is only one condition—one string to this offer. *Your order must come in promptly.*

Naturally, we cannot continue this price on coats made during the regular season. It holds good only on those made up in advance.

So it's very important that you fill in your height and weight on the enclosed card and mail it right away.

This won't put you under any obligation, you know, for if you don't like the "Keepdry," you have only to return it at our expense and that ends the matter.

Will you send this postcard for a free trial? *Today?*

I'll be waiting,

That letter sold a good many thousands of AnyWeather Coats, even in the Spring season. Spring, by the way, is only half as good as Fall for selling topcoats or suits. And the same letter will bring in twice as many orders in the Fall as in the Spring. The above letter pulled well, however, even in the Spring.

We followed it with a mailing on shirts, using the letter we had tested the previous Fall. And how those shirts did sell! In a couple of years we brought our shirt sales up to more than 350,000 a year! Here is the letter that started them:

DEAR SIR:

In our fathers' day, you know, all fine shirts were hand-made—that meant quality, but high cost.

Today you can buy as good a "LongWear" Shirt—all "ready-to-wear," and perfect-fitting—*at about half the cost!*

For when we fit you in a shirt, we don't take merely your neck measurement, and trust the rest to chance. No—we figure out from your height and weight and collar size, how much you need across the shoulders to give you free swing, and yet look trim and well-tailored; just how much to allow you around the waist to make your shirt look right SITTING or STANDING; how long your sleeves should be; how long the body.

You see, we're not confined to a few standard sizes like a retail store. Where they cater to a few hundred or a few thousand customers, we have 308,000. Where they carry shirts in a few standard sizes and a few sleeve lengths, we have *45 sizes and sleeve lengths!*

That is why "LongWear" shirts look as different on you as a custom-made suit of clothes. That is why they fit you so well "all over "—neckband, shoulders, chest, waist, sleeves.

But that isn't all!

"LongWear" shirts are made of *woven madras* instead of printed percale. For that reason they will hold their color in spite of repeated launderings. The madras cloth is woven fine and firm—there are more threads to the inch each way than in many shirts.

More than that, though. By concentrating all our efforts on three desirable patterns (the finest looking we can find) and selling three to a box (just as they are original-ly packed in the factory), we are able to offer you these

241

"LongWear" shirts DIRECT-BY-MAIL at only $4.95 for the three, *postpaid.* (Though fine woven madras shirts are known to sell in retail stores for much more.)

And if you will drop the enclosed card in the mail at once, before the heavy Fall demand begins, we will send the three shirts to you *at our own risk and expense* for a week's inspection FREE!

Send no money—pay nothing on delivery. Just tell us how tall you are, how much you weigh, and what size shirt you usually wear. Then sit back and watch results!

But you will have to mail the card right away!

Hastily yours,

What is there about shirts that makes some finer than others

The point in the letter which seemed to have the strongest appeal was the fact that we had so many sizes and sleeve lengths that we could easily fit any one. Yet as it worked out, we had fewer complaints about fit in shirts than in almost any other product that required fitting.

Notice the circular. We tried several different illustrations for that first page, and much to our surprise, the one of shirts hanging on a line considerably outpulled any other.

On the inside we found that our most effective way of driving home the selling features was the 1, 2, 3, 4 method, while the pointing arrows made the strongest appeal of all.

On the last page, we tried always to bring home the "free-trial-no-money" feature, and when possible, we put in a good, strong testimonial or two to make our assertions more convincing.

Another product we tried alone for the first time that Spring was silk socks. You would think, easy as it is for a man to go into any store and buy himself silk hose, that it would be difficult to sell him a dozen pairs at a time by mail. But it was not. That Spring we sold some 20,000. And that was just the start. Silk hose, too, came to be one of our big sellers. And here is the letter that started them

DEAR BUSINESS MAN:

I am going to send you within the next few days a box of twelve pairs of "LongWear" Silk Hose.

This "LongWear" Silk Hose is probably not like the silk socks you are now wearing because:

1. "LongWear" Hose is made of Pure Thread Japan Silk, while lots of "silk" hose nowadays is made partly of artificial silk to cheapen it.

2. The silk in "LongWear" hose is 11-strand, which makes it heavy and rich looking, instead of 9-strand with invisible metal loading which becomes brittle and soon makes holes.

3. The feet of "LongWear" Hose are made OVER-SIZE— just like good automobile tires—actually larger than most hose, so they will wear much longer.

4. The sole is double thickness and the heel and toe and top are made of fine mercerized lisle that wears and wears and wears.

I am going to send this hose to you—with no obligation on your part—for you to inspect and actually see the difference between it and the hose you now wear.

But—there's just one thing—I can't send the hose until you tell me the size you wear. You can do that in a jiffy on the enclosed postcard.

When I send the hose, there's absolutely no obligation on your part to pay for them. You can return the hose for ANY reason, or for no reason at all.

But Here's the Most Important Part

If you find these "Long Wear" socks are everything I say about them (and you're to be the sole judge), how much would you expect to pay for them? 75¢ a pair? No sir, that's what you'd expect to pay for silk hose with all the tricks of "loading" and "skimping." $1 a pair—the price that other real good hose sells for? That's more like it.

Well—if you decide to keep the "LongWear" socks, you need send me only $7.95 for the twelve pairs. That's the entire cost to you. Only sixty some cents a pair.

How can we do it? First, we sell the hose only in the "wholesale" lot of one dozen—the same amount that hundreds of dealers buy at a time. Second, you deal direct with us by mail and you pay none of the costs of selling through Jobbers and Traveling Salesmen who call on dealers, to say nothing about the heavy costs of ordinary retailing.

Just fill out the enclosed card and shoot it back. The "LongWear" Hose will come by Parcel Post (prepaid, of course) with no obligation on for you to keep them. You can't lose a penny. *I'm* the one who is *asking* to send them. Won't you let me?

Send the card NOW! Then sit back and watch results.

Yours for "LongWear" in GOOD Hose,

That brought us to the traveling bag season. All through the Spring we had been testing different letters on traveling bags, hoping to find one that would enable us to duplicate our sale of 50,000 bags of the year before. But not one of our appeals seemed to register. Apparently we had sold every one in our lists who had any idea of buying a traveling bag.

But we knew there must be some appeal that would put bags over, so we kept trying, and presently we found it.

You must know that one of the things we had learned in sending mailings to our customer lists ten or twelve times a year, was the need for varying the appearance of our letters and circulars. We found that if we used the same style of envelope and the same old letterhead month after month they were never even opened; but when we changed everything about them, even their size and color

245

and the corner cards, it was like circularizing a brand new list—so much better were the results.

That is what finally gave us the idea for our successful circular on traveling bags. If, as it seemed, our last offer had been so good that it had combed out of all the available lists every possible order, then our only chance for more was to make our next offer as different as possible from the previous one.

And that is what we proceeded to do. Instead of a letter, circular and card, we used a "giant letter," 9 by 14 inches, with a doubled sheet like a four-page letterhead, and on the inside pages we put a full-size picture of the traveling bag, opened so as to show the convenient arrangement of the pockets, and with a full description alongside calling attention to every feature. Here is the letter and the illustrations that went on the inside pages:

MY DEAR SIR:

Once in a blue moon the announcement is made of a new invention of such great importance as to warrant calling your attention to it—IN ADVANCE OF MANUFACTURE!

Word has just come from the inventor that a patent has been granted on a new LOCK for Traveling Bags which we believe will revolutionize the whole Traveling Bag industry.

For this new Lock has automatic clasps and does away with all the bother incident to closing the ordinary Traveling Bag, snapping the clasps and fastening the lock. It is AUTOMATIC—and it is SAFE.

But that isn't all!

This new "Statler" Traveling Bag has 10 *handy, moisture-proof pockets* to hold your comb and brush, shaving set, toothpaste and tooth brush—even your shirts, underwear and collars!

With this new "Statler" everything is right at your fingertips. You can pack your bag in *half* the time it used to

246

take. Bottles can't tip over. Your clothes will not be wrinkled. There's "a place for everything and everything in its place."

AND IN ADDITION TO THIS, the new "Statler" Bag has all the improvements that made the old "Statler" so famous—the genuine cowhide leather, so tough and durable it will last a lifetime, the double handles, the solid brass hardware.

YOU WON'T BE ABLE TO BUY A BAG COM-BIN-
ING ALL THESE FEATURES IN ANY STORE' THIS
YEAR FOR $25!

But to those of our friends who will send the enclosed Reservation Card at once, we are going to make a special Introductory Price on the first of these new Bags to come from the factory, of $14.75—lower even than our old "Statler" sold for last Summer.

This special price holds good on the first few Bags. The fact is that we don't know how much more expensive these new locks and frames are going to be to make than the old ones. These first bags will enable us to find out. *You* benefit by our need, if you reserve your bag now.

And it's all at our risk. You send no money—obligate yourself in no way. Just your name and address on the enclosed Reservation Card are all that is necessary. But your card must be mailed right away!

Yours—for SERVICE,

Again this was a case of adapting an idea from the book business, and showing that an idea which will sell one product successfully is just as potent in moving others. The "Once in a Blue Moon" announcement had been used in bringing out a book of unusual interest. It worked even more successfully in announcing a new feature on a traveling bag, for with this and a similar letter we sold another 50,000 traveling bags that Summer!

There were two or three details about this giant letter that added materially to its pulling power. The sample of the cowhide was one. We found that putting it on the letter added from 15 to 30 per cent to the number of orders.

Another was a "$1,000 Reward" featured on the last page. That created more comment and seemed to do more towards satisfying prospective buyers that the bag was all we claimed than any other feature of the letter. It worked so well that we used it later on other items such as rain coats, overcoats and the like. You will find it illustrated in a later shirt letter.

While we were testing different letters on the traveling bag, and before we had hit upon the successful giant form of appeal, we tried several other forms of bags, among them a Gladstone. This was a new product with us, so we decided it was another chance to try the value of that "will you do me a favor" appeal. It worked, of course. I have seldom known it to fail. So we added something like 15,000 Gladstone bags to our 50,000 sale of regular traveling bags. Here is the letter that did it:

DEAR CUSTOMER:

This letter is purely personal and does not seek business. Rather, it invites a courtesy from you, appreciating the fact that if—in your considerate way—you can help another by a simple act of politeness, you will do so— and gladly.

Here is the way of it:

For three years now, you know, we have been selling the famous "Statler" Traveling Bag direct to the consumer at a saving of a good many dollars from the usual retail puce.

But many of our customers have written us that they want a bag that will hold a couple suits of clothes without wrinkling, besides their clean linen, shoes, toilet articles, etc., in a size that will fit easily under a Pullman berth, and of the right weight for carrying by hand.

So this Spring we are bringing out a fine new "Gladstone" Bag, made of genuine cowhide leather—so sturdy it will last a lifetime—over a steel frame, with massive solid brass hardware, *sewed* leather edges and heavy leather corners.

But here, I believe, is the *Biggest Improvement* ever put into any kind of Gladstone Traveling Bag. This new

"Gladstone" has 8 handy pockets which give you a special place for each of your toilet accessories—comb and brush, shaving set, tooth brush and tooth paste—even your shirts, pajamas, underwear and collars! Not only does it put everything right at your finger tips. Not only can you pack your bag in *half* the time. But everything is kept separate! Your clothes are never mussed or wrinkled. Bottles can't tip over, and even if one breaks no harm is done, for each of the tidy pockets is *rubber lined.*

For anyone who wants an unusual piece of QUALITY Luggage, built to endure, I don't believe he could find the equal of this new "Gladstone" Bag for less than $30.00. At a very low price like $19.85, I believe these Bags will "sell like hot-cakes." But you know how it is in merchandising—you can never be sure of such things until after you have sunk a lot of money in them.

Which brings me to the courtesy I want to ask of you:

I'd like to make sure of the demand—or lack of demand— before we sink too much money in this new bag. So I'm writing to a number of our own customers to ask each of you this:

Will you try out one of these new "Gladstone" Bags for me for a week—USE IT—take it on a trip, notice its convenience, its fine appearance—see how it compares with bags that retail in stores for $30.00? And then write me?

Needless to say, I'll send you a Bag you can be proud to take with you to the most exclusive home or hotel—a Bag that in appearance as well as quality and convenience will compare with any you meet on the Twentieth Century Limited.

Just put your name and address on the enclosed "Special Privilege Card" and I'll send you one of these new "Gladstone" Bags by prepaid Parcel Post—to be used for a week *at my risk and expense*—FREE!

At the end of a week, if you should like the Bag so well that you want to keep it, you can pay—NOT the $30 or $35 you are accustomed to paying in stores, BUT OUR SPECIAL INTRO-DUCTORY PRICE TO YOU OF ONLY $19.85.

Otherwise just send it back at our expense, and in payment for the week's use, tell me frankly your honest opinion of the Bag and of its salability.

Naturally, however, your opinion will be of value to me only if I get it NOW—when the Vacation travel season is just opening—before we definitely authorize the manufacture of any great quantity of these new "Gladstone" Bags.

Won't you, therefore, fill in your name and address on the card *tonight if you can,* and mail it? On second thought, better mail it right away—while you have it in your hand— so there will be no chance of forgetting it.

I thank you for your courtesy.

Yours for mutual cooperation,

The Fifth Feature.

One amusing feature of this sale was an experiment we made with special delivery stamps. We filled in 1,000 letters very carefully, and instead of the usual 1 or 2 cent stamp, we sent the letter special delivery. The results jumped from the 3 per cent we got on ordinary postage to 9 per cent from the 1,000 special delivery letters.

That was too good to pass up, so we made our entire mailing special delivery. Wow! What a roar went up! When a man is wakened out of a sound sleep in the middle of the night by the ringing of his front door bell, and stumbles down the steps to find a messenger with a special delivery letter, you can feel sure you have his attention. Visions of sickness and sudden death flit through his mind. He tears open the envelope in fear and trembling, reads a few paragraphs and finds that the only thing wrong is that we want him to try a new Gladstone. Oh, boy, what a feeling!

It was a good thing most of our customers lived a long distance away, so they had time to cool off before they reached us. But distance did not cool the letters they wrote. They just about took off the hide! We did not try that again, for in the first place, on the big run our orders dropped down to 6 per cent, and in the next we angered so many of our customers that even double the number of orders would not have been worth the price.

That Summer there was hardly a product that did not go well. Silk socks, shirts, underwear—everything we could think of in the line of men's wear.

Then we came into the Fall and the coat season. Giant letters had done so well on traveling bags that we decided to try them on topcoats as well. Sure enough, they greatly out-pulled the ordinary letter and circular, so we made our big sale that Fall with giant letters. Here is the one. that did the trick on topcoats.

DEAR SIR:

I'm writing you this "Giant Letter" because I'm very anxious to get your frank opinion concerning a new product which we're just about ready to market. It's the "AnyWeather" Topcoat.

To attempt to produce a really fine-looking light overcoat of all-pure-wool cloth at less than half the price that topcoats usually sell for may strike you as presumptuous. It did *me* at first—after fifteen years experience in the cloth

252

line. Nobody had ever done it before. But along came a happy combination of circumstances. And I grew enthusiastic over the job.

Wool, you know, has been high ever since the War. Last February it hit the toboggan. *The first of June, it was selling for 36% less than in February!* Then it went up again. We were watching it so closely that we got in almost at the very bottom.

With our wool costing about a third less, if we could only cut the manufacturing cost as much, we could possibly afford to sell all-wool topcoats for half the usual price—the sales would be so big. And the factory tells us it CAN cut the costs *if we'll let them gear up to make as many as 20,000 Topcoats at a run.*

So I'm writing this "Giant Letter" to you and a number of other representative men in different sections of the country to ask you this:

Will you please look at one of the sample Coats the factory has made up—try it on—WEAR IT FOR A WEEK at my risk and expense—and then tell me what you think of it?

You see, I'm anxious to find out now—in advance of the Fall season—how many of these coats I can hope to sell this Fall. And it's on your opinion, and that of these few other selected business men that I'll base my plans. Will you help me, please, by using the enclosed card right away? If you think the "AnyWeather" equal to or better than topcoats you've seen for $25 or $30, I'll deeply appreciate your telling me so, and I'll be further grateful if you'll give me your judgment as to what selling price I should try to figure these coats down to, in order to sell 20,000 of them in a single season. $19? $18? $17?

If you should want to keep the sample "AnyWeather" after your week's tryout, I'll make you a special INTRODUCTORY PRICE on it of $14.85. Otherwise you can just return it at my expense and accept my thanks for your courtesy and advice.

Will you try this out for me, and then drop me a line—as one business friend to another?

Sincerely yours,

When we came to overcoats, however, we found the giant a bit passé. We had been working it too hard. So we changed back to the letter and circular and had our usual big sale of overcoats. The following is the letter that worked best:

Coats that Will Last—
In a Sale that Won't!

DEAR CUSTOMER:—

Here is one of those "Specials" that we let our customers and friends in on every once in a while.

Wool, you know, has been high ever since the War. This Spring it hit the toboggan. At the end of May it was selling for fully 36% less than in February. Now it is back up again.

But while it was down, we got in our orders with the Mill for enough fine, double-texture all-wool cloth for 4,000 "KeepWarm" Overcoats! We tried to get more, but the Mills wouldn't tie themselves up for any bigger quantity at this low price.

Then during the Summer, when the factory would otherwise have been idle, we had them make up these Coats in this Winter's new model, with its long, flowing lines, set off by broad lapels and deep patch pockets.

The result is that, while in style, in workmanship and in fabric these Coats are as fine as any we have ever offered, we can sell them to you *for only* $26.50! The equals, mind you, of coats we have sold in the past for up to $40.

And that isn't all. So sure are we of their unusual value that we will send you one of the coats themselves—in your own exact size—for you to SEE, to EXAMINE, to ACTUALLY TRY OUT AND WEAR FOR A WEEK at our risk and expense!

255

There is only one string to this offer—one condition of any kind. You must use the enclosed Special Reservation Card *at once*. Naturally, bargains such as these will be snapped up quickly. We got only enough cloth for 4,000 coats. We couldn't get any bigger quantity without paying a lot more money for it. When these 4,000 coats are gone, the sale closes.

All you have to do is pencil on the card how tall you are, how much you weigh and what size collar you wear. By return mail, your "KeepWarm" Coat will come to you—not merely in your exact size, but in the right length for a man of your height and weight. No money. No risk. No obligation.

But use the card today! Cards received too late will be acknowledged with a note of regret, for we have only 4,000 of these good "KeepWarm" Overcoats to sell at this special price, and it may be years before such a happy combination of circumstances occurs again.

Yours—for SAVINGS,

In between the mailings on these more important products, we sent out small efforts on such items as woolen socks, underwear, bath robes, etc., most of which did well enough, but not to be compared in volume with the sales of coats and bags.

To show you the limitations we labored under, one of the things we tried was trunks. We got the orders all right, but the trunks were so bulky we had to ship them by freight. It was a couple of weeks on the average before the customer received his order, and by that time he was so disgusted with our service and the trunk was so scarred from handling that he fired it right back to us. So we never proceeded beyond the test.

At times we tried clocks, watches and the like, too, but found that mechanical defects caused so many complaints and returns that they took too much of our time. So we dropped them.

For Christmas we had our perfume offer from the previous year's test, so we merely tried a few other items with an eye to the following year. Remembering what a sale we had had on traveling bags in the Summer, you would hardly think these would make a good Christmas offering, yet of all the tests we made, the following on traveling bags pulled the best results:

DEAR CUSTOMER:

"What on earth shall I give him?"

Choosing the "just-right" Christmas gift for business associate, or brother, or son is a perplexing problem. You want to put your personality into the present, to give some-thing that possesses individuality, something that will be a pleasant reminder of your thoughtfulness for years to come. We know how you feel, and for you we have a gift that will please any man.

You know how every man admires a really fine Traveling

257

Bag. Most Traveling Bags are just plain carry-alls. You dump everything into the bottom of the bag, and then you rummage through the mass for what you want.

All of that has been done away with in the new "Statler" Bag. Along one side of the bag are 8 moisture-proof pockets for your every toilet need. Along the other are three long, deep pockets, for shirts, ties, handkerchiefs, underwear, papers, etc., leaving the whole bottom free to pack clothing or bulky objects. It is the biggest improvement, we believe, that has been made in Traveling Bags in twenty years.

And now a new improvement has been added—a patented. AUTOMATIC LOCK that does away with all the bother incident to opening or closing the old Traveling Bag. Lock and clasp all spring open at the mere pressure of your thumb. And close the same way. They are AUTO-MATIC—and they are SAFE!

3 Distinguishing Marks

For a really distinctive gift, I don't believe you can find the equal of the "Statler" within $10.00 of its price. Certainly, if the half of our customers' letters are to be believed, you cannot find it in the luggage field.

So sure are we of this that we will gladly send one of the new, improved 1926 Model "Statler" Bags to you—at our own risk and expense—*for a week's* FREE TRIAL.

Send no money. Pay nothing on delivery. Just your name and address on the enclosed "Special FREE-TRIAL" Card are all that is necessary. But it will have to come in promptly, for we had the factory make up only 1,000 of these new 1926 Model "Statlers" especially for Xmas gifts, and they won't be working on them again until after the Holidays.

While these 1,000 Bags last, we're going to make it— "First come, first served!"

Sincerely yours,

That marked the end of a successful year—the biggest and most successful the company had ever had. It showed that the only limit to its sales was the limit of its ingenuity in presenting its sales appeal. That—and the number of names it could lay hands on of people who had bought other products by mail.

XVIII

The Third Fifty Thousand

Beating records is a contagious disease. The moment you have broken one the urge comes upon you to show how much better than that you can do, if only to prove that breaking the first was no accident.

We had come to look upon our traveling bag sale as our business indicator. Two years in succession we had sold 50,000 bags a year, besides the Gladstones and ladies' cases which went in no small volume. Could we do it another year? Competitors were betting we could not. Towards the last of the previous season they had introduced in luggage stores all over the country a bag as like ours in appearance as two peas in a pod, which they offered as a "Special" at $1.00 less than our price!

Of course, it hurt our sale. It would have been disastrous for us if it had appeared early in the season, for the stores advertised it extensively. But our sale was practically finished before theirs started. It gave us notice, however, of what we might expect the following Summer.

True, the other bag was made of shoddy material and would not stand up under hard usage. But who was to know that by merely looking at it. On the outside it looked as good as ours. And it was priced at $1.00 less. What was the answer?

The answer came from our tests of the previous year. Looking over the records, we found that the tests we had mailed in late January and February had done just about as well on traveling bags as the same circulars mailed in June—which was the best part of the regular traveling bag season!

So we stole a march on our competitors. While they were making preparations for all the things they were going to do to us in the Summer, we got out our big mailings on traveling bags in February! And sold more than half of our 50,000 quota!

When the regular season came we mailed a few tests, of course, just to see if we could sell some more then, and found that our competitors' tactics had done just what we expected—made orders so hard to get that it did not pay us to make a mailing. So we let traveling bags rest all through the season. Then, when their campaigns were all over, we started again, and before the end of the year had disposed of the last of our 50,000 bags!

That was putting one over on them! Yet we did it with the simplest, most ordinary of letter appeals. Here is copy of one of them;

DEAR SIR:

Only once in 50 years comes a Luggage improvement like this:

You know how often you have had to struggle with the locks and snap on your Traveling Bag. You know how they catch at times—how you have to use both hands and knees to get them closed?

Here is a new Traveling Bag frame that does away with all that bother. Lock and catches are in one piece—and they are AUTOMATIC! Snap the lock and you snap them all!

A more convenient, a better-looking frame has never, we believe, been devised. So simple that any child can work it, so easily operated that it snaps open or shut at the mere pressure of your thumb and forefinger, it is still so safe that it defies the cleverest thief.

THEN IN ADDITION, this new 1926 model "Statler" Bag has all the improvements that made the "Statler" Bag famous —the genuine cowhide leather, so tough it will last forever, the double handles, the solid brass hardware, the ten handy, moisture-proof pockets that almost pack themselves.

Naturally, these new bags cost a good deal more to make than the old ones. So the price must go up. But on the first bags to come from the factory we are going to make the same low price as on the old model "Statler" Bag—*only $14.75 delivered to you!*

This price holds good only on the first bags. It is subject to withdrawal at any moment. We make it in order to introduce these new model bags quickly, knowing that with them to be seen is to sell.

The "FREE-TRIAL Card" has been numbered and recorded. If mailed at once, it will bring you, without one cent of cost or obligation, a 1926 model "Statler" Bag for a week—to be seen, to be examined, to be TRIED OUT and USED for a week at our risk and expense.

But you will have to mail it right away.

Yours—if you are prompt,

But don't imagine we were idle while the regular traveling bag season was on. Starting in late January, when we mailed our first tests on the bag, we sent nearly 18,000,000 circulars of one kind and another during that year and brought in gross orders in the neighborhood of $6,000,000. That was our banner year.

After the traveling bags we sold "AnyWeather Top-coats "—scads of them. There seemed no end to the number of topcoats the market would absorb. We sold them profitably each Spring. We sold them twice as profitably each Fall. And then the next year would roll around, and we would do the same thing over again.

Here is the letter and circular we used this time. It is the last we shall give on topcoats because, while we changed their tenor and form, the idea behind the later ones remained much the same.

DEAR CUSTOMER:

I am going to send you within the next few days one of our famous "AnyWeather" Topcoats.

This "AnyWeather" Topcoat is probably not like any Topcoat you have ever had before because:

1. The cloth in the "Any Weather" Topcoat is not only all-wool. It is *full-weight wool*—16 ounces to the yard.

2. The "Any Weather" Topcoat is designed like the lat-

262

est imported English Topcoats—therefore stylish right up to the minute.

3. The "AnyWeather" Topcoat is carefully tailored in every detail. The lining of genuine Lustra serge makes the coat slip on and off easily.

4. But here's the biggest difference: The "AnyWeather" Topcoat is *shower-proofed* so it will withstand thirty minutes of steady rain.

I am going to send this coat to you—with no obligation on your part—for you to examine and actually see the difference between it and the Topcoat you now wear.

There's just one thing—I can't send the coat until you tell me three simple measurements. Just your height, weight and collar-size. You can do that in a jiffy on the enclosed postcard.

When I send the "AnyWeather" Topcoat, there's absolutely no obligation on your part to pay for it. You can return the coat for ANY reason, or for no reason at all.

But here's the Most Important Part

If you find the "AnyWeather" Topcoat is everything I say about it (and you're to be the sole judge), how much would you expect to pay for it? $22.50? No sir, that's what you'd expect to pay for cheap "sale" Topcoats. $25 to $45—the price that most good Topcoats sell for nowadays? That's more like it.

Well—if you decide to keep the "AnyWeather" Topcoat, you need send me only $14.85. That's the entire cost to you.

How can we do it? First, we hit the wool market just right, when wool was down a few months ago, and placed our order for 60,000 yards of this fine all-wool cloth. This was probably the largest order ever placed for one kind of Top-coat cloth and a tremendous saving was made. Second, we had the factory make up more than 20,000 coats from this cloth *all at once*. We could thus take advantage of great savings in production.

Then, of course, when you deal direct with us by mail, you pay none of the costs of selling through Jobbers and Traveling Salesmen who call on dealers, to say nothing about the heavy costs of ordinary retailing.

Just fill out the enclosed card and shoot it back. The "AnyWeather" Topcoat will come by Parcel Post (prepaid, of course) with no obligation for you to keep it. You can't lose a penny. *I'm* the one who is asking to send the coat. Won't you let me?

Yours for "Any Weather,"

Two Tests
of a
Good Coat—

Then came shirts. The previous Fall we had tested the giant letter on shirts and got such good response that we decided to make a big mailing at the first opportunity. And the Spring is the best time to sell shirts. So we made our mailing. And a goodly part of our quota of 340,000 shirts was hung up then and there. Here is the letter that did it:

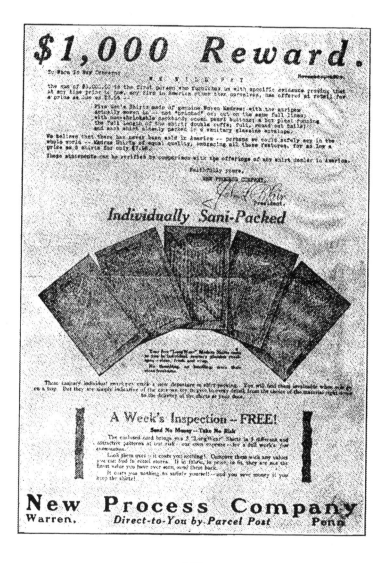

Before the Price Goes Up!

DEAR SIR:

A short time ago one of the old, reliable mills that makes the finer qualities of woven madras for shirts began sending out S. O. S. calls.

They had kept their plant going steadily for months, thinking that the usual demand would easily take care of their excess output.

But, with the weather so generally unseasonable, the usual demand didn't materialize. And there they were, heavily overstocked—and needing money.

If we would take *all* their surplus stock of the finer grades of woven madras, amounting to a *quarter of a million yards*, they offered to let us have them at away below any price we had ever paid for shirtings in all our years in business—at *far* less than they could make the materials and sell them today.

We took them—the whole quarter-million yards—at a tremendous saving in cost. There were five different patterns—as fine looking as any we've seen.

By concentrating all our efforts on these five desirable patterns and selling five shirts to a box (just as they are originally packed in the factory), we can offer these "Long-Wear" Madras Shirts delivered right to your door at only $7.95 for the five, *postpaid*.

A Bargain You May Never Get Again!

Of the quarter-million yards of fine woven Madras we got at this low price, nearly two-thirds are gone. The rest won't last long.

If you will drop the enclosed card in the mail at once, while our range of sizes is still complete, we will send

266

you a box of these fine shirts *at our own risk and expense* for a week's inspection FREE! Delay—and we don't believe you will be able to find their equal at a third higher price.

Send no money—pay nothing on delivery. Just tell us how tall you are, how much you weigh, and what size shirt you usually wear. Then sit back and watch results!

But you will have to mail the card right away, for at the rate orders are now coming in, these fine Madras shirts will all be gone in another couple of weeks.

What was it sold these? The bargain appeal, of course. But a bargain offer is of no use unless you make it convincing. We had a real reason for our bargain, so it succeeded. And we backed up the bargain with seven points, which showed the buyer that despite the low price, he was getting every feature of a fine shirt.

That is even more essential, you know, than the bargain, for though low price is a lure, it never gets far unless backed by reasonable quality.

In the Summer we followed this with a sale of broadcloth shirts, and they went even better than the Madras. With them, you will notice that our sales talk was aimed more at comfort and fine appearance and quality than at any bargain appeal. Of course, we always had in the back of our minds the fact that no man is going to the trouble of sending away for things he can just as well get around the corner unless he feels that he can save money by so doing. So we never failed to bring in the money-saving. But many times our most successful pieces were those on which we sold the quality or comfort or usefulness of the product, and then brought in the money-saving as an after-thought.

DEAR CUSTOMER:

In every man's wardrobe is some particular article—a tie, a shirt, or a suit—that he likes best to wear, because he looks his best and feels his best in it.

That's the way you'll feel about these "LongWear" Broadcloth Shirts—once you've worn one of them.

In the past couple of years, you know, fine quality white Broadcloth shirts have taken the place of silk as the finest "dress up" attire for men.

The Broadcloth in the new "LongWear" Shirt is imported from England, where the finest Broadcloth is now made. It is snowy-white in color, with a lustre that rivals that of silk, and it has a subdued softness of texture that one loves to feel.

There is no way of duplicating the rare lustrousness, the durability of this genuine imported English Broadcloth.

No imitation can tailor so superbly, can retain its snowy whiteness and silky finish after repeated launderings, as can the English cloth.

An Offer We Can Never Make Again!

Last Spring, when Sterling Exchange was low, we contracted for enough fine quality English Broadcloth for 10,000 shirts. It was necessary to place that large an order to secure this fine cloth at the lowest possible figure.

Now Sterling Exchange has gone up to par, and the indications are that it will stay there—or above! If we had waited until now to order, these shirts would probably cost us—in wholesale quantities—little less than the price we can now offer them to you in lots of one-third dozen (just as they are originally packed in the factory)— only $7.95 *for four shirts*, postpaid.

But 10,000 shirts don't go far among our more than 300,000 customers. Already half of them are gone. The remainder won't last long. If you will drop the enclosed card in the mail at once, we will send you a box (1/3 dozen) of these fine shirts *at our own risk and expense* for a week's inspection FREE!

Send no money—pay nothing on delivery. Just tell us how tall you are, how much you weigh, and what size shirt you usually wear. Then sit back and watch results!

But you will have to mail the card right away, for at the rate orders are now coming in, those 5,000 will be gone in another couple of weeks.

Hastily yours,

Notice one thing in all these circulars. There is never any choice in quantity or price or any other essential feature. Occasionally we gave a choice of color, or, in the case of shirts, of collar—attached or neckband style. But when we did so, we made no mention of this in the letter. We put it inconspicuously on the order card.

The reason for this we have explained before. There is only one way you can sell a man by mail. That is to get him to act at once. Nine times out of ten, the deferred order is a lost order. You get a few of them, of course, but, they are not worth counting on. So we never intentionally put anything into a letter that would cause a man to hesitate. We centered our talk on one article, of one quality and design, one price. Where there was a group of articles, as with shirts and socks, we offered a definite number at a group price. Never a choice of—would you rather have this, or do you think this would be preferable. We centered our whole appeal upon the one unit, and stood or fell by that.

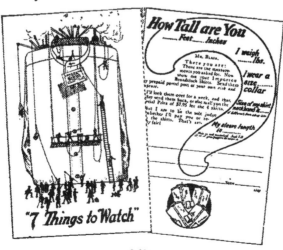

In the old days, the company had enclosed with many of their letters a circular offering a dozen other allied products. We were able to prove by conclusive tests that while this method brought a greater number of orders, the actual volume of sales was not as big as when we specialized on a single product. So for a while we confined our efforts to one product at a time.

Then came the time when we took on some women's and household products, and it occurred to us that as long as we were writing the head of the household about something for himself it might be a good idea to enclose something he could hand to his wife. But it had to be done in such a way as not to take one iota of his interest away from the product we were trying to sell him. So again we adopted an expedient of the book business and put a separate sealed envelope in with our regular circular. On the outside was some catch-phrase indicating that it was for the wife only; inside was a separate letter and circular describing blankets or linens or towels or lingerie.

That is the one way I have ever seen in which you can sell two separate and unrelated products in a single envelope, without interfering with the pulling power of your main offer. It added not merely to the number of orders received, but to the volume of actual sales. It worked so well that it has been in use ever since.

That was just one of the things we discovered that year. In the Summer we sold some 30,000 pairs of men's silk socks. Here is one of the letters that did this:

Do you know how to distinguish pure Silk Socks from "loaded" or "fibre" silk? There are three ways:

1. By fire test. Pull our a loose end of silk and touch a match to it. If "loaded" or "fibre," it will burn with a flash and leave a white or grayish ash. If pure silk, it will curl up and leave a round black ash.

2. By water test. "Fibre" silk, when wet, will easily pull apart. Pure silk, wet, is stronger than ever.

3. By feeling test. "Fibre" and "loaded" silk both have a hard, slick feeling, a flashy, glossy appearance. Pure silk is soft and yielding to the touch, with a subdued lustre all its own.

By fire test, by water test, by feeling test and by the final test of long, hard wear—" Long Wear" Silk Socks have established themselves among men who know and regard value first as the standard of quality.

And the quality is more than label deep. It permeates every thread of every sock. Just listen:

a. Made of pure thread Japan silk—and pure thread silk is stronger, strand for strand, than steel wire!

b. The silk in "LongWear" hose is 11-strand not 8 or 9-strand as in many silk socks that are priced merely to SELL.

c. Investigations show that 90% of all socks wear out at the toes first. That comes from wearing socks too small. "LongWear" Silk Socks are made slightly over-size—not enough to notice—just enough to keep that energetic big toe from stretching and pushing its way through.

d. The sole is double thickness for extra comfort, and heel, toe and top are reinforced with fine mercerized lisle for extra wear.

For the man who seeks foot-ease, "LongWear" Socks give that rare combination of ease, style and long life— all at reasonable price.

But that isn't all.

By selling these fine silk hose in wholesale lots of a dozen— the same amount that hundreds of dealers buy at one time— with none of the cost of jobbers, or traveling salesmen, or high store rentals, we are able to give them to you at the low Direct-By-Mail price of $7.95 for the dozen—only 60-some cents a palr.

And if you mail the enclosed card at once, while the season is at its height, we will send the socks to you for a week's examination at our risk and expense.

But to get "LongWear" Silk Hose on approval your card

271

must be mailed NOW!

Yours 'til then,

Then there were the broadcloth shirts mentioned above, and broadcloth underwear, and bath robes, and several other items. The bath robes proved an amusing experience.

We had tested them earlier in the season and the test had shown up well enough to justify buying some 10,000 robes, with slippers to match. But when we started to make the mailing results fell off badly. Probably the reason was that the time to sell bath robes is when the weather is cooler.

However this may be, we did not want to carry them over until Fall if we could help it, so we tried the device of offering the

*Strand for Strand--
Pure Thread Japan Silk
Is Stronger
Than Steel Wire*

slippers as a free premium, if customers would send for and try out the bath robe! You would be surprised how beautifully it worked. Those 10,000 robes melted away like snow before the Summer sun.

In the Fall we ran all our usual products and a few extra ones too. Fancy woolen socks were one of these latter. They went over very well, and here is the letter that sold them:

I am rushing out to you the first news about one of those "Specials" that we let our regular Customers in on once in a while—

This one is for the man who is used to paying a dollar a pair for his hosiery—

Only this time you need pay but 74 cents—

For the closely knit hosiery that you need for Fall and Winter—enough wool in it to make it comfortable, just enough lisle to keep it from shrinking. The design is woven in lustrous Rayon to give that dressiness of appearance that is so essential.

As good looking, as long wearing, as comfortable hose as a man would want to put on his feet. You'll never know what luxurious comfort a foot can enjoy on a bitter winter day, until your feet have snuggled into a pair of "LongWear" Socks for Fall and Winter.

Last year they sold in lots of places for $1.00 a pair. This year we can offer them to you, in special wholesale lots of 8 pairs to a box, at the amazing price of 74¢ a pair only $5.95 for the 8.

Don't think this is going to be a regular thing! It is a special offering. We have only a limited quantity to dispose of at this astonishingly low price. You can imagine how long they will last.

Don't decide now. You can do that later. Just drop the enclosed card in the mail and your 8 pairs will come to you for a week's inspection FREE. Plenty of time then to see whether you like them so well that $5.95 couldn't induce you to part with them.

Cordially yours,

Solid Comfort.
Good Looks. Too!

Topcoats, of course did well, but when it came to bed blankets, we again ran into one of those unaccountable cases where conditions change so between the test and the time of mailing that we found ourselves with 20,000 pairs of woolen blankets on our hands, and the letter we had counted on to move them was proving a "dud."

You would never guess how we got rid of them. I happened to be in the President's office one day when the stock clerk came in to complain that the blankets were not well wrapped and the ends of many of them were getting dusty. It brought to mind at once the good old damaged-set letter. So we sent out a damaged-blanket offer. Would you believe it—we sold not only those 9≥0,000, but an extra 10,000 to boot?

That brought us into the overcoat season—quite the biggest one we had ever had. And when you read the follow-up letter, you can easily see why:

DEAR DOCTOR:

Ever since I started this business, years and years ago, I've been dreaming of the time when I could offer a really good quality, fine-looking, all-wool Overcoat for less than $20.

Not, mind you, a cheap coat. But a coat that you or I could wear. A Coat we would be proud to be seen in anywhere. A snug, warm all-wool Overcoat, such as you'd never expect to meet with for less than $40 or $45.

Sounds impossible, I know, but I believe I've done it.

And to prove it, I'm going to send one to you for a week's free examination and trial. Of course, I'll need to know your height and weight in order to be able to fit you accurately, but you can easily give me these on the enclosed card.

Naturally I can't keep this up long, for it was only an extra-ordinary combination of circumstances that made this marvelously low price possible. And even then we got enough really fine-quality cloth for only a few thousand coats.

274

While they last, you can SEE and TRY OUT one of them with-out cost or obligation—merely by using the card.

If you've ever bought its equal for double the price-just send ours back, that's all. Otherwise mail us the special sale price of $19.85.

No need to tell you that bargains like these won't last long. And first come, you know, is best served.

May I hope you will mail your card today—now?

Sincerely yours,

That, with the Christmas sale, ended our biggest year, but before closing this chapter, I want to give one more example of the many products we tried out successfully, but abandoned because of the difficulty of giving a proper fit. This one was men's suits.

It is hard to imagine any one living within a few blocks of good department stores sending away out to a small town for a suit of clothes. Yet that is exactly what happened. It was not the rural districts that our orders came from. It was from the towns and cities. And we got as many orders in proportion to the number of names on our lists from big cities like New York and Chicago as from so-called "hick" towns.

Knowing that fact, perhaps the result should have been foreseen. We got the orders without difficulty, but we promptly got back about 40 per cent of the suits almost as fast as we sent them out. And the reason? *Fit.* It is comparatively easy to fit a man in a topcoat or overcoat, but when it comes to a suit he is far more particular. There are so many different places where it has to fit him, and if it fails in any of these, it is a lost sale.

So we quickly gave up the sale of suits. But the attached letter and circular may be interesting merely as examples of successful sales literature:

DEAR CUSTOMER:

Will you try this experiment?

275

Tear off the sample of "LongWear" Worsted from the inside of the folder herewith. Pull out a few ravelings of wool from one end.

Then cut a strip from the inside seam at the bottom of your trousers and pull a few strands from it.

Notice the long, strong fibres in the "LongWear" sample— Virgin wool—just as it comes from the sheep's back. Compare them with the ones from your own trousers. See how many little, short, broken looking ones there are among yours.

Wool—yes—but wool adulterated with "shoddy" taken from worn out garments, ground up and used over again!

A "LongWear" label in your suit means that it is every thread of pure Virgin wool—that it will not shrink or pucker or lose its shape—that the collar has been hand-tailored to make it fit right around the neck—that the sleeves have been hand-felled to make them comfortable under the armpits—that in style, in fit, in wearing quality, it will compare with any suit you have ever had at any price!

Try to tear that bit of sample cloth. Ever see a piece as strong? All the longest fibres of the Virgin wool are put aside, you know, for spinning into Worsteds, for only the long, strong fibres can be twisted into those compact, smooth strands. The result is a weave so firm, so crisp of finish, that it will not merely resist wear and tear, but will hold its shape and keep that new looking lustre long after any other suit would have been thrown away.

But that isn't all!

Have you ever stepped into a suit in a retail store and been able to walk right out with it without alteration of any kind? No—and neither have many other men. That's because the stores can carry suits in only 12 to 15 different sizes.

Where they have a few hundred or a few thousand customers, however, we have 318,000. Where they can carry 12 to 15 sizes, we have "LongWear" Suits in 90 different sizes and 10 different lengths!

That is the reason 'LongWear" Suits fit you as though molded to your form by your own tailor. That is the reason that the few simple measurements given on the enclosed card are enough to insure you a perfect fit.

The price?—$26.85.

And if you can match one of these suits anywhere at half as much again—well, just send ours back, that's all. The wear you have had out of it will not have cost you a cent!

You see, selling in such huge quantities as we do, we get not merely the lowest manufacturing costs, without having to pay commissions and profits to any middlemen, but we go beyond that—we get the benefit of bed-rock prices on the cloth itself! In short, we eliminate any needless middleman, selling direct to you, saving you a good share of the price— and if we don't give you as perfect fitting, as handsome looking clothes as you could get from your own tailor we don't want you to pay a cent.

To prove it, all you have to do is to fill in the few simple measurements on the enclosed card, stamp and mail. After seven days you MAY return the suit—if you want to—*and it won't have cost you a cent!*

Try it out! Never mind what we SAY about the value and fit of "LongWear" Suits—FIND OUT! It's easy. Just fill out the form and mail it. No money—no obligation.

But mail it right away, if you can. For every Fall just about October 1st, we offer some such opportunity as this to some of our old customers until a certain percentage of our output has been booked up. Naturally, such opportunities are snapped' up quickly. So it is important that you mail the card at once.

Nothing to sign. Don't send any money. Just fill in the few simple measurements on the card and mail. Your name's already on it.

At your Service,

If ever there was a business which required, as the price of success, eternal alertness and vigilance, selling by mail is it. The only thing about it you can be sure of is that you never know what you can do until you try. So we tried anything once. And some of the things we learned were surprising.

On the very day, for instance, that we read in a bulletin from some convention the speech of an expert on advertising and selling, in which he stated that no one but a fool would try a certain form of mailing, our tests showed that this particular form added 35 per cent to the pulling power of our circulars! Reminds one of the man who prayed: "Oh God, give me young men with brains enough to make fools of themselves!"

We determined early in the game that we would be guilty of every sin in the Decalogue rather than the one unpardonable sin of knowing it all. So nothing was too bizarre for us to try.

Why, we even tried addressing every man on a several hundred thousand customer list by his first name, starting our letter "Dear Jack," or "Dear Dick," and got a remarkable number of orders, but also angered so many customers that we were afraid the losses just about counterbalanced the gains, so we bracketed that with the special delivery mailing under the heading "experience," and did not try it again.

But some of the experiments did not turn out so badly. One time our purchasing agent picked up a big bargain in mufflers. When we tried to sell them, we found why they were such a "bargain." That particular type of muffler just was not selling that season. So the P. A. started to look around for a place to "job" them. Meantime, just as an experiment, and because we did not know any better, we put a slip in with every overcoat we shipped, offering the muffler at a special low price. Instead of jobbing those on hand, we had to look around for more mufflers!

We tried different styles and sizes of envelopes and found on one mailing that a picture of the town—which looked more like a picture post card than anything else and had no relation to the product we were offering—added some 10 per cent to the orders! Why? Because it attracted attention and made it easier for the reader to believe that a concern located in a little town like that ought to be able to serve him more economically than stores paying high rents in big cities.

We tried pictures on the letterhead and found that the old mail order letterheads, of which so much fun is made, showing the picture of the founder of the business, have a sound psychological reason back of them, and frequently increase orders anywhere from 5 to 10 per cent.

We tried everything—metered mail against stamped. Precancelled stamps against plain. Pen signatures against facsimile. Fill-in against running heads. Kier processed letters against stencil and typewriter fill-ins. Black ink against purple and blue and red. Printing through ribbon against type. And the trend of all the tests seemed to be that anything which tended to make your letter seem more personal added appreciably to the number of your orders.

Testing Hooven work against the best fill-ins, as' an instance, brought no extra orders for Hooven—*unless the reader's name was worked into the body of the first page two or three times!*

In other words, processed letters have become so perfect that people do not pretend to distinguish them from typewriting. But still they do not believe they are personally typed unless they see some allusion to themselves down in the *body* of the letter. Then they will believe it is personal. Then they will read it. As a rule, we found that such use of the Hooven doubled the number of orders.

These were just a few of the tests we made. There were literally hundreds of them. A book could be written about them alone. But by the time it came out it would be of little value. For the fascinating thing about this selling by mail—the thing that makes it impossible for any man or set of men to know all about it—is that it is continually changing. What you learn today you must unlearn tomorrow. You have to keep trying—and testing—and then just when you reach the point where you can arise and state with authority: "This you can do, that you cannot," along comes some darned fool who knows none of the rules and sells a million on the very plan you just said could not be worked!

XIX

Will You Accept This Little Gift?

When you have been selling one article for five or six years, when you have pushed that sale so hard that you have disposed of 50,000 a year for three years in succession, and when competition on that item has become so keen that it has come down to a cut-throat basis, it is time to see if you can not substitute some new item that will start the ball rolling all over again.

At least that is the way we felt about traveling bags. So for some time we had been testing a smaller edition of our traveling bag, to sell at just about half the price. We called it the "HandiBag."

It really started as a doctor's bag. We had lined one side of it with pockets to hold all sorts of small bottles and packets and the other side with three large pockets for papers, stethoscope and the like; and since it was a new product, we had tested it on doctors with our good old standby, the "Will you do me a favor?" letter. Here is copy of the letter, circular and card we used:

DEAR DOCTOR:

Will you do me a favor?

For several years now, you know, we have been selling Physicians' Leather Bags by mail, at a saving of a good many dollars from the usual retail price.

This year we have changed these bags so radically-- arranged the pockets and the inside so conveniently for Doctors—that I honestly believe no Physician or Surgeon can examine one without wanting it for his own.

Just listen—

On one side of the bag, five moisture-proof pockets lined with hospital rubber. You can put a bottle of iodine or acid or antiseptic solution into any of them without any fear of what will happen if the stopper comes out. On the other side, one big long pocket the full width of the bag, containing four heavy folders capable of holding your history sheets, prescription blanks, Call List, rubber gloves, etc. And the folders are easily removable, so the pockets can be used for stethoscope or surgical instruments.

The whole bottom of the bag left free for larger instruments and bulky objects.

Adjustable lock, that opens or shuts at the mere pressure of your thumb.

A more convenient bag for Physicians or Surgeons has never, we believe, been designed, but you know how it is in merchandising—you can never be sure of such things until after you have sunk a lot of money in them.

Which brings me to the favor:

I want to make sure of the demand—or lack of demand--before we sink too much money in this new "Handibag." So I've come to you with this favor:

> Will you try out one of these new Doctor's "Handibags" for me for a week—USE IT—see how convenient, how time saving, how handsome it is? How it compares with bags you have bought at $12 or $15? And then write me?

Needless to say, I'll send you our newest and finest bag, made of tough, outer "grain" cowhide--the kind that wears for years—with a richness of appearance that will not look out of place in the most exclusive home on the Avenue.

At the end of the week, if you should like the bag so well that you want to keep it, you can send me—not the $12 or $15 you would probably expect to pay for such a bag—BUT OUR SPECIAL INTRODUCTORY PRICE TO YOU, ONLY $7.95!

Otherwise just send it back at our expense, and in payment for the week's wear, tell me frankly your honest opinion of the bag and its salability.

Naturally, I am not making offers like this to everyone, so whether you accept it or not, I should feel obliged if you would return the card so as to insure against its falling into other hands.

Naturally, too, your opinion will be of value to me only if I get it NOW—before we are definitely committed for any great quantity of these new model "Handibags."

Won't you, therefore, fill in your name and address on the card TONIGHT, if you can? On second thought, better mail it *right away*—while you have it in your hand—so there will be no chance of forgetting it.

I thank you for your courtesy.

Yours for mutual co-operation,

It pulled well enough—around 4 per cent. On that basis our orders were costing us something less than 90 cents apiece, which, on a $7.95 sale, meant a selling cost of about 1 1/2per cent. That was not bad, but it was nothing to set the world afire, either. We were looking for something that would go so well that it would more than make up for the temporary dropping of the regular traveling bag. And presently we found it.

Looking over the past records one day, I came across the letter in which we offered the bedroom slippers free if people would send for the bath robe, and it occurred to me that something of the same kind might be tried with the HandiBag. You see, the bag was really so convenient and such a bargain, that we felt sure if we could once get it into a doctor's hands he would never let a little matter like $7.95 interfere with his keeping it. So we started looking around for a premium that would not cost us much, yet would have an universal appeal to every doctor.

And in a circular that drifted to my desk a few days later we found the answer. The circular described a new machine that would die-stamp names in raised letters upon such things as fountain pens at a cost of 2 to 4 cents each.

What could suit us better? Fountain pens are just about as necessary to a doctor as his prescription pad and they are continually getting mislaid. What more welcome gift than a fountain pen with his name die-stamped upon it? We would try it at once.
So we wrote to each doctor:

Will you accept one of the new, large-size, self-filling? Fountain Pens, with your name die-stamped upon it in raised letters, in return for a little favor I want you to do? The favor is a simple one, pleasant and easy to render. Here is the way of it:

And then we went on with the rest of the "Will you do me a favor" letter given above.

Did that pull? Does honey draw flies? Instead of 4 per cent our new letter brought in 12 and 14 per cent of orders! We worked our entire list of doctors. We changed the letter to make it suitable for our regular customers and worked them too. In the first two months of that year we sold 60,000 HandiBags! Here is the letter, without the fountain pen premium, as changed for the customer list:

DEAR FRIEND:

Before giving this offer wide publicity, we are laying it before a number of men whose judgment we value, with a request that they pass judgment upon the idea.

For four years now, you know, we have been selling the famous "Statler" Bag the greatest improvement, we believe, that has been made in Traveling Bags in the past 20 years.

But many friends wrote us that they had no need for as large a bag as the "Statler "—that all they wanted was a sturdy, conveniently arranged bag for overnight or week-end trips. Couldn't we give them a bag made along the same lines as the "Statler," of the same long-wearing *cowhide leather*, and with the same wonderfully handy interior arrangement—but somewhat smaller and at about half the price?

We can—and will--if we can only be sure of the demand for these *smaller-sized, lower-priced* bags before we sink a lot of money in them by putting them on the market in a "big" way. So I have come to you as a past customer of the house to ask if you will be good enough to help us out by giving us the benefit of your judgment on this new "Handibag."

Will you try out one of these new "Handibags" for us for a week--at our expense, our risk? Take it with you on a trip. Put it to any test you can think of. *And then write us*?

Needless to say, in both appearance and quality this "Handibag" is one you can feel proud of anywhere.

14 inches long by 7 inches wide and 12 inches high, it is made of tough outer "grain" cowhide--the kind that wears for years--over a shiny steel frame. Its deep, black leather, its carefully sewn seams, and its heavy, gold plated lock give it a richness of appearance that will not seem out of place in the most exclusive home.

But its unique value lies in the special arrangement of pockets on the inside—the feature that more than all else has made the "Statler" Bag so popular. These little pockets give you a special place for your every toilet need. Not only that, but if tooth-paste happens to leak or a stopper come out of a bottle, no harm is done, for these handy pockets are each one lined with moisture-proof hospital rubber!

All we want you to do is try out this new "Handibag" for a week. If at the end of that time, you should like the bag so well that you want to keep it for yourself, you can send us—NOT the $12 or $15 you would expect to pay for a genuine cowhide bag in a store—but our special Introductory Price to you—ONLY $7.95.

Otherwise all that is necessary is just to ship it back in its original container at our expense, and in payment for the week's use, give us your judgment of it's salability.

Naturally, we are not making offers such as this to everyone. Naturally, too, your advice will be of value to us only if we can get it soon—before the vacation season opens up.

Won't you, therefore, mail the enclosed card today? Better still, put your name and address on it NOW— while it's right before you, while you need but reach for your pen or pencil and then drop the card in the outgoing mail.

I thank you for your courtesy.

Yours for mutual cooperation,

286

But while one of the most profitable sales we had ever run, it proved to be indirectly the cause of the greatest debacle the company ever had.

Some time before, I had started a little publishing business of my own, and it was taking so much of my time that I felt I had best give up my out-of-town "Consultant's" work. So after the HandiBag campaign was successfully under way I withdrew. I am lucky to be able to say that, because I would probably have been as easy a victim of the new idea as were the others. Here was the way of it:

I had never been able to sell to women on a large scale as with men. Special lists like the women on our customer lists, or the wives of customers, or good mail buyers like the Davis Fish list, I could write circulars for and show as good a profit as with men. But when it came to picking up lists of women by the hundred thousand and the million, I had never been able to write anything that would bring back the orders in profitable volume.

But when the HandiBag went over so successfully on a premium appeal, it occurred to some bright soul that women were even more

"Try This in a Pullman."

susceptible to *free* offers than men, so why not pick some likely woman's product and put over a big sale on it?

Sounded reasonable, and excepting for an unfortunate experience of the kind I had had once before, I am sure I would have fallen for it as readily as did the others. Be that as it may, they scouted around for a suitable product and finally hit upon silk stockings.

They wrote to miscellaneous lists of women:

Will you accept a pair of beautiful silk stockings, pure thread silk from top to bottom, in return for a little favor I want you to do?

The favor is a simple one, pleasant and easy to render. Here is the way of it:

I am going to send you in the next few days a box of six pairs of the finest pure silk stockings, in the newest pastelle shades. When they arrive, look them over, pick out the pair you like best and put it on; actually *wear* it for a day; then wash it and wear it again:

Then if you don't agree with me that it is as fine a pair of silk stockings as you have ever had on your feet—if in lustre and feel and wear it is not the equal of any you can buy in stores *at any price—keep that pair as my gift* and return the box with the other five pairs at my expense.

Of course, there was more to the letter than that, but those were the salient points. Did it pull? I leave you to guess. In three months' time it brought orders for more than 600,000 pairs of silk stockings!

For a while it looked as though all we had done in the past was merely the efforts of pikers. On a single product, going to people we had never been able to sell successfully in any large way, they had orders amounting to more than $750,000. Then came the morning after--and oh, what a headache! It looked for a time as though the whole works were going by the board. Talk about the time we stood $80,000 in the red on the first of June! That was mere chicken feed. It looked as though they stood to lose three or four times that now!

I had a hurry call to drop everything and come up for a couple of months at any price. I found that of the more than 100,000 boxes of stockings shipped, 72 per cent were being returned, *minus one pair in each box*, and of the balance, some 10,000 accounts were uncollectible.

A sad enough prospect, truly, but when we tried to "job" those returned stockings it looked even more so. We could not get even half the price that had been paid for them. One-fourth was the best we were offered, and to add that tremendous loss to the amount already dropped on the sale would almost swamp everything. So we decided that we would have to sell the stockings by mail. And at a price that would leave us at least a slight profit.

Some undertaking, I think you will agree. Selling 360,000 pairs of silk stockings is a hard enough job at best, but when you have just worked all your available lists on an offer such as the one that had been used, and when those stock-mailings are "returns," it makes the difficulties look almost insurmountable.

But it is surprising what you can do when you have to. We had to sell those stockings. So we did! Though it took every different kind of "sale" I had ever heard of and some I had not.

To begin with, we sat down and wrote every manner of sales appeal on stockings that we could think of. Then we tried them all—some twelve or fourteen of them. Of the lot, four pulled surprisingly well! So we took them in order and used each on our entire available list about a month apart. By the end of the year the stockings were gone, and instead of a tremendous loss, we showed for the year's efforts a net profit of $18,000.

That looked pretty sickly after the big figures we were accustomed to, but ~any sort of black figures looked good to us then. It had been hard scratching, and we were thankful enough to be so well out of it.

To give you an idea of the endless methods we had used:

We had never been able to sell to teachers. But some one suggested that we offer them a special discount in return for their giving us the names of five parents who would make likely prospects for our silk stockings. The result was that we not only sold this new list at a fair profit but disposed of a large number of stockings to teachers, on which we made a slight profit as well!

Then we happened to be moving into new quarters, so of course we used that to stage "The first removal sale in our history." From that we went on to a 1 ct. sale, a combination sale—every kind of sale, in short, excepting a fire sale. And if the new building had not been so fireproof, we might have been tempted to have one of those too.

We managed to get out with a whole skin. But it was a close shave.

That is one of the great things about selling by mail. It puffs you up one day so you think you are the greatest thing on two feet. The next, it pricks the bubble and lets you down with a dull, heavy thud. Talk about a little knowledge being a dangerous thing! A little knowledge can drop money faster selling by mail than gambling in the stock market.

And yet, properly run, there is no safer business on earth. You need never risk anything but the cost of a test. At the Review of Reviews, for instance, when Wells' "Outline of History" was offered to us, we didn't need to say: "All right, we'll gamble on that," or "We can't afford to risk that much money." No indeed! All we said was: "Give us a sixty-day option and we'll find out!" So we gambled the cost of a couple of tests, found that we could sell so many sets to each thousand names we circularized, multiplied that by the number of names available, and knew just what we could safely contract to do.

There was no manufacturing cost, no inventories to worry about, no commitments. If the test had been a failure, we would have bought enough of the bookstore edition to fill the orders received and been out nothing but the small cost of the tests. If the bookstore edition had not been available we would have returned all money received, notified those who ordered that circumstances made it impossible to go ahead with the project, and closed the matter. Is there any other business where future projects can be forecast with such certainty and at such small expense?

XX

One Million Dollars' Worth of Orders in the
First Six Months

IN THE last chapter we mentioned how easy it is to try the sale of any article by mail and how safely the selling possibilities can be forecast. It was this that tempted us into starting a little publishing business of our own.

For a long time we had had the idea for a set of books on practical psychology. Like most such ideas, it seemed likely to stay in the back of our mind and that nothing would ever come of it. Until one day we got an idea for a sales letter that would sell such a book! That was a different matter. Sales letters were our daily bread and butter. Sales letters were unlike books in that when you got an idea for one of them, you used it! So we got that one down on paper as quickly as might be.

Even in the cold light of the next morning it looked good. In fact, it looked so good that we decided to try a few thousand as a test. Of course, the books were still in nebulous form, but we knew what they were going to contain (when and if issued) so we proceeded to outline all of that in our letter and circular. Then we mailed 1,000 to each of ten different lists. Here they are!

Mr. J. Kilgore,
317 Dover St.,
Hot Springs, Ark.

DEAR MR. KILGORE:

Would you like to see $1.00 grow to $60.00—$8.00 grow to $500.00—by next April?

Let me tell you how:

I am going to send within the next few days a set of seven little books.

These books are probably not like any you have ever seen before because:

1. They are about YOU!

2. They show you that you have been using but a small part of your real abilities—that back in your "subliminal mind," as the scientists call it, is a sleeping Giant who, awakened, can carry you on to fame and fortune almost overnight! A Genie-of-your-Brain as powerful, as capable of satisfying your every wish, as was ever Aladdin's wonderful Genie-of-the-Lamp of old.

3. They make your Day Dreams, your visions of wonderful achievement, of fortune, health and happiness--COME TRUE--not five, ten, or fifteen years from now, but TODAY, A. D. 1926!

I am going to send these little books to you—with no obligation on your part—for you to read and ACTUALLY TRY OUT for a week at my risk and expense.

But--there's just one thing—I don't want to send them without first getting your permission. You can grant that in a moment on the enclosed special "Courtesy Card."

When I send the books, there's absolutely no obligation on your part to pay for them. You can return them for ANY reason, or for no reason at all.

But Here's the Most Important Part:

If you find these little books are everything I say about them (and you're to be the sole judge), how much would you expect to pay for them! $30.00? $50.00? $100.00? That's what ordinary courses, which merely promise to show you how to do some special kind of work, cost you. Certainly if this one will do the half of what I've promised you, it will be worth all of that—and more!

292

Well if you decide to keep these books, you need send me--NOT $50.00 or $100.00, not even their regular price of $13.50 --but my SPECIAL INTRODUCTORY PRICE TO YOU, good only on this ADVANCE EDITION, of $7.85!

And that isn't all!

> If within six months your $1.00 hasn't grown to $60.00— if you can't credit to the $7.85 you pay for this Course at least $500.00 of ADDITIONAL EARNINGS—send back the books and I'll refund to you cheerfully and in *full every cent you have paid to me for them.*

There are no conditions—no strings of any kind to this offer. If within six months these little books have not brought you the pot of gold at the foot of the rainbow, then they are not for you. Send them back and get your money!

So don't decide about buying now. You can do that later. Send me only the FREE-TRIAL "Courtesy Card," with your name and address on it. Then, AFTER the week's try-out--AFTER you have summoned your Genie and put him to the test--you can send me your dollar or return the books. I'll pay the charges both ways.

But you'll have to send the card right away, for I'm printing only a small number of Autographed Sets for this "Advance Edition." And advanced orders are coming in so fast now that I'm afraid all of them will be spoken for even before the sets are ready.

So if you want to try out your hidden powers *without cost and without obligation*, you'll have to mail the enclosed card *now* —TODAY!

Yours—for DREAMS COME TRUE,

Did they pull? The returns from that letter and circular almost gave us heart failure. They pulled as high as 9 per cent from lists of people who had never heard of us before! They pulled so well that we worked every night for the next month or so getting our books written. And as soon as they were ready we arranged for the mailing of a million circulars, following these as soon as might be with a second million.

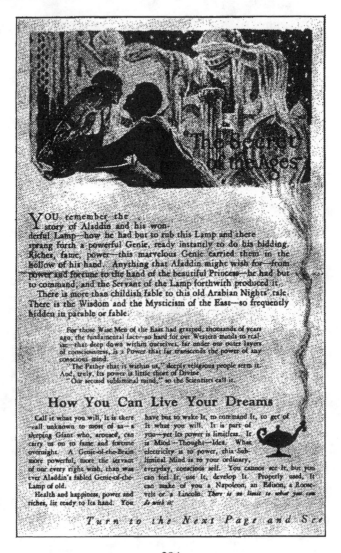

Within 6 months after the books were ready we had received more than $1,000,000 worth of orders for them--all in answer to the letter and circular quoted above!

Of course, a lot of the books came back. They would, when oversold as much as this letter and circular did oversell them. The idea had been excellent, but no book ever written could quite come up to such a promise. But those who did like the books did not think they were oversold. Judging by some of the letters we received, they felt that everything we had promised them had come true.

So it is a question how much of a mistake that overselling was. When the cost of shipping averages only 16 cents, it would seem better to get from 4 to 9 per cent of orders and have 40 per cent of them returned, than to receive the 1 or 2 per cent most publishers are satisfied with and have only 10 per cent of them come back. At any rate, the former is certainly the quicker way to build a customer list. And build one we certainly did in short order. By the end of the first year we had well over a hundred thousand names on our books.

The second year we extended the sale by the simple expedient of finding new names and mailing the same offer to them. Meantime, we had found it necessary to change the name of the books. The first set had been called "The Book of Life," but after selling it for a year we learned that another concern had been marketing a book of that name for years, so we changed the name of ours to "The Secret of the Ages." (In the letter quoted above, the title is given as "The Secret of the Ages," though the original edition was offered as "The Book of Life.")

As long as we had to change the name, we took advantage of the opportunity to radically revise and enlarge the books and then brought out an advance edition of the new set in a paper binding which we offered to the buyers of "The Book of Life" at the special price of $1.98. Of course, we used the tried and proven "will you do me a favor" appeal, and, as usual, it more than justified itself, Here is copy of the letter:

R. Naury
143 E. 39 St.
10925 Allerton House
New York, N. Y.

DEAR SIR:

Will you do me this favor? You can help me a lot if you will.

I'd like to have your opinion of the following:

I *have re-written "The Book of Life."* Parts of it I revised. Parts I explained. All of it I greatly added to. Where the old edition merely stated certain fundamental laws, the new set actually shows you how to put them into practice. Where the old told you that riches and happiness and success were your birthright, the new edition shows you, step by step, how to go about the actual GETTING of them.

In short, the new edition not only states the theory, but gets. right down to ACTUAL PRACTICE. It tells you the how and the Why and the Where, and WHAT TO DO!

Now Here's Where I Need Your Help!

Before I put a lot of money into advertising this new edition, before I give the Bindery word to start manufacturing on a big scale, I would like to have some of my friends let me know frankly what they think of it.

> Will you, therefore, do this for me? Return the enclosed card and let me send you a set of the new edition for a week's examination, so you can give me your opinion?

I'd do the same for you were our positions reversed. In fact, I intend to return the favor in a manner sure to please you.
Here's the way of it:

The new edition is twice as big, twice as good as the old. Naturally, too, it sells for more money.

For those buyers of "The Book of Life" who will help me

296

now by examining it and giving me their opinions of it, I have printed a few hundred sets in heavy paper covers, and I'm going to let you have one of them—NOT for the regular price of $15.00--NOT even for the price of the Advance Edition of $9.00, but for the special "Old Subscriber's" price *of only* $1.98.

That's just about cost, so of course I can't afford to add any bookkeeping charge to it, and I'm going to ask you to pay the postman this low price, with the small postage charges.

Your money will have a string to it. It's not mine until you say so. You get it right back if for any reason you send back the books.

And just listen to what they have done for others:

"Since receiving your first books I have made more than $100,000.00 in a little over 6 months' time. My previous income over a period of years has been approximately $7,500.00 a year. "—M. D. C., Capitola, California.

"I must write and tell you that what you promised has happened. My husband has not only doubled his salary from $225.00 a month to $500.00, but in addition, has turned a business deal where his commission meant $10,000.00 in one day's time.

"We have paid for our home completely. Bought us a fine automobile, a radio, new house furnishings and now have not only the necessities but also some of the comforts of life. "—Mrs. C. S. N., Indianapolis, Indiana.

You will forgive me if I seem insistent, but—will you use the post-card now? I'm afraid you'll mislay it. And I thank you most heartily and sincerely for your help.

Appreciatively yours,

That done, we felt that our original letter and circular were about done with. They had begun to show signs of wear. So we had recourse to the idea which had done so well on the HandiBag. We offered a premium as a reward for examining the books.

That revived the flagging interest with a vengeance. Quite too much so, for we found we were making the same mistake as was done on the silk stocking sale described in the last chapter—giving too valuable a premium without committing our readers to anything. So we promptly changed. We had started by offering a fountain pen as a premium. Instead, we gave to prospective customers a copy of Richard Harding Davis' short story, "The Man Who Could Not Lose."

That seemed to strike the happy medium. It greatly increased orders without increasing the proportion of returned sets, whereas with the pen, one of the first lists we tried gave us eight times as many orders with the premium as without—*but no more sales*! Luckily it was one of the first we tried, so no great damage was done.

Between the premium offers and our original letter we brought in some 300,000 orders. Then we tried selling the books in combination with a year's subscription to the Review of Reviews and sold an additional 30,000 that way. Here is the premium letter as adapted to sell in combination with the Review:

DEAR FRIEND:

Will you accept a copy of "The Man Who Could Not Lose"—in return for a little favor I want you to do?

The courtesy is a small one, pleasant and easy to render.

You know, of course, that the Psychologists declare that most of us use but a tenth of our brain power—that it is only the occasional Napoleon of politics or business or finance who, by using all of his powers for a little while, soars to heights so far above ordinary mortals that he is looked upon forever after as a genius.

But do you know that YOU have it in you to he such a Genius? That back in your brain is a Genii as powerful, yet as easily controlled, as was Aladdin's fabled "Genii-of-the-Lamp" of old?

298

Dr. Frank Crane calls this Genii the "Man Inside You." Robert Louis Stevenson referred to him as his "Mental Brownies" and gave them credit for all the wonderful things he wrote. Scientists call it your second subliminal mind, and estimate that it is to your ordinary conscious mind as a million is to one.

I am going to send you in the next few days seven books that give you the few things you really need to know to use this vast power that is within you. They are short; they are interesting as any Arabian Nights tale; and the best of it is--*they* are TRUE!

Which brings me to the courtesy I want to ask of you:

I'd like to make sure of the demand before I put a lot of money into the regular edition of these books. So I am writing to a few representative men in different sections of the country to ask each of you this:

Will you glance over one of the Advance Sets of the "Secret of the Ages" that I am going to send you—TRY OUT THE "GENII-OF-YOUR-BRAIN '—see what He can do for YOU?

It is a small favor, but it means a great deal to me, and I believe it will mean even more to YOU, for nearly every man has some pet ambition—some day-dream he entertains in idle moments. "Bubbles "—you probably call them. But they need not be "Bubbles" for you. Read the seven books I am sending you. If you don't find in them the way to make those dreams come true, just tell me so and they'll have cost you nothing.

And that isn't all!

The appeal of these books is to ambitious men and women—live, alert, forward-looking citizens. And such men and women are interested not alone in money success, but in keeping up with all that is best in Science, in the things that cultured people talk about, in the real news of the world. So I have arranged with the Review of Reviews Magazine for a special offer to those who first mail the enclosed FREE TRIAL CARD. Here is the offer:

50% Discount Offer!

Mail the enclosed card—without money. I will send you postpaid for FREE examination—a beautifully bound set of "The Secret of the Ages," and enter your subscription for one year to the Review of Reviews.

If you like the books and the magazine so well that you want to keep them, if you find in these seven volumes the way to the pot of gold at the foot of the rainbow, you can pay—NOT the usual $4.00 price of the Review of Reviews— NOT the price of the regular edition of the "Secret of the Ages," but 50% less than these-only $7.85; or $1 at the end of a week and $2 a month for 4 months.

That is what you save by using the enclosed card at once.

The Review of Reviews is, I believe, the one monthly that best presents the progress of the world in the most interesting, most readable way. It gleans from the great mass of newspapers and magazines all that is worth while and presents the gist of it to you. It ties together the scattered items of news, shows you their relation one to another, gives you a clear, connected picture of what has happened in the world during the previous 30 days. "The Secret of the Ages" brings you material success. The Review of Reviews provides the everyday knowledge that gives social poise to the successful man.

And mind you—if for any reason you don't find in these books the way to make your dreams come true, you don't need to keep them. You don't need to pay for them. You can send them back at my expense and cancel your subscription.

300

The Man Inside YOU

HAVE you ever read the story by Richard Harding Davis of "The Man Who Could Not Lose"?

It tells how one man, faced with the prospect of losing all that he held dear, stumbled by chance upon the secret of his own inner powers, and without really knowing how he did it, found the "Open Sesame" to fortune.

There is more to that story than even Davis dreamed, for, all unknowingly, he hit upon the one way scientists have found easiest to get in touch with the subconscious mind —the "Man Inside You" that Dr. Jung of Vienna claims knows not only everything you have ever learned during your lifetime, *but all the wisdom of past ages as well!*

Of course, it requires something more than the methods given in Davis' story, but the way to put "The Man Inside You" to work for you is really so simple, so easy, the marvel is that more people have not found it and used it. The few who have learned the secret have been like "The Man Who Could Not Lose." People thought Dame Fortune had camped on their doorstep. They called them lucky. When the whole fact of the matter was simply that they had established their contact with the subconscious; they had found the way to make "The Man Inside" work with them and for them.

The Acre of Diamonds

You remember the story of the Persian farmer of olden times. Someone showed him a diamond, and told him that these valuable stones could be found by merely digging for them. Afire with ambition, the farmer rented out his vineyard and roamed the world in search of diamonds. Years later, coming back a ragged and a wiser man, he found his vineyard neglected, his vines withered and dead.

Realizing then how foolish he had been, he started to dig up the old vines in order to plant new ones. But on digging deeply to get out the old roots, what was his astonishment to find that just beneath them were DIAMONDS—scores of diamonds—wealth such as he had been seeking far afield for years. And all the time it had been right beneath the surface of his own ground, needing only a little deeper digging, a little extra effort, to reach it!

Most of us are like that Persian farmer. Deep down within each one of us are all the essentials for complete success. You have the power to make of yourself what you will. You don't need outside help to enable you to succeed. You but need light. The "Man Inside You" is big enough, brave enough, strong enough to get you any thing of life. All you need is to learn how to get in touch with Him—how to use Him every day and hour.

Read In The Next Few Pages—

Naturally, I am not making offers like this to everyone. Naturally, too, your judgment will be of value to me only if I get it NOW—before the Winter book-selling season is over —before I start on the big regular edition of the books.

Won't you, therefore, put your name and address on the card TONIGHT *if you can*, and mail it?

On second thought, better mail it right away—while you have it in your hand—so there will be no chance of forgetting it.

I thank you for your courtesy.

Yours for mutual cooperation.

P.S. And whether or not you keep the "Secret of the Ages," I want you to keep "The Man Who Could Not Lose" as a present from me, *entirely free of charge*. It is in return for your courtesy in passing judgment upon the Advance Edition of the books.

That pretty well ended the big sale. We tried numbers of letters after it, of course, and some of them sold books with reasonable success, but none of them in anything like the quantities the first ones had. Here is one of the more successful of these efforts:

```
┌─────────┐
│ Coin    │
│ Attached│
│ here    │
└─────────┘
```

MY DEAR SIR:

It's a wonderful thing—the power of money to make money.

Just this little, insignificant penny invested at the birth of Christ, at interest of only 4% compounded semi-annually, would today amount to more than

302

$200,000,000,000,000,000,000,000—many times the wealth of the world!

It's too late now to date back your investments to then, but you can do the next best thing—you can invest a few minutes in wisdom that was old when Christ was born, and collect dividends from it now to almost as unbelievable an extent.

For those ancient Wise Men uncovered certain truths that we, with all our education, have overlooked or forgotten. Present day psychologists and metaphysicians are "re-discovering" them and shouting them to the world as something new and wonderful.

They are wonderful—but they are not new. They were ancient when Jesus came into the world. But mankind is only now beginning to get a glimmering of their power.

> When Prof. Wm. James of Harvard told us that we are using only a tenth part of the power that is ours—both physically and mentally—people smiled unbelievingly.

> When Judge Troward followed this with the startling statement that Universal Mind or God is to each of us exactly what we look for in Him a God of happiness and plenty or one of poverty and misery—and Emerson enunciated his theory of the Oversoul, people shook their heads uncomprehendingly.

> When Churches were founded, based on mental healing, people laughed. But these churches have grown, and the number of successful followers of the new psychology doubles continually--all *because they show actual results!*

What is the law back of all this? When drugs fail, is there a force we can call upon to restore health and strength? When our money is gone, when creditors are hounding us until there seems no way out, is there a power that can open up hidden channels of riches, uncover treasures we never dreamed of?

The Wise Men of the East taught that there is. Psychologists today are re-discovering the truth of their teachings. And ordinary men like you and me are *proving it.* One man whose hearings before the Referee in Bankruptcy had actually commenced had his business rehabilitated at the last minute.

Another needed $1600.00 by a certain time—and received $2000.00. A third asked for $500.00—and it came in a way that seemed almost miraculous. And these are only three of thousands of similar cases. I could fill a book with them.

How did they do it? Have you ever been in a serious accident, where everything looked black for an instant, but by some superhuman effort you managed to pull through with a whole skin? You didn't stop to reason out the right thing to do, did you? The prompting came from within— and you just did it, that's all!

Well, that prompter is just as potent a helper in sickness or in business as in sudden emergencies if only you learn to call upon him.

This is the knowledge the Wise Men of the East left for us. This is the knowledge that is the Secret of the Ages. And this is the knowledge that is yours--FREE--to read and to try without one cent of cost or one bit of obligation, if you will mail the enclosed card at once.

The Secret of the Ages consists of seven small books, easily carried, easily read. There is no mysticism, no involved passages. A child can understand it, yet it holds such depths of wisdom that Doctors, Ministers, Bankers, College Professors have read it a dozen times over and each time gotten something new and valuable from it.

Will you read it, if I send it to you for a week—FREE? If then you like it as much as half a quarter of a million others, if money won t tempt you to part with it, what would you expect to pay for it? $30? $50? That is what most Courses along similar lines of thought sell for. But if you like these books, you need send—NOT $30 or $50 not even the regular price of $15, but the special price for this Courtesy Edition in red Artcraft Leather of ONLY $7.85 (or $1 then and $2 a month for 4 months.)

"Your 7 volumes are the keys which have opened the doors of the Treasure House for me," writes Macon of Buffalo, while the Business Magazine of New York says of them: "Here at last is a man who has given to the world a practical method of having happiness on earth."

"Now what am I to do?" you ask. Simply put your name and address on the enclosed card and drop it in the mail. There's nothing to puzzle about, because you don't have to send one penny or promise anything other than that if you don't see where every penny and every minute you may put into these books will come back to you in dollars, you will send them back.

That's easy, isn't it?

Never mind what we SAY--just see what the Secret of the Ages will DO for you. But please mail the card right away to get one of the "Courtesy Edition" sets at the special low price.

Sincerely yours,

The real profit in selling by mail lies not in the first sale but in the succeeding ones. If you cannot sell a second product to something like half the people who bought your first one, then there is something wrong with your methods or your product. Repeat sales on books or merchandise are analogous to the renewing subscribers on a magazine. The magazine that cannot renew somewhere near half its subscribers is headed for a fall, and the same is true of the mail order merchandiser who cannot sell a second time to a high percentage of those who first bought from him.

About the time our first set of books was showing signs of being through, we finished our second set, which we called "The Life Magnet." So we were quite willing to forget the "Secret of the Ages" sale for a while in busying ourselves getting in the orders on this new set.

As usual when we had a new product to offer we tried half a dozen letters, then used the best of them: Here are the three most successful of the letters we tried:

DEAR FRIEND:

Is your address, as written above, correct?

If so, please return the enclosed card immediately, then sit back and watch results!

Within a few days, I'll send you seven new books, published only a few weeks ago, which already have brought to hundreds a secret that men have struggled for, fought for, died for since time began—" How to Get What you Want!"

These seven books put you in possession of a Money Magnet—a power capable of drawing to you anything of good you may desire.

Impossible? Just listen:

"I've had 'The Life Magnet' only a few weeks, but already it has proven to be a veritable Money Magnet. "—H. I. Lovett, Lily Dale, N. Y.

"The Life Magnet" will show you *how to get what you want*—how to draw to yourself riches and power just as surely as the magnet draws to itself every filing of iron that comes within its reach. There is nothing of good you can ask for, that it cannot bring you.

Do I promise too much? It is because I have seen this Magnet work—I have tried it in my own life—I have tested it on others. And I tell you again—*there is nothing of good you can ask for that it cannot bring you.* Riches and honor, health and happiness—you have but to charge this great Magnet with your particular desire, magnetize it in the way these seven books show you, and the result is as certain as the morrow's sun.

What These Books Will Do for You

Scientists tell us, you know, that all mankind is created equal--that the brain of one man is exactly the same as that of another. The only difference between a failure and a successful man is that the successful man's brain is more developed.

But here is the important part— These scientists tell us that *no man* has found the way to use more than *one-tenth* of the giant power of his brain. And the prime purpose of "The Life Magnet" is to point out in plain language the way to harness the vast reserve power of this Giant Inside You—the way to *use* it to bring you whatever you want.

There are no vague theories in these books. They show you first just what is this giant unused power within you, then how to reach it and finally how to make it work for you every day and hour.

Read the Books at No Expense!

I have so much confidence in "The Life Magnet" that I will send the seven volumes for you to read and study for 7 days FREE--without a single penny of payment from you.

Keep the books a full week. If you *think* they'll do what I promise, send me only $7.85 as payment in full. (Or $1 then and $2 a month for 4 months). Otherwise, just return them at my expense and owe me nothing.

If you decide to keep the books and remit the $7.85, your

307

money will be refunded to you *any time within a year* if you cannot then attribute at least $1,000.00 of additional earnings to the books.

Could anything be fairer than that?

Try it! You can't lose. You don't need to send a penny or take any risk. Just your name on the enclosed card will bring the seven volumes of "The Life Magnet" to you—subject to a week's reading *and* TRIAL!

Costs nothing to TRY them and if you want to make more money, achieve real success, you owe it to yourself to mail the enclosed "FREE TRIAL" card today!

Yours for greater success,

DEAR FRIEND:

Would you like to add $1,000.00 to your net income during the next year?

It doesn't make any difference whether you are in business for yourself, or whether you are working for someone else.

You have but to read seven books—the seven volumes of "The Life Magnet "—and I'll guarantee that *these seven books* will increase your earnings at least $1,000 a year, or you don't pay a single penny!

Unusual, yes! But the books are even more unusual for, to the best of my knowledge, such vitally helpful books have never been published before.

You have heard, of course, of Robert Collier's "Secret of the Ages," which sold well over 200,000 copies in its first three years.

Now, after further years of study, after testing the effect of those ideas on scores of thousands of followers, Robert Collier has prepared a new set--bigger and better, far more complete and much farther advanced than the old. Those who have had the privilege of seeing the advance sheets declare that now, indeed, the Age of Miracles is with us again—that the man who, with these books to

guide him, cannot take what he wants from life is indeed
a tyro.

What These Books Will Do for You

Scientists tell us, you know, that all mankind is created
equal—that the brain of one man is exactly the same as
that of another. The only difference between a failure and
a successful man is that the successful man's brain is
more developed.

But here is the important part—

These scientists tell us that *no man* has found the way to
use more than *one-tenth* of the giant power of his brain.
And the prime purpose of "The Life Magnet" is to point
out in plain language the way to harness the vast reserve
power of this Giant Inside You—the way to *use* it to bring
you whatever you want.

There are no vague theories in these books. They show
you first just what is this giant unused power within you,
then how to reach it and finally how to make it work for
you every day and hour.

Read the Books at No Expense!

I have so much confidence in "The Life Magnet" that I
will send the seven volumes for you to read and study for
7 days FREE without a single penny of payment from
you.

Keep the books a full week. If you *think* they'll do what
I promise, send me only $7.85 as payment in full. (Or $1
then and $2 a month for 4 months.) Otherwise, just return
them at my expense and owe me nothing.

If you decide to keep the books and remit the $7.85, your
money will be refunded to you *any time within a year* if
you cannot then attribute at least $1,000.00 of additional
earnings to the books.

Could anything be fairer than that?

Don't judge the books by this price. The regular price will be much higher after this Introductory Edition is exhausted. The $7.85 price is ridiculous when compared with the riches and the health and the success this great "Life Magnet" will bring to you. I firmly believe that after you have read them, you would not be willing to part with these 7 volumes for ten times their small price.

Costs nothing to TRY them and if you want to make more money, achieve real success, you owe it to yourself to mail the enclosed "FREE TRIAL" Card today!

Yours for greater success,

DEAR CUSTOMER:

Although I have never met you, I am going to write to you as if you were a personal friend.

You can help me to make a very important decision, and I am sure you won't mind it when I explain. I know I would gladly do as much for you if you asked me.

I have just brought out a small Advance Edition of a new set of books--much bigger, much better than anything I have ever published before. It is called The Life Magnet.

It treats of the same Psychology of Success, of Happiness and of Health as does The Secret of the Ages, but it carries the thought much farther along, and—even more important—it shows far more clearly how to APPLY these methods and principles to your every-day problems. In it are no more theories--it takes you right down to the bed-rock of ACTUAL PRACTICE. Here is what one of the first buyers of these new books wrote of them:

"They are just what I seemed to lack. I have been a stu-

311

dent of Psychology for years, and taken two courses in it, but I learned more—at least I have had more success in *actual application*—from your books than from both the courses."
—C. C. Showalter, Pittsburgh, Pa.

While A. D. Methven, Jr., of San Benito, Texas, wrote:

"They are virtually worth their weight in gold. Each time I pick them up I get something new and good out of them."

Now this small advance edition is almost gone, and what I want to find out is this: HOW BIG AN EDITION SHALL I PRINT NEXT?

In other words, how many of our Secret of the Ages readers want to go further into this subject—want to learn more about APPLYING the principles outlined in the books they have?

That is where you can help me. You have read The Secret of the Ages. Now I want you to read--at my expense, of course--the new Life Magnet. I want you to TRY OUT the actual methods it gives you in your business, in your social life, in your health. I want you to put it to every test you can.

Then send it back to me, and in payment for your FREE TRIAL, include a line telling me what you think of it, how big the market you believe there is for it.

The enclosed is merely your agreement to TRY the books--and return them. There is no expense—just a courtesy between friends. If you should like the books so well that you want to keep them, you can send me—not the $15 price of the regular Andalusian leather edition, but only $7.85 (or $1 in one week and $2 a month for 4 months) for the same fine effect in a red Spanish leather binding.

312

This first Advance Edition was not a big one to begin with, and there are only a few sets now left in that fine, red Spanish leather binding. I want you to see one of them, for I want your opinion, so won't you use the enclosed card right away?

I don't like to be so insistent, but I'm afraid you'll put it aside until it is too late, so please put your name and address on it *now*—while you have it in your hand and drop it in the mail.

I thank you very heartily and sincerely for your help.

Appreciatively yours,

All three of them pulled well, though none quite came up to the results of the favor letter which we used to sell the first paper-bound "Secret of the Ages" to "The Book of Life" buyers. However, the price was higher, so that may have had something to do with it.

We had sold the "Secret of the Ages" successfully for three years, but that usually marks the life of any set of books that has a big, popular sale. Even Wells' did not do much after the third year until it was brought out in a $1 volume, when the sale revived all over again. We skimmed the cream off the "Life Magnet" sale in a little over a year. Then we began to look around for new worlds to conquer. And presently we found them in a new and unique little magazine.

The idea of the magazine was based upon a test we had made of a series of lessons, a week or a month apart. They had shown such life that we decided to try them on a large scale, and instead of ordinary lessons, put them in a little magazine, letting the lesson be the central feature and accompanying it with a couple of stories that would illustrate the point we were trying to bring out. We decided to call the little magazine "Mind, Inc."

Before starting it, we planned some 15 lessons, which gave us our central theme and enabled us to look around well ahead of time for the sort of story material we should need. Then we decided to offer the first lesson or copy free, on the understanding that the reader was to either notify us within two weeks that he did not want the subscription or else send us $4.85 in full payment for the first twelve lessons.

Here is the letter we used, and one that brought a higher percentage of orders would be hard to find:

Here Is a New Way
To Get What You Want!

Will you let me send you Absolutely Free the first gainful Lesson in getting riches, from the new "Key to Life" Course? Yours at no cost whatever--yours to use—*yours to keep forever!*

Getting riches is not a matter of Saving money. You know that. Opportunity is not the answer. Even ability does not necessarily bring riches--as witness the number of geniuses who starve to death.

Then what is the secret?

The ancient Egyptians used to teach, you remember, that to grasp the Idea behind anything gave you the power over it, for it put into your hands the *Soul* of that thing.

The first Lessons of the "Key to Life" course give you the idea behind the getting of riches. They put the Soul of them into your hands. They show you

314

how to "cast your nets on the right side" and fill them to overflowing, even though you have labored all your life before and caught nothing.

Roger Babson says that one of the 70 opportunities still open to Americans to become millionaires lies in the utilization of the power behind prayer to bring you what you want in life. These Lessons will show you—Not how to pray—but how to use the power which is back of all successful prayer, to bring you what you want.

I am so sure that these practical Lessons will give to *You* the basic methods of How To Get What You Want that I make you this unusual offer:

Simply mail the enclosed card, and I will send you the first Lesson of the new "Key to Life" Course Free and Post-paid—*yours to keep forever.*

Read it—Try it—put it to the test! If you feel then that you are truly on the trail of the Aladdin secret--if you can trace directly to it additional earnings or additional opportunities worth a hundred times the regular price of the Lesson, send only $4.85 for the full year's Course of 12 Lessons. Otherwise keep the first Lesson Free.

I am making this offer just to you and those like you who have shown their faith in the power of Mind, because I feel that anyone who has taken one step in that direction will never be content until he has attained his goal. He knows he Has the power to be anything he wants to be. He knows that all of good is his for the taking. So he is willing to Try these practical Lessons in *Putting That Power To Actual Use!*

Whether I extend this offer to any other groups will depend entirely upon your response. Won't you, therefore, mail the enclosed card today, if you can? Better still, pencil your name on it Now--before you run any chance of forgetting it—and drop it in the mail! It's already stamped.

I thank you for your courtesy.

Appreciatively yours,

Of course, we had no intention of pressing for collection at the end of the two weeks if we failed to receive a cancellation or a remittance. Instead, we planned a series of follow-up efforts, each a sales letter in itself, to bring in the price of the subscription. These follow-ups are given in the next chapter.

To most of our readers we felt that the first lesson would be the best to send, but for certain classes, later lessons had a much stronger appeal. When we found this to be the case, we used the stronger lesson, of course.

With the heads of business concerns, for instance, our July lesson was particularly effective, because of one striking story it contained. So to the heads of some 10,000 business- concerns, we sent this letter:

MY DEAR MR. JONES:

At some desk in your Bank sits a man on whom you have your eye.

He shows promise. And you are hoping to see him develop one of these days to the calibre Vice Presidents are made of.

There is a story in the July issue of MIND, INC., which will help to put him in that class. It is called "The Magic Story." I should like to send you a complimentary copy of the July "MIND, INC.," so that YOU may hand it to him.

"This story is worth $25.00 to any man," wrote the General Manager of the Pratt & Lambert Co. of Buffalo. "To a few men, it is worth a fortune."

If you will mail the enclosed card, Mr. Godfrey, or drop me a line on your own letterhead, I will send you a complimentary copy of the July issue the moment it is out.

There is no cost or obligation attached. Our sole object is to get this story into the hands of men who are "up and coming," knowing that if they read it, they won't stop there. They will want every issue of MIND, INC.

Won't you, therefore, put your name on the card now and drop it in the mail? It's already stamped.

Appreciatively yours,

Something over 10 per cent of the list ordered copies. We followed them up promptly in an effort to sell them copies for every one in their organization and quite a few did order in reasonable quantities. Here are the two letters we used:

John Jones, Esq., President,
Bank of Commerce,

317

Monrovia, La.

DEAR MR. JONES:

The July MIND, INC., containing "The Magic Story,"
was mailed to you a couple of days ago.

If you have found time to read it, I know you have
thought of a dozen men in your organization (and some
outside) who need just the stimulus "The Magic Story"
gives, to wake them to their real possibilities.

Will you give them that stimulus, Mr. Jones? We don't
care what you pay for it, or whether you pay at all.
MIND, INC. is priced at 50¢ a copy, but we will bill the
copies to you at 25¢ each, or let you set your own price.

All we want is to get this story into the hands of the men
who need it—AND WILL USE IT!

Will you send us such a list of the men YOU know?
You'll be doing them a greater favor—you'll be actually
GIVING them more—than if you handed each your
check for $100.00.

Some of them are going to date their start from the time
they read "The Magic Story "—and YOU, John Jones,
will be the man back of it!

Sincerely,

DEAR MR. JONES:

"If you have not already sent for it," wrote Tom Hanlon,
Sales Manager of the Super Maid Cook-Ware
Corporation of Chicago, to his force of 1,500 salesmen,
"stop everything this very minute and send for a copy of
the July MIND, INC.

"I want to tell you that when you read 'The Magic Story'
in that issue, you will agree with me that it is worth $5.00

318

of any man's money.

"You will miss what I consider one of the greatest stories ever written if you do not read it. Many men will be able to trace their success from the day they read 'The Magic Story.

"Read it once, and I am sure you will read it at least once each week!"

That letter is from one of the most successful Sales Managers in the country to his field force. When a man like him will so strongly urge a story upon his salesmen, it must have properties of unusual value in "pepping up" a sales force.

Wouldn't that same enthusiasm be of help to your men, too, Mr. Jones? Then send us a list right now of all the men you want to infuse new life into and we'll have it on the way to them within twenty-four hours.

Sincerely,

Then the September and October lessons brought out some ideas on the question of the healing art that we felt every doctor would be interested in, so we circularized doctors, osteopaths and chiropractors first on the September, then on the October lessons.

This time, however, since there was no chance of quantity sales of the same lesson, we felt that they should be willing to pay something for the one they received; so we enclosed a coin card order form, and required payment of 25 cents. with order. That pulled too, pretty nearly as well as the July issue free. In fact, on one list, it did better than that, bringing in 12 per cent of orders!

What is more, where on the July issue we sold only additional copies of that one number, with these two we were able to close a goodly percentage of subscriptions.

Here is copy of the October letter. The September one was just about the same, the only change being in the title and description of the lesson.

J. Frankl, Esq.,
13929 Glendale Blvd,
Los Angeles, Calif.

DEAR CUSTOMER:

May we send you a copy of the October issue of "Mind, Inc.," which explains for the first time the two factors necessary to the cure of sickness or deformity?

If you have ever wondered why some people can so easily shake off sickness, while others suffer for weeks and months —if you have been at a loss to account for the miracle-cures you read so often in the daily news—if you are looking for the hidden factor in all healing—then mail the enclosed card for a copy of the October "Mind, Inc.," giving the law back of all these.

This Law is as fundamental as Einstein's Law of the Universe, as revolutionary as was Harvey's discovery of the circulation of the blood. When you have read it, we believe you will say it is as important to the cure of disease as Einstein's Law is to the study of Physics. It accounts for every so-called miracle, every case of healing. It shows how YOU can work miracles with your body.

We are giving to a few old customers the chance to read and try this newly discovered law--NOT at the regular price of 50¢ a copy, but for HALF that—only 25¢. YOU are one of the few who can get a copy of the October issue at this special price.

The enclosed card will bring you this specially priced copy if mailed at once. There is no obligation attached. The only essential is that you put your 25¢ into the card and mail it right away, before these special copies are all spoken for.

Sincerely yours,

320

That idea of selling one lesson at a time showed such life that we then tried asking full price, and since it is just about as easy to get $1 as 50 cents, we offered two lessons for $1.

The first that lent itself particularly well to this idea was the lesson for the following July. It was called "The Secret of Youth." And here is the letter we used on it:

DEAR FRIEND:

Will you risk $1 for the Secret of Youth?

There is such a secret—make no mistake about that. How else has Dr. Carrel, by two simple processes, kept the heart of an embryonic chicken not merely alive, but vital and youthful for 18 years!

The secret lies—NOT in dieting, NOT in surgery or monkey glands, NOT in exercise—but in something far simpler and easier than any of these.

Why do animals live to five and six times their maturity, while men and women average only two to three times theirs? Why do the wilder animals keep their vigor and youthful appearance until five-sixths of their span of life is gone, while men and women begin to look old when scarcely half their lives are gone?

Can you tell? No? Then send for the Secret of Youth. It requires no diet, no exercise, no appliances. What is more, if it does not do all you expect of it, you can send it back and get your money back!

On that understanding, will you risk $1 on it? Then fill out the form on the next page, or just wrap a dollar bill in this letter, and return it in the enclosed envelope.

If abounding youth and health and strength are worth a dollar to you, use the enclosed envelope--not next week, or next month, but Now—TODAY!

Sincerely,

321

That sold! It did so well that we quickly disposed of 25,000 extra copies, and orders for them are still rolling in. Of course, in making the sale, we could not divide the interest by saying that with the "Secret of Youth" we were going to send an extra lesson. But when we delivered the lesson, we sent with it a copy of another one which elaborated the same idea and thus left the reader even better satisfied because he got more than he expected.

Those orders, too, had the great advantage that a far higher percentage of them subscribed to the rest of the lessons.

Life Is Youth!

WHY do so many women of today live in a state of chronic half-health? Why do we hear thousands complain of constant lassitude and gloom that takes all gladness from life? Why does Beauty fade so fast, driving mere girls to the cosmetic counter to imitate the dainty flower-like complexion that Health alone can bring?

Ignorance of the simplest law of Nature is the answer. Without Health you cannot be strong, nor beautiful, nor successful, and certainly not happy. And without this most important of all of Nature's laws, you cannot be healthy.

In the last analysis, beauty is based upon health and vitality—upon clear, red blood and the normal activity of all glands and organs. The exterior of the body simply expresses the condition of the interior. Beauty is the natural expression of purity and wholesomeness.

Vitality and Success

The man or woman who possesses abounding vitality has the most valuable asset in life. No obstacle, no handicap can hold such a one back.

Most of our great men have been men of unusual physical energy, possessing the most hearty and powerful constitutions. They have developed a virile strength, a youthful force and vitality that have carried them over every obstacle.

On the other hand, thousands of men and women of exceptional ability fail because of the lack of physical power. The pathways of life are strewn with the devitalized and deficient who have fallen behind. Real youth means unlimited vitality. It means capacity for endless work. It means exuberant spirits. It means a pleasing, forceful, magnetic personality. It means a clear head and an active mind.

You can be brisk, active, youthful at an age when your mates are gray and broken. You can have abounding vitality, and the abundant vigor and energy that go with it. You can cheat time of twenty or thirty years, merely by learning Nature's simplest, yet most important law. But simply wishing will not do it —you must act. Send NOW for the *Secret of Youth!*

ROBERT COLLIER, INC.
599 FIFTH AVENUE   NEW YORK, N. Y.

322

Even where they did not, we made a little money on the $1 orders, for our circulars cost us only 2 1/2 to 3 cents apiece in the mail, and they pulled from 5 to 10 per cent of orders, so that each 2 1/2 or 3 cents. brought back 5 to 10 cents worth of business. On a $1 item, that is doing well.

Following the "Secret of Youth," we had two lessons covering "The Lost Word of Power." These lent themselves so well to the $1 idea that we offered them together and promptly sold an additional 15,000 of them. The following letter did the work:

DEAR CUSTOMER:

What would you give to be the "biggest" personage in your community, the greatest in your line anywhere?

Would you risk reading a law so important, that it is given in the Bible as part of God's labors on three of the six days of creation, and is repeated no less than six times in a single chapter?

Would you risk the time to go over another page which gives clearly and unmistakably the directions for success? Not in ambiguous language, but in short, cryptic words that a child could understand and follow.

Would you risk that much? Then send the coupon on the last page. It will bring you—not only the most important lesson life can teach, not only the clearest, surest directions for success ever given, BUT IN ADDITION—

"The Lost Word of Power"

Since time began, mankind has believed there was some magic formula, some talisman, that would open all doors to its possessor. That belief runs through all the legends and folklore of the ancients. You see it in the story of Aladdin and his lamp, in the "Open, Sesame!" of Ali Baba, in the Cabala of the Jewish Rabbis, in Longfellow's poem— "Sandalphon."

323

For a belief to persist through so many ages and countries, it must have some basis of fact. And in "The Lost Word of Power," *you get that basic truth.*

"My word shall not come back to me void," says the Bible, "but shall accomplish that whereunto it was sent."

"The Lost Word of Power" not only proves to you the truth of that statement, but shows you exactly the same principle working in physics, in electro-mechanics, in surgery—*in all of nature*! You can PROVE it—in your own life, with your own career—NOT in some dim and distant future, but RIGHT AWAY!

I know a man who had not a cent to his name nor enough food for another meal for his wife and three children, when this law was brought home to him—and through it he has made a fortune! I'll tell you his name and his full experience in "The Lost Word of Power."

I know others who have won from it fame, fortune, honors, happiness. I'll tell you some of their stories, too, and who they are.

What would YOU give for the power and success they have won? Would you risk $1 for it—if you could get it right back if the talisman failed to work for you?

If you would then mail the coupon on the next page, *with that distinct understanding*—that you get it right back if for any reason the Word of Power fails to work for *you*.

Sincerely,

The next two lessons fit together very well, too, so we tested them as a $1 unit. With a letter alone, their pulling power was disappointingly low. But we added a little booklet and jumped the results two and a half times!

That is one of the few cases we have seen where the letter did not account for somewhere near 75 per cent of the orders. Ordinarily, a good sales letter will pull about 75 per cent as many orders if mailed without a circular as it will with even the best descriptive circular. But occasionally the circular is the thing that does the pulling. And this was one of these rare cases. Here is the letter:

DEAR MR. JONES:

What would you give to be rid of every debt and obligation? What would it be worth to you to shed every limitation that hedges you around, and face the world as free as a butterfly that has just shed its cocoon? Would you risk $1 for it?

It can be done—make no mistake about that. As a matter of fact, it is the way all of Nature works. Only man clings to his troubles, and so reproduces them in ever greater and greater number. Only man hugs his chains, and so binds them tighter around him.

Yet it has been proven time and again that it is just as natural for man to shed wrong conditions and start afresh, as for a lobster to shed a broken claw, or a snake its skin. And it can be done without injustice to anyone—in fact, the Bible adjures us in many places to do that very thing!

How can it be done? How does the snake shed its old skin? By first forming a new skin beneath, does it not, then letting go of the old? How does the lobster get a new claw, a child grow a new tooth? By starting the new conditions under the shell of the old, then when they are far enough along, *letting go of the old!*

The outer shell is always dead. It is only underneath it, where the new' conditions are forming, that there is life. Your present circumstances or conditions do not matter. There is no life in them. *It is what is forming beneath them that counts!*

What conditions are taking shape under the shell of YOUR present circumstances? Are you hugging the same old debts and lacks and unhappiness to you, and

325

reproducing them over and over again? Or are you growing a set of brand new conditions, of riches and happiness
and success, ready to split the old shell and let go of it at
a moment's notice?

 You can shed the old, you can grow new and perfect condition, and you can do it right now. You don't have to wait
until someone dies and leaves you a million. You don't
need to depend upon outside help of any kind. The power
is *in you*, just as it is in every other form of life. It needs
using—that's all.

And the way to use it--the simple, clear, easily understood method of getting the things you want and ridding
yourself of wrong conditions, is given you in the next two
Lessons of Mind, Inc.

Send for them. The coupon on the last page brings them
to you, subject to 60-day's EXAMINATION and TRIAL.
At the end of that time (or any time between), if they have
not done all you ask of them, if for any reason you are not
satisfied, *send them back and your dollar will be refunded immediately and in full.*

$1 to make your dreams come true! $1 to rid yourself of
the old shell of debts and lacks! Will you risk that much?
Then pin it to the coupon on the next page and return it
in the enclosed envelope. You get it right back, if for any
reason you return the two Lessons.

Sincerely,

That is as far as we have gone with the idea. I have a belief that
by picking the right sort of lessons for our efforts, we can keep feeding in new $1 orders indefinitely, and of so varied a character as to
keep the whole list alive and responsive.

"The Secret of Youth," for instance, brings one type of reader.
"The Lost Word" an entirely different grade. While, judging by the
quality of orders received, the third letter appeals to a different class
altogether.

That keeps the list alive, and us, too, for as long as we must keep bestirring ourselves for an entirely new and different appeal every couple of months, there is no danger of our being guilty of the unpardonable sin of stagnation— *standing still!*

XXI

Taking the Guess Out of Advertising

THERE is a concern in New York called the "Tested Selling Institute and Word Laboratory, Inc.", whose purpose it is to take the guess out of selling. The writer once listened to a lecture by its founder, Elmer Wheeler, in which he showed that selling as it is usually practiced is the world's biggest guessing game. Not one salesman in a thousand, he said, can tell you exactly what words and phrases sold his customer. He merely guesses that this word or sentence will sell, and some-times it does, and sometimes it doesn't.

We have high salaried executives, Mr. Wheeler pointed out to buy the merchandise and place it at the counters, and other high salaried executives who advertise it and bring the people to the counters. So far so good. Then what happens? The actual selling of the merchandise is entrusted to a humble $15.00 a week sales clerk!

This is retailing's oldest weakness. It's biggest handicap. The answer to this problem, is to control the spoken word by placing in the mouths of the $15.00 a week sales clerks the words and expressions a $50,000 a year executive would use were he behind the counters selling your merchandise!

Within a period of time we have amassed upwards of 100,000 selling phrases, from over 200 lines of industry. The sentences that have made sale after sale we called "TESTED SELLING SENTENCES".

All of us are consciously, or unconsciously, using "TESTED SELLING SENTENCES" from morning, noon till night. Some of us use them to sell ideas, others service, and others actual merchandise.

Little Willy wants an extra slice of bread and jam; sister wants 15¢ for the movies; Dad is scheming how to get out of the house for lodge that night, and Mother is planning to have Dad sweep out the cellar--while around the corner the Preacher is planning a visit on the household to make it more church conscious and one and all, have their own pet "TESTED SELLING SENTENCES" they plan to use on one another!

The butcher, the baker, the candlestick maker, all trades and professions have their "TESTED SELLING SENTENCES." The dentist says, "Now, Willy, this won't hurt you—*much!*"

The doctor, the lawyer, the undertaker uses them. The barber says: "And now how about a NICE shampoo?" When you refuse with your best "TESTED SELLING SENTENCE" about being in a hurry to meet the wife, he proceeds to poke you in the eye with his elbow.

Hidden in every spool of thread, or row of safety pins, are reasons why customers will buy.

One sales person says: "These safety pins will not burst open in the garment and injure baby."

Another says: "This thread is waxed, Madam, and will not twist in the hand while sewing."

Another has found real magic when he says: "This suit has long pants, Sonny, like your Dad wears."

Another says: "This fly swatter is square, not oval, and gets them in the corners!" How many times have you missed a fly by only a fraction of an inch? Well, they are making fly swatters square~ now, to get 'em in the corners!

"This union suit is buttonless, and the child can put it on by himself!" What a "TESTED SELLING SENTENCE" for the woman who has to dress and undress little Johnny five times a day!

Only last week I bought some cigars in the chain store down the street. The sales clerk said, "How about a pipe today, Sir, only $1.00?"

"Not interested," said I.

I surmise the clerk had had many a refusal that day from using the inane approach, for he began to tap nervously on the counter with the pipe, when a man came up and said, "Say, is that pipe non-breakable?" "It sure is!" said the clerk, coming to sudden life, "Why I've been tapping it on the counter all day!"

"I'll buy one," said the man.

By accident, the clerk had hit upon a real "TESTED SELLING SENTENCE". He sold so many pipes that week using the sentence that he was placed in the advertising department of this national chain of stores, and this is a true story!

But I ask you, gentlemen, why should this company or any other take such chances? Why not give this salesman, and all others, sentences tested to make sales more sure-fire, so that sales persons will say something else of our products than, "How about a pipe today,

Sir, only $1.00?"

Just because a sentence sounds reasonable to you, does not necessarily indicate it will sell! Why gamble with unknown sales phraseology? Why not take advantage of modern science?

The above are only a few excerpts from Mr. Wheeler's interesting talk. But what he says about word-of-mouth selling is just as true of the printed word.

We have found, for instance, in selling through the printed word, a number of tested openings that almost invariably win the attention of the reader. And of all the different types of openings, the "How" appeal seems strongest. E. Haldeman -Julius, in selling his little Blue Books by mail, found that putting a "How" into a title frequently doubled or even quadrupled the pull of that title. A book on Success, for instance, would sell twice as well if its title were "How to Win Success" than it if were called merely "The Rules of Success

Here is the way we worked that "How" idea into the opening of a letter selling a facial cream:

How a New Kind of Cream Makes the Skin Soft, Clear, Lovely—
For Reasons That Every Woman Will Understand!

DEAR MADAM:

Women who "know it all" are not invited to read this page, for it holds nothing of interest to the wise young woman who is perfectly satisfied with her complexion and her beauty aids, and who feels like the man that resigned from the Patent Office back in '86 "because everything had been discovered that was ever going to be discovered."

This page is a personal message to those women who are worried about lines or spots or blackheads or blemishes that threaten to ruin an otherwise beautiful complexion.

Once in a blue moon, a discovery is made of such importance as to revolutionize the methods ordinarily used to beautify the skin. Such a discovery, we believe, is the new So-and-So Bleach Creme treatment.

330

You have four organs, you know, whose function it is to cleanse and purify and sweeten the body. Of these four, the skin is most important—more so even than the lungs. Sometimes called "the second lung," the skin throws off an unbelievable amount of impurities.

So it is essential that the pores of your skin should be kept open, that they should have a chance to breathe, that they should not be clogged with dead tissue or dust or cosmetics.

BUT HERE IS THE MOST IMPORTANT PART:

The outermost layer of skin is dead. It is exceedingly thin and transparent, but it is quite dead. And it is this outermost layer that, if left alone, brings on spots and patches. Not only that, but by clogging the pores with its dried tissue, and stopping the cleansing flow of perspiration, it tends to cause blackheads, pimples, splotches and the like. So the first step in bringing back a soft, clear, lovely skin is to rid your face of all that dried up layer of dead skin. And this is the purpose of So-and-So Bleach Creme.

So-and-So Bleach Creme is not an astringent. It does not burn. It requires no rubbing. It dissolves only dried, dead tissue. You spread it on lightly at night. You rub it off in the morning. It is purposely made so mild and safe that it will not remove all the dead skin in a single treatment, but after two or three treatments, you notice the difference, and at the end of a week, you are amazed at the baby softness, the creaminess, the loveliness of the new skin that all this time had been hiding behind that mask of dead tissue.

So-and-So Bleach Creme does not pretend to work miracles. Only Nature can do that. But So-and-So Bleach Creme does remove the mask that hides your natural, lovely skin.

You see, sun and wind and strong soaps dry up your outer skin and leave it muddy and lifeless. Yet that dead outer

331

skin remains firmly attached to the true inner skin and keeps it from breathing properly, from ridding itself of impurities. Is it any wonder that your complexion becomes dull, that it develops freckles and blackheads and the like?

Mind you, this is no new and untried theory. The base of this unusual cream was first employed many years ago by a prominent southern physician. Since then, special research has given additional value to it, more than thirty well-known beauty-culturists, scientists and physicians having contributed of their knowledge to perfect the formula. Today it is backed by a $200,000.00 company, and more than fifteen million So-and-So Bleach Creme beauty treatments are given EACH YEAR in homes and beauty parlors throughout the country.

Will you TRY it—if I send ft to you subject to 30 days' trial, your money to come back to you in full if you are not more than satisfied?

"Before I used your creams," writes Mrs. D. B. G., "I had a muddy, broken out skin. Now it is just like velvet. Everywhere I go, I get compliments on my complexion, and I felt it my duty to let you know what a wonderful product you have on the market." And her letter is only one of hundreds.

Just your name on the enclosed card, with 50 cents in coin or stamps, will bring you a large jar of So-and-So Bleach Creme—the same large jar that formerly sold for $1.00. And if you mail it right away, we will send with it—as our gift—a generous size sample of So-and-So Almond Lotion, to keep the hands soft and white.

Sincerely,

It is said that Demosthenes used to taunt his rival orator Aeschines with his cleverness—but ineffectiveness. "You make them say," charged Demosthenes,
"' What a wonderful speech!' I make them say

'Let us march against Philip!' "

The same thing is likely to be true of letters. Beware of the letter that everyone admires for its cleverness. It may bring you a great meed of praise—but few orders. The good letter is one that leaves your reader hardly conscious of the letter itself, so interested is he in doing the thing you want him to do. Judged from that point of view, here is a good letter:

Show Me One of Your Rejected Manuscripts,
And I'll Show You the Secret of
Making All Your Stories Successful!

DEAR WRITER:

In order that you may realize at the outset the peculiar importance of this letter, let me inform you, before taking up the details, that only one hundred of those who receive it can have the benefit this month of the personal analysis and the invaluable suggestions which it offers.

Under the supervision of Dr. John Jones, Editor, University Professor, successful Writer and Teacher of Writing, the Faculty of the John Jones School has agreed to read and analyze ten stories each day (not over 5000 words each), to point out why these stories were not acceptable and to tell you *the secret of making them successful.*

This letter is being sent to a limited number of writers. To the first three hundred of them who respond, it offers the chance to get a personal detailed analysis of their strong points and their weak ones, the factors which make their stories good and those they must change before they can be financially successful.

It offers you this personal analysis under the direct supervision of perhaps the most successful teacher of writing in the world today—NOT at the usual cost of $25 or $50—BUT FOR ONLY $1.00!

Pick one of your most promising stories or articles, not

333

exceeding 5000 words in length. Send it with $1.00 (and 10¢ for return postage) to Dr. John Jones, Jonesville, Mo., pinning a slip to it marked—"For Personal Analysis and Suggestions.

To ten of these each day, the Faculty will give their personal study, analyzing the strengths and the weaknesses, criticizing, suggesting, pointing out how the stories can be made successful. They will take the stories in the order in which they are received. If they come too late for them to reach them within a month, we shall return them to you with your $1.

Remember, only ten stories a day are all that the Faculty can find time for. And it's going to be "First come, first served!" So if you have a story which you know to be good but which the Editors keep sending back, *mail it in*. Find out what is wrong with it.

There may be only some minor weakness standing between you and success in writing. There may be some rule Dr. Jones can give you, some one thing to watch for, which will change your stories overnight from failures into successes.

Will you risk $1 to learn the truth about what is holding you back? Will you invest $1 for the secret of literary success?

Sincerely,

Of course, there is the occasional letter that combines cleverness with a really effective appeal. When you get one of these, you have a sure winner. As clever a letter as we have often seen, and at the same time as effective, was one received from the Advertising Club of New York:

DEAR MR. COLLIER:

The Directors of the Advertising Club of New York have

agreed to accept my proposal of a few important names for membership in the club WITHOUT HAVING TO PAY THE INITIATION OF $100 and your name is one of those I have suggested.

This means that your signature on the enclosed application will permit me to submit your name to our Admissions Committee and in due course place you on the same basis as our present members, with your first quarter's dues of $18.75 paying you up in full to July 1.

I am certain that you will appreciate this action of the Board, and welcome the opportunity of becoming associated with the membership of this Club.

Your joining the Club is a matter of interest to me and I look for the return of your application with keen pleasure.

Most sincerely,

That same idea can be used in many ways to advantage. In getting subscribers to a magazine, for instance, here is a way a client of ours used it with considerable success:

I Wonder If You Can Qualify
As A "Player Patron"?

DEAR MR. JONES:

You have been designated as one qualified to serve on our Board of "Player Patrons", and our Directors have authorized me to invite you to become one of this select group of amateur sportsmen.

The requirements are simple—for those like yourself who are interested in sport for the fun of it rather than for what they can get out of it.

You see, The Players has from its inception had an Advisory Board consisting of such well known gentlemen as So-and-So, Such-and-Such, Whoozit, and others equally important in the world of sport. The idea now is merely to enlarge this Board by having back of it a group of men and women well known in their local fields, at least, and many of them nationally known, who will form a "Patron's Group" and to whom difficult questions may be referred for judgment.

The purpose of this group will not be monetary support, but to have back of us the judgment and the experience of men and women known in the world of sports for their integrity, their knowledge of sport and their sportsman-ship.

Will you kindly fill out the enclosed card, putting a check mark against the sports you are most familiar with, so we may know which questions to refer to you?

It is, of course, essential that all of our "Patrons Group" should be readers of The Players, but because our idea is not monetary support, we are going to enter the names of this special group on our lists at half the usual price—$2.00 a year instead of the regular $4.00.

Will you fill out the card right away, please, so we can get your name among our "Players Patrons" group at once, and have the benefit of your judgment on the questions that are constantly coming up for decision?

Sincerely,

There are numerous variations of this method that can be used in a dozen ways, and all effectively. Here is another of them:

Will You Give Me a Little Information About Yourself—
Just the Sports That You Go In for Most?

DEAR SIR:

This letter is purely personal, and not primarily con-cerned with business. Rather, it invites a courtesy from you, appreciating the fact that if—in your considerate way— you can help the good cause by a bit of co-operation, you will do so, and gladly.

You know The Players, of course. It was founded six years ago to give a very limited group of Americans, a publication that should be peculiarly their own. It numbers among its subscribers the best known patrons of amateur sports in this country.

The editors are now thinking of restricting its field to a few major sports, but before coming to a definite decision, they want to determine accurately the sports in which you and other representative sportsmen are most interested.

Will you help us? Will you put a number against each sport listed on the enclosed card, to indicate the order in which they interest you?

There is no obligation of any kind attached. We want your preferences, whether you ever read The Players or not. But to show our appreciation of your courtesy in giving us this information, we shall be glad to enter your subscription to The Players for the next year for half its regular subscription price-only $2. The Players Almanac, which comes in each issue, will alone be worth that small amount to you.

Send no money. Just your name on the enclosed card, with your preferences checked against the list on the side, are all we need. Will you jot these down now, please, and drop it in the mail? It's already stamped. We shall greatly appreciate your courtesy.

Sincerely,

We all like to feel important. Anything that raises our ego, that makes us feel more necessary to the general scheme of things, is sure to please us. The cleverness of the foregoing letters lies in their ability to feed our vanity, without making it too apparent that this is the real purpose of the letter. The letter that follows had a similar purpose, and used on different magazines and with special lists, pulled amazingly high returns:

I Wonder If You Would Be Good Enough
To Give Me the Benefit of Your Experience?

DEAR SPORTSMAN:

Will you give me the benefit of your judgment on a matter of considerable importance to us?

Most magazines, as you know, are edited by a very small group, dominated by one man. He thinks he knows what his readers want, better than any writer or group of writers can tell him.

And he may be right. But we should like to try an experiment. We are going to get together a select group of hunters and fishermen from different sections of the country, and *have them practically edit Hunter & Fishermen for us* for a few months.

We want to see if a magazine for red-blooded men, edited by a select group of men who are sportsmen in the true sense of the word—men who find their greatest pleasure with rod, gun, tent and canoe—will not have a greater appeal than stories picked because they measure up to the standard of any one man.

Will YOU help? Will you accept a place on our Advisory Editorial Staff?

Mind you, this is no mere bluff. This will require some real work on your part. You will have to read enough of every story in Hunter & Fisherman to criticize it if it is not up to your standard, or if it is not the type you regard as interesting.

We shall want you to treat the magazine as your own— condemn everything you would not accept if you were the sole editor, and tell us WHY you condemn it; suggest

338

the type of article you would put in, and the authors you consider worth while.

We mean this. We want the benefit of your judgment, your help in making Hunter & Fisherman a magazine for every true sportsman who really cares about his shooting and fishing and camping and woodcraft, and who wants all the skill and knowledge he can get. We want to make Hunter & Fisherman a magazine that every member of the Editorial Staff can be proud of, and can feel that he has had a part in the making of. We want you as a co-worker—not merely as a reader. Will you join us?

Your reward? We'd like to make it a complimentary subscription to Hunter & Fisherman. We can't do that, on account of the Post Office regulations governing second class mail. But we are going to do the next best thing. Instead of the 50 cents a copy which 50,000 newsstand buyers pay for it every month. . . instead of the $5.00 a year paid by our regular subscribers. . . we will send Hunter & Fisherman to you at exactly HALF PRICE— *two years' subscription for the price of one!*

Not only that, but you need send us only $1 now. The balance of $3.50 for your special two-year subscription price you can send us when we bill you six months from now.

That is the only thing we shall have to charge for. We can send you prepaid reply envelopes for all correspondence, but under the Post Office regulations, we cannot mail second class to more than a very small percentage of our subscription list, unless those subscriptions are paid for.

The special low price of $5.00 you will pay for a two years subscription will come back to you many times over, however, in the contacts you will make with other hunters and fishermen, and in the greatly increased value you will get from the magazine yourself.

As John Jones Doe put it—"No man can hope to master woodcraft in one short lifetime. Always he is learning.

No small percentage of my own knowledge of how to kill game and catch fish has come from the lips or the writings of other sportsmen."

So in helping others to learn more of woodcraft, you will be increasing your own knowledge of the art, too. And instead of enjoying only two or three weeks of hunting and fishing, you will be re-living your experiences the whole year through.

Will you TRY it? Will you give us the benefit of your judgment and experience in making Hunter & Fisherman the most practical of all out-door magazines? Only a few men from each section can be selected to make up this Advisory Editorial Staff. Your name has been suggested for one of them. Will you serve as a member?

Just your name and address on the enclosed Acceptance Form, with your check or a $1 bill attached, are all that is necessary now. After you've had time to examine a copy or two, we'll write you about suggestions and the like. Will you put your name on the Acceptance and mail it back NOW? Thank you!

Appreciatively,

While most people lack the courage for real leadership, few there are who do not long to be looked up to, as being a bit above their fellows. Organizers of Lodges and Clubs realize this predominant trait in human nature and capitalize it to the fullest degree. And publishers have not been backward in giving their readers the chance to become "Founders" or "Charter Subscribers" or Members of some more or less exclusive group. Here is a membership offer by the Literary Guild which we understand was particularly effective:

DEAR FRIEND:

You have been elected to full membership in The Literary Guild of America for one year. Here is your membership certificate. It is made out in your name and is non-transferable.

340

Your membership entitles you to all advantages of the Guild—including the special NEW features that have been so enthusiastically received by thousands of other members. It entitles you also to one of the most entertaining and brilliant books ever published, AN AMERICAN OMNI—BUS, a library of the best of Americana, ABSOLUTELY FREE.

You now need only sign and return the membership certificate to put your membership into immediate effect and to receive the beautiful GIFT volume.

Probably you are already familiar with the Literary Guild— the book club which has become almost a necessity to thousands of readers. The new membership plan makes the Guild far and away the most satisfactory, convenient and economical method of obtaining the books you most want to own.

As a member of the Literary Guild you are entitled to all of these advantages:

1—Every month you receive, free, a copy of the Guild magazine, WINGS. This interesting little magazine contains original articles by and about the important writers of today and many delightful photographs and art reproductions. In addition, you will find a full description of the book which the Editors have selected as the outstanding one of the following month. This book is selected from the manuscripts submitted each month by all leading publishers. The best book is chosen and a special edition is made in an exclusive Guild binding—usually more attractive than the regular retail edition.

2—With your copy of WINGS, you receive an "Announcement Slip." If you do not care to receive this following month's selection, you simply return the Announcement Slip. Otherwise, destroy the slip and the book will come to you, postage paid, on the first of the month.

3—When the selected book arrives, take five days to read it. Then if you wish, return it at our expense and owe nothing. If you decide to keep the book, send $2.00 as payment in full. IT IS NOT NECESSARY TO BUY THE BOOK UNLESS YOU WISH TO.

4—Guild members save up to 50% and more. The price of Guild selections, in the regular retail book store runs as high as $5.00. Yet you never pay more than $2.00 for them, through the Guild.

5—Each month, in WINGS, the Editors of the Guild review briefly about twenty current books OTHER than Guild selections. You may purchase any of these recommended books at the regular publisher's prices. They will be sent postpaid.

6—In fact, you may purchase, through the Guild, any book published and in print in the United States, at regular publishers' prices. Such purchases will be promptly executed and the books will be sent to you postage prepaid.

7—You may purchase as few as four books a year through the Guild and still meet the requirements of full membership. These books may be either Guild selections or recommended books, or any other books of your choice.

8—Membership in the Guild is free. There are no dues, assessments, delivery costs or incidental charges of any kind. You pay only for the books you choose. You pay only $2.00 each for the Guild selections which you accept, although their regular retail prices range up to $5.00. You are never required to take a book you do not want.

9—The Editorial Board, which selects one outstanding book and keeps you informed of *all* the best books each month, is composed of four prominent authors, editors and critics—Carl Van Doren, Julia Peterkin, Joseph Wood Krutch and Burton Rascoe.

10—As a new member, you receive,

FREE, AN AMERICAN OMNIBUS,
Edited by Carl Van Doren

In this gigantic volume of 1488 pages is included a full length novel, short stories, essays, poetry, humor, mystery and even a play. Sinclair Lewis, Booth Tarkington, Ring Lardner, Marc Connolly, George Ade, Dorothy Parker, Don Marquis, Mary Austin and many other important writers are included in this omnibus of literary Americana, prepared to be read for sheer enjoyment.

This entertaining volume will be sent you free as soon as you have signed and returned your membership certificate.

IMPORTANT. Protect yourself against rising book prices. The cost of raw materials for the manufacture of books *is being advanced* 30%. Yet we guarantee to protect our members against any increase in the price of Guild selections for one year.

We urge you, therefore, to sign and return your membership certificate at once.

Sincerely yours,

A few years ago, Nelson Doubleday sold a million copies of the "Book of Etiquette", on a "Keeping Up with the Joneses'" appeal. And since he blazed the trail, hundreds of products of all kinds have been advertised and successfully sold in the same way.

One such ad that we remember was "Can You Talk About Books with the rest of them?" Knowing its success, we used the same appeal in writing a letter for Stage Magazine. Here is the way it went:

Can You Talk About Plays
And the Like With the Rest of Them?

DEAR READER:

An innocent looking Questionnaire—just a little ink on a piece of paper—is enclosed with this letter.

This Questionnaire, when answered and returned to us, will enable us to tell you whether you rate as a drawing-room Sphinx, with whom conversation is a lost art unless the talk turns to business, or as an all-around-man-of-affairs, as much at home in the world center of entertainment as in the marts of commerce.

The brightest hours of the day should be those after dark— if you know where to spend them. The Stage tells you each month what's new, what's interesting in the whole round of metropolitan life after dark—theatres, movies, radio, supper clubs. It covers the world of entertainment, informs you infallibly what to see and do. Rich, lavish and colorful, it is at once beautiful and diverting. It insures your enjoyment when you are out, keeps you in touch even when you stay at home.

For the Stage reports each month the whole dazzling world of amusement—all the vast apparatus of the relaxation and gaiety, which enframes the night's fun. It visits the friendly cocktail spots, the dinner, dancing and supper places, pictures the modes and manners of all the gay pilgrims to Baghdad, tells you where to go, what to do, before the theater and after, to get the utmost of fun and entertainment.

Will you try the next five issues—if I send them to you at the special price of $1.00? And will you fill out the enclosed Questionnaire, so we can tell you just how high you rate today in your knowledge of where to go and what to do to get the most fun for your money?

Make no mistake about this—Broadway is vividly alive,

even though it is Summer. And scattered over the country are hundreds of small playhouses that are well and entertainingly run. Everything that is bright, tuneful or interesting will be reflected in the colorful pages of Stage. The enclosed card will bring you Stage for the next five months at the special price of $1.00—just about half what it would cost you if you bought these issues on the news-stands. Will you TRY it? Will you see for yourself how it saves you the time and money wasted on mediocre performances, how it gives you the vital news on all that qualifies as valid entertainment?

Just your name and address on the enclosed card is all that is neccessary. Will you jot these down and drop it in the mail—NOW?

Sincerely,

The above letter illustrates the point that Mr. Wheeler made—that when you find an approach that is unusually successful, it pays to develop it to the utmost; to develop it—and then to extend it as far as possible to ideas of a similar nature.

At one of the Direct Mail Conventions, for instance, a speaker told us that the only letter from which his company had been able to get a satisfactory response was one beginning— "I wonder if you would be good enough to do me a favor?" So every letter they used started with some variation of that appeal.

When the writer was with the New Process Company of Warren, Pa., we found letters of that type to be successful, but we could never afford to stick to it or any one type of opening. We wrote to the same people too often, and they would soon have tired of it.

So we tested continually for new starters. And of a similar nature to this one, we found a dozen others that pulled just as well, while many of an entirely different style greatly outpulled it.

There is no one best method of approaching your reader. And no one knows all the successful methods. But experienced advertising men have learned a number of ways that work well in a large majority of cases and unless you know better ones, it pays to use these tested methods. They go far towards taking the guess out of advertising.

You have seen numbers of advertisements, for instance, starting—"Give me Five Minutes, and I'll give you this or that." So successful has this approach been found, that it has been put among the proven order-getters. Why not adapt it, then, to your offer? Here is the way we used it for one client:

Give Me Two Minutes—And I'll Give You
The Secret of a Goodly Profit Without Investment!

DEAR SIR:

I am going to send you, in the next few days, a book of Christmas Cards that are DIFFERENT, for your most particular customers.

This book is unlike any you have ever used before, because:

1—It has the new plastic style of binding that opens flat and makes it easy for a woman to hold; small in size, light in weight, it is an easy book to handle.

2—Many of the cards are illustrated with beautiful etchings, hand-colored, of new and original designs that will be in great demand among those who want their cards to be distinctive. Here are no duplicates of other Christmas books. The cards in this book were, for the most part, made especially for us.

3—An outstanding feature of this new book is the number of ENGRAVED cards. With their appealing designs, their beautiful coloring and their happily-phrased messages, they need only to be seen to be appreciated.

I am going to send this new and different book of Christmas cards to you—with no cost or obligation on your part— for you to examine and actually put to the test in your Christmas Card department.

There is only one thing: I don't want to send it without your permission. You can grant that in a moment on the enclosed card.

Mind you, there is no charge of any kind for the book, in spite of the fact that it is amazingly expensive to make up. We send it to you at our own risk for your FREE USE. All we ask of you is that you give it a chance to show what it can do, that you put it where your customers can see it, where they can compare it with the cards offered by others.

These cards, though so distinctive and beautiful, are in the popular price class—5 cents, 10 cents and 15 cents each. The margin of profit is the same as you get from your other Christmas Card books, and they have this big advantage:

> Ten years' experience has equipped us to handle quickly and efficiently as much business as you can send us, and to turn out all orders promptly, right up to the last minute before Christmas.

Only 125 of these Christmas Books are made up each season. Only 125 stores can handle our cards—never more than one in each section of the country. So there is no danger of duplication.

We should like you to be the store to handle our Cards for your section. May we send you 'our Christmas book?

Just your name on the enclosed card is all that is necessary. But please mail it soon, for we shall have to make it "First come, first served."

Sincerely,

That same client had recently received a letter which struck him favorably. It started with the story of a Klondyke miner who had struck it rich, and wanting to show his importance, walked into a restaurant in Seattle and ordered $25 worth of ham and eggs. The waiter, not to be outdone, told him he was sorry, but they didn't serve half-portions. And the story was used to point the moral that no matter how much you try to outdo the other fellow, there is always someone to cap your tale with a stronger one.

This client was so struck with that idea that he wanted a letter along the same lines, so we wrote the following to test against the more proven appeal of the previous letter. The proven approach won, but he had the right idea. It is always worth while to keep trying something new against the old. With every big mailing we ever made on New Process Company products, we always included tests of new letters. And it was surprising how often we developed new approaches that outpulled anything that had been used before.

DEAR MR. JONES:

You've heard the story, I know, of the proud fisherman who was trying to impress a couple of guides with his piscatorial proficiency.

"I had a big tarpon on the line," he was explaining, "when along came an enormous shark, opened his mouth and just swallowed that tarpon whole. Did I have a time landing that shark!"

"Hmm!" grunted one of the guides, expectorating disgustedly, "where I come from, we bait with sharks!"

Which goes to show that no matter how strong one makes his story, there is always someone ready to go him one better.

If I told you that our new 1937 Book of Christmas Cards is better than those you now use, someone else would just make a stronger statement.

So I shall say only that our book is DIFFERENT. To begin with, it is easier for a woman to handle, because it has the new plastic style of binding that opens flat.

An outstanding feature of the book is the number of ENGRAVED CARDS, with beautiful etchings, handcolored, of new and original designs made especially for us, that will be in demand among those who want their cards

348

to be distinctive.

Lastly, there is no charge for the book, in spite of its cost-liness. We send it to you at our own risk and expense, for your FREE USE. The margin of profit is the same you get from your other books, the cards are in the popular price class—5 cents, 10 cents and 15 cents —and we can offer you this big advantage:

Ten years' experience has equipped us to handle quickly and efficiently as much business as you can send us, and to turn out orders promptly, right up to the last minute.

Will you TRY it? The enclosed card will bring this amaz-ingly attractive book of cards to you without cost and without obligation. There is only one thing: We make up only 125 books each year—no more. We send only one to each territory. We should like to send the one for your territory to YOU. May we?

Sincerely,

The one thing that should always be borne in mind is that it is not merchandise you are selling, but human nature, human reactions. The movie people have found that people always respond to certain motivations, so they have their guaranteed laugh producers, their guaranteed methods of turning on the tears, and so on.

It doesn't matter what the play, they can drag in a scene showing a dignified butler carrying a tray, have him stumble and dive into the whipped cream, and they are sure of a good laugh. Or they can show the little boy kneeling at his mother's knee, praying— "God bless daddy and bring him back safe," and be sure of wringing a tear from every woman in the audience.

In the same way, you can take an approach that has successfully sold a set of books, and with very little change, adapt it to selling shoes or socks or luggage or any one of a thousand other products and be just as successful in disposing of these!

The "Give me 5 minutes" approach, for instance, used in one of the foregoing letters. You can use it to sell a relief for Athlete's Foot, as in—"Give me 5 days, and I'll give you relief from itching feet." Or a new dance step "Give me 15 minutes and I'll give you the

secret of dancing to the new slow-time music." Or a new car—
"Give me 5 minutes and I'll give you a new sensation in riding comfort." Here is the way it was adapted to selling a new set of books:

Give me Five Days—And I'll Give You
The Secret of Learning Any Subject!

DEAR READER:

Men who know it all need go no further into this letter
than this paragraph, because it is not for them. Neither is
it for those who are satisfied with their present positions,
and the progress they have made in life.

This letter is for the man whose ship has not come in,
who WANTS to get ahead, and who realizes that he will
earn more only as he learns more. For this letter gives you
the secret of the most important yet least known of all the
arts—THE SECRET OF LEARNING!

America spends two billions a year on its public schools,
other millions in training teachers how to teach, *but very
little in showing students how to learn!*

Is it any wonder that most people forget all they have
been taught in classrooms within five years after they
leave school? Is it surprising that students should dawdle
through four years in College to learn what, in the opinion of Professor Pitkin of Columbia, any man who understood the art of learning might grasp in six months?

For here, according to Professor Pitkin, is the
amazing fact: When you know how to learn, half
an hour daily is enough to master the fundamentals
of any science WITHIN A YEAR!

Never before have the rewards for high-speed learners
been so great. When you know how to learn, you put
yourself in position to master the intricacies of any job or
any problem—quickly, easily. You equip yourself in the
race of life to keep a jump ahead of the crowd. And that

350

is all the lead you need in life or in a race to pull down the biggest prices the world has to offer. The old adage of "Live and Learn" might well be changed to "Learn—and then live as you please!"

What IS the secret of learning? HEADLINE TREATMENT—sharply outlined, quickly digested resumes of each subject. With these as a framework, it is easy to add a thorough understanding of the details of the subject.

Notice the way a newspaper picks the high spots of the day's news, puts them in headlines, then follows with a brief resume that tells the essentials of the story in a dozen words. That is the secret of quickly learning any subject— getting the headlines that put the idea across, following these with a short resume, and then filling in the details. It is simplified study—*study made easy.*

And that is what we offer you in the COLLEGE OUTLINE series—*Headline Treatment* that gives you the important facts, illustrations that sum up whole chapters, pithy resumes that cover the essential framework— and then additional particulars to fill in the picture.

Years ago, the late President Eliot of Harvard University startled the world by saying that he could put all the books essential to a liberal education on a five foot shelf. If he had lived to see the COLLEGE OUTLINES, I think he would have cut his shelf to two feet instead of five.

For in the twenty-six volumes of the COLLEGE OUTLINE series now published, you get the essentials of a cultural education. They carry with them the mark of the educated man. Whether you have been to College or not, you need these handy volumes. If you are a College man, you need them to recall in interesting fashion the things you were taught there. If you are not, you need them to give you these facts that are so necessary to the successful man of today.

Each day in College, according to President Ferry of Hamilton College, is worth $100 in later life. Yet, as Ex-President Lowell of Harvard points out, it is not the College classroom that is necessary. "All true education," he says, "is self-education."

You can judge for yourself how valuable the COLLEGE OUTLINES are considered by educational authorities from the fact that practically every College and University throughout the land now uses them, and they are endorsed by more than 2700 College instructors. "I am a strong advocate of OUTLINES," writes a well known instructor from the University of Denver, "as furnishing the skeleton of a subject both to the student and teacher, *giving the subject a backbone.*"

For many years after he had made his millions, Andrew Carnegie used to employ a tutor to give him the cultural background he was unable to get as a youngster. COLLEGE OUTLINES take the place of a first class tutor in giving you a quick and thorough understanding of a subject. Each one gives you a fistful of pertinent reading covering a particular subject, as compared with the usual armload of reference works. Their plan of head-lining the essential facts gives you a grasp of the subject in the same way that the headlines in your newspaper give you the background for the story that follows.

> With your permission, I am going to send the 26 volumes of the COLLEGE OUTLINE series to you— to read, to try out in your own home for a week, at our risk and expense.

Mind you, there is no obligation on your part to keep them. You can return them for any reason or no reason. All I want you to do now is to TRY them, to put them to the test of actual use, to see for yourself how their head-line treatment gives you a thorough grasp of each subject quickly, easily—and how it shows you the secret of learning any subject.

352

If you were to buy all the books from which the 26 volumes of the COLLEGE OUTLINES were taken, you'd have a library of hundreds of volumes by 119 different authorities, that would cost you thousands of dollars. In the COLLEGE OUTLINES, you get the headline facts from all those books, and they cost you—NOT thousands, not even hundreds, but only $1.50 at the end of your week's examination, and $2 a month for nine months. (Or $17 in one full cash payment.)

Every man wants to get out of the rut, to grow. Yet who is the one that wins promotion? Is it the man whose knowledge is limited to his own routine work? Or is it the man who, like the famous psychologist Wm. James, realizes that at bottom there is but one science, and that until you know something of all subjects, you cannot know everything about one. So he broadens his knowledge by taking in the essentials of all important subjects.

That is what every man must do who wants to be regarded as educated in the broad sense, or even as an authority on some one subject. He must learn something of all. And nowhere can you get such a rounded knowledge so readily or so quickly as through the pages of the COLLEGE OUTLINES.

"The only worthwhile liberal education today," says Dr. Conant, of Harvard, "is one which is a continuing process going on throughout life." And he goes on to say that "If knowledge is to be advanced in a democracy, the leaders of opinion and the intelligent voters must be kept in touch with what scholarship and research really signify." To prove that, all you need to do is to mail the enclosed card. The card obligates us only—not you. Will you TRY it? Will you put your name on it and drop in the mail?

Sincerely,

P. S—To those who mail the enclosed card at once, we are going to send a copy of our latest COLLEGE OUTLINE, covering every essential phase of JOUR-

NALISM.

Most of the books you get on this subject cover only one type of writing such as editorial work, reporting, feature writing, etc. This new book covers all. Not only that, but it gives you a digest of the most successful methods of learning Journalism, by the very men who originated those methods.

To get a copy of this new OUTLINE, with our compliments, *just mail the enclosed card right away.*

A knowledge of your product is essential, of course. But familiarity with human reactions, human responses to familiar stimuli, is even more important.

Oftentimes when we have been asked to write a letter about some new product, we have sketched the first rough draft of it without seeing the product at all, or knowing any more about it than our average reader. We put into that first draft everything that we should want in the product if we were buying it. Then—after we had our mental picture of the ideal product from our point of view as a user—we took the product itself, studied it, and determined how it compared with our ideal. Many times it has been an approach developed in this way that has proven the most effective way of selling the product.

Magic Words That Make People

In changing the titles of his thousand and more little Blue Books, experimenting with first this and then another title, E. Haldeman - Julius found certain magic words that were more effective than any others in making people buy. "Truth", "Life," "Love," were among the strongest of these. As part of a title or headline, they always increased the pull. "At last" was a big help, as was "New", "Advice", "Facts you should know about—", "Cultural Help". But "How to" led them all.

As an instance of this, Haldeman—Julius shows how the changing of the name of "The Art of Controversy" to "How to Argue Logically" vastly increased the sale of the book. The same was true when he changed "Essay on Conversation" to "How to Improve Your Conversation". "Evolution made plain" was a flop, but "Facts you should know about Evolution" made the book sell in the big volume class. And everyone knows how "The Story of Philosophy" put Philosophy among the best sellers.

How can you apply the same idea to letters? Here is the way George H. Cole, of Syracuse, N. Y., did it. He had a series of collection letters to sell—a dry enough product, in all conscience. But is his letter dry? Just read it and see how he puts life into the very first line, and into every line that follows:

> Want to raise money? While they last,
> The Famous "Notes on Financing"—FREE!!

GENTLEMEN:

Would you like to see bigger and better collections in a few short weeks?

Let me tell you how:

I am going to send within the next few days a choice collection of marvelous letters—the cream of the very best collection letters ever written.

These letters are probably not like any you have ever seen before, because:

1. They actually are the 'pick' of the most effective collection letters ever used—and especially valuable right now.

2. They are the ones which have produced the best results ever attained—in actual use.

3. All are friendly, courteous—preserving and often creating good will.

4. They substitute experience for experiment—and are suitable to any business without revision.

I am going to send these wonder letters with no obligation on your part—for you to read and ACTUALLY TRY

OUT at my risk and expense.

But there's just one thing—I don't want to send them without first getting your permission. You can grant that in a moment by penciling the Courtesy Card enclosed.

When I send the letters there's absolutely no obligation to keep them. While I want you to know first hand the great results they will obtain in actual use—you are perfectly free to return them for any reason or for no reason at all.

But here's the most important part:

If you find they are everything I say about them—and you are to be the sole judge—how much would you expect to pay for them? $25.00? $50.00? $100.00? That's what they will be worth to you based on actual RESULTS they'll get for you. Use them side by side with those you are now using—and compare results! Certainly if they will do half of what I've promised you they would be worth that and more.

Well, if you decide to try out these letters, you need send me, not $25, or $50, or even the regular price of $10, but MY SPECIAL INTRODUCTORY PRICE TO YOU of $3.85.

And that isn't all—

If within three months your $3.85 hasn't grown to many times that amount in collections made and good-will preserved—send back the letters and I'll refund to you cheerfully and in full every cent you have paid for them.

Remember, there are no strings of any kind to my offer. If within three months they haven't helped you to the pot of gold at the end of the rainbow by collecting many, many times their cost, then they are not for you. Send them back and get your money.

And I want you to note this:

356

These wonder letters are by no means an ordinary 'series'. They are not a series of threats or ordinary 'dunning' letters. Nor are they the familiar 'tear out forms'. They ARE the aristocrats of the collection field.

And just listen to this:

"The letters are the work of geniuses—and worth thousands of dollars." So writes Chas. Hardman, of Chicago.

For they are the best of the best—and gotten together, I assure you, only after the expenditure of much time and effort.

The Famous Notes on Financing Free

And for good measure—while they last—I'll send you the very unusual and practical "Notes on Financing the Business of Moderate Size", with my compliments, at no cost whatever. You'll find them interesting and very valuable if you ever want to raise money for your business.

But you'll have to send the Courtesy Card right away for we're running off only a limited number of sets for this Advance Edition. And advanced orders are coming in so fast that I'm afraid all of them will be spoken for very quickly.

So if you want these WONDER LETTERS without risk of loss and the NOTES ON FINANCING free, you'll have to mail the Courtesy Card, NOW—TODAY.

Yours for better business,

Selling a Boring Machine is a dry subject. Offhand, you'd say it would be difficult to inject much life into lt. But just listen to this. Whether you are interested in Boring Machines or not, wouldn't it stop you? Wouldn't it hold your interest?

When Millions Were Actually
Thrown Into the Gutter!

DEAR SIR:

"The most expensive gutters in the world"—that is what
they called the canals of 1830, which cost
$200,000,000.00 to build, and were doomed by the loco-
motive. What do you suppose they will call the trenches
of today, where whole gangs of laborers take days to dig
up stretches of expensively paved streets, *just to lay pipes
or cables or drains under them?*

"The most expensive ditches in the world"—probably.
FOR THOSE SAME HOLES COULB BE BORED AT
A TENTH OF THE COST WITH A Boring Machine.

All the work of tearing up paving, all the expense of re-
surfacing, might just as well be thrown into the ditch, for
all the need there is of it or all the good you get out of it.

> You see, the ....bores UNDER the street. It
> can make any size hole from 2 1/2 inches to l0 1/2
> inches. It can bore any length up to 120 ft. It works
> as fast as a foot a minute, and it costs only 10 cents
> a foot!

"In 1930, we made plans for installing water mains in a
newly incorporated borough," writes the So-and-So
Town-ship Water Co., of Smithtown, Pa., "through which
passed three paved highways. Our permit was condi-
tioned upon *not breaking the paved surface of the high-
way.* Thirty or more crossings were necessary. The
Boring Machine enabled us to do the work in 1931 at
minimum expenditure.

We know of no better or more economical machine for its
purpose. We completed the entire job for less than half
the estimated cost of tunneling.

We can save more than half for you, too. May we tell you how? Your name on the enclosed card will bring full information by mail, without obligation.

Sincerely,

"Some men are born gamblers." There's a start for a letter. There is a phrase that gets under the skin of most readers. "A born gambler"—we all feel that we are ready to take a chance when the risk is worth while, yet that we know when to gamble, when to play safe. How can we tie that very human trait into our letter in a way that will appeal to our readers? Here is the way the Clinton Carpet Company of Chicago, did it:

DEAR SIR:

Some men are born gamblers—always willing to put their money on a long chance.

But there aren't many Hotel Men—no matter how strong their sporting instincts—who voluntarily turn their backs on a sure thing.

That's one reason for the success of Ozite Carpet Cushion. There isn't any gamble about it at all. You know when you buy it that Ozite will double the life of your carpets— and consequently *double your money*!

After all, your carpets are pretty high stakes to gamble with and the odds are all against you if you lay them without Ozite. What's more, if you put your money on a "just-as-good" carpet lining, you simply raise the ante and increase your risk!

In the important matter of carpets and carpet cushions— just stick to OZITE Carpet Cushion and luck will always be yours!

Cordially yours,

John Caples, author of "Tested Advertising Methods," is authority for the statement that the headline of an advertisement accounts for 60% of the pull of that advertisement. In the same way, the start of a letter makes or breaks the letter, for if the start does not interest your reader, he never gets down to the rest of your letter.

Personally, our concern starts with the outside of the envelope. If we can find a good enough catch-phrase, to correspond with the headline of an ad, we'll put it on the outside of the envelope. If not, we will try to make the envelope look like a personal letter, or use a novel size or design that will attract attention. A miniature letter, for instance, when used with an envelope about the size of a calling card, is one of the most effective pieces we have ever used. An imitation hand-written letter, with hand fill-in to match the body, is next. Then Hooven letters, with the recipient's name repeated in the body of the letter. After these come the stunt letters, like those with a penny pasted at the top, or a new dime or German mark or whatnot. All designed to win attention and thus get themselves read.

As to the motives to appeal to when you have won the reader's attention, by far the strongest, in our experience, is Vanity. Not the vanity that buys a cosmetic or whatnot to look a little better, but that unconscious vanity which makes a man want to feel important in his own eyes and makes him strut mentally. This appeal needs to be subtly used, but when properly used, it is the strongest we know.

Next to it, perhaps, is the premium or "Gift" idea—starting your letter with the gift of some unimportant article, to lead your reader on to the buying of your real product.

Selling, you know, is just a matter of making people WANT some one thing you have, more than they want the money it costs them. And the easiest way to make them want it is by sugar-coating your offer like a doctor sugar-coats a bitter pill—for it is oftentimes a bitter pill to dig up money for something you do not really need. This sugar-coating takes many different forms. The gift or premium is the most common form. Here it is used to sell a magazine subscription:

DEAR MR. JONES:

As you will see from the enclosed Reservation Card, we are putting aside for you, with our compliments, a set of three books which for timely value and business interest have seldom been equaled.

Thousands upon thousands of these books have been sold at regular retail prices. Thousands more will be sold at the same high figure. But our rights to them cease with the end of our one big edition—*and there are less than four hundred sets in our stock room now!*

These three volumes include the famous "Obvious Adams", as well as such popular stand-bys as "The Sixth Prune" and "The Subconscious Mind in Business". They contain some of the choicest nuggets of business philosophy and homely common sense ever written. They are called "The Library of Self-Starters", by Robert R. Updegraff.

> If you will mail the enclosed Reservation Card at once, calling for the next 24 issues of System, the Journal of Modern Business Management, at its regular price of $5, we will send you—*with our compliments*—a 3-volume set of Updegraff's "Library of Self-Starters," beautifully printed on heavy book paper and bound in thick board covers.

The only reason we can make this offer is that we are very near the end of our big edition, with not enough sets left to justify printing circulars and letters to sell them alone. So we decided to use them as a special inducement to introduce the new System to a few select business executives whom we have not been able to reach with our regular offer.

L. F. Loree, President of the Delaware & Hudson, says that during the past year 20% of the higher managerial staff of industry have been destroyed or totally disabled as industrial leaders. He believes it will take four or five years' training and experience for their juniors in the ranks of management to replace those fallen leaders.

But will it? If they depend upon ordinary training and experience—yes. But if they study each month the proven plans and practical methods of the most successful leaders of today—then we believe they can follow in

361

those leaders' footsteps at once! And not merely in their footsteps, but the enthusiasm and fresh viewpoints they can put into their jobs should enable them to quickly outstrip these leaders' pace.

That is what the new System gives you—the practical methods that are producing results for others. It is a clearing House for all that is timely and usable in the most efficiently run offices and successful businesses. It is a new deal—in business conditions and in a business magazine. It brings you the chance to get in on the ground floor of the new business cycle, with all that this signifies of opportunity and of profit.

Will you use the enclosed Reservation Card to TRY it? Will you accept a 3-volume set of Updegraff's "Library of Self-Starters," with our compliments? Then put your name on the card and drop it in the mail NOW! You will never have another such opportunity.

Sincerely,

Gifts or premiums can just as readily be used to sell dental supplies, or groceries, or furniture, or lots. In fact, the principle is as old as selling. Down in Louisiana, they have an old French word for it—"Lagnappe." When you buy a peck of potatoes, or a dozen eggs, or anything else down there, the merchant throws in a little something extra, just as a good-will offering, and a merchant is judged largely by the amount of Lagnappe that he gives. Well, here is Lagnappe as applied to dental supplies:

DEAR DOCTOR:

With your permission, I am going to send you FREE a New, Self-filling Black Beauty Fountain Pen-Pencil, with your name stamped upon it in 24 carat solid gold leaf.

You will like this good-looking, smooth-working Pen-Pencil. It has all the fine appearance of a Five Dollar Pen, and your name stamped upon it gives it a distinctiveness that expensive pens often lack. Practically unbreakable, it will give you smooth and satisfactory service for years.

Your name on the enclosed Coupon will bring this Pen-Pencil to you, postpaid, *with my compliments.*

I'm going to send this Gift to you—without cost or obligation on your part—upon receipt of your next order for —PRODUCTS amounting to $5 or more.

You can make up your own selection of Supplies. The inside pages illustrate and describe *many* money-saving offers— *50% below Dental Depot Prices.*

I only have 500 of these Black Beauty Fountain Pen-Pencils. Among over 10,000 customers of mine whom I am writing to—this quantity will not last very long.

But while they last, I will send you one FREE immediately upon receipt of your next order amounting to $5.00 or more, AND IN ADDITION, I will stamp your own name on it in gold.

Play safe. Send in your order AT ONCE and be sure to print your name *CLEARLY* on the Pen-Pencil Coupon, so that you will be sure of getting yours—before it is too late.

> Cordially yours,

And here is that same idea so cleverly worded, that it makes an ordinary prospectus sound like a most worthwhile gift. It is hard to get inquiries from the right kind of prospects. It is often difficult to get your literature into the right hands. So when you can make your logical prospect ASK for it, when you can make him look upon your advertising matter as a worth-while gift, then indeed have you accomplished some-thing to crow over. And in the following letter, the Limited Edition Club has done just that:

DEAR MR. JONES:

I have a present for you. To get it, you must ask for it, and it would be nice if you would say Please.

You don't have to guess what it is; if you did, you'd guess it to be a bank for the baby's pennies or a folder for your insurance policies. No, I'll tell you; it is a copy of a handsome printed prospectus, setting forth the plans of The Limited Editions Club for its sixth year.

If you have a real interest in literature; if you derive delight from the fine printing of books; if the presence of beautiful books in your home or anybody's home gives you a thrill, you'll want to ask for this lovely prospectus (it *is* remarkably handsome!) and you'll be willing to say Please.

For in it you will find the announcement of a First Edition of a hitherto unpublished work by Mark Twain. You will find plans for new editions of works by Chaucer, Dickens, Emerson, Hudson, Sterne, More, O'Henry, Lewis Carroll, Hawthorne, Melville—and James Joyce! You will find the promise of original critical work from Christopher Morley and H. G. Wells, William Beebe and Carl Van Doren, Stephen Leacock and Van Wyck Brooks. You will find the announcement of book illustrations by John Tenniel and Miguel Covarrubias, T. M. Cleland and George Grosx, Edward Wilson, Valenti Angelo, Gordon Ross—and Henri Matisse!

Such a prospectus is treasure trove for you if you are the kind of person I suggested in the third paragraph of this letter. I have a copy to present to you, and I'll pay the postage to get it to you, too. Naturally, I am anxious that you should read it, in return.

So, if you will simply write "Send me that prospectus, Please" across the edge of this letter and return it to me, I'll do the rest. I ask that you do this promptly, for only five hundred copies of the prospectus are available for the people who answer this coy letter from me.

Cordially yours,

To sum up—one of the strongest traits in human nature is the desire to be somebody, to feel important, to be necessary to the community and those around us. And many proven ways have been found of successfully approaching people through this harmless strain of vanity that is in all of us.

That being so, why take the hard way when there is an easy one open to us? Why blaze new trails, when there is a paved road already laid?

For twenty-five years or more, the Literary Digest used a letter that started along the following lines:

> The enclosed card is of real value to you, and has been registered in your name. It is for your personal use only. If you cannot use it, we should feel obliged if you would return or destroy it. For it brings to you and a select group of well-known book-lovers, the chance to examine the new this or that, etc.

The writer used the same idea time and again, and almost every book publisher has mailed repeatedly some modification of it. This has been going on for years and years, yet still the reading public seems to accept it at face value, still it is one of the most successful approaches that we know.

This was graphically proved this Spring when the new Commentator Magazine was brought out. The following letter which, as you will see, used the same general type of approach, is reported to have brought an average of nearly 9% orders:

> DEAR READER:
>
> Because your name is included on a selected list of those we should prefer to have as our Charter Subscribers, we invite you to receive the next six monthly issues of The Commentator at the special introductory price of only $1.00. The regular price is $3.00 per year—25c a copy.
>
> (Here follows description of the new magazine.)

We tell you sincerely that your name has been included at this time because of its special significance to us as a Charter Subscriber. We have segregated a known and selected group of readers, preferred as first subscribers. With this key group at the start, the merits of the magazine will be discussed in the right circles by people whose opinions are respected. For that reason we offer *you* this initial reduced price of $1.00 for six months' issues.

Accept our invitation NOW. Just fill in your complete address on the convenient form enclosed. No postage stamp is needed. Drop it in the mail in the envelope provided herewith.

Sincerely yours,

Editor, THE COMMENTATOR.

There is an old ditty to the effect that—

> "He who whispers down a well
> About the things he has to sell
> Will not make the shining dollars
> Like he who climbs a tree and hollers."

Not to advertise is like whispering down a well, but advertising ineffectively, is even worse, for you are spending good money to get no better results!

Follow in the footsteps of some of these users of TESTED approaches, PROVEN appeals, and you will take the guess out of your advertising and put profits into your tills.

XXII

We Help to Start a Store

Who can use the mails to best advantage? To what businesses and for what purposes is it best adapted?

You hear that question asked frequently, and the answers are as varied as the people who give them. Our own experience indicates that any one who has something to sell can use the mails in one way or another to further that sale.

That point was well illustrated in the experience of a young fellow who came to us for help some years ago. He was assistant to a resident buyer of ladies' ready-to-wear dresses. In the course of their buying for out-of-town stores, they ran across innumerable odd lots of dresses that could be picked up at discounts of anywhere from 40 to 75 per cent of the regular wholesale price. Some of them were original models which had been copied and now were no longer needed. Others were samples, slightly soiled from being exhibited by mannikins. But most were odd sizes of regular models, perfect in every respect—but left-overs.

The trouble was that there were only a few of each—not enough for any merchant to advertise. And anyway, by the time the buyer could write one of his out-of-town stores and get permission to send along the dresses, they would probably have been snapped up by some one else. So most of the out-of-town buyers passed them up.

But some ten years before, the head of this resident buyer's firm had conceived the idea of picking up a few of the best of these bargains, gathering them together in his own office, and then handing out cards telling of the bargains to girls working in near-by offices. It did not take long to work up quite a following, for by judicious picking he was able to offer every dress at less than its regular wholesale price! In ten years' time he was selling $1,000 worth of dresses a week!

But while this proof of Emerson's famous saying was enough for the head of the concern, our younger friend felt that the world could be brought to their door far more quickly by finding some better and more comprehensive way of telling people of the bargains to be had there. To him, the side-line seemed far more important than the resident buying and offered greater possibilities of development. But the "boss" was satisfied with the progress they were making, and the young fellow not only had nothing on which to make an independent start, but there was also a wife and child at home who had to eat.

Eventually, however, our young friend (whom we shall call Jones) persuaded a couple of his friends to put up $3,000 to back the idea, and with this $3,000 he launched out on his own. Mind you, with this $3,000 he had not only to stock an office with dresses, pay rent and help, but in addition, he and his family had to live on it while the business was getting started.

So there was not much left for advertising. Yet some advertising must be done, for it was essential that trade start at once, because every week ate into the small capital for unproductive expenses. After long and prayerful consideration it was decided to risk $20 a week as an advertising appropriation, and we were entrusted with the spending of it!

Not much you can do with $20 a week to launch a new business, perhaps you will say. And yet $20 can be made to cover a thousand letters when they are mailed third class. And that is exactly what we did with it.

We got names of business girls, feeling that they require more dresses than the average housewife, yet have less time to shop around for bargains. And to 1,000 business girls each week we sent one of the following letters:

DEAR MADAM:—

You know that being well dressed is not merely a matter of money. Right among your own acquaintances you can pick out a dozen women who spend more than you do on their clothes, and yet look far less well dressed.

Yet, you are spending twice as much for your clothes as you should!

How can we prove it!

By giving you two smart, new, modish dresses—lovelier,

more exquisite than any in your wardrobe for the price you now pay for one.

Impossible? No, indeed! You know what bargains you can pick up even in the regular stores by continually "shopping around." Imagine, then, what your opportunities would be if you were continually "shopping" among the dress manufacturers themselves.

Yet that is what we are daily, hourly doing as Resident Buyers for twelve out-of-town Department Stores. Every day we pick up Original-Model samples, "close-outs" of which only two or three are left in stock, or Designers' Model-Gowns, and because the manufacturers have no time to bother over single dresses, we get them at such bargains that we can pass them on to you *at actually less than the wholesale prices!*

That means we can offer you the prettiest, smartest dresses to be found in the big stores—beautiful frocks of the finest fabrics, that you'd pay them $25 to $85 for—at from $7.50 to $29. And not one among them that isn't priced at less than half what you'd pay for the same dress in any store!

Not only that, but you have a bigger selection to choose from in all sizes, all colors, all kinds of materials. There are beautiful summer frocks of fascinating freshness; chic, modish street dresses; exquisite afternoon gowns of the finest fabrics; pretty, dainty house dresses.

And remember, many of these are individual, specially designed models not the kind that is turned out by the thousand and that you meet on every passer-by. They are distinctive, charming, unusual, not only in price but in that far more elusive quality—style.

Come and see for yourself. There is no cost—no slightest obligation to buy. Just drop in and "shop around "— see all the authoritative new modes—satisfy yourself that these are the wonderful values we claim—compare the prices with those you've found in the stores.

But come soon if you can, for while we get in new and captivating models every day and there is never a time when you can't pick up some delightful bargain, yet the showing we have now is our best. If you want the pick of it, come soon while the choicest creations, the loveliest and most distinctive designs are still here. You will find the ladies in charge always glad to show you, never urgent that you buy.

Sincerely yours,

DEAR MADAM:—

Every woman, no matter how much money she spends on her clothes, likes to pick up special bargains when she can do it without sacrificing quality or style.

You know that.

You know, too, that being well dressed is not so much a matter of money as it is of having the gift for picking out chic, modish garments *with style to them.*

Many women have that gift. More have not.

If you are one of the lucky ones that have it, you can save half the price on every dress you buy. At the same time you can get individual, specially designed models, made up for samples or Designers' models, of special materials and workmanship.

You know what bargains you pick up occasionally even in the Stores just by shopping around. Imagine, then, what. you could do if you were continually shopping among the Dress Manufacturers and Designers themselves!

Yet that is what we are daily, hourly doing as Resident Buyers for a dozen out-of-town Department Stores.

Every day we pick up Original-model Dresses, Designers' Model-gowns or Coats, and because the Manufacturers have no time to bother with single dresses, we get them at such bargains that we can pass them on to you at actually less than their wholesale prices— *half what they would cost in any regular store!*

Not only that, but we give you a better selection to choose from—in all sizes, in the most fashionable colors and materials. There are lovely Fall and Winter frocks; chic, modish street dresses; exquisite afternoon and evening gowns; pretty, dainty house dresses; smart coats and wraps.

And, of course, there are all the regular models among them, too, just like those in the stores. Only ours are priced at half the Store prices. For in our rounds of the Manufacturers, we pick up many a special little "close-out," many an "odd lot" at 30, 40, *even 50% off the regular wholesale prices!*

Come in and see for yourself. Patty Prim invites you! There'll be no cost—no slightest urge or obligation to buy.

Just do as we do at the Manufacturers' showrooms—" shop around." See all the latest and most distinctive modes; com-pare the prices, the designs, the quality, with anything you can find in the stores.

Come soon if you can, for while we get in new and captivating models every day and there is never a time when you can't pick up some delightful bargain, yet the showing we have now is our best. If you want the pick of it, come soon while the choicest creations, the loveliest and most distinctive designs are here.

You will find the ladies in charge always glad to show you, never urgent that you buy.

Sincerely yours,

P. S. Remember, we are on the sixth floor now, in a much larger suite—No. 603. Take elevators #2 or #3. We are directly in front of the center elevator.

DEAR MADAM:

What size dress do you wear?

If it's a 16, an 18 or a 36, I can save you half its cost and at the same time give you as distinctive, as stylish, as unusual a model as you can find the whole length of the Avenue.

Even on the larger sizes I can sometimes do this, but if you wear a 16, an 18 or a 36, you can always find your size here.

You know how the Dress Manufacturers work. Their designers submit scores of different models each season— beautifully made, hand-worked, specially designed models. Some are discarded because they cost too much to make up. Some because they don't happen to appeal to the manufacturer's fancy. Only a few are copied and made up in quantity. The rest are sold for what they will bring.

These are the "Original-Models" we offer you. These are the dresses that, in our daily rounds of the manufacturers as Resident Buyers for out-of-town stores, we pick up at such low prices that we can offer them to you at half, or less than half what similar garments would cost you in any store.

There's only one or two of each, so no big store can take the time to bother with them. But by getting them from so many different manufacturers, we have a complete selection always on hand.

Come in and see them—if only to see what a range of lovely styles and materials they cover. Frequently they

372

are made up in the larger sizes, so there is every chance that out of our 400 dresses you'll find just the style, just the material and just the size you want.

Costs nothing to see them, anyway—and it's certainly worth while to SEE if you can save half and still get as lovely a dress as ever you've bought for double the price.

Sincerely,

DEAR MADAM:

Have you ever had some friend in the Dress business take you around to a manufacturer's, and let you pick the exact model you wanted *at the wholesale price?*

Remember what a bargain that was—how far below the regular Retail Store figures it was priced?

Well, that is the service we offer you on ALL your Dresses and Coats. We don't take you to one manufacturer. We do better. We bring the best from the stocks of a hundred manufacturers here, for you to choose from, *at wholesale prices.*

Now, here is the point. As Resident Buyers for a number of out-of-town Stores, we are making the rounds of the manufacturers every day. You know yourself what bargains you can pick up even in the Stores just by shopping around. Imagine, then, what we can do when we are daily shopping among the manufacturers themselves! Whenever they bring out some "Special," or whenever they have only a few of a style left, or whenever they finish copying their Designer's Model-Gowns, *we get them.*

At such a time the manufacturers, who cannot afford to bother with such small lots, are willing to let us have them at our own price. The result is that we can offer you many of the season's loveliest and most distinctive models, in all sizes, in the most fashionable colors and materials, *at actually less than their regular wholesale prices!*

373

Come and see for yourself. It costs nothing to be shown. And if you can save half on all your Dresses, you want to know it. Be sure to look here before you buy that next Dress.

Sincerely,

From the very first week those letters brought in a fair amount of business—some $200 to $300 worth each week. And the bargains were so real and so evident that many came back with friends.

Jones had figured that it would probably be a year before he could show any net profit, after allowing for the cost of getting started and for his own living expenses, but at the end of the first 7 months he had not only earned enough to cover all those expenses, but his books showed a net profit of $18 besides! Not much, of course, but from that time on it was one steady growth. By the end of the first year his sales had mounted, through consistent advertising, to the volume it had taken the original firm ten years to attain— $1,000 a week!

There were special sales now and then, of course, and on these the list of customer names made the letters even more productive than the regular ones. Here are three of these "Specials" that produced unusually good results:

Here is our first CLEARANCE SALE!

200 chic, modish dresses, all of the latest winter models, at from 33 1/3% to 50% *less than wholesale prices!*

The Manufacturers are finishing up their Spring stocks now, and by the end of the month they will be turning over to us all their sample dresses, designers' model gowns, etc., in the latest Spring styles. Nobody will want to buy Winter dresses then, so we must clean out our entire stock of more than 200 winter models before the Spring gowns start coming in.

That means that for this one month we are going to forget all about profits—sell everything at exact cost and exact cost with us is little more than half wholesale prices!

For we never buy anything that is not a bargain, and in our daily rounds of the manufacturers as Resident Buyers for fifteen out of town department stores, we are able to pick up some wonderful bargains for ourselves.

Modish street dresses, chic afternoon frocks, beautiful evening gowns—they are all here, more than 200 of them, in all sizes, for you to choose from. And remember—they are specially designed models, most of them, distinctive not only in price, but in that far more elusive quality, *style*.

Come and look them over. It is an opportunity such as you will find in no store that we have ever seen. Better come quickly, though, while our stock is at its best. Every single dress in the lot is a remarkable bargain, but by coming now you can get that wide choice of styles and designs that every woman wants, and that will be impossible after the stock has been picked over.

DEAR MADAM:

"Name your own price," said the manufacturer.

And we did.

This manufacturer had thousands of dollars tied up in the new Fall and Winter models of Ladies' Dresses. A big manufacturer's and a good one. Over-stocked with beautiful goods, in the styles and colorings sponsored at the recent Paris openings. Vast quantities of them—but money needed.

"The goods must be sold," he decided, "at once!"

We picked out 300 of his choicest models and named him a price on them. It was accepted without cavil or question. The result is that we can offer you some of the prettiest, some of the most exquisitely styled and fashioned dresses to be found along the Avenue at not merely less than retail, but actually at little more than *manufacturing cost prices!*

A windfall—not just for us—but for you. Understand, these are new Fall and Winter models—new fabrics, new linings, the latest versions of the strikingly new silhouettes—that were expected to appear in Department Stores throughout the coming season. No odd lots or clean aways. New goods— the Paris-accepted modes—complete.

You can't tell the quality story from the printed page, of course. You CAN from the garments. From a glance at the seams—hand-stitched. From the soft, beautiful, rich fabrics, from their splendid style—and, we might add, from the maker's reputation.

Come and see for yourself. Costs nothing to be shown, you know, and any time you can pick up some of the season's loveliest models at wholesale prices, it's worth looking into at least.

Better come soon—while the stock is at its best, while you can have a wide choice of models and designs.

Cordially yours,

DEAR MADAM:

Every season when the rush of order taking is over, the big dress manufacturers draw a deep, long breath and begin to straighten up their stocks preparatory to making up their samples for the next season.

And they always find dresses set to one side during the rush for one reason or another—reserved on some salesman s request for a particularly good customer and then cancelled; or marked "hold" and the reason forgotten; or often just pushed out of sight by accident.

These dresses are generally the very best of the stock, but

376

they have to be disposed of quickly without regard for cost, to make room for the coming season's stock; for space is more valuable than clothing.

If there were more of them and if they ran a complete line of sizes, the big department stores would snatch them up like lightning. But each manufacturer has only a few—perhaps six or eight—perhaps a dozen. So the department stores can't bother with them.

As Resident Buyers for a dozen out-of-town department stores, we are constantly calling on scores of the manufacturer's and by selecting the best of these dresses from each, we make up a complete stock that for distinctiveness of design, for fashionable colors and quality materials, can scarcely be equaled along the whole length of the Avenue.

And the prices—you know yourself what bargains you can pick up even in the regular stores by shopping around. Imagine, then, what prices we get on these "close out" lots from the manufacturers. A third off—even a half off the regular *wholesale price* is nothing out of the ordinary, so that we can pass these dresses on to you at half—or less than half—what you'd pay for the same models in any retail store.

And while the manufacturers sell them out because it's the end of the manufacturing season, the *Wearing Season has only just begun!*

The manufacturers are starting now to work on Summer Dresses and we are just getting the best of their Spring Models—colorful frocks of fascinating freshness, beautiful gowns of the finest fabrics, costumes for every mood and occasion that would cost you in any store from $25 to $75.

And we can give them to you for half, or less than half price— actually less than the wholesale price!

377

Whatever material you have set your heart on—crepe-de-chine, canton, roshanara, jersey—you will find it here. Tan, navy, grey, green—whatever color you fancy—you will find it among these charming, captivating dresses in some distinctive model. They are a showing of all the authoritative new modes—they make your Spring shopping one delightful adventure.

Come and see for yourself. Never mind what we say—come and prove the truth of it with your own eyes. There is no obligation to buy. Just drop in and "shop around."

Costs nothing to be shown, you know, and if you can save half on all your Spring wardrobe or get twice as many dresses for the money as you had expected, you want to know it, So LOOK in here any day before you buy that next dress.

Sincerely yours,

In the course of the next year he found it necessary to double the size of his office. A year later another office was added, followed soon after by a third.

That is one answer to what businesses can use the mails profitably. We have seen so many others that it is hard to pick the best examples of those worthy of inclusion here.

Perhaps one of the best would be on a boy's suit, for these are especially difficult to sell by mail, because it is so hard to find a list of people in the right circumstances with boys of an age to buy your suits. We solved that by arranging with the publishers of a magazine that appealed to boys of ten to fourteen years, to use their list, and we mailed them the following letters:

DEAR PARENT:

You know how an active boy can go through a pair of knickers. Seems no time before the seat is worn through, or one knee has a big, ragged gap in it. We used to think that nothing short of cast iron would keep a healthy youngster covered.

378

But over in England, the Admiralty was faced with this same problem over sailors' trousers. Sliding down ropes and climbing around boats and getting soaked with salt water are even harder on cloth than the average boy, and keeping sailors in trousers was one of the Admiralty's big expenses until a few years ago. Now they have perfected a fine woolen weave so tough and sturdy that it outwears any ordinary cloth four and five times!

We heard about this new weave, and got some to try in our Boys' Suits. And found that it defies even a boy's ingenuity to wear through! Trees, briars, fences, boards—nothing seems able to break those long, strong strands of pure virgin wool. Yet this fine fabric is good-looking as only an English Worsted can be, with all the style and swank that none but the real, imported woolen can show. No imitation will tailor so superbly. None will hold its shape and keep its fine appearance in spite of hardest wear half so long.

> I am going to send you, in the next few days, a complete new Spring Suit for that boy of yours, made of this fine imported English Worsted, so you can SEE FOR YOURSELF how good-looking and becoming it is, how perfectly it fits, how well it sets off the manly lines of his figure—*and yet how it will wear!* I am going to send this suit to you—with no obligation on your part—for you to examine and try on and actually SEE the difference between it and the suit your boy is now wearing.

There's just one thing—I can't send it until you tell me how old he is, and his height and weight. You can do that in a jiffy on the enclosed postcard.

When I send you the suit, there's absolutely no obligation on your part to pay for it. You can return it for ANY reason, or for no reason at all.

You see, this factory of ours specializes on Boys' Suits.

379

Our company has been making boys' clothes for more than 100 years, so we know all the things a healthy boy can do to a suit—better even than you do.

We know how to sew seams and buttons so securely that even a boy can't rip them. We know how to tailor a suit so as to give his active arms and legs free play, and yet have a style and a "set" that will make your youngster look his manly best. But until we found this imported English Worsted, we didn't know a cloth he couldn't wear through. Now we have found it.

So, as an Introductory Special, we offer you this new Spring suit of imported English Worsted, pure wool and all wool. The color is a rich, dark blue. The style as up-to-the-minute as Fifth Avenue designers can make it. The tailoring true Smith & Smith, cut and sewed as only tailors who have been making Boys' Suits all their lives can do it. Coat, vest and trousers, all three at the low "Direct-from-Factory-to-You" price of only $13.85!

AND IN ADDITION, *we will send you an extra pair of Knickers* —FREE! Not that your boy will need them— he will never wear out the first pair—but so you can alternate when one is being cleaned.

This is a special Introductory Offer. It is made only to a select list, *and it is not transferable*. We make it to a few families of influence, as an inducement to them to TRY this new, imported English Worsted, knowing that once its reputation spreads, we shall have no difficulty getting all the orders we can handle.

No Money—No Risk

Just mail the enclosed card—without money. By return Parcel Post, will come a suit of deep blue English Worsted, pure wool, in the exact size for your boy—at the Direct-from-Factory-to-You price of only $13.85. And with it—FREE—an extra pair of Knickers of the same fine fabric.

380

Will it
stand
this?

and
still look
like this

Try the Suit on your youngster. Compare it with any other he has —any you can find in stores. If for any reason you are then willing to part with it—SEND IT BACK! If you can equal it anywhere for less than $25 .00—SEND IT BACK!

But if you feel, as we do—and we have been making Boys' clothes for more than 100 years that you are saving at least $10.00 on that suit, then send us only $13.85, and KEEP THE KNICKERS FREE!

No money—just the Post Card. But remember, it's good only if mailed at once! We have enough imported English Worsted for only 450 Suits. It will be eight weeks before we can get another lot. You must mail the enclosed card NOW, or you will be too late.

Sincerely yours,

DEAR PARENT:

Will you give me a little "inside information" about that boy of yours—just his height and weight and how old he is?

381

I want to send him a new Spring Suit of imported English Worsted, to examine—FREE OF CHARGE. But I can't send one in his exact size without knowing his height and weight.

In the past fifty years, we have fitted more than 1,000,000 boys, in all parts of the world, with Smith & Smith Suits. Many of them have never worn any other make, for Smith & Smith Suits are the kind of well-made, perfectly-fitting clothes that every parent likes to see on his youngster.

You see, in our 106 years as tailors to boys, we have learned how to give a perfect "set" to a boy's coat while still leaving free play to arms and shoulders, how to fasten seams and buttons so even the most active boy can't tear them out, how to fashion a suit that not only wears well but LOOKS well on him up to the very last.

But Here, I Believe, Is the. Greatest Improvement Ever Made in a Boy's Suit:

A new, imported English Worsted that WON'T WEAR OUT! Actually, we mean it—*it won't wear out!* Your boy will out grow it before he can wear it out!

> It is a cloth that was perfected for the British Admiralty. You know the hard usage a sailor's trousers are put to— sliding down ropes, scurrying around boats, scrubbing decks and getting soaked with salt water. They never could find a cloth that would stand it until they made this. Now they can't wear it out!

Of a deep blue, soft and rich-looking, there is no way of duplicating the rare beauty, the durability and wearing-quality of this genuine imported English Worsted. No imitation can wear so superbly, can retain its style and shape after hard usage as can this English cloth.

Carefully cut, beautifully finished and tailored as only

382

Smith & Smith know how to tailor boys' clothes, this suit gives the *appearance of a custom-made, and a wear that has never been equaled.*

Yet our "Direct-from-Factory-to-You" Introductory Price, good for just 10 days, is—NOT $25.00, not even $20.00—BUT ONLY $13.85! We don't believe you could find its equal in tailoring and fine appearance alone within $10.00 of that low figure.

How can WE do it? Solely by cutting out every unnecessary item of overhead and middle-men and selling expense and selling *direct from Factory to You.* In style, in tailoring, in fine appearance, and most of all, in WEAR, this suit is worth $25.00. That we are not charging you that figure is due only to the savings we effect by selling and shipping direct from the Factory, and letting no unnecessary item of expense come between us and you.

Won't you fill in your boy's height, weight and age on the enclosed postcard and mail it at once? Then we can send him one of these fine, new, imported English Worsteds— in his exact size-by pre-paid Parcel Post for a week's FREE EXAMINATION.

You can see it then at your leisure, with no insistent clerks at your side. If it isn't the best-looking suit you have ever seen on your boy—*send it back*! If you can find its equal in style or cut or fine appearance at less than $10.00 more— SEND IT BACK!

Doesn't that strike you as a fair offer? We believe it is so unusually fair that all the suits we have cloth for, will be snapped up within a week at this bargain price of only $13.85. And it will be two months before we can get another lot from England.

Hadn't you better drop your card in the mail RIGHT NOW— while you can take advantage of this Special

Offer?

Sincerely yours,

P. S. If your card is received within 10 days, we shall put in an extra pair of Knickers—FREE! Not that your boy will need them—he will never wear out the first pair— but so you can alternate while one is being cleaned.

Like the boys' suit appeal was one we used on a Book-of-the-month Club for boys and girls. The letter followed the general lines of the one we used on the "Junior Classics" back in the days at Collier's, but the circular was new and different. Here is the letter. The circular follows:

DEAR PARENT:

You know how the little folks just love a good story— how they'd rather listen to one than eat or play or sleep— how they beg you, sometimes, to tell them a story, to read to them.

They will read something, you know. And it is what they read now that determines what they are to be. It is their heroes, their ideals, the men and women who are made to seem to them wonderful and worthy to pattern after, that form your children's characters, that leave the greatest impress upon their after life.

If you could pick from all the literature of the world the books that have helped most in moulding the characters of our greatest men and women—if you could tell what books would be of most help in later school and college work—you would not hesitate for a minute in getting them for your children, no matter what their cost.

Few parents have the time to pick such a library—in fact, few educators could do it without years of reading and research. BUT NOW, *after two years of preparation*, IT

HAS BEEN DONE FOR YOU—with the collaboration of a Board of Editors of such world-wide fame, with such distinctive qualifications, that Libraries, Schools, and Colleges all over the country are as one in acclaiming the idea and subscribing to its service.

The folder enclosed gives you the names of these world-renowned educators. The basis of their plan is that the real purpose of schools and colleges is not to cram the student's head full of facts and figures—BUT TO MAKE HIM THINK!

That this can be done, you who have listened to the eager questions of your own children know. But what• you may not know so well is how quickly the right books start their avid young minds questing along paths that lead to happiness and success, where trashy literature and comic supplements all too often start them on the opposite road.

If the greatest child experts in the world offered to direct your children's reading in such a way as to start their education a-right, you would gladly avail yourself of their help, no matter what the cost. Six of the greatest experts in America in child-training *have* made this offer, but instead of having to pay them big fees, *you pay only for the books they choose!* And even these you get—not at their regular bookstore prices—*but for from 40% to 60% under those figures*!

How does The Junior Foundation accomplish this? Very simply:

The Board of Editors has divided the children into three groups. The first group is for boys and girls 5, 6, 7 and 8 years of age; the second is for boys and girls 9, 10 and 11 years of age, and the third group is for boys and girls 12, 13 and 14 years of age. For each group the Board selects one book each month—THE one best fitted to win the children's interest, to inspire them with right ideals, to give the best groundwork for their school studies.

This book is printed in the big size, in large, readable type, on excellent paper, handsomely bound in cloth tough enough for hard usage, and beautifully illustrated in colors by artists who know how to reach the child imagination.

The books will in every case be the equal in size, in binding, in printing, and in illustrations, of those you find in stores costing as much as $5.00 each. But instead of $5.00, members of The Junior Foundation will receive them FOR LESS THAN $1.43 EACH!

Why! Because where the store book is printed in lots of one or two thousand, ours will be printed in runs of 25,000 and 50,000! Where the retailer has all the usual expenses of big stocks, high rentals and selling costs, The Junior Foundation deals direct with you by mail. You get your books at but little more than actual printing and binding costs!

The enclosed Certificate is an invitation to enter your child as a *Charter Member* of The Junior Foundation. It is worth real money—not only because it brings you the guidance of six of the greatest educators in America, not only because it enables you to get the finest illustrated editions of the right books at about half price or less—but because it protects you from any future increase in price that it may be found necessary to effect. Will you fill it in, put your name and address on it, and drop it in the mail?

It will bring to you each month a book your children can be proud of, a book that will hold their interest and yet educate them as well, a book that will be the start of a real library, and the foundation of a fine character. Ben Franklin used to say, you know, that—

> "Schools give us the rudiments, *but books teach us how to think!* No one can be truly educated or successful in life unless he is a reader of books."

No price is too high to pay for the right training of your

children. But when the BEST training is also the simplest and the cheapest, it pays to lose no time in starting it. Your children *are* reading something *now*. They will be reading other somethings tomorrow. They cannot start too soon reading the *right sort* of books.

Will you make that start possible SOON by mailing back the enclosed Certificate today? The return envelope requires no postage.

Sincerely yours,

Is Your Child Reaching for
NOTHING?

YOU KNOW how often you have heard business men complain that the average boy or girl, straight from High School or College—is trained for nothing in particular.

They have absorbed a lot of "education," but very little of it seems to fit into the work of the world. They have been working hard—*but aiming at nothing!*

Every ambitious youngster wants to hitch his wagon to a star, but instead of picking the particular star, most of them throw their ropes into space, figuring that there are lots of stars—but forgetting that there is a million times as much space as stars.

Your Children CAN Be What They WANT To Be

Your children have enough gray matter in those heads of theirs to be anything they make up their minds to be. They have enough innate ability to carry them to any height. The great need is the URGE that will fire their ambition, that will set them dreaming, thinking, planning for their goal.

How are you to supply that URGE? How are you to pick the goal?

Through their heroes, their ideals! All children try to emulate their heroes. All children try to reach for their ideal. Give them the right sort of heroes—show them how they can follow in their footsteps—fire them with ambition to do as their heroes did—and you will never need to worry about your children's future.

And the way to give them those heroes, those ideals—the way to show them how to follow in their footsteps—lies through the pages of good books. Books that EDUCATE as well as entertain.

Every child loves a good story. And some of the most intensely interesting stories ever written are the very ones best calculated to fire your children's ambitions in the right direction, to lead them on to happiness and success.

Will you let world-famous Authorities, those best fitted to pick the RIGHT reading material, pick the books YOUR child is going to read? Will you let these eminent men and women who have given their lives to the study of the new way of child-training help to lead your child to success?

And we must give our prize letter the one that pulled the highest returns we have ever heard of—200 per cent in actual number of books ordered! Of course, there is a catch in it, as in all those phenomenally high returns we have seen. The catch is that there were only 1,500 names, and they were of people who had written Pelley expressing an interest in his article when first it appeared in the American Magazine. We could not do the same with any other list—in fact, we could not get more than ordinary returns with other lists. But from those 1,500 letters, we got orders for 3,000 copies of Pelley's book! Here is the letter:

DEAR MISS SMITH:

May we send you the Aftermath to "Seven Minutes in Eternity" by William Dudley Pelley, telling the outgrowth of his extraordinary experience; together with a special Autographed gift copy of the real facts of that experience?

You understand, of course that to a general audience like the readers of a magazine, he could not tell the whole story. Facts so startling as to sound unbelievable to the average man, had to be deleted. We have persuaded Mr. Pelley to retell the episode, giving not only every thing that happened at the time, but, what is more wonderful still, the After-math, which he has never before allowed to be published.

We are putting the story and the Aftermath into a little gift book, together with an interesting biographical sketch of Mr. Pelley and his latest portrait.

But Here, We Believe, Is the Most Important Part:

Mr. Pelley has promised to AUTOGRAPH the first thousand of these little gift books at no extra charge!

I am writing to you first, Miss Medland, because you expressed such an interest in the article when it first came out. I know you'd enjoy the complete story yourself, and more especially the Aftermath. If you would like also to get some for gifts to your friends, I'll be glad to send you as many of the autographed copies as I can—provided

388

you order right away. I'll have to make it "First come, first served," of course, but I am giving you first chance.

The price? you'll smile when you hear it. 25 cents a copy, post-paid! But—the price is the same for Autographed copies or for plain. And you get the Autographed copies only if you order right away. I'll hold a few of the Autographed copies for you for one week—but no longer. May I hear from you at once, please, by letter or wire?

Sincerely,

As different from merchandise and books as anything we have ever tried is selling stock. We had always refused to have anything to do with stock fluctuations because, having been burned a few times ourselves, we had a fellow feeling for the victims, and did not care to be a party to adding any new ones to the list. But upon one occasion, a friend persuaded us that we should be doing the public a service if we helped him to place a certain issue and we finally fell for his arguments. Here was the result:

DEAR SIR—

I should like to buy $10.00 worth of your personal prestige— and here is an Option Certificate for one share of Bonus stock as payment in advance.

Here is the way of it:

You have heard, of course, of John Jones, Director of the Blank Theatres. You know that under his skilful direction these great motion picture enterprises have proven tremendously profitable, The Blank alone being reputed to earn 100% each year upon their equity.

But have you seen his new Theatre "The Jones Theatre" —the largest and finest in the world, that is now nearing completion at the corner of —Ave. and —St., New York, right in the heart of the new Theatre District?

There are only six other "first run" motion picture the-

389

atres in this whole Square district, and so great is the concentration of amusement-loving population in and around Manhattan, that these six theatres are filled to capacity *four* times each on Saturdays and Sundays, and approximately two-and-a-quarter times a day on every other day in the week!

Naturally their earnings have been so large that the securities of these enterprises are held very closely by capitalists. But Mr. Jones wants to POPULARIZE The Blank Theatre, and he realizes that the surest way to do that is to let the public share in these generous earnings on exactly the same basis as the capitalists—in fact, if it can be done, he would like the general public to be the only capitalist behind the enterprise.

His idea is to finance The Blank Theatre in the same way that the Smith and Brown theatres in Chicago were financed by the public a few years ago. These ventures proved so profitable that the Preferred Stock was presently retired at a handsome premium and five shares of a new Common Stock were given for each share of the original Common. This new Common Stock now sells for around $70 a share!

Which brings me to the subject of this letter:

> To start the subscriptions successfully, we need a few representative names from each section. Your name has been suggested as one that would be of help. So I am writing to you today to offer you FREE—as a bonus—one share of the Common Stock of The Blank Theatre in return for your sending in your subscription now for three shares of Class "A" Ownership Stock.

This Common Stock is selling right now for around $10.00 a share. The Class "A" Stock for $40.00 a share. The Class "A" Stock is entitled to cumulative preferred dividends of an additional $1.00 per share. It cannot be "called" for less than $50.00 a share.

390

Even if the Theatre should be filled to only *half* capacity, its estimated net earnings are almost five times the total dividends payable on the Class "A" stock, leaving approximately $4.00 a share available each year for dividends on the Common!

As for your money investment—it's safe enough. For the Class "A" Stock is protected not only by the business itself, but also by the real estate and the building. As long ago as the early part of 1925, William Green, one of the leading Real Estate men of New York, appraised the value of the entire completed property at $8,950,000, giving a total value to the company's property after installation of fixtures of over $10,000,000.

Real estate values have been increasing rapidly in this section, and it is not unlikely that the property today would be appraised at a considerably higher figure.

So the real estate alone makes your investment in the Class "A" Stock safe, even if the business itself, the Good Will of the Jones name and the contracts with entertainers and producing companies are valued at nothing.

So much for the safety. The important part is *what you get* from your money. From $120 invested in 3 shares of Class "A" Stock in The Blank Theatre you should get: —

1st. $3.50 a share each year, or a total of $10.50—8 3/4% dividends on your money.

2nd. An additional $1.00 per share after the first dollar of dividends has been paid on the Common Stock, bringing your total dividends on the Class "A" up to $13.50—11 1/4% dividends on your money.

3rd. If you use the enclosed Option Certificate within 10 days, you get IN ADDITION one share of Common Stock FREE with every three shares of Class "A" Stock that you reserve now. This Common Stock has a present market value around $10.00 but if the estimated earnings—based on only HALF capacity houses—are anywhere near correct, approximately $4.00 earnings should be available each year as dividends on every share of Common.

The Smith & Brown Common Stock which was given away in the same way as this, returned over $400.00 a share to investors!

So when I said that I wanted to buy $10.00 worth of your personal prestige, I was putting it conservatively. The enclosed Option Certificate should be worth many times $10.00.

But it will be worth that to you only if you use it at once. In a few weeks, The Blank Theatre will be opened. When that is done, when people have seen it thronged with the thousands of enthusiastic followers, when the wireless is again broadcasting "Jones and his Gang," the selling of what stock is left will be no problem. In fact, the problem will probably be to find any to sell, for once the Theatre is opened, the value of the stock should go up by leaps and bounds.

For that reason, I've had to put a limit on the time for which the enclosed Option Certificate is good. Mail it within ten days, and the prestige of your name will be worth to us the value of the stock. After that—'twould be too late to do us good.

So—you'll forgive me if I seem insistent, but—will you use the Option Certificate NOW? And thank you, most heartily and sincerely for your help.

Appreciatively yours,

Safety

The safest security on earth is the earth itself.

And when your particular section of earth is located in the middle of that most densely populated island on earth—Manhattan Island—right in the heart of New York's new Theatre District—

And when you have built upon it the largest Theatre in the world, with a seating capacity of 6,000 and a spacious rotunda capable of accommodating 3,000 more—Then indeed can you be said to have SAFETY in its ultimate form.

That is what we offer you in The Blank Theatre.

The popularity of motion pictures and the limited number of "first run" theatres has made investments in these projects extremely attractive. Usually the securities of these enterprises are held very closely by capitalists and hence their earnings are not made public. It is stated upon good authority, however, that the Smith and Brown theatres earn 100 per cent each year on their equity.

The Hub of Nine Millions

In the five boroughs of New York City alone 5,873,356 persons make their residence. In the surrounding suburbs, nearly 3,000,000 more are only a few minutes from Manhattan. Each day railroad and steamship lines bring thousands of visitors to the city. They are travelers from the four corners of the world who are pleasure bent and "out for a holiday."

This concentration of a huge population affords an opportunity to amusement projects that is unique in history. A public, craving entertainment, is spending millions of dollars each year. And the vortex of it all is the "Times Square District" in New York. Here the theatrical business has become a giant industry.

There are 70 theatres in the Times Square District at the present time. Of them, however, there are only six so-called "first run" moving picture theatres. As a result these theatres fill their capacity four times on Saturdays, Sundays and holidays. The general average throughout the week in all of these theatres is approximately two and one-quarter times the capacity each day.

Location

The Blank Theatre will occupy a large part of the block bounded by— and—Streets,—and—Avenues. It has a frontage of 290 feet on—Street and 190 feet on—Street. This property is owned outright by the corporation and in addition to that it has a lease for a term of 84 years on an entrance through the—Hotel at the northeast corner of—Avenue and—Street with a frontage of 40 feet on—Avenue and 100 feet on—Street.

The theatre is located one block from—and—Street Station of the— Line, and one block from the—Street Station of the—Line. — Avenue surface cars pass the door and the—Avenue surface cars are but a few yards away.

With the general uptown movement of the theatres The Blank Theatre will be in the heart of the theatrical district for many years to come. The district bounded by—and—Avenues,—and—Streets seems destined to become a district given over almost exclusively to theatres. The Blank Theatre will be in almost the exact centre.

What Others Have Done

In Chicago, the Smith and Brown theatres were financed by the public a few years ago. The Common Stock of this enterprise was given away as a bonus with the Preferred Stock. Later the Preferred Stock was retired at a handsome premium and five shares of a new Common Stock were given for each share of the original Common Stock. The new Common Stock now sells on the New York Curb for around $70 per share.

Investments in theatrical properties are unusually safe. The Bonds and Preferred Stock are protected by very desirable real estate. Even if the theatrical enterprise itself should fail, the real estate usually can be sold at a profit. If the enterprise is successful the Common stock-holders share in the huge profits that always come to "hits" in the theatrical business.

The Class A Stock

The Class A Stock of The—Theatre Corporation is preferred both as to assets and dividends. Each share of Class A Stock entitles the owner to a $50 interest in both, the building and the business. New York real estate is a sound, conservative investment—and in this section the values are increasing rapidly.

When the division of the yearly earnings takes place each share of Class A Stock first receives $3.50 each year. (At the present quoted price of $40 this is 8 3/4 %). This $3.50 each year is paid before any dividends are paid on the Common Stock. Then, after each share of Common Stock has been paid $1.50 the Class A stock-holders participate in the earnings again and receive another $1.00 per share. That increases the dividend to $4.50 per share per year (or 11 1/4% on the present price).

The $3.50 dividend is cumulative. The Corporation agrees to pay dividends on this Class A Stock at the rate of $3.50 per share each year from December 1, 1925. No dividends are paid to the holders of the Common Stock until the $3.50 per share is paid on the Class A Stock from December 1, 1925.

Each year 15 % of the net earnings of the Corporation are set aside as a sinking fund with which to purchase the Class A Stock. It is paid for at the rate of $50 per share.

The dividends are payable March 1, June 1, September 1, and December 1.

The Director

Of the six "first run" motion picture theatres in the Times Square District, Jones has been the director of four, . . . Probably the entertainment in those four theatres is the standard by which all other moving picture entertainments are judged. Yet all were conceived and executed by the one man: Jones.

Now the same man who created these entertainments will find his fullest scope in the presentations of The "Blank Theatre." The largest theatre in the world will seat over 6,000 persons. When you contrast this with the capacities of the other houses formerly under the direction of Jones you will see that it is possible to spend considerably more on programs and still make a far larger net profit than the facilities of the other theatres permitted.

Under the stage a complete broadcasting room is being built and—and his Gang' will continue the entertainment to Radio fans that has brought thousands of patrons to The—.

One of the leading Real Estate men of New York has appraised the value of the entire completed property at $8,950,000. This sum gives a total value to the Corporation's assets upon completion of the building and installation of fixtures of over $10,000,000.

That alone assures the safety of the investment in Class A Stock, even if the business itself, the Good Will of Jones' name and the contracts with entertainers and producing companies are valued at nothing.

It is a well known fact that Real Estate values are increasing rapidly in this section. The conservative estimate of Mr. Green was made early in 1925, and it is not unlikely that the property today would be appraised at a considerably higher figure. With the continued uptown movement of the theatrical business this site should become one of the most valuable in the entire district.

Earnings

The management of The Blank Theatre estimates the annual net income to be $2,105,875 after the payment of all operating expenses, including insurance, city and federal taxes, depreciation and mortgage interest and amortization. This sum is equivalent to over 4.8 times the dividend requirements of the Class A Stock, and indicates that approximately $4.00 would be available each year as dividends on each share of the Common Stock.

This estimate of $2,105,875 is not based upon a "capacity house" for every performance, but upon only one-half the capacity of the giant theatre. If it can be found that the theatre can be kept filled every day in the year, the earnings will be correspondingly larger.

The Blank Theatre is not like an ordinary business which has to build up a patronage over a period of time. The first night it is open thousands will be attracted. The novelty of the new building and the popularity of Jones will be sufficient.

As it turned out, he was right, so we let him persuade us into helping him put over another issue, which proved to be no better than some of those on which we had burned our fingers in the past. From then on we left such offers severely alone. While we were waiting for the results of these circulars we wrote for him another letter which out-lines a method of placing a new country club on its feet in a way different enough from the ordinary to be interesting. Here it is:

Will you give me a little information about yourself—just your favorite form of sport or recreation?

We are getting together a little group not to exceed

395

400 of men who stand high enough in the business or professional world to be able to take a bit of time off now and then for real outdoors—for hunting and fishing, for boating and swimming, for riding, golfing and tennis, off where they are not overrun by the casual week-end mob, yet close enough to reach their offices by train or motor within a couple of hours.

> Just listen:—5,000 acres of hunting preserve that has been posted and patrolled for 27 years. Adjoining an additional 5,000 acres of wooded state land. A lake that has been liberally stocked with fish for years and never opened to the public. Two excellent trout streams. Duck and wild geese, deer and other game in abundance. A 9-hole golf course over high rolling country. Two tennis courts. Good boating. Fine swimming. Miles and miles of wooded lanes for horseback. A Clubhouse and wonderful sites for permanent camps. *That* is "Moon Mere."

A play-ground for millionaires. Only we are not looking for millionaires. There will be some among us, of course, but this is not a money-making scheme. It is a real effort to get together a group of interesting, congenial people of the type —socially and professionally—that you will be happy to be with. The cost will be the smallest part of it. And for that very reason, every name proposed will be subjected to the very closest scrutiny.

Your name has been suggested as one interested in outdoor sports, and at the same time of such standing as to pass the most captious Board of Governors.

I have prepared a booklet, beautifully illustrated, that gives the details of this natural play-ground—as many details as a mere booklet can give of the wonders of hill and lake, stream and forest. It is expensive, so we printed no more than are actually needed. While they last, the enclosed card will bring one to you, without cost and without obligation.

May I send it?

Sincerely yours,

P.S. The membership of "Moon Mere" is limited to less than 400. When that number is completed, the books will automatically close. So it is important that you use the enclosed card at once.

While stocks offered by mail do not seem to turn out well on many occasions, if ever there was a place where good mail literature is sorely needed, this is it. A deadlier lot of stuff was never put out in the name of advertising than most of the pieces we have seen, which purported to describe financial issues.

Of course, it is all done in the name of dignity, so it cannot descend to such subterfuges as finding the motives that will make men act, or working out a clever approach, or any of the other steps we consider necessary in selling so ordinary a thing as a book or a coat.

Dignity! Whenever any one springs that word on us we feel like a St. Patrick's day Irishman who has just run into an Orangemen's parade. Dignity is a cloak for every jackass in high position. Dignity is the screen behind which every incompetent tries to hide. Dignity is just an excuse for lack of initiative and progressiveness; for complacent stagnation.

It is no more effective in selling stock than it would be in offering books—and if you want to see how successful it is in offering books, turn back to our first offer on Wells' "Outline of History" and see what the difference in results is between the dignified letter and circular, and any of those others that forgot all about dignity but were interesting.

The friend referred to above had offered his stock in the usual dignified way, and judging from the results, it had attained the usual result of dignity—*no one even knew it existed!* So we re-wrote the circular in what we conceived to be the interesting way, and the results were as different with stock as with Well's "History." Here is the first page of the re-written circular:

In the next chapter we shall show you a campaign aimed at the topmost executives of the biggest businesses in America, to see if we cannot show that they are no more concerned over dignity than you or we. It is interest you want and it is interest they want—and it is only when you interest them that they will read—or order!

The Fountain of Youth

ONE of the first tales that met the Spaniards when they landed on the shores of the New World was the legend of a marvelous Spring with waters of such miraculously healing qualities that the Indians had named it the Fountain of Youth.

Rumor had it that this Spring was located on the mainland, far to the North. The Indians of the Islands had never seen it, but all had heard of it and all vouched for its miraculous qualities.

So firm were they in their conviction and so consistently did the story run, that a number of hardy spirits among the Spaniards finally formed an expedition, and under the leadership of Ponce de Leon set out to find this marvelous Spring.

Having no idea of the extent of the continent before them, however, they felt they had gone far enough North when they reached the coast of Florida, and the tangled masses of the Everglades soon cured them of any desire to explore further.

So the story was relegated to the forgotten limbo of an Indian legend, and there it rested.

200 years later, Colonel William Byrd, founder of the City of Richmond, Va. (ancestor of Commander Byrd of Polar flight fame and of the present Governor of Virginia), while serving on the Virginia-North Carolina Boundary Commission, earned the gratitude of his Indian guide, and in return the latter disclosed to him a wonderful spring which, so the guide assured him, had the property of curing all manner of diseases.

Tradition has it that among the Indians this Spring was known as the Fountain of Youth. Certain it is that its waters have a marvelous efficacy in the treatment of stomach and kidney disorders, than which there is no surer destroyer of youth.

Three other springs were found in the immediate vicinity, and upon examination it was discovered that all four were highly mineralized.

The springs soon became the Mecca of those of the "Quality" of the Southland who suffered from gout, from rheumatism or from stomach disorders. Newspaper accounts of over 100 years ago show that so well were the medicinal properties of the water known that the proprietor "deemed any eulogy on the waters unnecessary."

"Several years ago I began to treat nervous cases with Buffalo Mineral Water with a result that was astonishing to me as it was beneficial to the patient."
DR. WILLIAM A. HAMMOND, Former Surgeon-General of the U. S. Army.

398

XXIII

How to Reach the Leaders

You often hear it said that the leaders of big business never read circulars—that they would be too busy to glance at them even if you could camouflage them sufficiently to get them past the private secretary's desk.

If that be true, pause for a moment to sympathize with the McGraw-Hill Publishing Company, who undertook in the Fall of 1929 to launch a weekly intended only for high executives of big business concerns. For which is harder— to find a salesman who can penetrate those august sanctums, or to write a letter that will reach all the way to the top of a big business?

As if they had not already attempted the impossible, the McGraw-Hill Company undertook not only to reach the topmost figures in the world of business but to land nearly half of them. They guaranteed to have on their subscription lists by January, 1931, 75,000 high executives of companies rated $75,000 or better!

Quality circulation has been attempted oftentimes in the past, but never on such a scale as this. Heretofore, the only index of quality was the content of the paper and the cost of the subscription. Any one who had the price and cared to read it was welcomed as a subscriber. Here for the first time was a concern actually refusing orders— accompanied by cash—that did not measure up to the standard they had set!

Of all the publishing problems we have seen, that was the most difficult—to get from a possible 200,000 leaders of big business, 75,000 subscribers to a business paper.

That it was done, and in so short a time, is a publishing achievement unequalled in its field.

Do not imagine we are handing bouquets to ourselves. We did not come into the picture until the job was more than half done. But even our part was sufficiently interesting.

When we were given charge of the mail order requirements, the cream had already been skimmed off the list with two good mailings. Further tests had shown little or no life. So to get some line on the efficacy of different appeals, we were allowed at the start to test a few outside lists of high quality in order to see how results compared with similar tests mailed to what was left of the 9200,000 names of top executives which the McGraw-Hill Company had compiled at great expense.

These 200,000 executives remember, were the presidents, vice-presidents, secretaries, treasurers, general managers and directors of companies rated at $75,000 and better. All were people who are not supposed to read circulars. All were supposed to have private secretaries intelligent enough to keep such trivial matters as magazine solicitations away from their desks. So to give them some excuse for regarding our message as one of import, we filled in each. man's name and sent the letters first class.

To get an idea of the most effective line of appeal, we tried six different letters, testing each on the list of business executives as well as on such lists as subscribers to financial "Services," buyers of business books that would interest only men high in business, and readers of magazines with a specialized business appeal.

All six of the letters did well and two pulled remarkably good returns. On the outside lists, one letter pulled more than 9 per cent of orders, another over 8 per cent, while 5 per cent and 6 per cent were little more than average. Even on the list of executives, one pulled 3 per cent, a second close to it, while the third went over 2 per cent.

Here are three of the letters, together with the folder that went with them. The folder is a bit crude. We had no time to wait for regular art work as we were anxious to get our tests out by a certain date. So we took what we could get in a hurry.

> To cause one of your employees to lose his job is not my intention. But if any one of your employees has MY job— then it isn't his—every man has a place somewhere, and I want my own.

> If you have assistants summarizing the news of business for you, who are NOT among the greatest experts in the basic lines of industry, then they have MY job, and their job is somewhere else.

> If you have accountants figuring estimates and quotas, who are not authorities on economic trends, then they

400

have MY job, and their work is something else again.

If you have secretaries to save your time, who cannot interpret the EFFECT of the day's news upon your business and investments, who cannot check the truth or falsity of each dispatch, then they have MY job, and their time would be better spent on other duties.

You see, I am the keystone of the arch of all the McGraw-Hill publications, with thirty-four different staffs of editors working for me, each a recognized authority in some basic field of industry, with engineers and financial experts and economists of world renown laying their findings upon my desk.

I am THE BUSINESS WEEK.

I watch the world for you, and bring you accurate, authoritative reports on everything of note in the basic industries and the happenings of business. Is there a flurry on the Tokyo exchange? I give you its probable effect upon the financial situation here. Is there a strike in France—a new cartel in Germany a hurricane in Chile? I show you their extent, analyze their effect.

I have unparalleled connections in industry, commerce, construction, engineering, finance—the basic activities. I have my fingers on the pulse of every important line of business. I feel the first symptoms of fever, I detect the first signs of recovery. I am reporter, interpreter and business analyst.

You are paying for my services whether you use them or not, but you are paying in lost time, in needless mistakes and worries. No busy man needs to spend hours on newspapers or business reviews if he reads my ticker-like summaries and analysis of the news. No executive needs to hesitate or worry about the effect of different events upon his business if he has before him the interpretations of my staffs of experts.

Will you TRY me for a while—with the privilege of firing me any time at your own pleasure? My salary? You'll smile when you hear it—10 cents *a week*, for as long or as short a time as you care to keep me on your payroll.

But—if you're like Andrew Mellon, Owen D. Young, David Sarnoff, Louis F. Swift, and other big business leaders, you'll be paying me that salary for a long time to come, for you'll find me the most invaluable assistant you've ever had.

Will you let me show you what I've done for them—what I can do for YOU? Then put your name on the enclosed card. It's already stamped. Thank you!

Sincerely,

What is the "Unpardonable Sir" in business? What one thing inevitably brings its own punishment? What most surely spells extinction?

> COMPLACENCY—becoming so self-satisfied with methods or product or service that you stop trying to better them, stop reaching outside for new ideas!

The only sure thing in business today is CHANGE. Money, organization, a dominant position in the industry—these may vanish overnight. Some new invention, some drastic change in style or trends may leave high and dry those unwilling or unready to keep in step with the demands of the moment.

But to the man whose finger is on the pulse of conditions, such changes spell—NOT disaster, but *opportunity*. He has the advantage of days or weeks of preparation. He knows how similar conditions have been met elsewhere, and he can draw upon the experience of dozens of authorities in arranging his own campaign.

It is for such alert, up-and-coming business men that The

Business Week is written. It watches the whole world for you, and brings you accurate news of every important happening in the basic industries. Not merely news so fresh that it is frequently in advance of the newspaper dispatches, but *what that news means to your business,* as interpreted by a group of economists and editors second to none anywhere.

You see, The Business Week is the keystone of the whole arch of the 34 McGraw-Hill publications. 34 staffs of experts, watching hourly for significant developments in the basic fields of industry, reporting their findings to one master group who analyze them, correlate them and then interpret them in terms of their effect upon YOUR business.

If your reading time is limited—if you have more publication now than you have time to get through—send for The Business Week. If you want only real news, authoritative news, each fact checked by experts, send for The Business Week. It summarizes the news for business. It gives you the things you must know, tersely, pointedly, authoritatively, then interprets the effect, they will have upon all business.

A secretary who could do this for you would be worth any money you could pay him. We offer you thirty-four staffs of secretaries, each among the greatest authorities in their particular line, for 10 cents a week. Will you risk 10¢ to let them show you how much they can save you, how many different ways they can increase your dividends?

Just your name on the enclosed card will put them on your staff for as long or as short a time as you may wish. You can fire them any time. On that understanding, will you give them a chance to show you what they can do— NOW?

Sincerely,

Have you tried the new "K. M. H." yardstick in your organization?

It is based, you know, on what an employee does in 1,000 working hours, and the results it has shown in some 14,000 plants have uncovered astounding inequalities of management.

Companies in the same line of industry show an average variation of 13 to 1, while the best plants sometimes produce 20 times as much per worker as the least efficient organizations doing the same work!

Can you wonder that so many organizations are finding it hard sledding now? Can you see how some of them make a profit even in the best of times?

But the remarkable part is yet to come. In 35 out of 53 industries, the prize for highest rate of production went— NOT to any of the giants of that industry, with all their money and fine equipment, not even to the medium-sized plants, BUT TO THE SMALLEST COMPANY IN EACH GROUP!

In only three industries did the largest company show the highest rate of output. In most of the others, the little fellows produced more goods per hour and at a lower cost than any of the great giants.

If business concerns were rated, not by their capital or promptness in paying bills, but by the "K. M. H." yardstick, how would yours stand? Could you get a G Aa rating? If you could, or if you are even interested in getting such a rating, then you are the type of Manager The Business Week is looking for.

For your reading time is limited. You already have more publications than you can get through. Yet you must keep up with what is new in business. And you must know how the news of the day is going to affect you and your interests. Only in The Business Week can you find the answer.

The Business Week is the keystone of the arch of all the 34 McGraw-Hill publications. Every hour of every day, in each of the hundred and more basic industries represented by these 34 magazines, scores of experts are busy digging out the significant happenings and analyzing their effects. Every day the gist of their findings, together with the cabled news from all parts of the world, is scrutinized by the trained economists and editors of The Business Week, and the result summarized for American business.

The readers of The Business Week have no time for long articles, or interesting theories. They want the facts, summarized in the fewest words; they want them interpreted in terms of their own business—*but first they want them verified!*

The McGraw-Hill organization, with its 34 different magazines in the basic fields of industry, is in better position, we believe, to gather the facts and to verify them than any group in the world today.

It gives you, in the pages of The Business Week, the net result of all its vast activities. And it gives them to you— NOT the week after or the next month, but frequently *before even they appear in the newspaper dispatches!*

How much would such a "ticker" service be worth to you? Would you be willing to pay 10 cents a week for it, with the privilege of stopping it any time you saw fit? Then use the enclosed card to start it NOW! You'll never invest any money that will pay you bigger dividends.

Sincerely,

Nine per cent on one letter would be enough to make almost any one we have known stretch a point to work that list into his schedule—but not these people. Nine per cent, or 6, they knew only one standard—the leaders of business America. When they analyzed the returns from our tests and found that no outside list could measure up to the standard they had set, they simply ruled them out and nothing we could say about costs or percentages seemed to make even a dent in their consciousness.

So we had to content ourselves with 2 and 3 per cent when all those high powered lists were just begging to be used. But we did not give up hope of hitting some high percentages, even if we had to do it on the business executive list. One of the offers that had been used with reason-able success before we came was a special introductory offer of seventeen weeks for $1. We tried two or three of these, and in one of them we at least partly realized our ambition— we brought the number of orders up to 7 per cent.

Here is the letter that did it, followed by another that pulled very well, too.

> I am going to send you, within the next few days, a forecast of what's coming in business.
>
> This forecast is unlike any you have seen before, because:
>
> 1. It is based not merely on Government statistics, Federal Reserve, Stock Exchange and Trade Association figures, but on the findings of 34 groups of independent investigators, in closest touch with the basic industries.
>
> 2. Back of these investigators is the McGraw-Hill organization, with its unparalleled connections in business, constructions, finance and the basic industries, and its reputation for careful investigations and accurate authoritative findings.
>
> 3. It dares to make definite predictions of what's coming in business, then shows you WHY it feels so safe in forecasting this. It is, perhaps, less a forecast than an explanation of the underlying trends and an interpretation of what they indicate.
>
> I am going to send this forecast or interpretation to you— with no obligation on your part—for you to read and

actually put to the test in your own business.

There's only one thing—I don't want to send it until I am sure you are interested in seeing it. I don't want to send it without your permission—but you can give that in a moment on the enclosed card.

When I send you this forecast, there's absolutely no obligation on your. part to pay for it. You need not even return it. Just notify us in the stamped, addressed envelope which we will mail you, you want no more, and that ends the matter.

You see, this forecast and interpretation of business condition- is an essential part of The Business Week—the keystone of the whole McGraw-Hill organization, with its 34 publications serving the basic lines of industry.

With all the usual indicators and business "Services" at its command, and with, in addition, 34 staffs of specialists searching the basic fields of industry for every event of import, and interpreting those events in terms of their effect upon business, it would be strange if The Business Week could not give you something unusual in the way of an interpretation of trends and conditions, a forecast based upon them.

That interpretation and forecast is a part of every copy, of The Business Week. It is being more widely quoted than anything of its kind in the country. As Paul Aldrich of The National Provisioner writes:

> "The Business Week is not only the best of its kind, but the first. I could not do without it. The best thing that could happen to business would be for every man to read and take to heart the material in The Business Week."

Will you TRY it—at least long enough to read next week's forecast and interpretation of conditions? Its price is 15 cents a copy, $5.00 a year, but if you mail the enclosed card now, you can get the special trial rate of 17 weeks for $1.

Not only that, but if the very first copy does not intrigue your interest, make you want to follow those forecasts through, check them against results in your own business, you can cancel your order right then, there, and owe us nothing.

On that basis, will you mail the enclosed card? On that understanding, will you risk a look at the next forecast?

Sincerely yours,

How's Business, Mr. Jones?

Heavy construction will equal last year's, judging by bonds issued. Bonds, you know, usually precede steam shovels by about four months.

Retail selling is holding up well, thanks to the reductions which are finally beginning to percolate through to the consumer. And installment sales are proving, instead of a weakness, one of the greatest factors of strength!

An interesting development is the sale of their own brand of tires at all their gas stations by the Standard Oil Co. of N. J. They have a great distribution machine, geared to reach the motorist at the time he needs it most. Why not use it to the full?

How far that will take them, no one can guess, but it seems to point in the same direction as Ford's experiment of a couple of years ago, when he opened his commissary to the public and undersold even the chain stores by 20% to 40%.

The drought in the West is the worst in years. Corn prices have responded to it, but wheat still sags. Why? You'd think the Farm Board would take advantage of such a situation to support the price of wheat, just as you'd expect the Federal Reserve to be putting more money into the market to stimulate flagging trade.

Those are the only two serious clouds on the horizon. They are the only two obstacles that stand in the way of a return to normal business by early Fall. They cannot permanently hold back the flooding tide, but they can retard it a lot.

Of course, that doesn't mean everything is rosy, or we can sit back and take it easy. On the contrary, there has seldom been a period which called for greater foresight and managerial judgment. Have commodity prices hit bottom? How about labor—is it coming down? What are other countries doing—Germany, for instance?

What happened to her big idea of cutting wages and prices simultaneously, so her home workers would not suffer, but she could undersell everybody in world markets?

These are just a few of the questions every keen executive is asking. And these are the questions The Business Week answers for you—better, we believe, than all the "Services" and statistics and bulletins issued the country over.

You see, The Business Week is the keystone of the whole McGraw-Hill organization, with its 34 publications serving the basic lines of industry, its 34 staffs of specialists searching their fields for every happening of import, then interpret those happenings in terms of their effect upon business. Commerce and Reserve statistics help, of course, as do the bulletins of the various Trade Organizations and Business Services, but they are mere side-lights compared to the first hand information constantly going across our desks from the direct contacts of our 34 staffs in the field.

What would their forecasts and interpretation of conditions be worth to you? Would you be willing to risk $1 for them? If you would, then send the enclosed card, without money.

It will bring you for 17 weeks the interpreted news of The Business Week. It will give you—*not* statistics, *not* a lot of unrelated facts—*but what is really happening in business,* the events of import *and their effect upon you.*

Would you be willing to risk $1 for that? Then mail the enclosed card NOW, while the tide is at the turn!

Sincerely,

In the early days of the magazine, quite a few of these introductory subscriptions had been taken and now they were beginning to expire. So it was necessary to write letters that would renew as many as possible of these. We tried a number and finally worked out a series of five that did very well. The following two alone renewed 20 per cent of the subscriptions on which they are sent:

Just a Few Weeks More, and Then— Right in the middle of one of the most important crises in business history, just at the time when conditions are coming to a head for better or for worse—

Your Subscription Expires!

4,000 years ago, King Darius of Persia could get one ounce of gold for every twelve ounces of silver he held in such quantities in his treasury. On down through the centuries since, those proportions have held with reasonable steadiness. Bryan put up his famous fight to standardize silver at sixteen to one.

Today those proportions have changed so greatly that *one ounce of gold buys sixty ounces of silver!*

What does that do to countries like India which are on a silver basis? What does it do to business here?

Last year this time most anyone could show a profit.

People who knew nothing of general trends or conditions made money, because business conditions made it for them.

But this year, only those skilled in reading signs are showing a profit, and to these weather-wise souls, The Business Week is like manna to wanderers in a desert.

For The Business Week watches the world of business for you. It brings you accurate news of every important happening in the basic industries. And not merely news so fresh that it is frequently in advance of the newspaper dispatches, but *what that news means to your business,* as interpreted by a group of economists and editors whose authority is second to none anywhere.

You see, The Business Week is the keystone of the whole arch of the 34 McGraw-Hill publications. 34 staffs of experts, watching the significant developments in 34 basic fields of industry, reporting them daily, hourly, to a master group who analyze them, correlate them and then interpret them in terms of their effect upon YOUR business.

Not even Andrew Mellon, with all his vast interests, had such a service until the McGraw-Hill organization started it a year ago. Yet today you can have that service for only 10 cents a week and one of the first subscribers for it was Andrew Mellon, Secretary of the Treasury of the United States.

When such men as he, and Owen D. Young, and David Sarnoff, and Louis F. Swift—men with whole corps of secretaries and assistants at their elbows—still find they can get their most thorough summaries, their most accurate interpretations of the business news, from The Business Week, I know you, too, will agree that it is as great a time-saver, as valuable a money-maker, for you as for them.

Worth risking 10 cents a week for, anyway, don't you

think? And that's all you ever have to risk, for you can stop it any time, for any reason, and get the balance of your subscription back in full.

On that basis, will you mail the enclosed card? On that basis, will you join Andrew Mellon, and Owen Young and David Sarnoff and Louis Swift in keeping up to the minute on the news of business, and what those news mean in terms of YOUR BUSINESS?

The enclosed card is your answer. Will you mail it now—TODAY?

Sincerely,

DEAR SUBSCRIBER:

Is your name and address, as given above, correct?

If so, won't you be good enough to return the enclosed card, properly checked, so that we may prove or correct our stencil?

Right now, with business at the turning point, it is more important that you keep your finger on the pulse of conditioning than for years past.

Never before has business recovered from a major depression until both prices and wages had been drastically cut. Can it do it this time? Henry Ford believes it can without wages being cut, and he has backed that belief by actually *raising* wages in his plants.

As far as his own business is concerned, the result has proven him right, for he is getting out 9,200 cars a day now with 108,890 men, where a year ago it took 120,000 men to produce only 7,500 cars a day. What is more, he and Chevrolet are dividing 65% of the country's automobile business!

But how about other businesses? How about your own?

Will you have to cut prices—and wages? And how much?

Will the basic industries cut their figures enough to save your line of profit?

These are facts you must know, and nowhere can you get them so promptly, so authoritatively, as in The Business Week.

You see The Business Week has back of it the tremendous resources of the whole McGraw-Hill organization, with thirty-four publications serving the basic lines of industry. Not John D. Rockefeller himself, with all his millions, not Andrew Mellon, with the resources of the U. S. Treasury behind him, has the means of analyzing basic conditions and interpreting the business news, that these great staffs of experts, engineers, economists and financial specialists give to us.

As a matter of fact, Andrew Mellon was one of the first subscribers to this new service—he and Owen D. Young and David Sarnoff and Louis F. Swift. When such men, with all their corps of secretaries and assistants, look to The Business Week for their interpretation of the events of the day, it surely ought to be worth all of 10¢ a week to you too, don't you think?

Just your name on the enclosed card, with a check mark to show that we have your address correct, will keep that ticker-like service coming to you each week, bringing you the news in brief—and not merely the news, *but what it means to you!*

I know you don't want to miss even a single one of those meaty, thought-provoking paragraphs—now, of all times, when seemingly innocuous news dispatches often hide so much of potent meaning. Won't you, therefore, mail the enclosed card at once? Then I can get your stencil back in its place on the list without the loss

413

of even a single issue.

Sincerely,

That pretty well took care of the number of subscriptions we were expected to write by mail on The Business Week magazine. Our next problem was to write a higher percentage of mail subscriptions for System, the Journal of Modern Business Management.

It was a simpler problem, for with it we were permitted to use the better grade of outside lists, lists like buyers of business books, subscribers to financial "Services," buyers of courses in business management and the like. With those lists to work upon, we tried the following letter:

YOUR PERSONALITY AND BUSINESS TRAITS ANALYZED

Have you ever been officially rated for Personality and Business Traits?

—for your capacity to achieve, for your power-pressure or ambition, for your ability to direct your energies into the most productive channels?

Have you ever longed for a frank consultation with an expert Business Psychologist who could show you how to make the most of your abilities?

The Carnegie Foundation, after a thorough study, reported that even in such technical lines as engineering, medicine and law, success is due only 15% to actual knowledge. 85% depends upon your *personality* and the way it expresses itself.

Have you ever been officially rated for *personality*?

Professor H. K. Nixon, Ph.D., head of a Department in one of the great Eastern Universities, author of numerous books and articles on the application of psychology to business, consultant for several large business organizations, has worked out a series of questions and tests that will astonish you by the hidden traits they bring out.

414

He calls it his "Capacity—Achievement Inventory." It reveals with uncanny cleverness your strong and weak points, helps you find the ways in which you are misdirecting your energies, suggests the salient points in your personality that lend themselves to greater development.

If you consulted Dr. Nixon privately, you would probably expect to pay from $15 to $25 for this information, and consider it cheap at the price. If you will mail the enclosed certificate at once, you can get this personality test and analysis *without charge!*

So important are the qualifications uncovered by this test that we have arranged with Dr. Nixon for a series of short articles running through the next six issues of System, the Journal of Modern Business Management, each explaining a different aspect of mental equipment in its relation to business success, together with methods for gauging personal and business qualifications.

These articles and methods will show you simple ways to determine how well you rate with your associates, with your customers, with all whose opinions count in the making of your success. They will in turn increase your ability to rate and to understand others.

But the first step in getting an unbiased picture of your own qualifications and capacities is the "Capacity—Achievement Inventory," and this the enclosed Certificate will bring to you at once.

Every test will be individually rated by Dr. Nixon and his associates. You will receive a rating chart, showing your standing in each part of the test, together with suggestions as to the significance of the various scores, and how best to develop the traits they indicate.

"Men are made," declared Emerson, "each with some triumphant superiority." Men are made that way, but most, never discover what their superiority is, so they go on being a square peg in a round hole to the end of their days.

The "Capacity-Achievement Inventory" will give you a measure of your present capacities and the extent to which you are using them, and it may uncover hidden powers in yourself that you never even suspected you had.

> Send *now* the enclosed Certificate, with a dollar bill in payment for the next six copies of System the Journal of Modern Business Management.

By return mail, the first copy will come to you, together with the "Capacity-Achievement Inventory." Fill it out frankly and honestly, with the full assurance that everything in it will be regarded as confidential by Dr. Nixon and his associates. They will study it, rate it, and report to you just as soon as they can possibly do so.

But remember this means *work* and a lot of it—for them. And there is a very distinct limit to the number they can handle. So we must confine this offer strictly to those who mail the enclosed Certificate at once.

You see, we cannot limit the offer to any special subscribers. It is part of System's service, and therefore open to all subscribers. Your advantage lies in the fact that this is an advance notice, and if acted on at once, insures you a prompt rating. Certificates which come late will be returned at once with the $1's accompanying them.

That pulled remarkably well. It gave us 6 per cent from the business book-buyers, better than 5 per cent from the students of business management courses, and as high as 10 per cent from one list of men interested in psychology.

In the days before the McGraw-Hill Company had taken it over, System had usually been sold with a premium. The McGraw-Hill Company feel, however, that the best premium you can offer any subscriber is something in the magazine itself, so they suggested that we try featuring series of articles on different subjects that were to appear in forthcoming issues of the magazine and see if subscription could not be sold on the strength of them.

We tried this, selling some special content of the magazine for the next six months or year in much the same way we would have described what was in a premium book we were offering, and found we could get as good returns by putting our premium in the magazine as by offering it separately! We took half a dozen excerpts from the early chapters of this book, for instance, worked them into articles to run in the magazine, and then sold the series as part of System with as great success as ever. In the old days, it had been possible to sell System with a premium. Here are the two letters that did it:

> When a man can turn an $80,000 loss of June 1st into a $121,000 Net Profit as of December 31st, entirely with letters—
>
> When he can sell, by mail, $3,000,000 worth of Traveling Bags—take 400,000 pairs of returned Silk Stockings at their regular dealers' price and dispose of them, by mail, at a profit—
>
> When he can increase gross sales in three years time from $2,000,000 a year to $6,000,000 a year for one concern, and then go and do just as big a job for two other companies in different lines of business—and all through the right use of good letters—
>
>> Then there must be something so fundamentally sound about his way of writing and using letters, that it would pay you as a business man to know what it is.
>
> If you could get this man to analyze his most successful letters, if you could induce him to point out the features that made them pull such enormous volume of orders, if you could persuade him to show you how those same factors could be applied to the sale of your products, the collection of your accounts, there is no price in reason you would not be willing to pay for this service, is there?

Well, that is exactly what he has undertaken to do in a series of articles in SYSTEM—analyze his strongest appeals, point out the factors that made them pay, and show how you can use those same factors and same appeals to increase the pulling power of your letters.

His name is Robert Collier, and he has been selling by mail for 20 years. In that time, he has sold considerably more than twenty millions of dollars' worth of goods by mail. He was the first to sell the Famous Five-Foot Shelf of Books by mail. He sold $2,000,000 worth of O. Henry stories, over $3,000,000 worth of Wells' Outline of History, millions of dollars' worth of all manner of products from coal and coke to ladies' dresses and men's socks.

> And now he has put the meat of his experience into a series of articles for System, the Journal of Modern Business Practice. And not the experience only, but actual examples of the way to apply it. A clearer, more instructive lot of articles on how to make your letters bring back bigger returns would be hard to find.

Will you *try* them? Three of these valuable articles have already appeared in System, and the demand for' them was so great that we had to reprint 4,000 copies. Of those 4,000, less than 600 are now left. If you mail the enclosed card right away—without money—we will send you one of those reprints with your first copy of System containing the current article.

If you like it—if you feel, as we do, that these articles alone will be worth to you a lot more than the subscription price of the whole magazine—send us $1 at the end of 30 days, and $1 a month for four months to cover the special price of the next 24 issues. Otherwise, you can mail us 25 cents for the copy you receive, and cancel the balance of the subscription. Fair enough? Then jot down your name and position on the enclosed card and drop it

418

in the mail. But please do it *now* if you want to get a reprint of the first three articles.

These first articles contain some of the most important essentials of resultful letters in the whole series, so don't miss them!

The card is already stamped. All you need to do is put your name on it and drop in the mail.

What is there about some letters, that makes them so much more effective than others?

A letter may have perfect diction, finished style—it may follow all the rules—yet the orders it brings back will be scarce as oysters in the stew at a Church supper. Why? Because writing letters that bring home the bacon is like fishing—it's not a matter of rules, *but of bait!*

Do you know how to bait your hook for orders—swarms of orders—all coming by mail? That is the Secret of selling by mail. That is the secret we have prevailed on Robert Collier to reveal in a series of articles, starting in the next issue of System, the Journal of Modern Business Management.

Robert Collier is the man who started the sale by mail of Dr. Eliot's famous Five-Foot Shelf of Books. Who followed that by selling a couple of million dollars' worth of O. Henry stories in two years, and then some three million dollars worth of Wells' "Outline of History."

Lest you think his methods good only for selling books, he took over the writing of the copy for a mail order house, and in seven months time turned an $80,000 loss into a Net Profit of $121,000. In the next three years he increased their gross sales of men's furnishings, traveling bags and the like from $2,000,000 a year to better than $6,000,000.

He has taken such different lines as a coal mine and a

ladies' dress establishment, and by applying the same fundamental rules of "baiting the hook" to both, he has made them eminently successful.

Now he has put those fundamentals into a series of articles that not only show you what they are, but how and why they work. You see, Collier is primarily a student of human reactions. He doesn't study merchandise—*he studies man!*

He may know very little about the product he is offering, but he makes it his business to know all about the people he is offering it to. That is why his "fundamentals" apply just as well to ladies' dresses as to coal, to traveling bags and men's shirts as to books.

Will you read the first of those fundamentals? The enclosed card brings it to you in the next issue of System. Send for it—TRY it! If you don't feel that Collier's secrets of mail selling will alone be worth the entire subscription to System, send us only 25 cents to pay for the one copy and cancel the rest of your subscription.

That's fair enough, I think you'll agree. If the first article doesn't make you feel that you must have the whole series, cancel your order, pay 25 cents for the one you receive, and that ends it.

But—if you want even to see that first article, you'll have to mail the enclosed card right away. We print only 1,000 extra copies of each issue. When they are gone, subscriptions have to start with the next one. So if you want to see the first and most important of Collier's "fundamentals," put your name on the enclosed card and mail it right away!

That question answered, we set about seeing whether we could not step up the percentage of subscribers who renewed their subscriptions at expiration and found that by depending less upon notices that their subscription was about to expire and more upon re-selling them on what the coming issues would do for them, we were able to just about double our percentage of renewals.

To do this, we used a series of six letters. Here are two typical ones:

What size hat do you wear?

Is it one any other man in the organization could clap on his head and never notice the difference, or would it come down over the ears of most and leave them looking like would-be clowns?

In every successful organization is at least one man whose place no one else can fill. He may be back of the selling policy. He may be the heart of the collection or merchandising end. But wherever he is, the success of the business turns on him.

Such a man usually has two things: 1st, IDEAS. 2nd, THE TACT AND FINESSE TO PUT THOSE IDEAS ACROSS.

Lots of men have good ideas. The difference between the wide-awake, progressive thinker and one who is looked upon as an unsound radical, lies more often than not in the way each presents his plan. The one feeds it out only as fast as his associates can digest it; the other tries to ram it whole down his hearers' throats.

In System, the Journal of Modern Business Management, you get only those sound ideas which have been proven - good in other organizations. You get hints for adapting those ideas to your work, and you get the authoritative backing often needed to "sell" a new idea to your organization.

In short, you get the means of becoming the "Idea-Man" of your concern, the one about whom all the activities of the company revolve. To such a man, the question is not— "What size hat do I wear?" but—" *How big a one can I fill?"*

Whatever your answer to that question now, it will be a lot better answer a year from now, if meantime you have added to your own original ideas the proven methods of other successful "Idea Men," from the pages of System.

I know you won't want to miss a single one of those timely suggestions now, of all times, when a new collection method, a new sales plan or money-saving idea, may make all the difference between red ink and black on your monthly Profit & Loss statement.

No need to write a line. Just your penciled "O.K." on the enclosed card will continue your name for the next twelve issues. Will you jot that down—NOW—and drop the card in the mail? Then the days may come and the weeks may go, but you'll be sure of your grist of workable plans each month just as surely as the mailman comes 'round.

Send no money—just the card. But to keep your name in its proper place on the list, you will have to mail that card right away!

Sincerely,

DEAR SUBSCRIBER:

Would you risk $1 for the most effective collection letter we have ever seen—a letter that brought in 85% of all past due money when every other appeal had failed?

Would you chance $1 to see a sales letter that pulled literally hundreds of thousands of dollars worth of direct orders?

Would you spend 16 1/2 cents each to get the six essential steps which a Master Salesman found most important in selling, or the plans which have proven most successful in job analysis, measurement of work, group bonus and "incentive " systems?

If you would, then send the enclosed card for the first six issues of the *new* System, Journal of Modern Business Management. For System has taken on new life, new pep, new interest.

You see, we are facing new conditions today. We've been in a rising market, where circumstances made money for many people who could never have made it for themselves. That's past. It's going to take real ability, a thorough grasp of modern management methods, to reach the top or stay there in the period now in front of us.

Such inequalities as one manager getting only a third as much from his labor-dollar as another will not be tolerated. The man who cannot produce will go—the manager, too!

The next few years will be hard on drones. They are going to be known as "the leveling years," for they will bring down many a man who is now in high place, and put the real workers in power—and by workers we mean not those who merely go through the motions, but those who PRODUCE!

In such a period, every man must look to himself, and System has set the example. The new System is different. It is more practical. It is, in effect, a continuous course in modern business management. It gives to the forward-looking executive the plans, the methods, the letters, the incentive he needs to meet the new competition of today.

Will you risk $1 to TRY it for six months? It doesn't matter if you have already taken it for the six years—YOU NEED TO READ THIS NEW SYSTEM! You'll miss an essential factor in your success if you don't! Will you risk $1 on that?

The enclosed card is your answer. Will you send it *now*—TODAY?

Sincerely,

But merely bringing in the orders is not enough. That is just the first part. The next part is getting paid for them. And it is just as important a problem to write letters that will bring in the payments as it is to get the orders in the first place. So our next chapter will be devoted to collections

XXIV

Collecting with a Smile

What is the hardest job a collection letter can have?

Collecting money people owe you when times are hard may be difficult. Collecting after something has happened to anger your debtor may be worse. But compared to one kind of collecting, both of these are easy. That kind is collecting for goods people have not sent for—and for all you know, have no use for.

If a letter will bring back the money from such a debtor, where the creditor has no standing morally or legally, it must be a good one. If it will work on him, it ought to bring home the bacon no matter where it is used.

You remember the flood of unsolicited merchandise that filled the mails a couple of years ago, until Chambers of Commerce and Better Business Bureaus began to advise people to throw the stuff away, and the post office threatened to refuse to handle it?

With such advice ringing in their ears, people could scarcely be considered in a favorable mood for good collection, yet it was at just this time that a company with which the writer was connected in a consulting capacity found itself with nearly 600,000 one dollar accounts on its books, collections getting slower and slower, and no possible redress in sight.

The merchandise sent was of three different kinds—a bottle of perfume, a set of initialed handkerchiefs, and an initialed cosmetic set, each selling for $1, and each sent to a likely list without order or other authorization.

It was poor business to send out merchandise that way - no doubt of that. Even the ones who first proposed it were willing to admit that then. But this was not the point that was worrying them. The important matter on the boards at the moment was whether there was any way of getting the money back

Threats, of course, were out of the question. There remained only persuasion, and even this had to be used with care, for the chances were that a great many of the recipients of that merchandise were feeling distinctly peeved at having things sent them they had never ordered, and would be a lot more so when they were asked to pay for them. They must be mollified first. And the best way to do it seemed to be with a smile. But even before that, some sort of a bill must be sent, to establish in their minds the idea that they did owe something for the merchandise. So the first notice took the form of a letter and bill combined. It read:

One Full Ounce Bottle—
Delightfully Fragrant Narcisse Perfume—$1

A person who is busy can be forgiven for forgetting a little bill like the above.

Our account will be off your mind, if you wrap a check or dollar bill in this letter and slip it in the enclosed envelope. Why not use it *now*? It's already stamped!

Appreciatively yours,

That idea was given a couple of weeks to percolate, then "the voice with the smile" was used. Here was the most successful of this type of letter that was tried:

Have you heard this one of Bud Fisher's?

"For the love of Mike!" exclaimed Jeff, looking at a letter. "Bad news in the letter, Jeff?" asks Mutt. "I'll say so. Terrible news. A fellow writes me that he wants my autograph. "I call a request for an autograph a compliment." "Yes," wails Jeff, "but he wants my autograph on a check for the eight bucks I owe him!"

May we not, like Jeff's creditor, request your autograph on a check for $1 (or just a plain dollar bill) covering the full ounce bottle of fine perfume we sent you a month ago? Thank you!

Gratefully,

That failing, it was necessary to become just a little more insistent, so the next two letters took on a slightly aggrieved tone.

426

? ?

That is the way we are beginning to feel about that bottle of fine perfume we sent you six weeks ago, with the privilege of keeping it or using the postage enclosed to mail it back to us.

We've written you several letters—but not a line from you have we had.

If you have merely neglected to take care of our previous letters—won't you please *pin* your *check* or a *dollar bill* to this letter and send it in the enclosed envelope *now*?

Yours hopefully,

A feather is not very heavy, but have you ever carried a feather bed upstairs?

One small account does not burden any one, but hundreds of them often make a tremendous load.

Besides—

A small account may be easily spent in postage and letters before it is paid.

That isn't fair, and I know you don't want to appear unfair for the small amount you owe us for that full ounce bottle of exquisite perfume we sent you a couple of months ago, with postage enclosed for its return in case you didn't care for it.
RSVP $1.

Expectantly yours,

Those letters brought home the bacon—or a sufficiently large part of it to keep the hair from going with the hide. They brought back dollars from something like 60 per cent of the people to whom they were sent, and the merchandise itself from about 25 per cent more.

427

Only about 15 per cent adopted the advice of local leaders to throw away or refuse payment on anything delivered without order.

Letters that will work on such difficult accounts must have back of them a fundamentally sound idea, and it seems to us that these four had. For what is it impels a debtor to pay you? Two things only—fear or persuasion. If you can stir up in him the fear that he will lose his credit, if you can hold over him the threat of a judgment and foreclosure or garnishee, you will get your money if it is possible for him to pay it. You will get your money, but you will lose his good will—and his trade when he is able to buy elsewhere.

How much better, then, to use the sort of persuasion that leaves a smile in its wake, that extracts the money, but instead of an aching void, leaves in its place the pleasant glow of a favor done for a friend.

But the fact that it is pleasantly expressed need not take the firmness out of your letter. On the contrary, it makes it the more necessary that you put it there plainly, unmistakably. If there is anything better calculated to lull a debtor into a sense of security than a "Trusting to hear from you" letter, I hope I never meet it. Just listen to this one:

DEAR MR. JONES:

You are undoubtedly aware of the balance due on your account. I believe you care little for dunning letters, and for me to personally write of the whole affair would consume considerable unnecessary time.

Extensive experience has led us to conclude that there is a positive danger in your failure to give regular attention to payments. When you fail to send them in promptly, it does not take long for back payments to accumulate to such an extent that it is a great inconvenience—and often an unanticipated impossibility—to pay at all.

Not having heard from you for quite some time, I ask you to please confer a personal favor by advising me when I can expect a remittance, or possibly make known the circumstances that have prevented payment.

Thanking you in advance for this personal courtesy,

I am—

No, we did not make that one up. It was actually a typical one of a series we were called upon to revise for a company that you would think had better sense than ever to mail such a screed as that. If you got it, would you not feel that while they might want their money, they would be too diffident ever to do anything about it, so you could safely put off payment until it suited your convenience? Compare that with this courteous, but forceful, definite request for payment:

DEAR MR. JONES:

Some people, the minute a delay or dispute arises in the payment of a bill of theirs, want to rush to the law about it. They think the only reason a person can have for not paying a bill when it is due must be dishonesty.

But we know better.

We have dealt with too many people not to know that only a very, very small percentage are deliberately dishonest.

But many perfectly honest people get classed with the "dead beats" simply because they are careless. They fully intend to pay—do pay eventually—but because the amount involved is small, they put it off.

Now we know that you fully intend to pay the $10 overdue on your account—we know that eventually we shall get the money—but that difference between "eventually" and "now" is what marks the line between the "gilt-edged" customer and the "poor pay."

You want to be in the "gilt-edged" class, even if you never buy another book from us or another dollar's worth of goods on credit. It's such a pleasant feeling to know that you are a "preferred risk"—that any merchant will be glad to extend credit privileges to you if you want them.

Get back into that class by pinning your check or money order to this letter now, and dropping it in the mail.

The greatest danger of collection letters is that after the first one, people recognize them for what they are from a glance at the corner card of the envelope, and throw them away unread. So it is well to vary the appearance of your collection appeal in every way possible. The Business Week, for instance, uses a miniature letter, envelope and bill that attract attention by their very novelty, then follows these with a letter in the ordinary form. Here they are:

DEAR MR JONES:

The attached bill is so small, that we don't want to take up much space in bringing it to the attention of a man in your position.

We know that a reminder is all that is necessary.

Won't you pencil your "O.K." on it and drop in the "Out-going" basket— NOW?

Thank you!

Gratefully,

THE BUSINESS WEEK

A MCGRAW-HILL PUBLICATION

Tenth Avenue at 36th Street, New York, N. Y.

SUBSCRIPTION INVOICE

John Jones
121 J St.,
Washington, D. C.

For 52 Issues to THE BUSINESS WEEK $5.00

Kindly return this

invoice with your
remittance or refer
to No.   121

With a man like you, it is not a problem of how to pay, but *when*—because you re so busy.

But that very busyness makes The Business Week the more invaluable to you, because it not only condenses into a few, meaty paragraphs, everything of import that happens in business, but it INTERPRETS those happenings for you in terms of their effect upon your business.

The Business Week is as necessary to the important executive as his bank statement and his sales charts. And your check (because it's one of thousands) is as necessary to the service The Business Week is rendering you.

Won't you, therefore, get that check definitely off your mind by penciling your "O.K." on the enclosed bill now and dropping it in your "Out-going" basket?

Thank you!

Appreciatively,

The famous string letters written by Louis Victor Eytinge owed their success in large part to the clever idea around which they were written—the idea of tying a string around your finger so you would not forget to send remittance, *and then tying letter and bill with the piece of string you were to use!*

Here is the first of his letters:

Do you remember how, when you were young and your good folks sent you down town after something, they were very likely to tie a string about your thumb to make certain you would not forget?

Those were the happy days, weren't they?

431

But—there s no reason why the days of NOW should not be as happy, and it is just as certain that some of us are liable to forget the little things of today.

Because of that, I am sending you this little reminder— NOT TO FORGET TO PAY the little item listed below.

I hope you enjoy the smile in my letter, and that I may have the pleasure of hearing from you promptly.

Cordially yours,

—Tie the string—and you won't forget!

Another good one is the "pin letter." It is an adaptation of the string idea and works just about as well. Here it is:

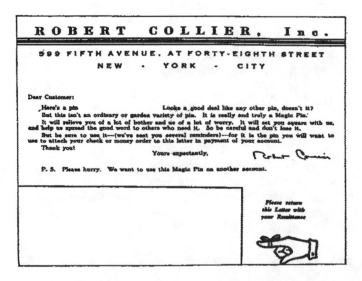

ROBERT COLLIER, Inc.

599 FIFTH AVENUE, AT FORTY-EIGHTH STREET
NEW • YORK • CITY

Dear Customer:

Here's a pin   Looks a good deal like any other pin, doesn't it?
But this isn't an ordinary or garden variety of pin. It is really and truly a Magic Pin. It will relieve you of a lot of bother and us of a lot of worry. It will set you square with us, and help us spread the good word to others who need it. So be careful and don't lose it.
But be sure to use it—(we've sent you several reminders)—for it is the pin you will want to use to attach your check or money order to this letter in payment of your account.
Thank you!

Yours expectantly,

Robert Collier

P. S. Please hurry. We want to use this Magic Pin on another account.

Please return this Letter with your Remittance

Then there is the letter in a blue envelope, printed on a blue letterhead, which tells the reader how blue you are feeling at not having received his expected check. This idea can be carried to extremes, as in the "gravestone letter," which carries a black border on envelope and letter, and is "Sacred to the memory of John Jones (or whatever the reader's name may be) whose account died after a lingering illness, etc." Down in the corner of the card, in small type, is a line to the effect that if there is any mistake, and Jones still lives, they will be glad to receive evidence of that fact in the form of a remittance.

Of course, stunts like that can easily be carried too far. But the idea back of them is sound—that the difficult part, and the important part, is to get your debtor's attention, and anything which will attract his attention long enough to get you a hearing will add greatly to your collections.

When you are selling something that requires further work on the buyer's part, it is frequently necessary to re-sell him on the desirability of your product before you can collect. This is especially true of courses of instruction, sets of books and the like. When collecting such accounts, an occasional inspirational letter of the right type is worth its weight in gold—and usually brings it back in the form of remittances!

Then there are always premiums for prompt payment, and cash-ups on installment accounts. A good cash-up will frequently bring in as high as 30 to 40 per cent of payments in full on accounts that without it would be slow in paying even the monthly installments. Here are a few that have been very successful for us:

Will you accept a 3-volume set of Updegraff's "Library of Self-Starters" in return for a favor I want you to do? The favor is a simple one, easy to render. Here is the way of it:

You owe us a small balance on your subscription to Mind, Inc.

You can settle that balance in convenient monthly payments,

BUT—
If you will mail us that balance in full NOW, we will give you—FREE and POSTPAID—a 3-volume set of Updegraff's "Library of Self-Starters."

These volumes sell regularly for $2.25 plus postage, and thousands upon thousands of them have been sold at this figure. They include such old stand-bys as the famous "Obvious Adams," "The Sixth Prune" and "The Sub-conscious Mind in Business." They are beautifully printed on heavy book paper, and bound in thick board covers. The only reason we can make this offer is that we are very near the end of the big edition, and have only two or three hundred sets now left. When they are gone, our rights to the books go with them, so no more will be printed. We are therefore giving away these last couple of hundred sets. The books are really good, however, and the few who get them will be drawing prizes worth while. To be one of them, you'll have to mail your remittance *right away.*

Sincerely,

A GIFT FOR YOU!
If you are prompt!

We have left from the last big edition a few hundred copies of the famous "Business Correspondence Handbook," edited by Prof. James A. Picken, Lecturer in Advertising at the School of Commerce of Northwestern University, and consultant in many a big business campaign.

This "Business Correspondence Handbook" is in three handy volumes, bound in heavy paper imitation leather. It is the same in every respect as the thousands of sets which sold for $5.00. But we have only a few hundred left—not even enough to print new advertising matter describing it. So we are going to give those few to the first of our subscribers who are prompt. Here is our offer:

> Send us NOW the full amount of the enclosed statement, rather than wait to pay it by the month. If you mail that balance right away, we will send you FREE and POSTPAID—the three volumes of the "Business Correspondence Handbook."

If the books are all gone when your remittance comes, we will return that remittance intact and let you take care of the payments as originally intended—by the months.

But don't delay! Don't take any chances on such an offer as this! Attach your check Now to the enclosed statement and mail it in the stamped, addressed envelope. You'll never have another such chance!

Sincerely,

Of course, the most successful collection series is the one that combines all these features to the greatest possible extent, alternating one form with another. When you threaten, for instance, you frighten a certain number of your debtors into paying, but the chances are you simply anger the others. If your next letter contains a stronger threat, or even the action implied in your previous one, its principal effect is going to be to make the recipients angrier than they were before.

It is like stroking a cat's fur. You can make the sparks fly by stroking it the wrong way. But then you must smooth it down again before you can make the sparks fly some more! The same with your debtors. Ruffle them up with a threatening letter. You will land a certain number of payments. Smooth them over with a cash up or inspirational letter or a stunt like the pin or string letter. You land a lot more payments. Stir them up again with a stronger threat, and keep alternating one with another and you will get every cent it is possible to collect from them.

All 39 Books of Shakespeare

in One Volume FREE!—

(No Premium—No Subscription—This is FREE! See Last Page)

In collection letters, as in everything else, it is well to remember that you can catch more flies with honey than with vinegar. And another thing the threat of action is even more effective than the action itself provided your debtor believes your threat is not mere bluff.

The law is a last resort, and unless a large amount of money is involved, it is seldom a profitable resort. A letter from a lawyer, on the other hand, is one of the most effective collectors of delinquent accounts that there is. But it seldom pays to go beyond the letter.

Close collections, as a rule, are good collections. If you follow up a man the moment his accounts start to lag, if you camp on his trail and keep reminding him courteously, *but firmly,* of that overdue balance, the chances are that as soon as he is able to pay you will get it.

XXV

The Ideal Sales Letter

You remember the newspaper editor's description of the ideal wedding:

"Take a beautiful heiress," he said, "have her elope with the chauffeur. Let the irate father pursue with a shot-gun and a high-powered car. Throw in a smash-up, a heroic rescue and a nip-and-tuck finish—and you have the ideal situation dear to tabloid readers."

And his advice to cub reporters was to go to every wedding with that ideal situation in mind, see how many of the dramatic elements from that situation could be found in the function he was attending and build his story around them.

Much the same thought can be used in writing letters. No matter what the product or service you are writing about, first put yourself in the place of your prospective customer. Think of every property you could possibly desire in such a product or service. Think of everything you would like to have it do for you. Work out the ultimate ideal, then write a letter that stresses every desirable point of that ideal product.

Here, for instance, is the basis for an ideal bargain appeal on linen tablecloths. Read it, then turn back to the old "damaged-set" letter and see how closely we came to the ideal in our offerings with it.

> We are manufacturers of Linen Tablecloths. We import the finest linen direct from Belfast—linen with the sheen of satin—so heavy it will stand alone, so strong it will wear forever.

> Linen like that is worth a king's ransom, and costs just about that in the best stores. But by selling it to you direct, with no wholesaler or middleman or high store expenses or service charges, we can save you half the usual price.

But that isn't all!

Even at half the regular retail price, this linen is so costly that you may feel you still cannot afford it. But in manufacturing thousands of these fine tablecloths, we turn out an occasional one with some slight flaw in it—perhaps an uneven hem, perhaps a slight discoloration in some tiny spot—not enough to be apparent to the eye of any but the expert, but still not up to our standard of perfection.

Over the past few months, we have accumulated perhaps thirty or forty of these technically imperfect tablecloths. While they last, you can have one for one-third off our already low price!

Remember, though, we have only 30 or 40 of these, and we may not have another for months, so if you want to even see one, it behooves you to use the enclosed order form quickly.

When you have your ideal letter written to your satisfaction, let it cool for a day. The next day, go over it and cross out every descriptive phrase and adjective that cannot honestly be applied to your product. You will be surprised at how many you have left—more than enough to write the finest sort of a letter that will build a picture in your reader's mind so desirable that he will scarcely be able to refrain from ordering.

There is an old saying, you know, that there is nothing you can say about a 50 cent cigar that you cannot say about a 5 cent one—and the Cremo advertising seems to be proving the truth of it. You see, the only difference between an expensive product and one of ordinary price is usually one of degree. In a general way, they look alike, they are made of much the same type of material, they will do the same things. The difference is in the degree of pleasure or satisfaction they will bring. And this is largely in the mind of the buyer.

So your job is to build a picture in his mind's eye of what he will get from your product or service. Build it with bricks he can handle, *i.e.*, with words and mental images that are familiar to him. Do not exaggerate—or he will refuse to believe in it and kick the whole structure over disgustedly, like a child trying to build with blocks a

438

house that will not come out right. But keep it attractive. Keep it desirable—more desirable far than the money or the time or the trouble it takes to build it.

Do not make the mistake of trying to stress in your letter all the points of your product. You can list them in a separate folder and make your letter the stronger for it. But find the one point on which your sale is likely to hang and build your letter around it. Let that be the focal point of your mental image, your picture, and let every word in it be a brush stroke that adds clearness and power to that one focal point.

Then remember that it is not enough merely to tell your reader to order now, or "Mail the enclosed card at once!" *Why* must he do this? What will he gain by doing it now? What will he lose by delay?

You must dangle certain bait before his eyes. You must hold over his head a "Sword of Damocles," the thread of which may be cut at any moment. Set a time beyond which orders will not be accepted. Or give a valid reason why the supply is strictly limited. Or announce an increase in price that takes effect on a certain date. Or make a special combination offer, good only for a limited time.

But whatever you do, make it sound as though you mean it. If you set a time limit, say positively that no orders will be accepted beyond that date. If you announce a raise in price, tell them there will be no last-minute concessions. All orders not mailed by a certain date will take the higher price. Be definite—and be positive! You will lose a few last-minute orders, but you will gain ten times the number in those who are impelled to act the moment they read the letter—while the order card is in their hands—for fear if they lay it down they will delay and be too late.

These are the important factors of a successful letter. There are others, however, that add to or take away from their effectiveness.

The first essential is to get your reader to look inside the envelope. That may sound simple—and is simple on ordinary correspondence—but when you have been circularizing in a large way and people recognize your envelopes as circulars at sight, then it becomes a problem.

Some people depend upon "teasers" on the outside of the envelope to arouse the reader's curiosity and make him look at the letter to see what it is all about. A really effective "teaser" is good, but the effective ones are scarce. As a general rule, it is better to try to make your envelope so personal looking and so attractive that the reader will at least want to know whom it is from and what it is about.

This can be done in various ways. If your name is too well known and your mere corner card brands the envelope as containing a circular, it frequently pays to use a box number in the corner, with an armorial design or a mono-gram or some such attractive insignia under it.

Using a window envelope sometimes helps, as does a change in the color of the envelope or in the size. If your mailings have been going in a No. 6 envelope, change to a baronial at times, from that to a Monarch, then to a No. 9 and back to your No. 6, varying your corner card on all, and sometimes changing the color as well as the size of your envelope.

One concern makes a specialty of letters on pseudo-telegraph forms, mailed in envelopes that look almost exactly like the yellow window envelopes the Western Union uses for telegrams. We have tried them and found them very effective as a variation from our usual forms.

Another makes a "giant" telegram of it, using 18-point type, a giant envelope and a pseudo-telegraph form inside to fit it. This in our experience has been even more effective than the other. But again it is just a novelty and will wear out quickly if used too much.

Such novelties, however, are invaluable to the man who does much circularizing, for they keep his appeal from going stale. People never throw away his letters unopened because they are never able to discount in advance what is inside them. But when they have taken your reader into your letter, their job is done. From there on, it is up to you to win his interest and turn it into a sale.

What is the most important factor in the making of your sale? Your letter! The circular helps, and the order card makes it~ easier—but the letter must carry the load. If you have not the stuff in it, it does not matter where else you have it. It will not do you much good.

So put your best efforts into your letter. Keep an "idea file" of good starters, good descriptions, good closers, good pointers of all kinds—not to copy, but to inspire you to new and better ideas. There is nothing like glancing over a few such ideas to stimulate your own brain cells into action.

And always remember that the point which sells your customer is not what your product is, *but what it will do for him!*

Remember, too, that the purpose of a letter is to put ideas *into* your reader's head, so be careful not to put in negative ones that you will have to take out again before you can make a sale.

Some people will tell you never to write long letters, others never to make them short. Both are wrong—as didactic extremists usually are. As a general proposition, it is advisable to make your letter short and snappy when you are trying for inquiries and all you want is to win enough of the prospect's interest to make him ask for further particulars.

Before a man will definitely commit himself to buy, however, he wants to know all about the thing you are offering, and you cannot tell him that in a short letter. So tell your story, no matter how long or how short it may be, striving simply to keep it interesting. The only safe measure you can apply is the one Lincoln gave when some one asked him how long a man's legs should be: "Long enough to reach the ground!"

XXVI

How to Raise Money By Mail

THE Charity Fund Raising organizations of New York once gave a dinner to the secretaries of all these philanthropies. Several hundred attended.

One of them had a niece who happened to be visiting him from the country, so he brought her along, expecting her to be much impressed. She was. Coming to the big dining room and seeing what a crowd was there, she turned to her uncle aghast. "Uncle," she exclaimed in a very audible whisper, "do the poor of New York have to support all these people?"

The Secretaries of Charity Organizations are, for the most part, an earnest, hard-working group, doing wonders in the way of money raising. And many of them do it at remarkably small expense. Dozens of effective methods of appealing for funds have been worked out, of which perhaps the best is that of showing the picture of some crippled child, telling his pitiful story, and then leaving it to the reader to multiply that story by thousands.

You see, it is difficult to get much worked up over statistics. You read with comparative indifference that 36,000 people are killed and 1,000,000 injured each year in auto accidents. But just let you witness a little child being run down, let you hear the anguished cry of its mother, let you look at the pitiful, mangled remains, and you will never feel indifferent again. Every time you read of an accident, you will see again that mangled child, you will think of the bereft mother, and you will resolve to DO something to see that this wholesale slaughter is stopped.

The same is true of any great catastrophe—of earthquakes, or floods, or famine or war. We cannot visualize them in the mass. The only way to make us feel them is to tie them into the story of one victim. The English have learned this, and in the Great War, they brought it down to a science.

First they tried us on broken treaties and the like. But these left us cold, for every European nation has broken treaties pretty much at will, when it happened to be advantageous to them to do so. They tried a dozen other angles, and then they hit upon the theme of young girls being attacked by the Hun soldiers. At last, they had something. From then on, their propaganda was resistless. They dramatized the case of Edith Cavell, and of a dozen other individuals, until they had this' country ready to war with Germany nearly two years before we actually got into it. In short, they appealed to our emotions by visualizing what was happening to some one poor victim of war, and then followed with argument that sounded reasonable in indicating what might happen to us if we did not do something about it.

And that is what the most successful Fund appeals do. They appeal first to the emotion, and follow that with a swift shift to the intellect. They work up your feeling of pity, and follow it with a logical reason why you should give, lest similar catastrophe come close to you. Here is the way it was done by one Tuberculosis Association. In a childish scrawl across the top of a letter, there was reproduced the following—

DEAR T. B. PEOPLE:

Thank you for helping to save my daddy's life and bring him home safe again and not being sick and coughing all the time like he used—

Then underneath it came the appeal—

DEAR FRIEND:

The above is an exact copy of a part of a letter received by the Association. We are passing the thanks along to where it belongs—To the people who bought Christmas Seals last year. For without their help we could not have arranged for "Daddy's" cure.

Will you help us to bring others back home, safe and well, by next Christmas?

We have already sent you your Christmas Seals, so you could help. In the rush of things, you have overlooked sending in your remittance in the addressed envelope we sent.

443

Your dollar can never do more good, nor be spent in a better way, than to help those who are sick and unable to help themselves. Won't you help us to finish the job by sending yours NOW? Please don't wait.

Sincerely,

If that does not bring back the money, there follows a letter with a snap shot of an under-nourished youngster in the corner, hopeful, appealing-looking, and this message from him—

DEAR FOLKS:

I am Junior Smith. This is my picture. I was sick for a long time, and it didn't seem that I was ever going to get well. Then the Blank Tuberculosis Association said they would help me. So last November they took me to the Tuberculosis Camp, where they help others like me to get well.

Now I am getting well and strong and will soon be able to run and play again. I can then grow up to be a big strong man. I hope a lot of people bought Christmas Seals, so a lot of other boys and girls in Smithtown can be helped to get well.

Thank you,

Under it comes the follow-up from the Association:

P. S.—We don't want to overburden you, but our former letter requesting a remittance for the Seals we sent you, was evidently overlooked. We will deeply appreciate a dollar, or any amount you wish to send.

Forgive me for calling it to your attention, but the need for tuberculosis work this year is unusually urgent. We must help hundreds of others like Junior Smith.

Please put your check or money in the enclosed envelope and mail it NOW.

Gratefully,

Summer Camps have worked out effective appeals along similar lines, many of them using the "Before and After" pictures. They show some poor, pale youngster from the slums as he looked in the heat of the big city. Then they show a picture of him after a month at Camp, with plenty of fresh air, food and exercise. With it, they show campfire scenes, swimming pool, fishing and all the things you loved to do when you were a boy, and end with a letter along the lines of the following:

DEAR MR. SMITH:

This is Phillip Jones' application, a good boy who wants to go to Camp but has no money.

His folks have had a very had time indeed this winter and Phillip needs good substantial nourishment.

One dollar a day will pay his way. I thought you might like to help us take him for two weeks.

If you would be good enough to return this Application with your contribution, I would appreciate it.

Sincerely,

It is a fact, which all will admit, that what helps one helps all, so even though the benefit be indirect, we all benefit from any good that may be done for the children of the slums, we all benefit from any help that may be given them to grow into healthy, happy, successful men and women. Knowing that, there is an appeal to our reason, so all we need is a strong enough emotion of sympathy to make us dig down into our jeans and give 'til it hurts. Here is a letter based largely on that appeal to reason:

This Plan Is Helping Thousands
To End Their Worry About Tuberculosis!

DEAR FRIEND:

Human beings do not come like buttons from a mold, but in individual packages. There is a prize in every package— but many people never seem able to find theirs.

This civilization of ours is based on giving every man a chance to find the prize in his packet of life. It is based on the strong helping the weak, on the fortunate sharing some of their gifts with those unable to fend for themselves.

That is why we are taking the liberty of sending you the enclosed Christmas Seals. You are one of the fortunate ones. You are strong. You are able. You have found the prize in your package. Will you share a little of it with those less fortunate?

The money you send for the enclosed seals will not be wasted on overhead and the like. More than 80% of it goes direct to the needy. It enables us to provide one or two clinics every week. To test for tuberculosis in the public schools. To give emergency relief in newly discovered cases. To prevent other members of the family developing the disease. To put many in sanitariums and help even more at home.

Will you help? Will you share a little of the good things you have won from life with these poor souls who are unable to help themselves? Will you act the part of the Good Samaritan, by helping to bind up their hurts, by making it possible for them to be healed?

The enclosed envelope is for your convenience. Will you put your remittance into it and mail it NOW? On the part of all those you are helping, I say sincerely—"Thank you!"

Gratefully,

446

Then there is the seldom used, but popular method of helping people to help themselves. Most of us have heard too many stories of families that sit back and wait for Relief Checks to come to them, refusing to lift a finger for their own help. A letter like the following sounds refreshing:

Here Is a Plan Which Is Helping
Thousands to Start Life Over Again!

DEAR SIR:

For three years now, you have been giving generously to help those in desperate need. And the chances are you are getting a bit tired of their continuous calls upon your pocketbook.

What a relief it would be to lend a hand to a man, who would use whatever you gave him to start afresh, and look after himself thereafter?

> That is what is happening down in the soft coal fields of Pa., Ky., and W. Va. The Quakers down there are teaching the miners how to earn a livelihood, *regardless of whether the mines run or not!*

They are showing them how to make furniture, to weave rugs, to take leather and make shoes, and especially they are making it possible for them to raise their own food. And they are doing it with a very little money. Largely they are using gifts of machinery and equipment and clothing—old sewing machines, spinning wheels, shop motors, grinders and the like.

Have you anything that would help to equip a shop to make these sturdy workers self-supporting? The Quakers aim to so equip each community that it will be able to supply all its own needs. Have you anything that will help? If not, will you feed one family for a week, to help them carry on until their little gardens produce?

$10 will feed a whole family for a week. Will you adopt

447

one for just one week—take its feeding upon your shoulders? The enclosed envelope is for your convenience. Will you use it *now*—TODAY?

Sincerely,

Lastly, there is the plan of getting together a central group of well-known citizens, and getting each to write a personal appeal in his own name to ten friends. For such, a letter along the lines of the following has been found effective:

DEAR JIM:

Will you join me in helping an old friend of ours out of a serious "hole?"

Dr. Jones came to me about it. I promised him I'd lend a hand, and told him I thought I could promise as much for you, too. He doesn't ask much of us, but if each one of those he is counting on does his bit, it will pull our friend out of the hole.

You see, it is the Blank Institute that is in difficulties. You know it, of course. It is one of the few places where a man down on his luck can still go and get a meal and a place to sleep and help in landing a job. . . without having to supply his birth certificate or dog license, and without putting up a cent.

So many people have been calling on this Institute for help this past year that it has had to spend every penny on them, with the result that it is eight months behind on its own rent, and the landlord has served it with a dispossess notice. And if that should go through, I don't know what would happen to a lot of these poor fellows who don't know where to lay their heads from one night to the next.

Dr. Jones has appealed to a number of us to each put up $10 to pay the back rent and start the Institute afresh. I promised for myself and assured him I thought I could

448

promise for you, Jim.

Will you join me in this? Will you send me $10 that I can add to my own $10 and hand to Dr. Jones for this really worthy work? Here is a stamped envelope for your convenience in mailing it. I'll be looking forward to hearing from you, Jim, SOON.

Sincerely,

These are some of the ways to raise money by mail. There are dozens of other methods of getting people to give, which we shall go into in another work—the principal among them being the appeal to vanity. Many a man will give freely if it means seeing his name blazoned across a newspaper page, when he will give for no other reason. Even small contributors can be given this same satisfaction. But that is subject for a chapter in itself.

Next to giving to charity is the plan of getting contributions for some worth-while cause like let us say the Liberty League or Prohibition or anything of the kind. One project we once worked on was a plan to interest people in a League to enforce public economy. Here is the letter we tried. It brought a good response, but as you may have noticed, it did not affect public expenditures in any noteworthy degree. Pasted at the top of the letter was a brand new penny.

Here Is the Most Profitable Invention Ever Made—
The Idea that Borrowed Money Must Pay INTEREST!

DEAR NEIGHBOR:

Just this little, insignificant penny, put out at 4% compound interest in the year One A. D., would today be worth $1,227,000,000,000,000,000,000,000,000,000,—many times the wealth of the entire world!

That shows how interest on borrowed money can mount up. Benjamin Franklin gave a graphic illustration of the idea when he bequeathed $1,000 to a charitable enterprise, with the provision that it be put out at compound interest until it amounted to a sum sufficient for the purpose he had in mind. At 6%, compounded quarterly, that $1,000 would today amount to $5,190,000.00!

If a single penny put out at interest can grow to such proportions, if $1,000 at interest can mount up so rapidly, imagine what Thirty-six Billions will amount to in a few years if left to grow compounded by budgetary deficits. The public debt of the U. S. Government is today more than $36,000,000,000. For the last year and a half, it has grown at a rate of more than $4,000,000,000 a year, and the indications are that next year will show an even greater increase.

Unless that mounting debt is speedily checked, the country will be in danger, and the depression now ended may be as nothing to the one we may still have to go through.

> There is only one way to avoid that. Put an end to the NEEDLESS spending that now threatens to wreck the whole structure of our Government. Spend for NECESSARY relief—yes—but cut out the unnecessary spending that has doubled the relief rolls and thrown billions into all manner of wasteful projects.

Will you help to stop that waste? You are paying for it now and you are going to keep on paying the rest of your days. No matter what your occupation or earnings, you are now working for the Government one day in every four—and not getting your money's worth. You'll be working for it half your time—or perhaps all your time—if something is not done soon.

The purpose of The Blank League is to do something to stop this waste. But we can't do it alone. We need help—the help of every intelligent voter, for it is only as we can show ourselves to be the voice of a large section of the public that we can have any weight with Congress. Will you join? Will you send $1 as your contribution for one year's work?

450

What can we do? Four years ago, we were instrumental in stopping most of the ever-mounting payments to veterans *not* injured in the war—and thus saving annually over $300,000,000 of the taxpayer's money. We can do even more now, we believe.

$1 put into this work will bring your country a greater return, we truly believe, than any you have ever spent. $1 now will help to save hundreds and perhaps thousands in taxes later—and what is more, it may help to save you a free Government, for who knows what form of Fascism or Communism might follow a real financial difficulty?

Will you help? Will you help protect the Treasury against the hordes who are trying to raid it? Will you use the enclosed blank to enroll in the non-partisan membership of the Blank League for the single purpose of checking Government waste and getting rid of those Old Men of the Sea— the twin threats of confiscatory taxes or disastrous printing-press money?

Sincerely,

Quite different from any of the above was a letter selling the Bonds of an Industrial Loan Company. The appeal there, of course, was SAFETY, with high return. And here is the type of letter that brought best returns:

You Can Laugh At Money Worries—
If You Use This Plan!

DEAR SIR:

This letter, coming to you in advance of any public announcement, is intended for your eyes alone. It contains information which we ask you to regard as confidential. You will see why in a moment.

In order that you may realize at the outset the peculiar importance of this letter, let me tell you, before taking up the details, that to a few men who have as little as $20 a month to spare, it brings the possibility of quitting work in ten years and retiring on a comfortable income.

Yet their money will be as safe, we believe, as in U. S. bonds, for it will be invested in one of the surest and strongest lines of business in this country today. For what is the safest place for your money? In one of the strong, conservative banks, is it not? The banks of this country have built some of the biggest, most profitable institutions in the world, and their business is based on just one thing—the power of money to make more money when lent out at interest. Yet despite their great size, they deal with only 15% of the population. An even greater and stronger institution, we believe, is being built on dealings with the other 85% of the population.

Here is the way of it:

You probably know that the Blank Foundation spent a number of years and a considerable fortune investigating the needs of the average family of moderate means. And they found that the greatest need of 85% of these families was a place where they could borrow money to tide them over the emergencies which arise in every man's life. Banks were for the most part closed to them, leaving them at the mercy of the pawnbroker and the loan shark.

So the Blank Foundation worked out what they regarded as an ideal law to cover the formation of Loan Companies which should lend to these people on adequate security and at fair interest. And 26 States have made it the basis of their "Uniform Small Loan Law."

A number of Loan Companies have been organized under this law, but so great is the demand for such loans, that it is estimated $900,000,000.00 would be needed to take care of all of them. This is true not merely in times of depression, but in good times as well, for regardless of conditions, there are always emergencies arising in the average family requiring the need of some unusual sum.

452

It is for this reason that the profits to be made in the Loan business are so unusual. It has no sales problem, no advertising or selling expense. There are no left-over stocks to be sold at lower prices, no inventories gathering dust on its shelves. Where other businesses have to worry about high sales expense, over-production and cut-throat competition, it has none of these. Its shelves are bare every night. Every dollar that comes in during the day is put back to work again before evening.

It has no worries about holidays or Sundays, about six or eight hour working days, for every dollar works .24 hours a day, 365 days a year, adding its little interest so steadily day after day, that in a few years it piles up into an amount greater than the original investment!

You see, there is always a waiting line of customers, ready to use the money as fast as old customers pay it back or investors put it in. There is no delay. The dollar you put in today is hard at work tomorrow, gathering interest from the moment it is received. It is like a snow-ball which grows as it rolls. Yet it is safe, too, for the loans are always small ones, never over $300, they are made to the FAMILY, and they are thoroughly secured. Over a period of eight years, the losses have been less than one-tenth of one per-cent.

Yet by keeping all its funds constantly at work, turning over the money into new loans as fast as the old ones are paid, it is able to show a gross profit on the money used of 36% each year! Any business which can earn this amount on its funds has no difficulty in paying 6% or even more to its bondholders, and constantly increasing dividends to its stockholders.

Some eight years ago, the Blank Industrial Loan Corporation was organized under the Uniform Small Loan Law of So-and-So for the purpose of making small loans not in excess of $300 each to families. For the first two or three years, it felt its way very carefully, putting out only a small amount of money, until it could be sure that its methods and its system were right. Since then it has been increasing steadily in size and earnings.

Today it finds that it could use ten times the amount of funds it has at its disposal—could keep them loaned out on a profitable basis every day of the year. What is more, it could do that at no increase in administrative expense.

To gradually provide these extra funds, The Blank Industrial Loan Corporation is going to put on the market a Convertible Gold Bond, carrying some unusual privileges.

1st, to begin with, this bond will pay 6% interest, in seml-annual payments.

2nd, it will share in the earnings, up to a third of the corporation's net earnings, to the extent of another 3%, as declared by the Board of Directors.

3rd, it will be convertible into fully participating common stock. on the basis of 5 shares of stock to each $100 bold bond, until July 1, 1939, and after that for another 5 years on the basis of 4 to 1.

In other words, if you use the attached Application form to apply for a single Gold Bond, payable $20 a month for 5 months, it brings you not merely a generous interest on your money, but the chance to share in the earnings of a business which we believe offers greater possibilities than any other in the country today. You remember how the big installment credit houses grew between 1910 and 1925, and how those who put their money into them early in their careers prospered. The next few years, we believe, are going to see as great an expansion in the business of the Personal Loan companies, and those who have money in them should prosper as greatly.

For the man who wants to quit work some day, for the man who wants to retire on a comfortable income, we know of no safer, surer way of ending money worries for

454

good and all than by sowing these seeds of future fortune.

One of the first laws given in the Bible is that everything increases after its kind. That law was considered so important that it was repeated no less than six times in the very first chapter of Genesis, and referred to frequently throughout the Scriptures. Everything increases after its kind. To reap dollars, you must sow dollars. Few men ever get rich on a salary. To make money, you must put money working for you.

Long before the time of Christ, this truth was known. Read His parable of the talents. What did the servants whom their Lord commended do with their money? Put it out at interest! And what did the unprofitable servant do with his? Hid it away—left it idle, doing nothing—even as most men do today!

For what is money in needless furnishings and luxuries but idle money? How many dollars are sitting around your home, staring at you idly, rotting away uselessly, when they might be bringing you their daily increase?

If you had been able to put out at interest even a single penny at the time Jesus walked the earth, it would today be worth over $200,000,000,000,000—more than all the wealth of the earth!

You can't pre-date your investment like that, but you CAN put your money *now* where it will enable you to laugh at money worries ten years from now. You can write your own income. You can say now when you are going to quit work, and retire to enjoy the rest of your days. And the enclosed Application form is the way you can bring it to pass.

For this Application enables you to put to work not only the few idle dollars you may have to spare now, *but in addition*, it brings to you first chance at every future issue of Convertible Gold Bonds, with their privilege of chang-

455

ing into fully participating stock.

Only 500 of these Gold Bonds will be issued now. Then for the next four months no more will be sold. Five months from now there will be another issue, and only those who have used the attached Application Form will have a chance at it. Thereafter, from time to time, additional issues will be brought out, and always present holders will get first chance.

You can laugh at money worries if you get your dollars working for you, reaping such a golden harvest. You can quit work one of these days, and retire, while your dollars go on working for you—if you plant them in such fertile soil as this.

The enclosed Application form is your opportunity. It is good only if used in 10 days. You can mail yours now—TODAY! *Will* you? You can withdraw it, you know, for any reason or no reason within 20 days, and any money you have deposited will be returned to you in full.

Sincerely,

Akin to it in its opening is the following letter on a mining stock. Here, of course, the investment is a palpable gamble. There is no factor of safety about it, but there is the speculative possibility of a high return. Offerings of this kind have been greatly restricted by the Security and Exchange Commission, but there are practically no restrictions when the amount to be raised is under $30,000, and even for a $100,000 offering, all that is necessary is to file a copy of your Prospectus with the Commission.

Here Is a Plan Which Has Helped Thousands
To End Their Money Worries for Good!

DEAR SIR:

Here is a plan which has already brought more than a hundredfold increase to those who were courageous

456

enough to take a chance on the Lake Shore Gold Mine, about two and a half miles away from us. Every 32 1/2¢ put into their stock when they were preparing for their first 50-Ton Mill in 1918 has grown to $58.50, besides receiving rich dividends from the very first year after the mill was installed right down to now.

The same plan showed a profit of many thousand percent to those who invested in the stock of Teck Hughes—less than two miles northeast of us and on a line with Lake Shore—back in 1921 when it sold for as low as 11 cents a share. It brought ten-fold increase to investors in Wright-Hargreaves—on the same ore-bearing strata about two and three-quarters miles northeast of us. In the past two years alone, it has multiplied by fourteen the money put into Macassa—just to the northeast of us. And it is paying goodly dividends to everyone who has followed this plan and invested money in any of the seven producing mines in this Kirkland Lake Area.

Today this same plan promises even greater possibilities of profit from seemingly the richest discovery in this Kirkland Lake Gold Belt—the Trout Creek "Treasure Chest."

BUT BEFORE TELLING YOU A THING ABOUT THIS VERY REAL CHANCE AT FORTUNE, WE WANT TO SAY THAT THIS LETTER DOES NOT ASK YOU FOR A SINGLE PENNY. ALL WE WANT FROM YOU NOW IS AN EXPRESSION OF INTEREST.

You see, most of the preliminary work has already been done on this Trout Creek property. A Mill has been bought and is ready to set up. It needs only to do this and the underground work necessary to block out large quantities of commercial ore, to bring the mine into active operation. But that, it is estimated, will require in the neighborhood of $100,000, and until we are assured that all of this will be available when and as we need it, we don't want to sell you any stock.

So the purpose of this letter is to learn if you will be interested in putting up $10 or more, up to $100—provided enough others will pledge themselves for similar amounts to make up the necessary $100,000.

It was back in August, 1928, that one of the most spectacular discoveries yet made in the Kirkland Lake Gold Belt, which is now the second largest gold producing area in the world, was made on the property of the Trout Creek Gold Mining Co., Ltd., near Swastika, Ontario. To quote E. H. Orser, the Mining Engineer in charge of the work:

> "In 1928, on August 14th, men working under my direction uncovered what has been one of the most spectacular gold finds in the north country. My assays on the surface of this material ran up to $1425 per ton, and records which I have seen of ore shipped to smelter indicate ore of exceptional values at this point. Channel samples taken by me over the top of the original show on a width of 12 inches gave as follows: $1425.00—$41.25—$29.20—$1163.00.00 per ton. Later assays by other officials gave the following results: $295.00 — $2231.00 — $2217.00— $280.00 — $44.20 — $5201.00—$1594.00 per ton. Test shipments to the smelter gave $14,295.60 per ton gold value. Another shipment of 47 lbs. with no free gold showing, averaging $3716.00 per ton value. Very little of this value of ore is ever seen around a gold mine which operates on what we call a high grade ore. This find was an exceptional one."

About 5,000 feet of diamond drilling and some 200 feet of underground development has since been done on the property, with the result that two important facts have been established. 1st, Trout Creek is in the same highly mineralized zone as the big gold producers of the area, like Lake Shore, Teck Hughes, Wright-Hargreaves, etc., and has the same geological conditions. 2nd, Gold values

458

typical of Kirkland Lake's average have been proven in underground development.

If Trout Creek had nothing more than these two facts on which to base its expectations, it would offer a wonderful chance at fortune, because out of this small district has already been taken $145,000,000.00 worth of gold. But Trout Creek has much more. Trout Creek has found at the surface gold ore of almost unbelievable richness. And ore does not rain down from heaven. It is forced up from the inner fastnesses of the earth. So if ore that rich is found at the surface, the chances are that even greater and richer finds will be encountered as the development work is pushed deeper 'and deeper.

That this belief is shared by mining authorities is indicated by the headlines that ran in the newspapers when the first discovery became known. "Croesus-like Discovery near Kirkland Road," read the Financial Post. "Remarkable Find near Swastika," reported the Northern Miner. "Spectacular Sample of Gold," said the Toronto Evening Star while the Mail and Empire wrote—"Your correspondent examined the rich material in the discovery on Trout Creek property, and is glad to confirm the earlier report that it compares with the richest surface discoveries ever made in the Kirkland Lake area.

Then why, you may well ask, have not investors' come forward with all the money we need to develop the property and bring it into profitable operation? For the same reason that most other rich mines went begging in their early development stages. The history of our own country is full of the records of small investments that quickly grew into fortunes, simply because people generally are looking for sure things, and are reluctant to take a chance. Back in 1926, for instance, the Sunshine Mine in Idaho was begging at 30c a share. Today it is selling around $19.00, and has paid big dividends in cash. According to the Spokes-man Review, a sixteenth interest in *the Hercules Mine was once offered for $160.00. Since then it has paid in dividends just about a million dollars!

What the Trout Creek Gold Mine will pay, nobody knows. We don't offer it as a "sure thing." It is a speculation. But it seems to us so good a speculation that we, the men now interested in it, have put into the company $90,000.00 of our own money. We believe it will be worth your while to put into it any money that you can spare, too.

But we don't want you to put in a penny until we are assured that we can get all the money we estimate will be needed to develop the mine up to commercial operation. Will you come in—IF we get that assurance? Will you invest $10 or more (not exceeding $100)— if enough other people pledge themselves to provide a total of $100,000?

If you will, please put your name on the enclosed card and send it back at once. The books close in two weeks. If we have not reasonable assurance by then that the money will be available, no subscriptions will be accepted, and we shall use other channels for raising the money.

We don't pretend to be prophets, and we are not going to tell you that the enclosed card is a sure key to fortune. But we do know a number of men and women who are today retired and living on comfortable incomes, solely because they saw the possibilities in the stock of our neighbors, Lake Shore, or Teck-Hughes, or Wright-Hargraeves. Now Macassa—which almost adjoins our property—has just declared its first dividend, and those who bought its stock only eighteen months ago *can sell it today at a profit of 1400%!*

Our mining claims are astride the same highly mineralized zone as these rich producers, and we believe are by far the richest yet uncovered. This may prove to be your chance to end your money worries for good.

Sincerely,

One of the most interesting trends of the last few years has been the growth of forecasting and interpretive agencies to tell you what the New Deal was going to do next and to interpret what it was doing. Some of these appealed to the "Gain" motive, so they properly belong with the money-raising letters. Typical of this class is the following:

How To Read the Future So You Can
Laugh at Business Worries In the Months To Come!

DEAR SIR:

You remember the tale of the Wall Street broker, who was asked what one thing he would wish for, if he could have anything he wanted. "To know TODAY," he answered, "what the market will do next Thursday."

Everybody wants to know the future—wants to learn ahead of time what of good fortune is awaiting him there. But to men in business or in the market, such knowledge, gained ahead of the crowd, is oftentimes of untold value.

For it is not personal ability that makes people rich or successful, so much as OPPORTUNITY. When Mr. Rentschler made $35,000,000 out of a $253 investment, it was through no unusual ability of his own. It was simply his "inside knowledge" of the profits likely to come to the aircraft companies through Government subsidy.

> And it is through "inside" knowledge and understanding of what is happening in Washington today, that you can plan your business and your investments so as to be able to laugh at business worries in the months to come.

Would you risk $1 for such "inside" information each week for the next eight weeks? If you would, then use the enclosed Trail Order blank at once.

461

You see, Wall Street is no longer the arbiter of American business. The nation's financial capital has moved from the banks of Wall Street to the banks of the Potomac. Wall Street is still a power, of course—but its sway is passing. It is what goes on in Washington that will determine the ups and downs of business in the future, far more than any schemes of the "money changers" who used to sit in the seats of the mighty.

So it is not the Market you need to watch today. It is the Capitol. And it is not the froth of speech-making. It is the quiet planning that is going on behind the scenes. That is where history is being made. That is where the future success of your business and your investments is being determined. You can wait for the news reports of those plans in the daily papers, and make what meaning you can out of them, or you can get advance information on them, with a thorough digest of just what they will mean to you and to your business, by reading—

The Private News Letter
Of the Such-and-Such Company.

For more than 40 years, the Such-and-Such Magazine has given in each issue a review of the events of importance of the previous month, showing their relation one to another, and how they affected the world plan as a whole. Today, history is being made so rapidly 'that the men who guide the destinies of business need not only a resume of the past, but what is being planned for the future. So we have arranged with the man who, in our opinion, shows the greatest insight into the meaning of the New Deal, and has perhaps the most valuable contacts in Washington—John J. Smith—to write for us a private News Letter each week, and then fill in each month in the Such-and-Such Magazine the entire background needed to understand what is going on in Washington today.

John J. Smith taught Economics for several years at Blank University. He has written a number of books on

462

Wall Street and Washington. He edited the Blank Weekly, and later the "So-and-So." He not only has a thorough grasp of the whole subject, but his wide contacts give him inside information impossible for the ordinary writer to obtain. To those men to whom others look to guide the destinies of their business, Smith's letters will prove indispensable. They will provide the information without which it is impossible to intelligently plan ahead.

Will you TRY them? Will you let us send them to you for eight weeks—just to PROVE to you how valuable they are, what a clear insight they give into what is going on in Washington and what it will mean to you?

The price of the Private News Letter each week is $7 a year. Of the Such-and-Such Magazine, $3 a year. Of the two together—the Weekly Letter and the monthly background—$9 a year, payable $1 with order and $2 monthly or $8 cash.

> BUT IF YOU WILL MAIL THE ENCLOSED SPECIAL 8 WEEKS' TRIAL ORDER BLANK AT ONCE. WITH ONLY $1, WE WILL SEND YOU BOTH THE WEEKLY LETTERS AND THE MONTHLY SUCH-AND-SUCH MAGAZINE FOR TWO MONTHS, AT LITTLE MORE THAN HALF THEIR REGULAR COST!

Never in our history has there been a time when the news of Washington held more of importance to you and to your business than it does today. The next eight weeks may bring revolutionary changes to many industries. To others, it will give opportunity such as they have never seen before. If you are one of these, the advance information given you by these weekly letters may be worth to you hundreds and thousands of dollars.

Will you risk $1 for eight weeks of such advance information? Will you send the Trial Order form NOW?

Sincerely,

To those who took advantage of this short-term offer, a series of letters was then written along the lines of the one that follows, urging them to subscribe for a full year:

DEAR MR. JONES:

1937 will be, for insiders, a "buying year."

You remember when Russell Sage was asked the secret of his vast fortune, he said it was—"Buying straw hats in January!"

Well, that's true, for buying straw hats in January means buying when stocks or commodities are a drug on the market, and then selling when everyone else is bidding them up sky-high.

It's sad to confess, but the mass of the people usually guess wrong. When stocks are at the peak, they buy. When they are on the toboggan, they sell.

Business moves in cycles, you know, and if past experience counts for anything, 1937 is a year in which to buy. Commodities, stocks, almost everything, are still near their bottom prices. They have started up, but they have a long way yet to go.

Next year, everybody will be climbing on the bandwagon. But next year, anybody will be able to read the signs which are understandable now only to the insiders. Bank deposits rising. Commodity prices going up. Big credit expansion starting in the banks. Business indicators suggesting a big increase in activity in October and November. Do these signs mean anything to you?

Over in England, they have been enjoying a stock market boom for months. Many stocks have advanced so far in price as to make new high records since the War! Why has not the market here been doing the same?

464

Because Wall Street is no longer in the saddle. The determining factors in the rise and fall of stocks and commodities come out of Washington—not Wall Street!

Washington wants no runaway stock market, so there'll be no 1929 boom. Washington already controls the issuing of new securities. It is going to have a large voice in the handling of those already on the market. cupidity. And people want to know the future, so if you can persuade them that you are any sort of a Seer or a Prophet, they will buy your forecasting servlce.

To keep in touch with the world of business and finance today, to even invest your money with safety, you must know what is going on under the surface in Washington. And we know of no better way to learn that than through the Weekly News Letters of the Such-and-Such Magazine, with the monthly background supplied by the magazine itself.

The price of the Weekly News Letter is $7 a year. Of the Such-and-Such Magazine, $3 a year. By using the enclosed card at once, you get both together for only $9, payable $1 a month, or $8 cash.

Just your name on the enclosed card will keep the News Letter and Such-and-Such Magazine coming to you for the next 52 weeks. You need send no money now. Bill for the first month's payment of $1 will be mailed you in due course. But to keep getting without a break your Weekly Letter, giving the inside information on what is happening in Washington, your card will have to be mailed right away!

Sincerely,

More and more restrictions are being placed each year on money-raising campaigns and on services being marketed by mail. But when properly done, both fields offer amazing possibilities.

People will give, when you have stirred their emotions. People will invest, when you have aroused their cupidity. And people want to know the future, so if you can persuade them that you are any sort of a Seer or a Prophet, they will buy your forecasting service.

It all comes back to the point we made in the beginning—"What do they want~" What is the bait that will attract your fish and make them bite? Find that —and you will be as successful in bringing back orders as any angler can be with a properly baited hook in bringing in the fish.

THE END